The American Symphony Orchestra

John H. Mueller

The American
Symphony Orchestra

A Social History of Musical Taste

Indiana University Press
Bloomington
1951

Preface

THIS IS A HISTORY of what has been termed the "monumental orchestra" in America. It is, of course, not a complete history of music in America; it is not even an exhaustive history of the American symphony orchestra. To do justice to the intermediate orchestras, as well as the numerous small civic orchestras which make music primarily for their own enjoyment and only secondarily as a professional activity, to render a report on radio performances, the circulation of recordings, and to evaluate the importance of orchestral music in American universities during the last several decades, a truly encyclopedic treatment would be required. The present account traces the growth of the symphony orchestra to its roots in European traditions, recounts the crises which it has overcome, the musical repertoires with which it has regaled its audiences during the past century, the social setting in which it has had its being, and finally offers a discussion of the elusive problems of aesthetic taste in terms of which the historical trends can be understood and evaluated.

This volume was about fifteen years in the making. It could not have been accomplished without the cooperation of many persons in strategic positions. The managers of the orchestras have assisted in various significant ways in supplying repertoires and programs, and patiently replying to interview questions of sundry types. The New York Public Library, the Newberry Library of Chicago, Indiana University Music Library, the public libraries of San Francisco, Boston, Indianapolis, Cincinnati, and other cities have cooperated in making available their files and facilities. Members of the orchestras, critics, and other musicians, have given valuable assistance in reconstructing the histories of their orchestras, and retired members have supplied the reminiscences and cues which are responsible for any lively interest which this history may possess.

v

Students who have been members of the author's classes have contributed more to the evolution of the aesthetic thought portrayed in this volume than they will ever realize. Furthermore, it is not as a mere conventional gesture, but as a genuine recognition of indebtedness that I add this inadequate expression of appreciation of the aid of my wife, Kate Hevner Mueller, who is a student and author in the field of psychological aesthetics in her own right. The intelligent preparation of statistical materials, the meaningful interpretation of cold figures, and the critical reading of the text, make her a real participant in this work.

The collation of the individual histories of the orchestras has entailed a scrutiny of numberless facts and critical judgments in which it would be impossible to avoid critical errors and disputed emphases. The author would, of course, be grateful for corrections of any significant errors discovered by specialized readers. Since the preparations of this history of orchestral repertoires of the major orchestras required a complete card catalogue of every piece played in the subscription series from their opening concerts to the season 1949-50, the author would be glad to continue to answer inquiries on the performance history of specific compositions of those orchestras that have not published their own cumulated repertoire.

The Graduate School of Indiana University has liberally subsidized this project with funds for travel, clerical assistance, and for the purchase of the necessary books and materials.

Although a skeleton monograph on the History of Musical Taste, published in 1942, constituted the point of departure of the present work, this work is entirely new in its scope and general function.

Finally, in the production of the book, the editor of the Indiana University Press, Edith Greenburg, must be credited with many of the qualities of the text which derive from meticulous reading of the manuscript and a patient discussion of the problems of publication.

Indiana University   JOHN H. MUELLER
July, 1951

Contents

vii

4

Life Spans of Composers in the Repertoire   182

5

National Sources of the Orchestral Repertoire   253

Illustrations

xi

INTRODUCTION

Tastes Can Be Accounted For

A CONCERT performance is never insulated from the milieu in which it has its being. It cannot function without a set of congenial circumstances—a social soil—which permit its existence and determine its content. The sources of its economic support, the traditional cultural values, the expectations of the audiences, the pedagogical institutions which propagate the art, the political climate, the technology which produced the instruments, the lure of competitive alternative pleasures, are only a few of the miscellany of factors that mold the concert system into a reflection of themselves. No one can hazard a responsible opinion on trends without adequate consideration of these, and other, determining conditions.

These convictions would seem to run counter to the popular cliché, that "there is no accounting for taste." Wholly aside from the disputed translation of that frayed Latin proverb, it is the assumption of the present work that tastes can be accounted for. In fact, scholars have for some time thrown considerable light on their formation. The discouraging doctrine that aesthetic taste is a mystical and elusive gift has been challenged by researches in the social function of the arts and in the social determinants of style. In recent years there has been an increasing degree of cross-fertilization between the arts on the one hand and the social and psychological disciplines on the other. The present work was planned in the spirit of this expanding trend.

Its contribution is in terms of an analysis and survey of the public life of orchestral compositions as performed in American symphony orchestras, with the intention of tracing their fluctuations and identifying, as far as possible in such a survey, some of the factors that condition these fluctuations. This is a particularly appropriate moment to undertake such a task. The American symphony orchestra

3

has been in existence about a century—a period long enough to uncover trends and to yield historical perspective. In this sense, the study is a contribution to musical Americana.

Since the symphony orchestra is anchored to our social institutions and to the principles of human nature that supply it with its vital energy, an understanding of symphonic trends is dependent upon a certain familiarity with the larger social practices. Hence, in addition to the profiles of the individual orchestras, extended consideration must be given to the ancestry of the American orchestra in European cultures, to the American economic system in which the orchestra has matured, to the class structure of the audience and its behavior, and finally to the social psychology of taste formation as it is rooted in human nature.

This work is not an encyclopedia of symphonic affairs. Many phases of orchestral life are touched but lightly when not essential to the main stream of thought. Thus, radio and records [1] as vehicles for the dissemination of orchestral music comprise such an extended field that they are mentioned only in passing. Although the destinies of "live" music and mechanical reproduction are interwoven, it is improbable that their respective taste trends coincide. The respective locales in which they are enjoyed, the population segments which they serve, the occasions and circumstances attending their enjoyment, the financial transactions involved in the purchase of the musical services—all constitute powerful forces which differentiate their operating conditions.

However, radio and recordings cannot very well by-pass the symphony orchestra, which is the very source of their documents. The orchestras cannot record what they do not play, and they do not play what they do not perform in public. However, when once the musical document is made, it embarks on a life of its own over the record bars, in the homes, and in the radio studio, from which it flows into an immense market that is not bounded by the limited geography of the local orchestra.

Actual musical performances are, of course, ephemeral and can only be recaptured by means of historical documents. In this respect they differ from architecture, literature, and other forms of material human achievement. Although it is difficult to recoup the public appreciation that accompanied them, effective efforts to comprehend their significance can be made by resurrecting contemporary critical comment. Musical programs can similarly be reconstructed, which permit the re-creation of past musical epochs for fresh study and for the analysis of the aesthetic attitudes that supported them.

A few musicologists have, in that manner, uncovered certain periods in early American musical history. O. G. Sonneck [2] has reproduced the colonial period, while Earle Johnson [3] has reviewed in great detail the early musical history of Boston from 1800 to 1825. The present work represents a continuation of these efforts. Programs have been itemized, contemporary critical comments have been exhumed, and news reports have been examined. It is hoped that the work of students who follow a century hence will thus be greatly facilitated by permitting them to recall more adequately the musical experiences of the nineteenth and twentieth centuries.

More specifically, this study should be useful to persons of various interests: (1) to historians, musicologists, and annotators who follow the popularity trends of composers and compositions; (2) to aestheticians and critics who can profit by the analysis of the fluctuations in taste that are discussed too frequently with more ecstasy than insight into the social and psychological orbits within which these fluctuations occur; (3) to the academic fraternity, for whom it should serve as welcome collateral in hitherto unplowed fields of musical taste, empirical aesthetics, and general musical Americana as the academic curtain between the conservatory of music and the liberal arts is gradually lifted; (4) to social scientists who are intent on dissecting the body politic in order to understand the principles of social change in the various categories of culture; and finally, (5) to the large audience of laymen who have been introduced by radio, recordings, and concert, to the composer and his music—a privilege formerly reserved for a small and select class propitiously located in culture centers. In being guided through the life history of orchestral societies, and through the maze of aesthetic trends, the cultivated listener should arrive at a new comprehension of the problems of the symphony orchestras and their programs.

The student, as well as the general lover of symphonic music, will be able to find in this work a discussion of the following, and other, questions:

Why do conductors almost universally choose programs "over the heads" of the audience? Was this true in the days of Bach, Mozart and Haydn?

Since when, and why, are composers composing for the future rather than for the current audience?

What is happening to Beethoven, Wagner, Tschaikowsky and other composers in respect to the volume of their music performed in the symphonic repertoire?

Is it true that great composers of the past eras were not appreciated in their day?

Can musical taste be accounted for? Can future tastes be predicted?

What is the history of the methods of economic support of the American orchestras?

To what extent is the American composer performed in the symphony orchestra? Is he successfully competing with foreign composers of comparable age?

What are the different schools of conducting? What is the history of the seating of the orchestra?

What was the nature of the programs played a century ago?

Why did the United States produce early sculptors, painters, and authors of international renown, but not musicians?

Is there such a thing as "national" music? If not, why do so many people think so? Why do other countries have "national" music, but not the United States?

When was the first musicians' strike in an American symphony orchestra? What were the circumstances?

Do cities differ in their repertoires? To what extent?

What are some of the principles of program-building?

Who are the forgotten masters of the past?

Is there a basic, standard repertoire? How rapid is the turnover in the repertoire?

How influential is the conductor in the determination of the repertoires?

What can one learn of the "qualities" that determine the survival of a composition? What other factors contribute to survival?

What is the probability of another "Beethoven" who will dominate the repertoire for a century?

I

History of Music as Performance

In 1838 Robert Schumann wrote in his *Neue Zeitschrift für Musik* (Leipzig):

In order to judge the spirit and taste which predominates in our subscription concerts, we need only to observe the choice of pieces performed and the masters preferred here. And, as is but right, we find Mozart's name oftenest (17 times), then Beethoven (15 times), 7 numbers by Weber, 5 by Haydn, from 3 to 5 by Cherubini, Spohr, Mendelssohn, and Rossini; Handel, Bach, Vogler, Cimarosa, Mehul, Onslow, Moscheles were each heard twice; Naumann, Salieri, Righini, Fesca, Hummel, Spontini, Marschner, and others played but once.[1]

Perhaps this is an oversimplified depiction of the taste of the Leipzig audience during the period of Mendelssohn's conductorship of the Gewandhaus orchestra. Certainly it is only a tiny fragment dredged from the flow of musical history. But it is a pertinent reminder that, whatever may be the professed aesthetic ideologies of composers, or their pretensions to pure self-expression, it is, after all, public performance that constitutes the life of music and is the consummation devoutly wished by every creator of music.

Conventional music history, however, assigns greater emphasis to the chronology of compositions, their classification into schools and styles, the formative factors in their creation, and the biographies of their creators. It is upon these areas that most scholarly research has been bestowed. There has been some interest, to be sure, in the practical musical life of the past as it pertains to the social institution of the concert and the taste of its audience. Research into the concert life of the American colonies and of the various communities in our early national history, has revivified our past and has portrayed the embryonic beginnings from which our own concert practices have evolved. Similar historical services have been rendered by Hanslick,

Schumann, Burney, and others [2] in acquainting us with the concert life of Vienna, Leipzig, London, Berlin, and other European centers, while snatches of such materials are found in innumerable other works.

It is therefore apparent that there are several equally valid approaches to the study of the history of music. The first is the evolutionary or developmental approach, which considers musical forms in their historical continuity. By this conventional method we discover, for example, the traces of Gluck, Weber, and Berlioz in Wagner, certain of whose characteristics find later reincarnation in Richard Strauss. It delineates the features of Beethoven that were inherited from Haydn and Mozart, who, in turn, recognized their own indebtedness to the experimenter, Karl Philipp Emanuel Bach. In this sense every work of art is but a culmination, or end-product, of a long series of antecedents, plus the new and individual increment, just as a scientific invention, such as the electric light, is but the culmination of many successive inventive increments cumulated throughout the history of physical science.

But there is more than mere lineal continuity and descent, a kind of ancestral heredity, to a work of art. This historical dimension is supplemented by a lateral relation, a sociological background, which relates the composer and his work to his own environment. For no composition escapes the imprint of its contemporary surroundings. It reflects the currently available instruments and their technological characteristics, the contemporary organization of society, the source of its economic sustenance, its political and social standards, all vaguely lumped together by certain mystically-minded authors as the "spirit of the age." A musical composition, therefore, not only contains many nonaesthetic ingredients, but is to a great extent molded by them.

The two foregoing broad approaches are primarily concerned with the analysis of the *production* of the work of art. But, as already implied, the history of music is incomplete and sterile without its fulfillment in the patronage of the audience. It is the consumer of the work of art who expresses his preferences and thereby determines the very survival of the created work. This aspect of music history is a third dimension that reflects the mutual relation between the composer and his audience, and their respective roles in the process of taste formation, together with the function of the smaller specialized groups of patrons, conductors, performers, critics, and connoisseurs who serve as mediators, without whom the inert printed notes would have no vital existence at all. The history of music from this point of view has been singularly neglected in spite of the fact that, because of the nature of its milieu, the very form and logic of music grows out of its performance history.

The mechanism of the consumption of music and of the other arts, such as dance and drama, that also require a personal interpreter, differs significantly from the consumption of the literary works on deposit in libraries and of the visual arts on display in the museums. The latter works of art are directly available to the consumer. But not even the most expert score reader can absorb in his own imagination, from the symbols on the printed page, the experience and pleasure of a performance, nor was it ever so intended. The absence of the performer, who recreates the work in the salon or on the concert stage, condemns the published work to eternal silence.

Although recorded music and radio broadcasts have greatly expanded the opportunity for such intermediary service, they have only modified, not eliminated the performance link between creator and consumer. For this technological centralization is a power that may cut both ways. A radio chain, for example, which had previously been hospitable to serious music may suddenly adopt a policy of restriction, and thereby raise an untraversable barrier where previously had existed a generous outlet.

Thus, the translation from inanimate symbols to aural performance has become a highly technical and elaborately institutionalized system, deeply immersed in our social and economic order. The act of performance is hedged about by a network of forces that constitute a complex filter through which must pass the musical repertoire.

There was a time when this gap between the fund of potential repertoire and the actually performed music was relatively negligible. In former times music-in-performance was essentially contemporary music. Such a situation is reduced to its lowest terms in nonliterate society, where all known music is performed at appropriate times, and is of such elementary and unspecialized character that nearly every man is a potential musical executant. Without a system of recorded notation, music could not repose unperformed and still survive, but had to be personally passed on from generation to generation. Even as late as two centuries ago, music was usually composed to order, or was written with good prospects for production, usually by, or under the direction of, the composer himself. If, at times, the public was indifferent to these offerings—as it was to a magnificent extent in the case of Sebastian Bach—it is still true that the composer intended that the audience be pleased at the first—and often the only—hearing of his work. Therefore, before the opening of the nineteenth century, a knowledge of available music of a given period would afford fairly reliable evidence of the taste of that period. Consequently, Percy Scholes could determine, with reasonable approximation, the character of British musical taste in the 1760's simply by analyzing the musical catalogues of the time.[3] Like the popular music of today, it was composed for the moment. The bold presumption of composing for posterity was an invention of nineteenth-century romanticism.

The spread of the techniques of music engraving in the eighteenth century, which facilitated the preservation of old scores, together with a multitude of other technological and social factors, permitted the injection of the now familiar discrepancy or "lag" between the audience taste of the day and the current style of composition that must compete with the past accumulations. Consequently, the volume of "latent" music on the library shelves is today much greater than can ever possibly be played. Not only the cumulated past repertoires, constantly augmented by musical archeologists, but also the currently composed works, constitute a reservoir from which only a very limited number can ever possibly see the light of production. This circumstance imposes upon the performers the necessity—or privilege—of choice from a wide latitude of musical forms and styles, extending over nearly three centuries, and disrupts the erstwhile more or less simple and direct relation between the composer and the consumer public that prevailed in the days of Bach, Haydn, and Mozart. This momentous shift, and the social forces that produced it, raise issues in public appreciation and suggest inquiries into the conditions that determine the resultant repertoire choices.

The history of the American symphony orchestra, which has been a central feature of American musical life for nearly a century, has not yet been written. There exist only a few accounts of specific symphony associations in several cities, usually characterized by polite anecdotal details rather than by a more fundamental and generalized perspective. Furthermore, valuable as are the cumulated repertoires published by several of these orchestras, their alphabetical array of composers is not a compilation from which trends can be discerned.

For practical reasons, this study of American symphony orchestras is limited to those major orchestras whose history is of sufficient length—arbitrarily set at a minimum of twenty-five years—to display a trend. Again, in the interest of homogeneity, the popular and other miscellaneous concerts have been segregated from the subscription series.

The orchestras, whose repertoires have been tabulated from the respective dates of their founding to 1950, are, in the order of age as follows:

The New York Philharmonic Society	1842
The New York Symphony Society	1878
(merged with the above as The New York	
Philharmonic-Symphony Society in 1928)	
The Boston Symphony Orchestra	1881
The Chicago Symphony Orchestra	1891
The Cincinnati Symphony Orchestra	1894
(season began January 1895)	
The Philadelphia Orchestra	1900
The Minneapolis Symphony Orchestra	1903
The St. Louis Symphony Orchestra	1907
The San Francisco Symphony Orchestra	1911
The Cleveland Orchestra	1918
The Philharmonic Orchestra of Los Angeles	1919

On the basis of the classified repertoires of these orchestras, of the hundreds of composers—old and modern, eminent and obscure, native and foreign—and of the thousands of compositions, durable and ephemeral, trend lines can be plotted and fluctuations in taste can be measured which then yield a perspective of a social history of music.

To some critics and aestheticians the changing repertoire is no great enigma. It is to them essentially a weeding out process of the inferior compositions that seep into the repertoire through the fallibilities of human judgment—while the more inspired works, which are fit to survive, will inevitably be selected by the "judgment of time." According to these critics, the intangibility of musical values and the poverty of our aesthetic vocabulary may render it impossible to describe those qualities which have survival value, but the fitness of certain works to survive is amply testified by the simple and obvious fact that they do survive. Even after a period of quiescence, it is alleged, the greatest music will rise again to claim its place in the hearts of those who are qualified to judge.

Now, such an "explanation" of the survival of the fit is as tautological in music as it would be in biology. The explanation is clearly a case of circular reasoning, in which survival is first explained by "fitness," and fitness is then explained by the fact of survival. It is an ex post facto judgment that does not uncover the mechanism, nor the specific traits, which are involved in the durability of a piece of music.

It must therefore be observed that "survival" is not a simple absolute fact. It is attached to time and space, and its existence embraces a whole range of gradations from the infrequently performed Geminiani to the almost annual occurrence of a Beethoven symphony—both of which may be said to have survived. Examination will reveal that the same compositions do not survive with the same durability, nor to uniform degree in different areas, and that the intensity of their appreciation varies by time and place. Hence it is evident that the fluctuations in popularity would have been different under correspondingly different circumstances. The quality of music is, therefore, not an intrinsic trait that alone makes for survival, but it is rather to be defined in terms of the social environment to which it caters. The dictum that "good music survives" inverts the logical process and thereby begs the question. Instead of good music surviving, we must put the horse back again before the cart by assuming that the music that survives (by right of certain determining conditions) is then called "good."

The general procedure of measurement consisted in reducing the repertoire of the individual composers and of the national groups to quantitative terms by calculating their respective percentages of the total repertoire; and tracing this volume for individual, or groups of, composers in the history of each orchestra alone, and in the composite of all orchestras considered here. The latter would yield a national trend, as a contemporary and continuous reflection of American taste.

Because of the tremendous range in playing time between the least of the preludes or overtures and the longest of the symphonies, mere frequency of appearance cannot fairly be taken as a measure of the composer's representation. In view of the inflexible limits of program time, the volume of Beethoven, for example, is more appropriately measured in terms of the total playing time devoted to the composer, rather than mere frequency of performance.

Precision in playing time is, of course, difficult and, in a sense, impossible to determine because of the variations induced by a number of different factors.[4] Various conceptions of the same work by conductors of differing temperaments will yield appreciable differences in timing. Different editions, or revisions, of the same work incur changes in playing time of some compositions. Cuts by individual conductors, diverse policies on observing "repeats," especially in the classic symphonies, produce discrepancies with the standard timings recorded in reference works. Incomplete performances of suites and the elastic "excerpts" are always sources of confusion. But in the end, none of these variations, interesting and important as they are from the interpretive point of view, is of sufficient magnitude to make impossible the determination of an average length, or to invalidate the conclusions that may be drawn from the findings.

The ranks and weights here advanced are, of course, not designed to determine the presumable "quality" of these works of musical art. The concept of "quality," in the commonly accepted connotation of the term, has here no meaning whatsoever. This is merely an objective story of the history of musical choices over a period of a century, with the view to adding to our knowledge of the subtle and evasive problems of musical taste.

2

Social Evolution of the American Symphony Orchestra

Growth of the Concert System

ACCESS to the public concert is today not a class privilege but rather a purchasable right limited only by the ability and willingness to pay the price of admission. This is one of the symptoms of the rise of the middle class and the growth of urban economy. It marked the invention of the box office, with its manifold social implications. A corollary to this economic transition was, of course, the atrophy of the feudal system, which, by a policy of personal employment and patronage, had nourished the institution of closed, private musicales in court and castle. This system had provided a livelihood for an innumerable host of *Kapellmeister*, instrumentalists, and singers, whose services were ordinarily restricted to the orbit of courtly circles defined by the prince, and whose productions were normally the property of their employer or patron. Johann Sebastian Bach in Weimar and Cöthen, his son, Philipp Emanuel, at the court of Frederick the Great at Potsdam, and Franz Joseph Haydn at Esterhaz, were illustrations of this type of feudal "servitude." If Mozart suffered from the lack of such a satisfactory and congenial appointment during most of his professional career, it was not because he did not seek one most fervently. Without this attachment he was, by the standards of the day, virtually an unemployed musician, dependent on the irregular commissions that came his way, which were insufficient to lift him from the poverty that plagued him throughout his life.

Roughly parallel to this decline of feudalism was the waning wealth, prestige, and consequent patronage of the church in both Protestant and Catholic centers, as it faced the growing competition of the secular institutions. The Church had been for centuries a steady consumer of the arts and an employer of artists. Like the murals of Michelangelo in the Sistine Chapel, some of the most magnificent creations of Bach and Mozart, to say nothing of earlier composers such as Palestrina, had been produced under strictly religious auspices, and these works were therefore bound to share the adverse destiny of their ecclesiastical sponsors. Their consequent passing into relative oblivion was often the result, not of any artistic insufficiency, but of the secularization of public interest. If, in spite of this new channeling of public activity, any have survived, it is only within the framework of the institutions of the new civil life. Thus the pious Bach, were he to return to us today, would, after recovering from his astonishment at seeing his music performed at all, probably be scandalized to witness the routine annual revival of the *St. Matthew Passion*, conducted by Catholic, Jew, or unbeliever, for the aesthetic edification of a miscellaneous population in Carnegie Hall for an admission fee of $3.60, federal tax included. This *Passion*, like the several hundred religious cantatas, was conceived as an integral and inseparable portion of the Divine service. Today the church is no longer the magnificent employer of creative artists, whose inspiration serves the populace both socially and aesthetically. Creative artists are now drawing their sustenance from a more profane source, and this is visibly reflected in the character of their works, the occasions for which they are produced, the mechanism of remuneration which sustains them, and the repertoire which finally emerges from them.

The chronological line of demarcation between the dissolution of feudalism and the germination of the new commercial order with its public concerts cannot, of course, be precisely drawn, first, because all historical transitions are gradual, and second, because these transitions did not occur simultaneously in all countries. It is commonly asserted that the earliest public concert took place in London in 1673, although Venice, as a very prosperous mercantile republic, was conspicuous for its public opera houses nearly half a century earlier. Other cities on the world's commercial highways similarly evolved the pattern of public concerts. In Paris were the extremely significant and prophetic Concerts Spirituels, founded by Philidor in 1725, which became the model for similar series in Vienna (1771),

Berlin (1783), and other centers. St. Petersburg organized its Philharmonic Society in 1802.

The industrial revolution, the emergence of private enterprise and an urban economy encouraged the public concert in England, while on the continent such ventures generally still remained in the private hands of royalty, nobility, and clergy within the walls of court and castle. By way of exception, Hamburg, undamaged in the Thirty Years' War, profited from its favorable geographical location and was rich, commercial, and secular-minded. As early as 1704 Handel's *Almira* was produced there and had a run of seven weeks, a great success for that day, or any other day for that matter. By 1711 *Rinaldo*, his first opera in England, enjoyed sold-out houses in London. From 1748 to 1840 the Oxford Music Room,[1] to mention only one of several public enterprises, presented a series of weekly subscription concerts of choral and instrumental music, both solo and ensemble with a permanent orchestra of sixteen to twenty players, the conventional complement of that day. After 1800 the emphasis on oratorio diminished in favor of the instrumental works of Mozart, Haydn, Beethoven, and other contemporaries. But not all the records of these series have been preserved for us in musical lore as have the brief subscription series of the Salomon-Haydn concerts in London (1791–95), or the Leipzig Gewandhaus series, which began so modestly in 1743, established itself in the old Gewandhaus in 1781, and flowered into one of the most brilliant orchestral series in Europe.

As compared to Europe, the American colonies were provided with almost none of these ingredients for a rich musical life. Private court orchestras and opera, the remnants of which stimulated the rising bourgeoisie of Europe to similar projects, had of course never existed in the Western world. There were no sophisticated institutions, no imperial courts like Vienna, no prodigal noblemen, no prosperous crossroads of commerce like Hamburg, Leipzig, and Venice, in the raw and hardy pioneer environment. There was no Catholic Church with sumptuous baroque traditions, nor a Protestant parish to employ a Bach. Finally, there was no reservoir of trained personnel in the musical arts, no orphan school for choir boys from

which might have graduated so many adult practitioners, no architectural conveniences for concerted music that could compare with
the spacious homes of the nobility or the public theatres in the large
urban centers of Europe. Austere American Protestant churches, in
which frequently even the organ was tabu, took the place of the
elaborate ritualistic musical ceremonies of continental traditions. Musical instruments, every last ounce and inch of them, had to be imported in cargo space that was not always ample and certainly not
cheap.

The very ideology of many colonists was totally incompatible
with the aristocratic public cultivation of the secular arts. While the
New England Puritans were engaged in such rudimentary musical
disputations, as whether the Bible sanctioned the reading or the singing of the psalms, and the organ in King's Chapel was threateningly
characterized as an "infernal box of whistles with the devil inside,"
Bach and Handel were composing their masterpieces for church and
concert stage. While Boston's "tanner-composer" William Billings
(1746–1800) was composing his "fugueing pieces" and compiling the
Psalm Singer, Haydn and Mozart were laying the foundation for the
modern symphony, and Beethoven was beginning his sensational
career as pianist and composer in glittering Vienna, the literal hub
of the musical world.

Few of the early patriots could see as clearly as John Adams that
several generations of effort would be required to realize the new
country's cultural potential. In 1780, he wrote to his wife from Paris:

I could fill volumes with descriptions of temples and palaces, paintings,
sculpture, tapestry, porcelain, etc., if I could have the time, but I could
not do this without neglecting my duty. My duty is to study the science
of government that my sons may have the liberty to study mathematics
and science. My sons ought to study geography, navigation, commerce,
and agriculture in order to give their children a right to study philosophy, painting, poetry, music, architecture, sculpture, tapestry, and porcelain.[2]

In contrast to the state of music, the achievements of the new
world in the realm of the other arts and sciences, after all, were not
so rudimentary. In painting, Copley, Peale, West, Trumbull, and
Gilbert Stuart had permanently enriched their field before the nine-

teenth century was well begun. In sculpture, Thomas Crawford, Horatio Greenough, and Hiram Powers had achieved an international reputation before the middle of the century.[3] At a time when the New York Philharmonic was still in its incubation period, the New England school of literature had attained early and respected maturity, not only at home but abroad.

Possible reasons for the precocity of these favored arts may be gleaned from an examination of their content, their social functions, and antecedent background. The early painters and sculptors celebrated the heroics of the new nation, a task which abstract tonal combinations were able to do less picturesquely. Further, these arts could be cultivated on an individual basis by individual patrons, while music derives most of its aesthetic sustenance from collective cultivation. Skills in painting and literature could and did easily migrate (West, Hiram Powers, and Horatio Greenough spent part of their professional life in Europe), but the whole constellation of institutions that had brought European music to such an exalted state of efflorescence was lacking in the United States. In Europe, the feudal state had bowed to the inevitable and relinquished its protective authority over the Muses, but its material and cultural heritage had been readily adopted by its new patrons and continued to flourish with almost no interruption. It was a heritage far too indigenous to be uprooted successfully and to transport across the seas to thrive in the new and different soil of America.

Musical beginnings in America were therefore bound to be rudimentary, but perhaps no more so than could be expected from the size of the population, the social opportunities, facilities for travel and communication, and above all, from the absence of the tradition and technical accoutrements of the hundreds of courts that dotted the continent of Europe. Late colonial America could exhibit four centers of commerce and culture, which were, in order of population, Quaker Philadelphia, commercial New York, Puritan Boston, and prosperous Charleston. Until about 1750 Boston had been the most populous town, then numbering about 15,000 inhabitants, while Charleston, the gateway to the rich agricultural south, with a population of only 8,000 enjoyed an importance out of proportion to its census returns.

In Boston, New York, and Charleston, the evidence of concert life, of a sort, extends as far back as 1731–33. Since records, principally newspaper articles, are both sparse and ambiguous, there is some ground for speculation that the earliest newspaper accounts do not necessarily coincide with actual historical beginnings. Philadelphia, however, in spite of the fairly complete files of newspapers since 1719, does not yield evidence of public concerts until 1757. So late an entry of the Quaker City into public music seems "doubtful, not to say incredible" to the most authoritative student of colonial concert life,[4] although it is freely granted that in "Philadelphia especially the Quakers were more inclined to reject worldly amusements than the southerners, or even the Puritans." Whether such doubts are justified will probably remain forever unknown, but after the 1750's, the city of "brotherly love" entered a period of unprecedented expansion and prosperity that, within ten years, placed her at the forefront of colonial communities, well in advance of Boston, and even ahead of New York, with whom she had been in virtual tie.[5] It is no doubt quite safe to accept this extraordinary growth as an index to other social changes, which would include at least a partial relaxation of her traditional austerity—a reputation the city has to this day not been able to shake off.

The concert "season" of two centuries ago was only an embryonic precursor of modern practices. Although various seasons may have been remarkable for individual achievements (a very abbreviated version of Handel's *Messiah* was given in New York, January 1770, about a year before its introduction into Germany), most of the concerts consisted of what are now deprecatingly referred to as "tutti-frutti" programs, an admixture of vocal and instrumental solo and ensemble numbers. In contrast to the present taste, the concert programs of the pioneer period evince a heterogeneity in type and quality that seems shocking to the modern ear. Sentimental and even ribald ditties are found mated with serious Haydn symphonies. The popular *Battle of Prague* of Kotzwara, one of the many battle pieces of the convulsed Napoleonic period, appears in all sorts of instrumental permutations and undoubtedly served as an exciting compensation for the more "cerebral" overtures of Gluck and symphonies of Christian Bach. Perhaps if one recalls that Beethoven's own forgotten *Battle* Symphony was launched in 1813 by the composer himself on the same program with his new Seventh Symphony, this sense of incongruity may be discounted as an aesthetic idiosyncrasy of our own time.

Orchestral numbers were usually pushed out to the beginning and the end of the programs to frame the more glamorous solo offerings. It required a full century for the various orchestral forms to differentiate themselves into independent status, eligible to stand alone in their own behalf. With Paganini, Liszt, and Clara Schumann, solo recitals assumed an assured position, but orchestral concerts, in spite of the jealous efforts of a Nikisch, Muck, or a Koussevitzky, have not even today altogether achieved a complete "solo" standing. In most cities the visiting star performers are still an essential part of a concert, who more than pay their way at the box office.

All in all, however, the repertoire of these provincial days does not suffer too much by comparison with that of aristocratic Europe. The symphonies of Haydn, Stamitz, the "London" Bach, Pleyel, and Gyrowetz, would constitute good ballast for any concert season in much more recent years. Nor were local composers lacking. Alexander Reinagle (1756–1809) of Philadelphia and New York, Francis Hopkinson (1737–1791), song composer and statesman, and William Billings (1746–1800), composer and compiler, were given, as some Americans are today, at least a courtesy appearance on the program.

Although some of the early concerts were given in series of several weeks to a season in duration, most of the concerts were offered as single enterprises. After 1800, with more abundant facilities, musical amateurs as well as professionals began to organize more permanent bodies to enjoy at regular intervals the exhilaration of musical participation and to share these accomplishments with friends or the general public. The Handel and Haydn Society of Boston was founded in 1815 for the purpose of "cultivation and improving a correct taste in the performances of sacred music." Its offer of a commission to Beethoven for an oratorio in 1823 testifies to an early affinity for serious music. Gottlieb Graupner sparked the organization of an instrumental group, the Philharmonic Orchestra, in 1810, which persisted for about fifteen years. The Harvard Musical Association (1837), which itself had fissioned from a previous society founded in 1808, was a forerunner to the Boston Symphony Orchestra. In New York, the Euterpian Society (1800–1850), similarly offered public performances that fostered a salubrious musical climate in which their descendents could flourish.

Background of the Symphony Orchestra in the United States

In December, 1909, just after he had assumed the direction of the New York Philharmonic Society, Gustav Mahler wrote to his protégé and friend Bruno Walter in Vienna, "*Mein Orchester hier is das richtige Amerikanische Orchester, talentlos and phlegmatisch.*" [6] Although on another occasion he enthusiastically characterized the Boston orchestra as "*ersten Ranges,*" the derogatory reference to his own musicians approximates more nearly the typical judgment of Europeans on the condition of music in the United States before and at the turn of the century. This evaluation of American art was, to be sure, not wrapped up in a phrase so cruelly laconic as the usual reference to England as *Das Land ohne Musik*, but that was merely because the more modest pretensions of the United States made such a formulation almost irrelevant. Both before Mahler, and many years after him, it was claimed in Europe and freely admitted by word and action in this country, that any merit to which American musical life might lay claim was largely attributable to the migration of men and ideas from across the seas. It holds true in cultural as well as in military matters that weaker countries are invaded by the stronger.

The long history of music in America is a saga of growth from the early embryonic dependence on the rich cumulation of European culture to the present era, which manifests an admirable degree of maturity, independence, and self-respect. To be sure, it has been only during the most recent decades that even this partial emancipation from European tutelage has been effected. But there has been a discernible and inexorable trend toward independence, which has gained acceleration from every political crisis in Europe during the last 150 years. Not only have these crises expelled from her midst some of the most energetic exponents of the arts; but, likewise, in more recent periods, they have left her fatigued and harassed with an ever diminishing potency for further accomplishment. The

French Revolution, the revolutions of 1848, and World Wars I and II are only the major and more obvious disturbances highlighting a continuous period of political and economic restlessness, which propelled in a steady stream of unprecedented volume the more volatile population in all the arts and crafts from their disorganized homelands into the fresh opportunities of a pioneer country. To this "push" from inside Europe one must add the "pull" of the fantastic economic expansion of the new world where dollars flowed like the "milk and honey" of old and promised fabulous rewards for every effort from coal mining to concertizing. This was a positive attraction for all who were either stifled by the monarchic atmosphere and other restraints, or crowded out by the saturated economic market of the old country. According to the Viennese critic, Eduard Hanslick, who never fumbled a chance for a sarcastic jab, "America was truly the promised land, if not of music, at least of the musician." [7]

To obtain, for the purposes of objective history, an honest and balanced perspective of the actual material rewards of this migration —a perspective which of course many a nervously optimistic immigrant never achieved—it is obviously necessary to set off against the spectacular rewards of a Jenny Lind (nearly $175,000 net in two seasons), of an Anton Rubinstein, a Paderewski, and a score of other luminaries, the insolvent integrity of a Theodore Thomas and the frustrated dignity of a Leopold Damrosch. Both of them held valiantly to the course without a Barnum to embellish their paths, setting the pattern for innumerable but nameless teachers, performers, and chorus masters whose modest and collective efforts laid the foundation for whatever indigenous musical culture has since been erected. But by and large they were all well recompensed, for there was established in the New World a musical standard which not only competed very successfully with the Old World in monetary considerations, but eventually equalled and often surpassed it in professional excellence, so that by the time of World War I there remained very few masters—performers, teachers, and conductors— who could not be prevailed upon to share its prospects for a brief or lengthy period.

The most conspicuous single phenomenon in the evolution of this

AN ENGLISH CONCERT IN THE 1840's
Until about 1850, the conductor customarily faced the audience. (The Bettmann Archive)

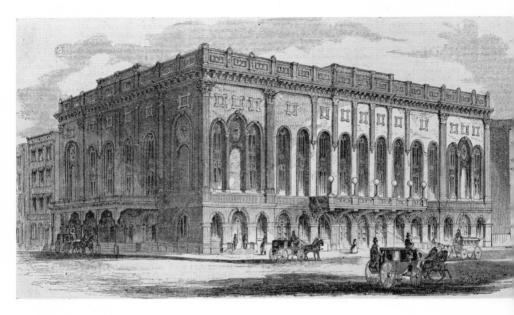

THE NEW YORK ACADEMY OF MUSIC,
FOURTEENTH STREET AND IRVING PLACE
*The home of the best music in New York for many years, until the
Metropolitan Opera House was built. (The Bettmann Archive)*

nineteenth-century American musical romance was the rise of the symphony orchestra. Although built on the German model, and although its basic repertoire has always been and still is largely Teutonic, it is nevertheless more peculiarly typical of America than is any other phase of serious music; and, similarly, there is no country in the world in which the symphony orchestra carries more prestige than in the United States. In no other country in the world has the symphony orchestra won the priority in status accorded it in the United States.

If this claim seems inflated, one must be reminded that even in Germany, its ancestral home, the orchestra assumed a rank second to opera, while in the United States the opera furnished only periodic competition to the orchestra. With few possible exceptions, such as the Leipzig Gewandhaus orchestra, the Meiningen orchestra under Bülow, and the Berlin Philharmonic under Nikisch and Furtwängler, most of the orchestras of central Europe, including the celebrated Vienna Philharmonic, were appendages to the opera, gained their livelihood from the opera, and could not compete with the opera in general patronage. That these conditions prevailed in early, as well as later days, is attested by Ottmar Schreiber, the historian of German orchestras, who explains the inferior position of the Munich orchestra in 1803 by the fact that the regular opera performances were the center of interest, which precluded the possibility of even a good orchestra attaining a high status in its own right. Later (1822–23), the Leipzig orchestra claims the "peculiar and unique virtue" of cultivating symphonic music as such, since in nearly every other orchestra it is considered secondary to other types of performances.[8] At the time of the launching of the Boston orchestra in 1881, it was proudly declared by Boston rhapsodists with approximate accuracy that

in Germany, no unsubventioned orchestra can maintain itself without offering the public the additional attractions of lager beer and tobacco. A symphony orchestra pure and simple does not exist in all Europe. That is to say, that in no city in Germany, Italy, France or Russia is there an orchestra which is made up of players whose *only* business it is to perform such music as is to be found on programmes of symphony concerts. . . . This sounds sweeping. . . . Bilse, supported by liquor, plays every day. But the orchestra is artistic bait merely. . . . All other orchestras are recruited from the opera.[9]

Even though German opera, from Mozart to Wagner, stressed the symphonic element as a copartner of the other arts, in contrast to the Italian opera, which subordinated the orchestra in the role of accompaniment to the vocal stars, such an emphasis was still far from according the solo orchestra a position of comparable dignity.

An examination of conductors' careers further underscores this division of public interest between orchestra and opera. From the latter part of the century down to the present day almost all noted German conductors, many of whom subsequently sought fame in the United States, were, during their German careers, opera conductors first and orchestra leaders secondarily. Among these were Richter, Seidl, Gericke, Muck, Mahler, Reiner, Fritz Busch, and Bruno Walter. Even Bülow, Nikisch, Furtwängler, and Weingartner, all of whom are associated by the American observer with the orchestra, shared their German professional life with the opera. Nowhere except in the United States do we find that almost lifelong, exclusive, and single-minded devotion to the orchestra that was permitted to Theodore Thomas, Stock, Stokowski, Goossens, Stransky, Ormandy, Koussevitzky, Mitropoulos, Golschmann, and a host of other conductors of the American symphony orchestras that have mushroomed "in the provinces" since the opening of this century. Others, like Walter Damrosch (very briefly), Seidl, Toscanini, Mahler, Hertz, Leinsdorf, Monteux, and Szell, gave their first services to the only opera company in the United States that survived to accumulate a history of dignified length and achievement. The continued growth of their reputations, however, proceeded not from the Metropolitan Opera Association, but from their consecration to their respective orchestras.

If the German orchestra had to content itself with sharing both prestige and conductors with the opera, this was all the more the case with the French orchestras and decidedly so in Italy, the traditional home of the opera itself. Habeneck, today remembered as the founder of the Société des Concerts du Conservatoire in 1828, and who "taught" Wagner how to conduct Beethoven's Ninth, was in his day best known as the conductor of the Paris Opera—a post to which Berlioz aspired, for it was "the only place where a French composer of that day could hope to find real fame and fortune." [10] The French interest in instrumental music, kindled by Habeneck and rekindled by Berlioz, Saint-Saëns, and César Franck, did not burst forth into a warm flame until the latter part of the century. Franck insisted on the dignity of chamber music and orchestral composition, but was hampered by the fact that the symphony was associated with the Germans who had ignominiously defeated the French (1871), a humiliation that solidified their musical sentiments by converting them into a patriotic issue.

In Italy, during the nineteenth century, there was almost no independent cultivation of the orchestra, though every town of any pretensions supported one or more opera houses. Thereby was created that prodigious demand for new operas, the setting in which Rossini, Bellini, and Donizetti spawned their numerous musical progeny and Verdi rose to the pinnacle as the "grand old man of music." It was Italian opera that inundated all Europe as far north as London and St. Petersburg, and left, like a receding glacier, the legacy of the Italian musical vocabulary, which has now become a sort of *lingua franca* for migratory conductors and musicians.

Even England, which boasts the oldest symphonic body in existence—the London Philharmonic was founded in 1813—could not show us an example of an orchestra competing successfully with the Royal Opera of Covent Garden for length of season and international eminence. The venerable "Phil," whose history is studded with the most brilliant composers and conductors, never played more than six to ten concerts a season until the 1930's. Though Sir Henry Wood achieved great popularity for the Promenade concerts in Queen's Hall, established in 1895, and Hans Richter and Hallé regaled London and Manchester with authoritative concerts for thirty years, Sir Thomas Beecham, the most scintillating of British conductors, has [11] divided both his allegiance and his personal fortune between his operatic ventures and his orchestral exploits.

Circumstances and situations such as these are in sharp contrast to the almost monopolistic orchestra of the American scene and confirm the claim that the symphony orchestra has found in America its most congenial home. But previous to the emergence of the

American symphony orchestra, which dates roughly from the middle of the nineteenth century, America, like Europe, generally accorded greater prestige to vocal and dramatic music.

When Wagner declared that Beethoven's *Choral* Symphony evidenced the exhaustion of the expressive potentialities of instrumental or "absolute" music, he was of course guilty of an egregious miscalculation of the trend. But what was more significant, he was merely echoing a sentiment that had not only been repeatedly formulated, but had never really lost currency. From Rousseau, through Gluck, Weber, and Wagner, the inseparability of music and poetry had been proclaimed.[12] Even the popularity of absolute music achieved by Haydn in England, the fame of the Mannheim orchestra, or the eminence of Beethoven—all of which loom large in the light of subsequent music history—could not shake the accumulated vocal traditions of Handel and of the Italian opera. The literal engulfment of all Europe in Italian vocal music during the early nineteenth century greatly embittered the declining years of the instrumentally minded Beethoven.

In France, according to Berlioz, instrumental music had indeed been regarded as "respectable, but distinctly inferior . . . Haydn and Mozart had achieved all that could be looked for in that direction." [13] When Habeneck first introduced well-disciplined performances of the sturdy Beethoven symphonies to the puzzled French, who had a sweet tooth for Italian vocal monody but no appetite for the heavy German symphonies, he was himself definitely cultivating a sideline. In a word, the general musical public, which was habituated to instrumental music as an expressive accompaniment to vocal themes, could not quickly accustom themselves to an autonomous and complex instrumental medium. An orchestra without a voice was like a pedestal without a statue. It had been suggested that, if instrumental music could emulate, or simulate, the voice, it could perhaps justify an independent existence. Therefore, K. P. E. Bach endeavored to compose in as vocal a manner as possible. Charles Burney, a follower of French Encyclopedist thought, declared that

of musical tones the most grateful are such as are produced by the vocal organs. And next to singing, the most pleasing kinds are those which approach the nearest to vocal, such as can be sustained, swelled and diminished at pleasure. Of these the first in rank are such as the most excellent performers produce from the violin, flute, and hautbois.[14]

When such convictions become well established in the unconscious experience of a people, theorists will rationalize an explanation for what everybody already accepts. Thus the English Busby in his *Dictionary* avers that

The music of the voice, when good, is universally acknowledged to be infinitely superior in its effect to that of any instrument, for the tone is not only more natural, and therefore gratifying in itself, but with the union of sense with sound, by means of the words, the mind is entertained while the ear is delighted. . . . Instrumental music is very inferior in its powers to vocal, yet it claims an honorable prerogative in having contributed so materially to the advancement of the vocal.[15]

There was some appreciation, however, for the fact that instrumental music was at least beginning to challenge this superiority, and that Germany was, of course, the leader in this development. Burney very early advanced the opinion that

though Italy has carried vocal music to a perfection unknown in any other country, much of the present excellence of instrumental music is owing to the natives of Germany, as wind and keyed instruments have never perhaps in any age or country been brought to a greater degree of refinement, either in construction or in use than by the modern Germans.[16]

Except for a few such rudimentary stirrings, the story in the United States after 1800 follows faithfully the European tradition. The pioneer period was safely past and the singing societies were gathering force. Even such organizations as the New York Philharmonic Society, founded in 1842 for the express purpose of cultivating the neglected instrumental field, garnished its programs liberally with vocal solos. That they dared not forsake the vocal art is evident from a complaint voiced in the Sixth Annual Report for that society: "We are living in a community where considerable prejudice exists unfavorable particularly to instrumental music."

As late as 1881, Theodore Thomas, frustrated temporarily in his mission to establish orchestral music on a firm foundation, confessed that "although the contrary has been asserted, I think that it is in the vocal direction, and not in the instrumental, that the present development of the art lies. . . . Singing . . . appeals to every-one." [17] A similarly discouraged pronouncement (1895) is occasioned by the inhospitable reception of the orchestral strivings of the St. Louis Choral-Symphony Society:

It is a well known fact that instrumental concerts, i.e. symphony concerts, are as a rule not well patronized. . . . As soon as it is known that only 'mysterious' symphonies and 'learned' overtures are offered, they take it for granted that such concerts are not intended for them. Here is where so many program dictators make a serious mistake. Why not compromise? Must people be converted in one season? [18]

Psychologically the reason for the allegiance enjoyed by vocal music is not remote. Vocal music in song, oratorio, or opera betokens dramatic action; it involves personalities and plots; there is "always something going on." On the other hand, abstract tonal patterns do not ordinarily revive personal experiences, do not deal with or solve life's problems. It is only after an adequate fund of tonal experiences has been accumulated that these tonal patterns awaken a meaningful reaction. That many instrumental composers have themselves supplemented their tonal creations with a "program" testifies to this. That program music is usually ranked low in the hierarchy of musical values is partially a result of the wounded pride of the instrumental purist for whom instrumental music is entirely self-sufficient, noble, and sublime, and who sees the literary element as an intrusion that corrupts the integrity of the tonal structure.

Again, much of the homage tendered vocal music was derived from the enthusiastic amateur participants in choral societies. Enormously less training and preparation were required for the chorus than for participation in instrumental ensembles. Some of the choral organizations, which always gratified social as well as musical aspirations, achieved a long and honorable history: the Handel and Haydn Society of Boston, the Liederkranz of New York, which later merged with the Arion Society, the Apollo Club of Chicago, the Choral-Symphony Society of St. Louis, to say nothing of the veritable rash of Männerchors in scores of cities, large and small, wherever there existed a minimum German settlement. From 1849 to the period of World War I the choral groups banded together in periodic regional and national festivals. But when these voluntary, amateur organizations were forced to compete with the diverse modern attractions that levy their claims on leisure time, even the strongest organizations perished, and only a few now remain as interesting relics of the golden age of song. In the history of the symphony orchestra, however, they have served a useful purpose, not only in the cultivation of musical taste in general, but also in their frequent collaboration with instrumental groups for presenting the masterpieces of Mass and Oratorio. This collaboration in some cases inspired the formation of the very instrumental orchestras that were destined to displace them.

This shift from popular participation to professionalism set the stage for the numerous orchestras founded since the close of the last century. It drove a fatal wedge between the lay audience, which during the choral days had shuttled rather easily back and forth across the footlights, and the highly trained orchestral body from which they were now barred. The chasm widened with the increasing preoccupation, on the one hand, of the audience in its own personal interests, and the increasing finesse of professional execution of the orchestral bodies on the other. To bridge this gap with a mutually acceptable repertoire, constructed on a common ground of aesthetic tastes and interests, it would be necessary, either for the unprofessional lay audience to reach forth to attain the maturity of the orchestra, or for the orchestras to condescend to the level of the audience which they left behind. It cannot be said that this problem has even yet been solved.

The ascent of instrumental music to its present exalted position required a century or more of growth and development from the epoch when a "symphony" was a mere instrumental fragment within an extended vocal composition, to the time when it had grown in dimensions and assumed an emancipated position. As in the case of every other shift in important social values, whether political, economic, or aesthetic, this canonization of instrumental music in general, and the symphony in particular, constituted a slow evolution in aesthetic values, and had to be ideologically defended and rationalized.

This defense appeared in the revival of Neo-Platonism in the romantic philosophies of the nineteenth century. Since Kant, and more particularly since Hegel, the fine arts were coupled with religion and philosophy as the human version of the Infinite, which only the properly gifted genius could to a certain extent fathom. This supernatural realm was the antithesis of the material world—according to the familiar division of Plato, of Christianity, and other cosmic philosophies—which was the concern of science. Scientific "truths," conditioned as they are by the limitations of human reasoning and observation, were changeable, unstable, and constantly subject to correction. Aesthetic and religious truths were, however, ultimate and therefore of a higher order. Any industrious person, according to Kant, could become a scientist; but only an inspired person could be an artist and a prophet. Since the artist and philosopher dealt in eternal verities while the ordinary people were concerned with the mutable physical world, the inspiration of the artist, logically, became a higher law than the taste and appreciation of the mundane consumer. Of all the arts, music was often held to be the most removed from the material universe, although Kant accorded this high position to poetry. According to Schopenhauer, music was pure spirit. Even architecture, when it escapes material limitations, is "frozen music," if Schelling is to be believed.

Music was not, therefore, mere entertainment and pleasure, as Burney and the eighteenth century had "mistakenly" surmised. Music, pure and instrumental, had a social mission, and its practitioners were gripped with the Messianic impulse to bring its finest examples to the people. Theodore Thomas epitomized the guiding philosophy of the nineteenth century:

A symphony orchestra shows the culture of a community . . . the man who does not understand Beethoven and has not been under his spell has not lived half his life. The masterworks of . . . instrumental music are the language of the soul and express more than those of any other art. Light music, "popular" so called, is the sensual side of the art and has more or less the devil in it.[19]

It was because instrumental music was considered the least sensuous, the least descriptive and mundane of all the arts, that it could never appeal to the masses as does vocal and "popular" music. That the symphony, which is only one of the many instrumental forms, should have won this position of honor and be sanctified as the ulti-mate fulfillment of musical expression is unquestionably owing to the influence of the nine symphonies of Beethoven. His deifica-tion by Schumann, Mendelssohn, and other romanticists followed within two decades after his death. Psychologically, furthermore, a symphony was a complete unit, as Berlioz, too, had emphasized; while overtures and other forms were short and fragmentary. By 1840, Schumann already referred as a matter of course to the sym-phony as the "highest style of instrumental music"; [20] by 1864, Theo-dore Thomas was announcing "symphonic soirées"; and in 1878, Leopold Damrosch for the first time incorporated the term in the name of an orchestra—a practice that has been all but uniformly followed by the other American orchestras founded since that time. Instrumental music had indeed "arrived," and the "symphony" orchestra was the most perfect vehicle for its promulgation.

Some Forerunners of the American Symphony Orchestra

The modern American symphony orchestras, which display so many similarities in their professional and economic organization, are obviously a culmination of a long series of experimental progeni-tors. Out of this struggle for mere survival, as well as the lure of professional excellence, there has evolved a form of symphonic organization that appears to have adapted itself moderately well to our current social order; but which will, by the same token, un-doubtedly undergo further developmental mutations in the future.

In comparison with European music, the beginnings of the American orchestra were, as already indicated, pathetically meagre. For in this country there were no luxurious courts and castles which could sustain a Haydn, nor a landed nobility which could pension a Beethoven, nor yet the rich tradition in which whole nations take pride, and are thereby automatically impelled to nurture the arts and set standards for emulation. Still awaited in the United States were the counterparts of their European forebears: the philan-thropic amateurs who were to deliver such a decisive impetus to the development of music a half century later, and the financiers and captains of industry who would seize upon the symphony orchestra to proclaim their civic pride.

Without such royal or industrial patronage, the early American (as well as English) orchestras were thrown upon their own resources. The Graupner "orchestra," of Boston, the earliest essay in "permanent" orchestral organization, today would hardly merit the name. A German who had migrated to London and played under Haydn in 1791–92, Gottlieb Graupner subsequently emigrated to Charleston and finally settled in Boston where, as teacher of oboe, flute, and violin and as proprietor of a publishing house, he established himself as the musical factotum in that city of 25,000 inhabitants. Not only did he inspire the founding of the Handel and Haydn Society, but he also gathered together a dozen musicians to play the symphonies of Gyrowetz and Haydn, and to study such other scores as were available in the incipiently cultured Boston of that day. His enterprise has gained for him from some historians the hackneyed but appreciative title of "father of the American Orchestra."

Every other city also sprouted its musical organizations, even though the cultural soil might have been more stony than that of the precocious East. Philadelphia, Cincinnati, St. Louis, San Francisco, and other communities, as they attained a modicum of wealth and leisure, and attracted German and French immigrants, cultivated the Muses. If the beginnings were usually modest, casual, and ephemeral, they still were harbingers of greater things to come.

At mid-century, there appeared from across the waters a source of energy that fertilized the American symphonic movement and accelerated its maturation. In 1848, as a precipitation from the German revolution of that year, a score of impecunious but competent musicians banded themselves together for a concert tour of America. Having gained their initial and greatest success in Boston, this Germania Orchestra responded to a demand from cities as far west as St. Louis, played the Beethoven symphonies together with an assortment of more or less serious music, and inculcated for the first time some appreciation for reasonably dexterous performance of the classics. The members of this group, however, soon became aware of the melancholy truth that traveling orchestras, then as now, were not necessarily profitable enterprises. At their dissolution in 1854, they scattered from Boston to Chicago, thereby continuing the work of fructifying American musical culture to its everlasting benefit. One of these members, Carl Bergmann, cellist and conductor, soon became the conductor of the New York Philharmonic. Bergmann was an ardent disciple of Wagner and Liszt, and according to Theodore Thomas, with whom he was associated for many years, he was "the first man in this country who gave proper rendering of Beethoven . . . and the first real conductor to give us an insight of our great composers." [21]

More sensational, but less durable in influence, was the French conductor, Louis Antoine Jullien, showman extraordinary, who brought his orchestra of European artists, including many of the most prominent instrumentalists, to the United States in 1853–54. This orchestra was augmented by an American contingent to one hundred players, with whom he presented nightly concerts in New York for a period of two months. After nine months sojourn, during which he conducted two hundred concerts and toured the country from Boston to New Orleans, the irrepressible Jullien instituted the first of America's "jumbo" concerts—later to take the name of "festival"—in New York in June, 1854. This "Grand Musical Congress," which was made up of 1,500 instrumentalists and sixteen choral societies, performed selections from the great oratorios as well as symphonic numbers. The less sophisticated of the 20,000 members of the audience satiated their appetite on this occasion with one of the Jullienesque "descriptive pieces," specially written for the occasion, the *Fireman's Quadrille*.

Jullien may have been a musical demagogue, for he was never unmindful of the psychological effect of such extramusical trappings, the jewelled baton and spotless white gloves for a Beethoven rendition, or the frenetic gestures for his many quadrilles. But he was definitely not a humbug, as was alleged by some snobbish observers. He received extravagant notices, even in the best press, for his serious achievements: "His fiddles all bowed together . . . he was painstaking and energetic in rehearsals . . . he attained a pianissimo, while the New York Philharmonic could not even achieve a *piano*, much less a *pianissimo*." He explored the means of reaching the masses, which the austere New York Philharmonic never dreamed of and the dignified Germania barely attempted. While crude megalomania never again reached such heights, it was by no means inconspicuous in the monster festivals of Damrosch, Thomas, or Patrick Gilmore the bandmaster, while the personal career of the virtuoso conductor down to the present day is never quite devoid of a subtle touch of it, intent on sending the music on its way more effectively.

In the local contingent of the Jullien orchestra was an eighteen-year-old violinist, Theodore Thomas, who absorbed his first impressions of disciplined rehearsals, and who was to continue the sowing so that a later generation might reap. Theodore Thomas was the first modern conductor to fulfill completely the promise of symphonic ideals. During the middle years of his pioneering career, this indomitable spirit launched, or participated in, three distinct experiments in symphonic organization, the third of which was destined to become the standard one. The Thomas biography is the evolutionary history of the American symphony orchestra.

As his first venture, in 1863, he founded his own organization, a permanent and fully employed body of men, presented in popular concerts in the famous Central Park Garden, Seventh Avenue near Fifty-eighth Street, and in serious concerts in Steinway Hall on Fourteenth Street. It was this well-disciplined band, held together with minor interruptions for about twenty-five years with modest material assistance from William Steinway and other friends, that imparted the first genuine and substantial impetus to the establishment of sound symphonic standards outside New York City. Essentially it was the product of Thomas' own financial and artistic responsibility, whose exciting history of alternating frustration and success has been repeatedly told.[22] Although it has been averred that the New York Philharmonic stimulated the organization of orchestras in other cities of the United States, [23] this is an overstatement. It was the migratory Thomas, with the Thomas orchestra, that whetted the appetite for disciplined performance in Boston, Philadelphia, Cincinnati, and Chicago.

After a second undertaking—the direction of the New York Philharmonic Society (1879–91), Thomas finally achieved the fulfillment of his dream in the Chicago Orchestra (1891) supported by philanthropic subsidy. (See profiles of the Chicago and New York orchestras.)

This, Thomas' third type of organizational experiment, bears pointed testimony to the tenacity of his purpose and the eminence of his ideals. Even this persistence would have availed little had it not been supported by resolute philanthropic forces, whose patience was fortified by the powerful stimulant of civic pride and the fierce determination of a frontier city to crash the company of the cultivated East.

In addition to the cooperative system of the New York Philharmonic and the private enterprise of Theodore Thomas, there appeared a variation of the philanthropic systems of administration that is today practically obsolete. This was the personal philanthropy practiced by such persons as Edward Bok in Philadelphia, William Clark in Los Angeles, Clarence Mackay, and H. H. Flagler in New York, but which attained its consummate perfection in the Boston Orchestra, the creation of Henry Higginson, the Boston financier. The first orchestra to profit from an almost unlimited philanthropy, it was modelled on the court troupes of Europe, and was established, owned, and administered by one man who looked upon and treated his musicians as his salaried employees. It differed from its European prototype, however, in two significant respects. First, it was in no sense functionally a private orchestra but was administered solely in the interest of public performance; second, it was dominated by an aesthetic idealism which entrusted the musical director with complete and autonomous jurisdiction, unrestrained by any economic, political, or personal consideration. Never has the theory of "artistic supremacy" been more perfectly implemented. It set the pattern of things to come. If detailed features have been altered, the general principle of philanthropic support, which permits a certain autonomy to an aesthetic standard, is now well accepted in orchestral administration.

The story of this long and gradual evolution is best told in the histories of the individual major orchestras.

3
Profiles of Major American Orchestras

THE IDEAL toward which American orchestral history has been moving is the "permanent" orchestra. The permanent orchestra may be identified by the following traits: (1) exclusively professional membership; (2) full season contracts; (3) the orchestra as principal employment of its members; (4) all other employment (e.g. teaching, concert, etc.) compatible with priority of orchestral requirements; (5) regular and adequate rehearsals; (6) financial base sufficient to insure the above conditions. The obvious intent of these conditions is to provide continuity of organization, without which high artistic standards are impossible.

This description represents, of course, an ideal which may not be completely attained. American orchestras range from the Boston orchestra, which is held intact practically throughout the year, to the small community orchestra made up virtually of amateurs who present several concerts per season.

In 1900, there were only four established orchestras closely approximating "permanency": Boston, Chicago, Cincinnati, and Pittsburgh. Six others fulfilled the requirements less completely. They were Philadelphia, which was founded in November, 1900; the New York Symphony, which was then temporarily suspended, but was revived in 1903; the St. Louis Choral-Symphony, which had had a continuous existence since 1880 but shared the repertoire with a choral society; the New York Philharmonic, founded in 1842, but whose members did not give priority to the orchestra. San Francisco, which had experienced a certain success under Fritz Scheel until 1899, was now stumbling along experimentally, and Los Angeles, which founded its symphony orchestra in 1897 and had won some philanthropic aid in 1899, complete a list of ten orchestras at the opening of the century.

The half century witnessed a general proliferation of symphonic orchestras, so that even small communities felt pressed to emulate the fashion. Major orchestras, with budgets exceeding $100,000, number over twenty; of minor orchestras, with smaller budgets, in which the membership is predominantly professional, there are several score; community orchestras, which testify to the grass-roots interest in concerted music, number six hundred, according to the American Symphony Orchestra League. Many cities have more recently founded orchestras which have attained professional dimensions: Denver, New Orleans, Buffalo, Kansas City, Houston, San Antonio; while others have suffered serious breaks in their continuity: Pittsburgh, Dallas, Seattle, and Portland, Oregon. Their basic problems, however, do not differ from those whose histories are here fully recounted.

In the history of American music there have been many orchestras which are not classifiable in the customary civic categories. Most of these orchestras were in New York. The Russian Symphony, under Modest Altschuler, was organized in 1904; between 1914 and 1919, this orchestra brought celebrated soloists and played a progressive repertoire. In the 1940's, with the blessing of the picturesque Mayor LaGuardia, the City Center orchestra under Leopold Stokowski and Leonard Bernstein purveyed music at popular prices. The radio chains likewise entered the active lists. While CBS had long featured the New York Philharmonic, NBC organized its own orchestra in 1937 for Toscanini, who usually functioned during about half the season. All these orchestras are, however, ancillary to the local orchestras distributed throughout the country. Often playing several times per week to their local audiences, they constitute the essential framework of American symphonic life.

The New York Philharmonic-Symphony Society (1842)

The New York Philharmonic Society, America's first and oldest extant professional orchestra organized exclusively for concert purposes, made its initial appearance December 7, 1842, in the Apollo Rooms (capacity 500), 410 Broadway, a few doors below Canal Street.[1]

Such a terse chronological statement hardly does justice to the functional beginnings of orchestral history in the United States, and contributes little to the understanding of the social forces that called it into being and fostered its survival. Substantially, its history embraces that of the symphonic orchestra movement in the United States, modified to some extent, of course, by the conditions peculiar to its local habitat.

New York, which during the pre-Revolutionary days had ranked third to Boston and Philadelphia in size and cultural importance, was soon to outstrip its two rivals. With the opening of the Erie Canal in 1825, New York was assured supremacy as the first port of America. Doubling its population during this decade, it was by 1840 a thriving and cosmopolitan commercial city of about 400,000 while Boston and Philadelphia were now left far behind with only about one-fourth of that population. All forms of entertainment were in a flourishing state. Opera and theatre began to supply a fine backlog of musicians and audiences for all types of musical projects, although before 1830 the city had suffered from a serious scarcity of instrumental artists.

Besides being supplied with adequate, if not abundant, talent, New York could show evidence that interest in instrumental and orchestral music was "in the air." The theatre had nursed along the small auxiliary orchestras which were now seeking emancipation and craved an opportunity to make music on their own account. A sumptuous repertoire lay ready. Haydn and Mozart had a long-established fame. Beethoven and Schubert had been dead about fifteen years; Mendelssohn and Spohr were at the height of their careers, while Wagner and Liszt were on the threshold of theirs.

England, France, Germany, and Austria, from which the New World received its inspiration, had already developed models to be emulated. The Philharmonic Society of London was founded in 1813 with the avowed intent to "rekindle in the public mind that taste for excellence in instrumental music which has so long remained in a latent state"; [2] Habeneck had founded, in 1828, the Société des Concerts du Conservatoire for the express purpose of performing the Beethoven symphonies; the Leipzig Gewandhaus concerts, which were destined to assume the highest dignity in the orchestral field in all Germany, extended back to 1781; and, finally, the orchestra of the Vienna Royal Opera under Otto Nicolai, composer of the still performed *Merry Wives of Windsor*, branched off on its own account in November, 1842, to present to the Viennese musical public "for the first time the symphonic masterpieces performed by a well-trained orchestra, with verve and technical perfection under the direction of a young, energetic conductor," [3] and thus anticipated the inaugural concert of the New York society by only a few weeks.

The tardy developments in New York and Vienna issued from quite dissimilar circumstances. Although Vienna was the ancestral home of the symphony, it was the opera that enjoyed priority in the patronage of the nobility and cultivated bourgeoisie. Even today, the Vienna Philharmonic is nothing more than the opera orchestra which undertakes to offer a half dozen concerts per season on its own responsibility. It was an offshoot from the opera in a musically mature community. In New York, on the other hand, the symphony orchestra was itself an original phenomenon in a musically immature community, which during much of its life maintained itself against all other competing forms of serious musical entertainment.

The occasion which precipitated the organization of an ensemble of professional musicians was a memorial benefit concert for the surviving family of Daniel Schlesinger, a respected musician, who had died in 1838. The whole musical fraternity seems to have cooperated in the formation of an "orchestra of unprecedented strength" which embraced "all the musical talent of this city, the managers of the theatres and W. Niblo, Esq. having kindly allowed their most distinguished performers to place themselves at the disposal of the committee." [4] The Overture to *Der Freischütz*, and the *Finale* to the Symphony No. 2 of Beethoven, as played by sixty professionals, made a stupendous impression upon the audience of 2,000 persons. That "no such orchestra had ever before been heard in New York, and no such effect ever before produced," is quite comprehensible when it is recalled that, in leaner days (1828), the *Eroica* had been performed as a septet. Although it was an undoubted achievement for that period, the modern concept of an orchestra as a thoroughly disciplined body had not yet touched their imagination, for even forty years later R. Osgood Mason could reminisce:

The performance was a success in various ways . . . but what is germane to the present subject, it demonstrated the fact that classical and even difficult music could be performed by a large number of New York musicians from various organizations without frequent rehearsals.[5]

Many years were destined to pass before the relinquishment of this comforting and complacent illusion.

This musical feast created the taste for a permanent fare, but it was not until April, 1842, that the Society was organized, and not until December 7 that it was prepared for its first appearance. The new group assumed the name of its English prototype by calling itself the "Philharmonic" Society, a Greek derivative consonant with its high purpose of cultivating one of the principal arts. It was then a designation commonly used, before the "Symphony" had usurped the place of prestige.

Like many of its European prototypes,[6] the New York orchestra was a "cooperative" or communistic body. The net income at the close of the season was distributed equally among all the active members from percussion to concertmaster. Only the conductor and the librarian, elected by popular vote, received salaries according to contract. It was also a self-governing group, in which new members were admitted only by the vote of the old. These circumstances are all of vital importance in the explanation of some of the dilemmas of the orchestra in its subsequent history. Well adapted as it was to its own times, it led a quiet and profitable existence for many years, but, like all the cooperative and utopian societies in the social and economic fields which sprang up in those decades, it could not endure the white heat of the fiercely competitive world into which it was ultimately propelled. Eventually, it too succumbed to the inevitable.

From the standpoint of its internal musical organization, its approximately sixty members represented a phenomenal achievement. For some decades such a number was to be assumed satisfactory, and even in the present century many reputable conductors—Thomas, Damrosch, Oberhoffer—who spread the gospel of good orchestral ensemble with their traveling orchestras, knew how to be content with less. However, the internal balance left much to be desired in terms of present-day standards. Instrumentation was top-heavy with an easily understandable excess of violins (twenty-two) to only four cellos.[7] The Society had to depend on the actual availability as well as the willingness of the musicians to participate in the public concerts.

The new orchestra by no means represented the principal activity of its members. The monthly concert was anticipated as a pleasant relief from more remunerative occupational duties, and the rehearsal periods were cluttered up with routine business matters, from which members could absent themselves with relative impunity. In his Fifth Annual Report, the secretary bemoans the fact that while

the number of Violin, Viola and Cello performers among the members . . . is quite sufficient for our concerts; but still for various reasons we have not had the proper number of either of these instruments at one concert during the season.

In the Eleventh Annual Report he continues to complain of a condition that remained to plague the cooperative orchestras for decades to come:

We need many more from whom we can at any moment fill a vacancy at a rehearsal or concert, so that whenever we meet we are sure of a full orchestra, and that, too, of our members.

For a long time the Society seemed to many a player at best a pleasant luxury and at worst a dubious venture, not worthy of causing interruption in his regular employment. Still distant was the time when a well-established orchestra, with adequate financial inducements, could import on almost immediate notice a needed woodwind from Paris or a string player from Vienna to perfect its balance in personnel.

The conductor of 1842—if we may call him such—had just graduated from the player's stand. As a profession of independent dignity, conducting was still in a primitive state, for Berlioz was still to write his chapter (1856) and Wagner his brochure (1869) on this métier. During the first New York season of three concerts, six different conductors officiated, selected according to qualifications upon which we can only speculate, but probably to keep every eligible candidate happy. Certainly they could not have been much more than *Taktschläger*, a kind of first among equals who were bound together by ties of friendship rather than the thongs of stern discipline.

If these first flights did not reach great artistic heights, they were at least impelled by a lofty purpose which many of the fashionable audiences seemed to reciprocate. In the prospectus of the twenty-ninth season (1870–71), it is reported that

inasmuch as the compositions of that class can seldom be fully appreciated when heard but once, the Society has for many years made the rehearsals preceding each concert open to the public.

But then, as now, there were those who had no inclination to soar to the heights of abstraction, who came to be entertained, not to worship. It was thus with great reluctance that the orchestra swerved from its original determination to cultivate the music which these instrumentalists loved.

. . . vocal music has been introduced only to satisfy the demands of those . . . who would not without it have been persuaded to contribute their support. . . . We are living in a community where considerable prejudice exists unfavorable to music in its highest state of cultivation, more particularly to instrumental music and to some musical instruments. . . . It must be acknowledged that the science of music . . . is not a human invention, but of Divine appointment. . . . Therefore, it should be cultivated equally with all our other faculties, and its pursuit is as useful and necessary . . . as that of the other arts and sciences.

The apostles of instrumental music bewailed the public defection toward the false gods of vocalism; and, in the same Sixth Annual Report, deplored:

. . . "Italian opera competes tragically with the Philharmonic."

But even purely instrumental music was given programmatic interpretations. To render abstract music more comprehensible in the absence of "words, action, and scenery," the music annotator of the day often invented a literary accompaniment, one of the earliest functions of what we now know as program notes. It is easy in our day to be condescending toward those who lived in the age of "the Dying Poet," and it might seem naïve and childish when the *Eroica*, in the second Philharmonic season, is described as a "portrayal of the workings of that extraordinary man's mind. . . . The winding up of this movement [the Funeral March] represents the faltering step of the last gazers into the grave, and the listener hears the tears fall on the coffin ere the funeral volley is fired." [8] It is hardly fair to make our tastes and aesthetic ideologies retroactive, unless we accord the right of future critics to prepare analogous obituaries for us. In the mid-nineteenth century theorists were burning with romantic ardor; they believed thoroughly in the merger of all the arts: literary, musical, and graphic—a tenet that found ultimate realization in the Wagnerian music-dramas. The present post-romantic sophistication, having repudiated this dogma for a stark neoclassicism, is hardly competent to sit in judgment over such an age.

In spite of early discouragements, the Philharmonic Society flourished quite beyond the dreams of its early visionaries. It not only supplied a sturdy education in serious music to those who desired it but, according to the Sixth Annual Report, soon began to appeal to the fashionable élite who found in the concerts an outlet for their desire for a symbol of exclusiveness, or who "recognized the duty of patronizing the fine arts with liberal appropriations from their affluence." By 1856 "opera-cloaks could be seen in the audience." The Society was now ready to move from Niblo's Theatre, at Broadway and Prince in lower Manhattan, to the fashionable Academy of Music, at Fourteenth and Irving Place, where it remained with minor interruptions until it moved still farther uptown to the Metropolitan Opera House in 1886.

The alliance of the social aristocracy with the promulgation of great music, which was to prove so fertile in later years, took tentative beginnings in the election, for the first time in its history, of a nonplaying associate member as president. Dr. R. Ogden Doremus, professor of chemistry at New York University, who had been associate member for twenty years, was elevated to this post in 1867 after exacting two promises: that the orchestra be increased to one hundred men, and that it engage prominent soloists. Up to this time many of the soloists had been local musicians who served gratis for the public distinction such an association conferred upon them. The orchestra concerts were almost immediately converted into a principal feature of the social season, to the great pecuniary benefit of the organization. In addition to the musical people and the fashionable set, the Society also attracted considerable patronage from those whose religious beliefs forbade their attendance at the opera and the theatre.

But, by no means all the best people harbored such pious aversions to theatre and opera. Consequently, the Philharmonic was not to be the only pet of society. New York was a fantastically expanding field. The city had grown from 400,000 in 1840 to one and one-half million in 1870 and two million in 1880. The Philharmonic was not keeping pace. Many factors, both internal and external to the Society, contributed to the stunting of its growth and ultimately to its very marked decline by the end of the century. Beginning about 1880, New York, with its fabulous wealth, was entering into its "golden age" of the opera. The old aristocracy at the Academy of Music, as well as the newly rich "Wall Street upstarts" who had built the Metropolitan Opera House (opened October, 1883), had generated an appetite for the distingué which the old Philharmonic could never satisfy. The glamour of the prima donnas furnished a more exciting and socially exclusive hobby than a plodding orchestra playing the intellectual Beethoven symphonies.

Other orchestras likewise entered the competitive lists. Discouraged with the desultory, sparse rehearsals and the absenteeism of the cooperative Philharmonic, Theodore Thomas, a leading member of that orchestra since 1854, surging with implacable ambition and musical idealism, had organized his own orchestra. He employed his men full time, inculcated a furious discipline in his ensemble, and infused imagination and variety into the repertoire, all of which quickly outdistanced the loosely knit Philharmonic, which *Dwight's Journal of Music* had labeled "antiquated and old-fogyish" as early as 1864. The lure of full employment and the prestige of membership in the Thomas orchestra attracted from the Philharmonic many of its important players.

Leopold Damrosch, one of the first mature musicians of note to settle in the United States, likewise provided a counterattraction with the establishment of the Symphony Society in 1878. Warmhearted and genial, carrying the prestige of friendship with Wagner, Bülow, and Liszt, Dr. Damrosch succeeded in enlisting the cooperation of certain elements of fashionable New York which neither the cold dignity of Theodore Thomas nor the uninspired Philharmonic could thaw. In fact, Damrosch was given a one-year turn (1876–77) at the moribund Philharmonic. The editor of the Steinway Hall Programme Notes

was glad to learn that the Philharmonic has been reorganized, non-competent members weeded out . . . engaged a thoroughly capable and conscientious conductor in Dr. Leopold Damrosch who, it is hoped, will put a little fresh vim into the Society.

These hostile forces were closing in on this venerable group and threatening it with annihilation.

In despair, the Philharmonic turned to Thomas, counting on the asset of his popularity with the New York public. He was elected in 1877, dropped out one year while engaged in the Cincinnati episode described later, and then was re-elected, polling 54 votes to 9 for Damrosch and 6 for Neuendorff, the interim incumbent who had defeated Dr. Damrosch the preceding year, 46 to 29. When, in 1891, Thomas was called to Chicago, Anton Seidl, the Metropolitan Opera conductor and "dean" of New York musicians at the time, became his logical successor and, like Thomas, played to crowded houses. The concerts were almost at once (November, 1892) transferred to the newly built Music Hall (later "Carnegie Hall") from the Metropolitan Opera House, where they had been housed since 1886 but which Theodore Thomas and other musicians considered too large, and the recesses of the stage too ruinous, for fine musical effect.[9] It was a profitable, if not brilliant period.

The lustre of the Philharmonic was nevertheless blemished by the fact that it carried within its own organization the seeds of its disintegration. After Thomas and Seidl had ushered in a period of hitherto unachieved prosperity, thereby postponing for a couple of decades the inevitable reckoning, the orchestra reverted to a period of drowsy torpor which even the occasional flash of inspired conducting could not shake off. Thomas and Seidl, both of whom had built up a loyal following, definitely marked the end of the period of efflorescence when seats had been at a premium and reasonable artistic integrity had been maintained. After the sudden death of

Seidl in 1898, Emil Paur, late of Boston, was elected with fifty-five votes against five for Walter Damrosch. But patronage declined, and the orchestra now seemed to have no other interest than to maintain itself, its form of government, its stodgy repertoire, and its complacent pace of existence. For these and other reasons it came about that, at the close of the century, when Boston and Chicago possessed virile orchestras of almost world renown, the New York Philharmonic, composed of musicians some of whom were superannuated, many of them tired, was an orchestra with no mark of distinction excepting its chronological seniority. This orchestra was not much more than a hobby of its members, an amiable diversion, a source of pin money, rather than an essential organization enlisting the primary energies and loyalties of its players, and actively fostering the progress of the art.

For decades it had presented only six concerts per season, in addition to public rehearsals, which were increased to eight in 1897–98. If Theodore Thomas and his permanent orchestra had stimulated Boston to put aside its obsolete system, it was now the Boston orchestra, invading New York annually, which pointed up the anachronism of the cooperative Philharmonic. Without financial subsidy, and the quality of its performances constantly subject to odious comparison with the Boston orchestra, it was eking out a threadbare existence, at the point of death from sheer inanition. No first-rate conductor could be attracted under such hopeless conditions.

But it would not be fair to conclude that this was willful stubbornness and sheer inertia. Two dominant forces were operating to buttress the status quo: (1) the strength of the obsolete system of the cooperative organization, and (2) the aloofness of wealth, whose indispensability was demonstrated in the experience of other cities.

Paradoxically enough, it was the very weakness of the organization that constituted its strength. If the orchestra did not yield much in financial and aesthetic returns, it was also true that not much was expected from it. With such a flexible foundation, it could absorb all the vicissitudes of fortune without collapsing. The members, who controlled its destiny by their votes, opposed change for a variety of personal motives. Some feared replacement, others resented disciplined rehearsals, and all were beset by the uncertainties of the proposed new order. They were essentially a group of democratically self-employed musicians who saw no reason why anyone should interfere with their enterprise as long as they were content to maintain it. As for fashion and wealth, it was preoccupied with the opera, which was still in its Augustan age, and had not yet developed solicitude for the orchestra and its affairs. When neither players nor civic leaders sensed a strong need for change, the mechanical law of inertia prevailed.

At this time, however, certain philanthropic elements were moving to capture the Society with a view to its reorganization. Andrew Carnegie had accepted the presidency in 1901, and his friend Walter Damrosch, who had relinquished his post in the Symphony Society and was always good for a half dozen votes in the annual Philharmonic elections, was finally elected conductor for 1902–03. This aroused hopes of financial relief from that segment of society in the city that had always been cordial to him.

One would suppose that an orchestra would seize with alacrity any opportunity of greater financial security. However, gifts come high, and conditions attached to such financial assistance were still considered prohibitive by the membership of the not quite lifeless Philharmonic. During that season, Carnegie and other friends had established a fund of $25,000 for four years, which was pledged to the Philharmonic under the stipulation that the Society would:

(1) admit to the fifteen-member governing board seven members representing the contributors
(2) make certain radical changes in personnel
(3) increase the number of concerts and rehearsals

This was correctly interpreted by the organization as an attempt to destroy the fundamental democratic system of control, and allegedly designed to place the incumbent as permanent conductor during the life of the proposed agreement. The offer was therefore rejected. When the dust had settled, and the outline of future events became clear, Damrosch superfluously announced his noncandidacy for re-election and proceeded to mobilize the forces for the resumption of the concerts of his own Symphony Society.

Year	NEW YORK PHILHARMONIC	NEW YORK SYMPHONY	BOSTON	CHICAGO	CINCINNATI	PHILADELPHIA
1840	HILL, TIMM, LODER AND OTHERS, '42					
1850	EISFELD, BERGMANN AND OTHERS, '49					
1860						
	BERGMANN, '65					
1870		NEW YORK SYMPHONY				
	L. DAMROSCH, '76 THOMAS, '77 NEUENDORF, '78 THOMAS, '79	L. DAMROSCH, '78	BOSTON			
1880			HENSCHEL, '81			
		W. DAMROSCH, '85	GERICKE, '84			
1890	SEIDL, '91		NIKISCH, '89	CHICAGO		
			PAUR, '93	THOMAS, '91	CINCINNATI	
					VAN DER STUCKEN, '95	PHILADELPHIA
	PAUR, '98	SUSPENDED, '98	GERICKE, '98			
1900	W. DAMROSCH, '02 GUESTS, '03	W. DAMROSCH, '03				SCHEEL, 1900
	SAFONOFF, '06		MUCK, '06 FIEDLER, '08	STOCK, '05	SUSPENDED, '07 STOKOWSKI, '09	POHLIG, '07
1910	MAHLER, '09 STRANSKY, '11		MUCK, '12		KUNWALD, '12	STOKOWSKI, '12
1920			RABAUD, '18 MONTEUX, 19		YSAYE, '18	
	STRANSKY AND GUESTS, '21		KOUSSEVITZKY, '24		REINER, '22	
	TOSCANINI-MENGELBERG, '27	MERGED WITH N.Y. PHILHARMONIC '28				
1930	TOSCANINI, '30				GOOSSENS, '31	
	BARBIROLLI, '36					ORMANDY, '36
1940	GUESTS, '41 RODZINSKI, '43			DEFAUW, '43		
	GUESTS, '47 STOKOWSKI-MITROPOULOS, '49		MUNCH, '49	RODZINSKI, '47 GUESTS, '48	JOHNSON, '47	
1950	MITROPOULOS, '50			KUBELIK, '50		

Tenure of Permanent Conductors
ELEVEN AMERICAN SYMPHONY ORCHESTRAS
1840-1950

MINNEAPOLIS						1900
OBERHOFFER, '03	ST. LOUIS					
	ZACH, '07	SAN FRANCISCO				1910
		HADLEY, '11	CLEVELAND	LOS ANGELES		
		HERTZ, '15				
			SOKOLOFF, '18	ROTHWELL, '19		1920
GUESTS, '22 VERBRUGGHEN '23	GANZ, '21					
	GUESTS, '27			SCHNEEVOIGT, '27 RODZINSKI, '29		1930
ORMANDY, '31	GOLSCHMANN, '31	CAMERON AND GUESTS, '30	RODZINSKI, '33	KLEMPERER, '33		
GUESTS, '36 MITROPOULOS,'37		SUSPENDED, '34 MONTEUX, '35				
				GUESTS, '39		1940
			LEINSDORF, '43 GUESTS, '44 SZELL, '46	WALLENSTEIN, '43		
DORATI, '49						1950

49

The aroused Philharmonic, in an heroic effort to reinvigorate its ebbing strength, resorted to a galaxy of guest conductors. Aided by contributions from John D. Rockefeller and others, some of the most eminent conductors of France, England, Germany, and Russia were invited: Colonne, Henry Wood, Weingartner, Safonoff, Richard Strauss, Mengelberg, and several lesser lights. Theodore Thomas, of Chicago, who had still retained some loyal friends—as well as enemies—in New York after ten years of absence, was to have conducted the last concert of the season of 1904–05, and only death intervened in the plans for his grand homecoming.

The public was thrilled with the relay race of conductors who passed the baton from one to the other. The first season was successful beyond the most sanguine hopes, and it was Vassily Safonoff, a more or less obscure Russian, who stunned the audience with his Slavic renditions of the well-known Russian works. But after the third year of guest conductors, appetites were again jaded, and Safonoff, who had appeared with great success in all three years, was elected permanent conductor with a three-year contract at $20,000 per year. In the end, he too failed to maintain his grip on the audience. When the stunned audience awoke—the thrill was gone! The daringly garish interpretation of his fellow-Russian composers by this musical Tartar turned out to be an impossible mannerism, aberrant and irresponsible, when applied to the general repertoire. Eschewing the baton, he employed a fistic style of direction, vehement and theatrical, which called for rude contrasts and extravagant rhythms and tempi.

After three years, in 1908–09, at long last, the members of the orchestra could not fail to see that the cooperative machinery, which had rumbled along for sixty-seven years, was creaking toward its final breakdown. It simply could not rise to modern demands, and was artistically and financially ruinous. Harassed by the memory of past futilities, and frightened by future prospects of the reorganization of the competitive Symphony Society under Walter Damrosch, the Philharmonic was ready to capitulate. It was, in a way, a pathetic denouement to an originally worthy, but now archaic, principle; for such is the irony of "progress," and so far had the world moved, that a group of likeminded friends, democratically banded together as a private enterprise in the service of their art, content with a modest pecuniary reward, was not permitted by a sophisticated society to persevere, but was now compelled to submit to the dictates of efficiency and discipline to fulfill its manifest destiny. Like many another private enterprise, it was taken over by society as soon as it was affected with the public interest.

Under the aggressive sponsorship of Mrs. George R. Sheldon, wife of a banker and Republican chairman of New York City, a guarantee of $90,000 for three years was raised among the "best families" of the city, which included such names as J. P. Morgan, Andrew Carnegie, and Joseph Pulitzer. The conditions of surrender were similar to the terms rejected six years previously:

(1) abandonment of the cooperative plan by which the members controlled the policy and elected the conductors
(2) establishment of an outside board of control, on which the orchestra was, however, to be represented
(3) retirement of the superannuated members, and the addition of younger members
(4) expansion of the season's activities
(5) replacement of Safonoff by Gustav Mahler, with absolute power over membership and musical affairs

All members handed in their resignation, subject to the acceptance of the new musical director.

Gustav Mahler, composer of symphonies and opera conductor, who had spent ten years at the Royal Opera of Vienna and since 1907 had been with the Metropolitan Opera, assumed the direction of this new venture with the highest hopes. He had not been entirely happy in Vienna. Being both a Jew and a very egocentric personality, his difficulties of adjustment were insuperable. Anti-Semitism in Austria was at that time more severe than in Germany. What aggravated the situation still more was that the greatest anti-Semite of them all, Dr. Karl Lueger, was Mayor of Vienna coincident with the tenure of Mahler at the Opera. His conversion to Catholicism was slight protection in such a case. He finally writes, July 17, 1907: "*Ich gehe nach Amerika, weil ich das Gesindel nicht mehr aushalten kann.*"

But he could expect great things from America, its tolerance and its unlimited resources—so he thought—and was highly encouraged by the initial enthusiasm of the orchestra officials. He therefore drew his plans in the grand manner. For the first time in the history of the orchestra it was to emerge from the dull routine of a short series of pairs. To the augmented subscription series, he added a Beethoven cycle, a historical cycle, Sunday concerts, and a tour.

But this first experiment in cooperation between conductor and lay board was doomed to disappointment on both sides. It was a stormy regime. Mahler, who in his artistically successful career had hardened himself to obstacles, and had at times defied royalty itself, was not likely to err on the side of diffidence when dealing with a group of social leaders of New York who "failed" in their comprehension of the principle of artistic supremacy. Unreceptive to interference, or even active criticism, he received a full measure of both. The ladies' committee entered where the Hapsburg Emperor himself had feared to tread. They, who laid down the cash for the project, took an unexpectedly personal interest in the new orchestra and entertained decided notions on matters of programs and soloists. According to Frau Mahler, the ladies ordered him about like a puppet—him, to whom royalty itself did not dictate. He ran afoul of critics such as Krehbiel, who should have known better, for doing what all conductors did then and now—editing the scores and modifying instrumentation.

Nor was the general competitive musical setting auspicious. The Metropolitan Opera was then enjoying one of the most brilliant periods in its history. Gatti-Casazza had assumed the headship and imported Toscanini as principal conductor. Among their stars were the glamorous Caruso, Farrar, Nordica, Homer, Gadski, Sembrich, and Melba. Another opera company, of brief existence, was the Hammerstein company, which crashed the orbit of the Metropolitan like a comet with Tetrazzini, Mary Garden, and John McCormack. As if that were not enough, a popular, preseason, Italian opera company held forth at the Academy of Music and siphoned off some of the city's musical enthusiasm. Between 1880 and 1910, New York was very fertile in the creation of new millionaires, some of whose metamorphosed mansions still speckle uptown Manhattan. This new wealth sought its social dividends in opera.

As for the orchestra, which had recently slipped out of the protective cocoon of the cooperative system, and had eased through three years of guest conducting, it was hardly ready for Mahler's savage prosecution of musical ideals and the continuous discipline of a leader of thorough experience and an abundance of self-confidence. Neither did his almost pathologically irritable temperament and blunt speech alleviate the tense situation. The final melancholy fact was that the attendance "failed to meet expectations." The spring of 1911, the time of Mahler's retirement and death, therefore found the long-suffering Philharmonic exhausted after its first brush with big-time company, and its vitality at its lowest ebb. It was drifting toward extinction, but was revived by one of those strokes of fortune that almost every organization requires occasionally, and of which the New York Philharmonic has enjoyed its quota.

This stroke of good fortune consisted in a bequest of almost $1,000,000 from the estate of Joseph Pulitzer, owner and editor of the New York *World*, who had died in 1911. The stipulations set forth in this—one of his many well-known benevolences—were as follows:

(1) establishment of a permanent orchestra
(2) a list of 1,000 contributing members
(3) low rates of admission
(4) less esoteric programs and "not too severely classical," with preference for his favorites Wagner, Beethoven, and Liszt

Within a few months, the conditions of the will were fulfilled and the court was petitioned to implement the bequest.

At this juncture, in its search for a conductor, the board turned to a relatively unknown young man. Having tried previously a mature musician of established eminence, and found him a partial, if not complete, failure, they now imported a relatively untried *Kapell-meister*, the thirty-nine-year-old Joseph Stransky from Germany. He turned out to be more than amenable to the stipulation of the Pulitzer bequest to lighten the programs. A person of affable demeanor and a good administrator, he enjoyed a large personal following. Given the benefit of more rehearsals than any previous conductor in the history of the orchestra, he was credited with being a good drill master even by those critics who did not impute to him more profound musical talents. There is no question of his unique service to his organization in reviving the old, and generating new, public interest in orchestral music. If higher criticism condemned him for pandering to the public taste by playing an excess of Dvořák, Liszt, and Wagner, it was exactly that policy which reflected itself favorably in the box office. While Aldrich of the *Times* soon began to lament the fact that the Philharmonic audience no longer included the passionate few of "the cultivated, the most exacting among the city's music lovers," the concerts were selling standing room. If he was not the "greatest conductor in the world" as some of his followers naïvely contended, there is still no doubt that he earned his $30,000 salary by contributing a service that was vitally needed at that particular moment. The seventy-fifth anniversary (1916–17) was less a pleasurable and triumphant celebration than an occasion for serious stock-taking of future prospects of the orchestra, and an evaluation and assessment of the widely divergent views on the conductor.

The Philharmonic could not escape odious comparison with its sister orchestras. The Philadelphia orchestra, with its sensational young conductor, Leopold Stokowski, carried the competition into home territory and was beginning to electrify New York audiences. Boston and Chicago had previously attained national and international prominence, and New York, responding to these rival pressures, could not hold back. In the meantime, New York had also absorbed the lesson taught it by the experience of Boston, Philadelphia, and Chicago, that no orchestra could attain the now generally established musical standards without adequate financial subsidies.

At this very time (1920) there were three subsidized orchestras in New York: The New York Philharmonic, which had enjoyed an inadequate subsidy since 1909; the New York Symphony under Walter Damrosch, which had been supported by Henry Harkness Flagler since 1914; and the National Symphony, whose financial sponsors were Clarence Mackay, president of the Postal Telegraph Company, and Adolph Lewisohn, copper magnate. The last-named orchestra was founded in the spring of 1919 with the rather Gertrude Stein-like title of "New Symphony Orchestra of the Musicians' New Orchestra Society," with thirty-five-year-old Edgar Varèse, a mod-

A print from the original of the very first program of the New York Philharmonic concert, December 7, 1842. Note the mixture of symphonic works, operatic arias, and chamber music, assisted by three vocal solos. In those days, the music was more important than the conductor, whose name was omitted from the program. The Beethoven Symphony was conducted by U. C. Hill (violinist); the Overture to Oberon, by D. G. Etienne (piano or horn); and the Kalliwoda Overture by H. C. Timm (piano or trombone). During the vocal solos, the orchestra was directed by Mr. Timm. (Courtesy New York Philharmonic-Symphony Society)

WALTER DAMROSCH AND THE NEW YORK SYMPHONY ORCHESTRA

Next to Theodore Thomas, Walter Damrosch was the most traveled conductor. Between 1885 and 1928, he covered the United States with orchestra and opera. Here, he and his orchestra are leaving Pennsylvania Station, about 1925. The bearded figure in the foreground is the famous flutist, Georges Barrère. (Culver Service) ern composer recently arrived from France, as conductor. Varèse, however, conducted only one concert and was followed briefly by Artur Bodansky, who had been associated with the Metropolitan Opera. In the fall of 1920, its ambitious guarantors secured William Mengelberg, who had not only had a brilliant career at the Concert-gebouw in Amsterdam, but who raised the pitch of excitement of the concert patrons in New York to a height never before experienced. That Mengelberg could realize his genius was, of course, the result of the generosity of the philanthropists who gave him the green light on expensive rehearsals and high salary scales—which was also the rock upon which his orchestra was destined to be wrecked. New York was only now learning the hard way that rehearsals, at union rates, constitute one of the "concealed" items in the budget of a competent orchestra. It was a magnificent season, the Mengelberg season of 1920–21, as long as it lasted. But it was too costly to endure. The significant features of this experience were, however, first that New York was taking an interest in orchestral music and showering it with the attention that had hitherto been bestowed only upon the opera, and secondly that standards of excellence, long since established in other cities, were finally being courted in New York.

Since the dispersion of the financial and musical resources over three large orchestras was disastrous, the solution obviously indicated their amalgamation.

With the avowed ambition of making the oldest symphony orchestra also the finest in the world, it absorbed Mengelberg's National Symphony Orchestra. Stransky, who had proven his great box office appeal, was retained for the first half of that season; Mengelberg, who had earned the respect of the critics and philanthropists, took over the second half. Arthur Judson, manager of the Philadelphia orchestra, was appointed manager.

The major competitor of the Philharmonic had long been the New York Symphony Society, founded in 1878 by Leopold Damrosch and enduring for almost fifty years, with only periodic interruptions, under Walter Damrosch. Much of its strength lay in the personal following of the Damrosch family, thereby dividing musical New York into two factions, both socially and financially. Many patrons had furthermore come to enjoy the Damrosch offerings, which, in the later years, were much richer in novelties than those of the more conservative Philharmonic. Musically, however, it could never challenge its senior rival. Now that Walter Damrosch had reached the age of retirement, and both organizations were beset with financial worries, and the Symphony Society had gratified normal sentiment by rounding out the half-century, the stage was set for the consolidation of forces that had been proposed as early as 1910.[10] The merger was announced in February, 1928. Both Mackay, who had come to the Philharmonic board from the National Symphony, and Flagler, who had spent over $1,000,000 on the New York Symphony during the preceding decade, were included in the reorganized board, thereby effecting an important consolidation of financial forces.

There were those who genuinely regretted the demise of the Symphony Society because they feared that the new orchestra would present a less enterprising repertoire than had Mr. Damrosch, that concerts would be less frequent, and that not all patrons could be accommodated in the telescoped schedule. Some even bluntly asserted that it was motivated primarily by the desire of the "impoverished millionaires" to get out from under. The merger was symbolized in the union of the names, the Philharmonic-Symphony Society, and Arturo Toscanini, the conductor of the hour, was entrusted with the selection of the personnel, twenty of whom were to be drawn from the Damrosch group.[11]

Toscanini had already stirred his audiences during his tenure at the Metropolitan Opera, 1908–15. He was known for his inflexible discipline, his unappeasable frenzy for technical perfection, his scoreless conducting, and his implacable demand that prima donnas, who had been traditionally considered a law unto themselves, be subservient to the conductor. Added to his phenomenal control of the score was an equally phenomenal repertoire of invectives hurled against his musicians, probably evident enough to the custodian who swept up the broken batons, but entirely unsuspected by those members of the audience who melted under the spell of the translucent perfection of the performance. Although Toscanini's experience had been almost exclusively operatic, he had conducted some concerts in

Italy,[12] and the Metropolitan orchestra in a few concerts in April, 1913. During the postwar season of 1920–21 he had also visited the United States with a handpicked La Scala orchestra in a goodwill tour of over forty concerts, from New York to Omaha. Suffused with all the trappings and sentiments of patriotic ardor, the occasion thrilled the old subscribers of the Metropolitan Opera who cherished memories of a decade and more ago. Most patrons readily overlooked the scattered comments, floated by a few critics when they had taken their second wind, that his orchestra was technically inferior, and, in fact, that the maestro had really not proven himself a symphonic conductor at all.

Toscanini made his debut with the New York Philharmonic as guest conductor on January 14, 1926—as had been announced more than a year previously—and made his last appearance on April 29, 1936. During these ten years, while serving either as guest or permanent conductor—never for a period longer than about half a season, often less—he evoked a frenzied adulation almost more characteristic of a sports stadium than of the dignified halls of a symphony concert. With crowds jamming the entrance way and cheers and exclamations from the audience, he, who had suppressed all grandstand play on the part of the operatic prima donnas, now became himself the supreme star featured above the orchestra. During the last season, the management, loath to lose the benefits accruing from this high-salaried (estimated at $100,000 for ten weeks)[13] sensation, added fifty cents to the price of the single ticket, which it guaranteed to refund on the "nonappearance of the conductor scheduled for this concert."

What was the secret of the fantastic and unprecedented grip of this virtuoso conductor on the emotions of the public? It would be too naïvely simple to answer that it was exclusively musical, for every discerning conductor and manager knows better, and every critic can cite conductors of high scholarship who do not obtain comparable deserts in adulation.

No pat answer is forthcoming, not only because the capture of public acclaim is a complex achievement, but also because not all elements of an impression ever rise into consciousness. Consequently, not all observers would agree on the diagnosis of his magnetism. An academic listing culled from contemporary critical commentary

includes both aesthetic and nonaesthetic ingredients: (1) absolute
finesse and vigor in rendition to the last detail, and razor-sharp precision achieved by no previous conductors; (2) noncontroversial, un-
complicated, almost reactionary repertoire, consisting of Beethoven,
Wagner, Brahms, some Mendelssohn, and a liberal condiment of
tuneful Italian overtures rendered with the aforementioned exquisite
precision; (3) absence of distorted and individualistic readings that
would draw critical fire, but rather fidelity to the "intentions of the
composer," and a characteristic forthright performance without
"crude rubatos" resorted to by "romantic showmen"; (4) colorful
personality, tales about phenomenal memory, the inexorable demands upon his musicians, his driving discipline, his temperamental
explosions, which date back to the "Met" days; (5) his open defiance
of the dictators Mussolini and Hitler,[14] which endeared him to a
large element of the New York population and visibly affected attendance at concerts at a time when both psychological satiety and
the depression presaged a lull in patronage.

It is clear that this conductor had something for everybody, including even the nonmusical, a kind of omnibus appeal that is necessary for those who would attain popular success. But public acclaim
was not without its discordant notes in press and corridor gossip.
Some critics observed that there was less emphasis on tone and more
on structure; less on poetry, more on meticulous cultivation of technique. To the modernist, his repertoire was utterly conventional,
threadbare, and unenterprising. Some deplored his neglect of the
American composer. To others, the virtue of meticulous clarity and
the chiseled, metallic contours became a passionate fault which inhibited the flexibility and mellowness of style so essential to genuinely satisfying performance. His vigorous execution often became so
strident that the pastel shades of gentler moods were entirely oblit-
erated; his tempi were often hurried when restraint was called for.
As for his temper tantrums, and his famous hour-long sulks in the
Green Room, it was not clear to the commentators whether they
were the manifestations of a divine frenzy of a supreme artist, a
dramatic hoax to "get results," or whether they derived from a
strange sense of showmanship.

However, such scattered criticisms never attained sufficient mo-

mentum to precipitate ugly and cacophonous public controversy—
as was the misfortune of almost every other conductor of comparable stature: Nikisch, Theodore Thomas, or Stokowski. He was
never torn between social factions, a kind of struggle which New
York had by this time outgrown. On the contrary, there was an
extraordinary unanimity of acclaim—rare for a public figure. After
sitting through a half dozen seasons of such uniformly noncontroversial performances, a critic might well have worried where his
next adjective was coming from!

Nevertheless, it is interesting to speculate how Toscanini would
have endured if, like Theodore Thomas, Frederick Stock, Stokowski, Koussevitzky, Monteux, and others with long tenures, he had
had to risk boring his audiences by conducting concert after concert, year in and year out, with only minor midseason vacations,
with a variegated repertoire, without "playing it safe" with standard works that are "sure to please." Be that as it may, the Toscanini decade was for the new Philharmonic-Symphony Society a
golden age during which it savored to the full the novel and exhilarating experience of flirting with greatness.

But even Toscanini could not escape the symptoms of economic
adversity of the depression years. In the fall of 1934, there were
rumors of still another merger—this time with the Metropolitan
Opera.[15] Both organizations were suffering the economic afflictions
of the threadbare 'thirties, and Gatti-Casazza had announced his retirement at the close of the 1934–35 season. The plan, however, never
jelled. Two obvious objections were that it would have meant the
dismissal of the "Met" orchestra, and that the Philharmonic orchestra could not possibly have acquitted itself well in both capacities.
Although such collaboration is rather general in Europe where the
symphonic season is shorter, the long and arduous orchestra schedule
in symphony-minded United States made such a project impractical.
Consulted on this desperate depression-born project, the Maestro
advised against it, and it was definitely abandoned almost before it
emerged from the rumor stage.

Toscanini conducted his last Philharmonic concert April 29, 1936,
amid a riot of public frenzy. It was generally, but mistakenly, assumed to be the end of his American career.[16] The farewell concert,

which was not in the subscription series, packed Carnegie Hall, and a thousand persons waited in line for standing room to which only 140 were admitted. Tickets had gone on sale at $10 top and $200 a box, in one final fantastic splurge. Mounted police and fifty foot patrols kept order. This episode is indicative of the incredible public ado that the orchestra and Toscanini had aroused. After the concert, he proceeded almost immediately to Palestine to conduct the newly organized Israel Philharmonic at the instigation of Bronislaw Hubermann, the eminent violinist.

No specific reason was publicly advanced for the retirement of Toscanini, except that he wished to be "free," that he was tired, and was of an age to retire anyway. On the other hand, it was "confidentially" asserted in the press that it was not entirely a secret that his resignation was the result of dissatisfaction on both sides, that the Maestro made demands as to salary, rehearsals, programs that seemed excessive—all of which was "officially" denied with equal facility, with the public as usual a perplexed bystander. It seems certain that management strove, for both artistic and commercial reasons, to retain the conductor.

There was no unanimous appraisal of his long-run worth. That he had a favorable effect on public interest was an unquestioned corollary to his unprecedented drawing power. However, the Toscanini cult produced possible harm in the prominence accorded the "star" conductor. His very popularity was a liability in that, both in the eyes of the public and in the esteem of the orchestra, he dwarfed every conductor who had to fill out his unfinished seasons. The rehearsal experiences of these "guest-of-the-month" conductors, and the untenanted seats in the auditorium, confirmed the folk wisdom that no orchestra can serve two masters. So obvious was the demoralization of both orchestra and audience that some critics actually declared Toscanini's departure not a catastrophe but a blessing in disguise if the orchestra management were only wise enough to learn its lesson. The choice of his successor was therefore a critical one.

In February, 1936, two weeks after the publication of Toscanini's retirement, it was announced that Wilhelm Furtwängler, Europe's most eligible conductor, would assume the baton the following year.

Then fifty years old, conductor of Europe's two most noted orchestras in Berlin and Leipzig, he was not unknown in New York where he had done a turn during the seasons 1924–27. His urgent desire to return to America was common knowledge. Furtwängler, however, had been embarrassingly involved in the Nazi regime which, since 1933, had aroused hatred, revulsion, and fear in the rest of the world. Although he had publicly espoused the case of Hindemith against the Nazis and had dramatically resigned his post in Berlin as a protest against their creeping control of things musical, his skirts did not seem sufficiently clean to appease the smoldering anti-Nazi sentiment in New York, which was about ready to burst into flame. To a certain extent, Furtwängler had patched up his differences with Hitler on the professed principle of the separation of art and politics, and had conducted only "as guest" in Berlin since the spring of 1935. But to clinch his embarrassment, the German government calculatingly heralded Furtwängler's "reinstatement" on the very evening of the New York announcement. Unable to ignore the powerful, but by no means unanimous protests, the Philharmonic, after an exchange of communication with Furtwängler, accepted his resignation because "political controversy [is] disagreeable to me." [17]

The position was again vacant. On the chance of securing a "find" who might be on the rise, the board's choice fell on a thirty-seven-year-old Englishman of Italian extraction, John Barbirolli, who had achieved precocious success in England both with opera and orchestra. To be catapulted into such a position—successor to Toscanini and substitute for Furtwängler—was a fate not to be wished on one's worst enemy. Not only would the new incumbent be vulnerable to comparison with his immediate predecessor, but he would necessarily expose his relative inexperience to his own orchestra. A steady grind of concerts is a physical and intellectual burden that is absolutely unknown to the European conductor. After the first year Barbirolli was entrusted with the responsibility of the entire season, with only a short midwinter holiday. The added fact that the depression had brought a decline in patronage, which had been felt even during the Toscanini regime, probably added its harassing and disheartening effects on the new incumbent. The task proved an insuperable one, and Barbirolli ultimately returned to England, with a few voices still proclaiming that he had been the victim of a raw deal.

The centennial year, 1941–42, was memorialized by a bevy of nine guest conductors for short turns on the rostrum. It was a feast for the sensation seeker, and a field day for the critics, who seized the unusual opportunity to assess the relative merits of conductors controlling exactly the same material. The podium was, however, again untenanted.

Artur Rodzinski, formerly assistant conductor in Philadelphia, who had acquired a reputation in Los Angeles and Cleveland for whipping orchestras into disciplined shape, and had "guested" for some weeks during Barbirolli's very first season (1936–37), received the new call, which carried the title of Musical Director, a status which presumably conferred more authoritative responsibility than the title of mere "conductor." Hired for the purpose of renovating an orchestra with which he was already somewhat familiar, he signalized his entry upon his new duties by dismissing, before the first rehearsal, fourteen men, including the concertmaster and a half dozen other first-desk men. Reasons were never made public, but surmises were plentiful. After an excited skirmish with the union, a compromise was reached by the reinstatement of five members.

The rebuilding proceeded apparently to the entire satisfaction of critics and public. All the more severe was the shock when, in mid-season of 1946–47 during negotiations for a new contract, Rodzinski submitted his resignation embellished with accusations against management of crass invasion of the province of conductorial responsibilities. Management shrewdly refrained from participating in the public recriminations, but its rebuttal consisted in an immediate release from his contract, while the press reviewed the general philosophy of the division of powers, managerial and artistic, and bemoaned this new "evidence" of the subjection of art to material considerations. Before discharging his parting salvo, Rodzinski had in his pocket an offer from Chicago where another "repair job" was supposedly in order. Thither he betook himself in 1947.

In search of a successor, the New York management again pondered the possibilities of dividing its heavy annual schedule between two co-conductors, as had been done in the days of Toscanini and

Mengelberg. The success of such a dual arrangement was, of course, difficult to assure. It is a real question whether it "worked" in the twenties and thirties. Mitropoulos and Stokowski shared the podium for one year (1949–50), but the following year the Minneapolis conductor was given full appointment as conductor-in-chief.

The fall of 1950 was marked by a very radical departure in concert policy, namely the appearance of the orchestra on the stage of the Roxy motion picture theatre for a four-a-day concert during a two-week period. Apparently conceived by Spyros Skouras, who was a member of both the Symphony board and the Roxy management, this engagement was a reply to the pleas of the orchestra personnel for a longer season, and to the desire of the Philharmonic to gain new friends. The orchestra for this occasion was no streamlined "pop" compromise, but included the complete roster from concertmaster to percussion, Mitropoulos conducting.

Editorial opinion was not unanimous on this break with tradition. The symphony orchestra had struggled for a century to attain an exclusive status, and had laboriously trained the audience to sit in silence during a full-length concert. It was therefore natural that many should regret the decision to accept the role of sideshow to a motion picture, however discriminatingly that picture might have been selected. It recalls the scandal caused by Richard Strauss in 1904 by conducting a symphony concert in the auditorium of Wanamaker's department store. On the other hand, the proponents of the venture view it as a method of bringing good music to that part of the populace that would not dream of coming to it. To them it is a clue to the "solution of the symphony problem." The readiness of the New York Philharmonic-Symphony to embrace on a small scale an opportunity to humanize the concert repertoire, may some day be considered the turning point in the history of the orchestra.

REPERTOIRE   A century of uninterrupted orchestral programs of the New York Philharmonic affords an extraordinary view of changes in musical taste. No other orchestra in America covers so long a span, but it is exceeded by the London Philharmonic, the Gewandhaus of Leipzig, the Société des Concerts of Paris, and equalled by the Philharmonic of Vienna, except that the last-named suffered several dark seasons. What the European orchestras gain in antiquity, however, they more than lose in the sparse number of concerts, the low volume of repertoire, and the heterogeneity of orchestral offerings. The American repertoire, especially in later decades, is mixed with less nonorchestral "chaff." As a consequence, the New York Philharmonic repertoire remains a unique phenomenon in the annals of world music. In depicting the life spans of composers in a greater variety of stages, and unfolding a complete turnover in certain styles of composition, such a hundred-year record discloses, in conjunction with the leaner records of other cities, the principles underlying the shifts in taste, which a snapshot observation would never disclose.

At the time of founding of the New York Philharmonic Society, Beethoven was supreme in solitary glory, although he has since that time shared his exalted status with Wagner, Brahms, and Tschaikowsky in various orchestras. In the first three years, his compositions occupied forty per cent of the repertoire, and were represented on nearly every program. Mendelssohn, a star of lesser magnitude, was also at the peak of his eminence, but faded perceptibly after his death (1847).

Several now totally forgotten composers were then still popular: Kalliwoda (1801–66), a German symphonist; Lindpaintner (1791–1856), a conductor and much respected composer of operas, symphonies, and overtures; Hummel (1778–1837), whose chamber music and brilliant piano concertos competed favorably with those of Beethoven in his day. Though never considered of first magnitude, they had not yet lost their places on the boards.

After its birth and infancy in Germany, the new romantic school was not long in shaking itself loose from the old anchorage. Though Beethoven was still revered as the father of romanticism, the more dramatic innovators, Wagner and Liszt, pushed forward aggressively and soon established a cult of their own. In New York, these names appeared on the program almost as soon as they did in Europe. Bergmann introduced Wagner in the early fifties and Liszt a few years later, to the dismay of the conservative members of the audience.

With the election of Theodore Thomas (1877) to the leadership of the Philharmonic, a new era was inaugurated. Without minimizing the services of Eisfeld and Bergmann, the first more or less regular conductors of the Society, it is still true that Thomas was the first American symphonic conductor in the modern disciplined sense. He embarked on a still more expanded repertoire and introduced many "first times" to the American audiences. Though he has gone down in history for his militant sponsorship of Wagner, this aspect of his regime has been exaggerated because anything pertaining to that controversial public figure engraved itself on public attention. Thomas embraced all other new figures as well—Richard Strauss, Dvořák, Tschaikowsky, and the resurrected Bach. He cultivated Beethoven in the traditional fashion, up to about twenty per cent of the repertoire, while Liszt, Schubert, Schumann, Berlioz, Rubinstein, and Mendelssohn, and a host of miscellaneous composers, made regular appearances with a range of two to seven per cent. A cold, quantitative calculation indicates that there has probably never been a conductor of the New York Philharmonic who has displayed a less distorted taste or presented a more balanced and eclectic series of programs.

A shift in soloist policy was introduced about 1870. Since its inception, the Philharmonic had always considered that it conferred an honor upon its soloists, which the latter were happy to reciprocate with performances rendered gratis. Many of these were undoubtedly the result of mild intrigue and marginal negotiation. The fact that many of these soloists were hardly likely to add splendor to the reputation of the orchestra, or even to themselves, had been a matter of public and critical comments. During the last quarter of the century, however, the glamour soloist emerged. Though the traveling virtuosos were not as abundant as today, such international artists as Anton Rubinstein, Wieniawski, Wilhelmj, Julia Rivé, Remenyi, Georg Henschel, Emil Fischer, and Lilli Lehmann trickled into the programs, beginning about 1875.

With the departure of Theodore Thomas for Chicago (1891) to found a new orchestra, Anton Seidl, coming from the Metropolitan Opera, introduced innovations of a different sort. He had come to the United States almost direct from the Wagner household, where he had worked and studied with the master himself. If, after Bergmann, Thomas, and Damrosch it was no longer necessary to introduce Wagner to the American audience, the new conductor was nevertheless able to import a new style of conducting. The romantic school of Wagner and Bülow charged the conductor with the responsibility of personal interpretation and expression, and Seidl flavored even the classics with flexible tempi and unconventional nuances; in short, he startled the sophisticates with the "Wagnerization" of the classics.

Quite in keeping with these personal predilections, he doubled the incidence of Wagner's compositions from four to eight per cent of the repertoire, and that of Liszt from two to four. As would seem right to a Wagnerite, Brahms was reduced from about six per cent in the previous five-year period, to three during the Seidl tenure. Haydn, Mozart, Schubert, and Schumann suffered analogously. Beethoven declined a bit, but was beyond much tampering. The most violent skew was the growth of Dvořák from four to twelve per cent, that derived from totally different circumstances. Dvořák was resident in New York from 1892 to 1895 as head of the American Conservatory. Seidl premièred the *New World* Symphony, December 15, 1893, and presented other compositions in deference to the distinguished visitor and to the undoubted delight of the public.

After the short regime of Emil Paur and the bevy of guest conductors corralled for the purpose of infusing vitality into the moribund organization, Safonoff electrified the public with his bombastic interpretation of Tschaikowsky's *Pathétique*. In a few years it was perceived that he had hardly been successful at anything else. The Russian composers occupied almost one-third of the repertoire. Tschaikowsky, alone, carried off about twenty per cent of the total, while Glinka, Rimsky-Korsakoff, Rubinstein, Glazounoff, and Scriabin, the last named a former pupil of Safonoff, bring up the rest of the Slavonic family. Brahms declined to the vanishing point; only Beethoven was sufficiently immune to maintain his approximate position, though exceeded by Tschaikowsky for the first time in the career of either of them.

The advent of Mahler (1909) marked an expansion in programming as well as financial administration. By adding to the regular pairs a Beethoven cycle and an historical cycle, the programs were given an educational tone; and the supplemental Sunday afternoon series, which since 1930 have been broadcast by CBS, compensated for this trend by expanding the audience to the less mature groups. The addition of a tour to the aforementioned innovations indicated the serious purposes and exalted ambitions of Gustav Mahler for this orchestra which he, himself, was not permitted to exploit fully. The building of an audience was left to his successor, Josef Stransky, a conductor of lesser capacities, but infinitely more adaptable in the implementation of his plans.

Stransky opened the season of 1911–12 in the spirit of Mr. Pulitzer's bequest, which had attached to it the provision that his favorite composers be given a hearing. Beethoven, Wagner, and Liszt, who had long ago survived their controversial period, were accorded most generous hearings. He featured other favorites—Tschaikowsky (nine per cent); Dvořák, his Czech compatriot (five per cent); and Richard Strauss (five per cent). The orchestra prospered financially. For the first time since the days of Thomas and Seidl, they experienced the luxury and thrill of sold-out houses. But if there is an incongruity between material prosperity and aesthetic progress, here was an illustration of it; and the more sophisticated members of the audience and critical fraternity clamored for a change.

Since 1923, when Stransky relinquished the post, nearly all of the world's great conductors have occupied the podium for a shorter or longer period. None, however, persisted through so long a period, nor lifted the public to such a pitch of frenzy as did Toscanini. The analysis of his repertoire, compared to the composite repertoire of the ten other orchestras for the same period, gives evidence of the degree of his conservatism, which indeed the conductor himself had always acknowledged. By his own declaration, he wished to "come nearer the truth of Haydn and Beethoven" and leave to younger men the responsibility to promote new music.[18] Beethoven constituted nearly a quarter of the repertoire, as against half that amount for the national average. His meager American repertoire comprised only the following items: Hanson, Symphony No. 2; Ernest Schelling, *Impressions of an Artist's Life*, for piano and orchestra (composer at the piano); Bernard Wagenaar, Symphony No. 2; Hans

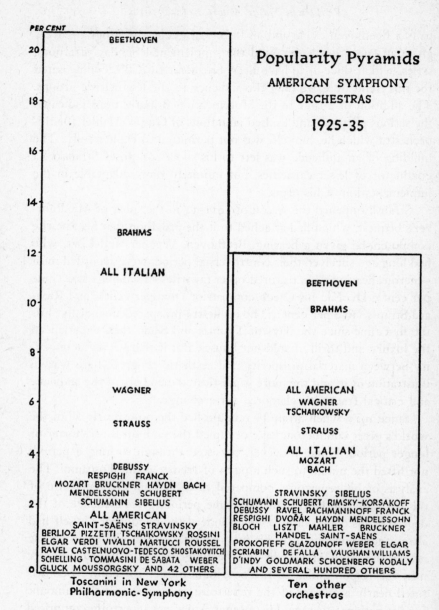

PER CENT

| Toscanini in New York Philharmonic-Symphony | Ten other orchestras |

Popularity Pyramids

AMERICAN SYMPHONY
ORCHESTRAS

1925-35

BEETHOVEN

BRAHMS

ALL ITALIAN

WAGNER

STRAUSS

DEBUSSY
RESPIGHI   FRANCK
MOZART BRUCKNER HAYDN BACH
MENDELSSOHN   SCHUBERT
SCHUMANN   SIBELIUS
ALL AMERICAN
SAINT-SAËNS   STRAVINSKY
BERLIOZ PIZZETTI TSCHAIKOWSKY ROSSINI
ELGAR VERDI VIVALDI MARTUCCI ROUSSEL
RAVEL CASTELNUOVO-TEDESCO SHOSTAKOVITCH
SCHELLING TOMMASINI DE SABATA WEBER
GLUCK MOUSSORGSKY AND 42 OTHERS

BEETHOVEN

BRAHMS

ALL AMERICAN
WAGNER
TSCHAIKOWSKY

STRAUSS

ALL ITALIAN
MOZART
BACH

STRAVINSKY SIBELIUS
SCHUMANN SCHUBERT RIMSKY-KORSAKOFF
DEBUSSY RAVEL RACHMANINOFF FRANCK
RESPIGHI DVOŘÁK HAYDN MENDELSSOHN
BLOCH   LISZT   MAHLER   BRUCKNER
HANDEL   SAINT-SAËNS
PROKOFIEFF GLAZOUNOFF WEBER ELGAR
SCRIABIN   DE FALLA   VAUGHAN WILLIAMS
D'INDY GOLDMARK SCHOENBERG KODALY
AND SEVERAL HUNDRED OTHERS

*The well-known conservatism of Toscanini is indicated by the high
proportion of Beethoven, the large amount of Italian music, and the
meager place given American composers.*

Wetzler, Symphonic Dance, *Basque Venus;* and Abram Chasins, *Flirtation in a Chinese Garden* and *Parade*. The Chasins and Wagenaar compositions were world premières. On his European tour in the spring of 1930, he played no American compositions. The most notorious novelty of his career was the first American concert performance of Ravel's *Bolero*, November 14, 1929, which he allegedly played about one-third faster than indicated by the composer.[19] Toscanini's detractors, however, seized on his warped proportion of Italian music, which comprised a list of twenty-two assorted composers, including repeated performance of seven of Rossini's overtures, and the revival of other and lesser known compatriots. (As conductor of the NBC orchestra, he somewhat liberalized his repertoire, and on November 2, 1942, actually played an American program consisting of the works of Loeffler, Creston, Gould, and Gershwin.)

After Toscanini's departure, the German and Italian compositions very quickly resumed their accustomed levels. Barbirolli, however, consonant with his English heritage, showed some favoritism for his countrymen: Elgar, Purcell, and several minor writers; while the American contingent increased a trifle, principally because the Toscanini level had been so depressed.

The New York Symphony Society (1878)

The history of the New York Symphony Society is practically coincident with the professional life of the Damrosches—Leopold, the father, and Walter, the son. At the time of his arrival in New York in 1871, the elder Damrosch found the musical affairs of the city dominated by the "benevolent despot," Theodore Thomas, who naturally looked upon the newcomer as a rival. We have his son's testimony for the subsequently oft-repeated anecdote that the forty-three-year-old Thomas, after being introduced to the newcomer, only three years his senior, expressed the threat: "I hear, Dr. Damrosch [Damrosch was an M.D.], that you are a very fine musician, but I want to tell you one thing: whoever crosses my path, I crush." [20] Whether or not it is true that the adherents of these notable men felt the rivalry more strongly than did the principals themselves, it is true that the conflict in the New York arena never did end in a clear-cut victory for either one. While Thomas dominated the orchestral field as long as he remained in New York, he was finally obliged to leave the city because his economic position was untenable in terms of his demands. On the other hand, Leopold Damrosch secured a good foothold in opera, gained the support of highly influential families, all of which redounded to the long-term benefit of his son, and assured the periodic financial security of his orchestra, while the New York Philharmonic was eking out an existence on its accumulated prestige.

Leopold Damrosch was a violinist, who had played under Liszt in Weimar and had acquired some conductorial experience in Breslau before emigrating to the United States at the invitation of the Arion Männergesangverein of New York. Of course, this position with the Arion society was never meant to occupy the full time of such an energetic and schooled musician. Damrosch' major opportunity came with the retirement and death of Carl Bergmann, who had been head of the Philharmonic. To Damrosch fell the task of resuscitating the flagging public interest in the Philharmonic. He failed and the dividends of the season 1876–77 sagged to the lowest point in history. His son, Walter, a lad of fourteen, played second violin in the orchestra "just for the experience." Some have declared that his first failure was due to circumstances beyond the control of the conductor—but the stigma had its effect, for when Thomas, who had succeeded Damrosch as conductor of the Philharmonic, departed for Cincinnati, the Society elected not Damrosch but Adolph Neuendorff, who had been conducting German opera in New York for some years. The vote of forty-six to only twenty-nine for Damrosch may not have been a too disgraceful defeat since a shift of nine of the seventy-five votes would have upset these results. But it definitely ended for two decades the threat of the Damrosch faction to capture the Philharmonic, a venture which was not again to be attempted until 1902 when the son, Walter, was involved. In both instances, they responded to the rebuff by establishing their own orchestras.

With the election of Theodore Thomas to the headship of the Philharmonic in the fall of 1877, which was to end the hostilities between the Thomas private orchestra and the Philharmonic, Damrosch collected an orchestra of his own from the supply of musicians remaining after Mr. Thomas had selected the best. With this orchestra Damrosch offered a series of symphonic matinees during the season of 1877–78. With Thomas safely (it was thought) ensconced in Cincinnati the following year, the opportunity seemed propitious to move into the vacancy left by the popular leader, and this, by inevitable Damrosch logic, led to the founding of the New York Symphony Society. According to its minutes of October 22, 1878, the Society was founded "to assure the continuance of concerts threatened by the departure of Theodore Thomas to Cincinnati." Steinway Hall on Fourteenth Street was secured for the dates which had been held for the Thomas orchestra, and it was offered rent-free by Henry Steinway. With the unexpected return of Thomas, Damrosch and his Symphony Society moved to the Academy of Music, which also housed the Philharmonic, now destined to be its rival, potential or actual, for the next fifty years.

As early as 1883–84, the minutes of the Society report informal discussion on plans for a Hall of Music adequate for the purposes of a symphony orchestra, a plan which was later to be fulfilled by Andrew Carnegie, who joined the Symphony Society board in 1886 and was elevated to its presidency in 1888. In later years he was to be joined by other equally impressive families: Rockefeller, Morgan, Roosevelt, Gould, and Vanderbilt.

The enlistment of such an array of wealth for the new society in a brief five years was an achievement the like of which Thomas never attained in New York. It has been ascribed in large part to its leader's personal characteristics. Leopold Damrosch had always carried the prestige of European training and was a friend of its most noted musical representatives, Liszt, Bülow, and Wagner. Later he conducted a successful Festival of Music, as well as a season of German Opera at the Metropolitan Opera House, which had been built by the rising generation of wealth, some of whose names overlapped with the previously cited Symphony Board. He was personally affable, a cultured conversationalist, and an enthusiastic romanticist. But his conducting never attained the finish of Theodore Thomas:

his beat was less distinct, and he never had access to the best players.
He was reputed to be at his best in Berlioz and Wagner.

"His nervous manner is quite suited to the nervous vigor of these composers. One is not annoyed by the windmill flourishes of his arms or the
wild waving of his hair when there is so much wind and wildness in the
music which he conducts." [21]

Thus he differed from Thomas in sponsoring the "flexible line" of
the Liszt-Wagner-Nikisch school—a line which classicists, such as
Thomas, deprecated as exaggeration and distortion.

His son, Walter, married well (a daughter of James G. Blaine)
and always had relatively free entree to fashionable society. Indeed,
the young Walter is credited with being responsible for inducing
Carnegie to invest some of his wealth to further the interests of
music by building Carnegie Hall. Walter's enemies often referred
sarcastically to his alliance with millionaires as the chief explanation
of his musical success.

Upon the passing of the elder Damrosch in 1885, Walter assumed
the responsibilities of the orchestra and Anton Seidl was secured
from Germany to direct the German opera. The twenty-three-
year-old son had inherited many of the personality traits that facilitated the successes of his father. He, too, was affable and gregarious,
charming and witty, and "had a way" with society; but he was never
able to achieve recognition as an outstanding conductor. In fact, the
contemporary critical press periodically loosed upon him some of the
most vitriolic slander in the history of American criticism, more akin
to the style of Hanslick in his bigoted moments than what might be
expected from tempered "objective" American reporting. In retrospect they seem so sadistic and abusive that they leave one with
more respect for the victim than for the guardians of art. But rival
claims were at stake. Newspapers and vested interests of various
types, the prestige of social cliques, personal reputations—all had a
share in the fate of musical personalities. Polite criticism, much less
objective and scholarly evaluation, could not thrive in the no man's
land between such contending forces.

The Symphony Society pursued a checkered and clearly oppor-
tunistic career. Not only were concerts suspended between 1898 and

1903, but the orchestra was organized along different lines at different times. In the early years (1878–1905) the number of concerts usually numbered only six pairs, the maintenance fund was relatively small, and the orchestral activity made only a small demand upon the musicians. After Theodore Thomas had finally and permanently left New York for Chicago (1891), Damrosch, with the aid of Carnegie, Vanderbilt, Rockefeller, Morgan, and others, strengthened the orchestra by importing Adolf Brodsky as concertmaster and Anton Hekking as cellist, and establishing daily rehearsals. It prominently advertised itself as the "only permanent orchestra in New York." Unfortunately, the guarantee fund expired after a few years and in 1898 the concerts were abandoned.

In 1902, a group of philanthropists extended an offer to the co-operative Philharmonic orchestra designed to reorganize its system and presumably to turn the baton over to Walter Damrosch who had conducted it in the season 1902–03. When the offer was rejected, this group of patrons aided Damrosch in reorganizing the New York Symphony Orchestra. The orchestra passed through a series of reorganizations (in 1903 and in 1907) by which the principal members were eventually placed on a fixed season salary—establishing it to all intents as the characteristic "permanent orchestra" of the time. In 1914, Henry Harkness Flagler, millionaire oil magnate, who with other donors had already carried a large portion of the financial burden, now determined to assume the complete responsibility up to a maximum guarantee of $100,000 per year.

It was in the subsequent period that Walter reached the pinnacle of his entire career. The number of concerts increased to as many as forty or more on the regular subscription series. He toured the country, emulating the barnstorming activities of Theodore Thomas of several decades previously. The orchestra was available for hire—as was the custom then with the best symphony orchestras in Europe—for accompaniment to solo recitalists, and for any type of public occasion. His concerts were presented in Aeolian Hall (on Forty-second Street, between Fifth and Sixth Avenues), in Carnegie Hall, as well as in the large auditorium of Mecca Temple (later the City Center).

He led an exceedingly busy life here and abroad. In 1920, now sponsored by his friend Flagler to the extent of $250,000, the New York Symphony of about ninety members toured the major European cities of our country's late political allies, where he was openly envied for his fabulous private support.

His lectures on musical topics were always popular with certain segments of society. He imported distinguished musicians for his orchestra, introduced many conductors as his guests to American audiences, and offered a repertoire which was much more imaginative and progressive than that of the antiquated Philharmonic. It is no detraction to suggest that the foreign guest conductors—Albert Coates, Bruno Walter, Klemperer, Goossens, Golschmann—were designed as counterattractions to Mengelberg, who was then mesmerizing the enlightened audience of the rival Philharmonic.

Whatever one may say of his musicianship, his casual and easygoing procedures as conductor, his limited comprehension of certain masterpieces, his lackadaisical rehearsals, or awkward beat, Damrosch nevertheless ranks next to Thomas in his permanent contributions to the cause of music in America during its pioneer and immature period. He toured almost as much as did Thomas, he—more than Thomas—was instrumental in mobilizing wealth to his support. He was an educator, lecturer, and impresario outside the concert hall, a field in which Thomas was exceedingly awkward. Moreover, he conducted and toured successfully with opera troupes, an area which Thomas did not cultivate except for his disastrous fling with the American Opera Company.

Although critics jibed at his propensity for didactic remarks on his concert novelties, there is no question that these contributed much toward keeping the audience in good humor, creating in many patrons an attitude of friendly experimentalism toward novelties that the austere and authoritative take-it-or-leave-it attitude of the disciplined Thomas had never achieved. To Europeans—whose languages he spoke—he was the "dean" of American conductors and was honored accordingly. He was one of the leading spirits in the establishment of the American conservatory at Fontainebleau, opened in 1921, which became the training center for scores of Americans. It attracted many of the most successful American composers, who received their theoretical training from Mlle. Nadia Boulanger, to the great enrichment of American creative music.

By 1927, many factors conspired to prepare Damrosch for retirement from active orchestral duties. The competition between the "second-best" Symphony Orchestra and the Philharmonic, which had recently waxed in prestige, was becoming more and more costly, however salutary it might have been for the advancement of music. The merger of these orchestras, to conserve the prestige and traditions of both, was a constantly recurring rumor, and it was certain that Damrosch, now sixty-five years of age and with a less than unanimous estimate of his genius, could not hope to head the new body, especially in view of the sensational accomplishments of Toscanini and Mengelberg with the reconstructed Philharmonic.

But he still deserved some homage. In March, 1927, a grand ceremonial concert was instituted in his honor, in which both the Philharmonic and the Symphony Orchestra participated, under the direction of Fritz Busch and Furtwängler, respectively the guests of the two orchestras. In reply to the remarks of Ossip Gabrilowitsch, who presented to the guest of honor a silver smoking set on behalf of the conductor colleagues of the nation, Damrosch acknowledged that he was tired of the labor and routine of a permanent conductor —he would henceforth be a guest conductor and "let the other fellow do the rehearsing." [22]

Though the orchestra continued its existence another year to fill out the half century, the plans for the merger went on apace. The exhilarating period of competition between Thomas and Damrosch was long past; the subsequent benefits of that competition between the rivals had been harvested abundantly. But competition can also be wasteful and expensive, and the fruits of this competition had at last become too costly.

After one more year of concerts, presided over by nine guests, including Damrosch, the orchestra ended its fifty-year existence in a nominal merger with its great rival, in which only a small quota of personnel was actually absorbed, leaving the great majority to re-enter the crowded labor market. Mr. Damrosch continued his professional activity by becoming the musical consultant of the National Broadcasting Company, and for some years conducted its children's symphonic hour. Then he went into quiet retirement. He died December 23, 1950.

REPERTOIRE The Symphony orchestra, playing side by side with the New York Philharmonic during its entire career, catered to a different audience and displayed many symptomatic differences from its neighbor. The New York Symphony took its competitive status much more seriously and therefore was more enterprising in its repertoire than was its venerable rival.

Walter Damrosch gave the Germans a cold shoulder, but warmed up to the French—exactly the reverse of the policy of the Philharmonic. Though his own personal background was German, he had shown, even before World War I, a fashionable affinity for the less hackneyed Gallic composers, Franck, Ravel, Debussy, d'Indy, Berlioz, some of whom he cultivated earlier and more generously than did his unimaginative rival. During the war, he was as French as was Boston with Rabaud and Monteux. He also espoused Rachmaninoff and Scriabin more liberally than any other orchestra. Nor were the English neglected, with Elgar a special favorite.

There was something of the showman and exhibitionist in Damrosch—not the brash and vulgar brand, but rather calculated, piquant, sly, and humorous. In the twenties he offered to the public, which always loves a contest, several annual concerts of "Modern Music—Pleasant and Unpleasant" in which Honegger, Milhaud, Copland, and others could compete in the "open market" with the traditional masters. In 1909, he boldly presented a double-header—the Ninth Symphony performed twice in one evening with fifteen minutes intermission as Bülow had done in Berlin in 1889. The "quartet" consisted of sixteen voices, stationed on a raised platform in the midst of the orchestra. It is reported that many of the audience remained for both performances.

At the time when jazz was a category of marginal respectability from the other side of the railroad tracks, but had started to influence the French moderns and to infiltrate the musical journals, Damrosch commissioned George Gershwin to compose a piano concerto, which he produced during the season 1925–26. Taking this flyer in what had been shortly before a risqué area, Damrosch suggested that the "musicians, in their attitude toward jazz, were behaving like the cat hovering around a saucer of hot milk, waiting for it to cool." He introduced other miscellaneous novelties without too much offense or complaint: Sibelius, Bloch, Bruckner, Schoenberg—always with tactful stage remarks; and it was under his auspices that many subsequently prominent conductors made their American debut: Walter, Klemperer, Coates, and Golschmann.

In the fifty-year history of the Symphony Society about seventy-five compositions appeared on the program "for the first time in America," and an equally large number were described as "new," which in many cases meant a world première. In his first ten years, Leopold Damrosch presented more than a dozen new works, including Dvořák's *Slavonic Rhapsodies* and new things of Berlioz, Raff, and Rubinstein. Besides Gershwin, Walter offered new works of the Americans Copland, Taylor, Dubensky, Hanson, Hadley, Hill, and a half dozen others. The "first" for Sibelius was *Tapiola* and for Rachmaninoff, the Third Piano Concerto. Tschaikowsky's *Pathétique* received its American première March 16, 1894. There were also many "firsts" for the British: Holsts' *Egdon Heath*, several from Elgar, Bantock, Vaughan Williams, and Goossens. Strauss, although on the average conspicuously low in the Society's favor, had two "firsts": *Macbeth* and the Prelude to Act II of *Guntram*.

If unfriendly observers have met these innovations in caustic manner, at the time of the merger, many concert patrons feared that they were on the threshold of a less exciting if not a positively dull season. Damrosch was in many ways a prototype of Stokowski, much more subtle and genial, but arousing in many of his followers the same anxious expectancy and stimulating satisfaction.

Though proclaiming his Americanism, his contribution to American music was modest when compared to that of Chicago and Boston. It should be recalled, however, that the American musical lobby was then not as strong as it was later. Since there were then far fewer American composers, it was not the accepted, much less the required, policy to gratify their urge for public performances. However, when in 1920 Damrosch led the first "conducted tour" of an American orchestra abroad, he was accompanied by John Powell,

American pianist, and Albert Spalding, American violinist—a considerate gesture which Toscanini did not emulate in 1930, when he toured Europe with the Philharmonic-Symphony without a single page of American music in his library.

The Boston Symphony Orchestra (1881)

In the spring of 1881, Boston was startled at the casual omnipotence lurking in the announcement of Henry L. Higginson entitled "In re the Boston Symphony Orchestra." The Boston financier therein proclaimed his resolve "to hire an orchestra of sixty men and a conductor, paying them all by the year" and anticipating a "deficit of $50,000, for which $1,000,000 would be needed in principal," which principal he of course intended to provide.[23]

Whether he then realized it or not, by this action Mr. Higginson had set the general pattern of financial support of all first-class orchestras for the next half a century. Not until an orchestra was granted the benefit of adequate private aid to supplement the insufficiencies of the box office, could it achieve the highest standard of artistic excellence. In this sense, the Boston orchestra was the pioneer "permanent" orchestra in the United States, founded at a time when the newly rich of New York were about to build the Metropolitan Opera House, and the Handel and Haydn Society of Boston had reached maturity in vocal music. Without detracting from the brilliance of the innovation, still such innovations do not come "out of the blue." There is a law of continuity in social affairs, as in evolutionary biology, to which all events conform. What, then, was the social climate which was so propitious for the new venture?

Boston had never been without its music. The early influence of Gottlieb Graupner, who is generally credited with founding America's first serious orchestra, cannot well be overestimated. Having played under Haydn in the Salomon orchestra of London (1790–91), this versatile musician and publisher brought to America a taste for the current continental repertoire and, what is more important, implemented it. His Philo-Harmonic orchestra of fifteen to twenty members was as rudimentary as the cultural frontier that nourished it. But it cooperated with the Handel and Haydn Society, presented

concerts in annual series between 1810 (?) and 1824, and was in its
way, a permanent orchestra with a permanent conductor.

Various orchestras followed, which the pedantic historian could
enumerate, of which the more important were the Musical Fund
Society (1847–55), the Philharmonic orchestra (1855–63), and the
Harvard Musical Association, founded in 1837 for the general advancement of music, but more directly responsible for the orchestral
series of 1865–81.

The Musical Fund Society, composed of about sixty musicians,
was devoted to the higher type of symphonies and overtures. According to *Dwight's Journal* (1852), "a band much larger would
fall into the modern monster category." The Philharmonic succumbed to the distractions of the Civil War. After hostilities had
ceased, the Harvard alumni undertook the responsibility for the
concerts which were to "appeal to persons of taste," and finally
withdrew when Higginson organized his orchestra.

Outside orchestras also exerted their impact on the taste and
ideals of the Boston public. Besides the immigrant Germania orchestra, which made Boston its adopted home while touring the country
between 1848 and 1854, the most sensational jolt to local mediocrity
was the Theodore Thomas Orchestra of New York, which made
its maiden appearance in Boston in 1869. While the critic was lament-
ing over the local Association concert that "a dozen members were
absent from the concert" because of "other duties," he could glow-
ingly describe the Thomas concert which manifested "such pure and
brilliant intonation, perfect ensemble and tone color, such sure attack
and vital unity in violins, all bowing alike." [24] When things were
looking dreary in Boston, the Thomas orchestra exerted a quicken-
ing effect upon the orchestra of the Harvard Musical Association.
Carl Zerrahn, the conductor, even imitated Thomas' seating order,
by grouping the cellos together in a solid body in middle front, the
basses behind them, and the wind band—raised in two long rows
above—in the extreme rear. But within a short time, the energy of
this fillip was dissipated, and musical affairs were again at low ebb.
Anticipating the new era in orchestral finance, the editor of the new
Boston *Musical Herald*, in its maiden issue, January, 1880, had already wistfully opined:

Considering the great value of the existence of a permanent (musical) organization to the city, would it not be well for wealthy and public-spirited friends of music to assure its continued success by the establishment of a guarantee fund, similar to that of the Handel and Haydn Society for its triennial festivals?

Higginson, who had been a music student in Vienna, was well aware what a paternalistic government could accomplish. However, in this country, according to his creed, this function should devolve upon paternalistic capitalism, through the efforts of those who had been financially successful. His new administrative arrangement made the orchestra member a full-time employee, engaged for the purpose of creating music, which would then be resold to the public, of course at considerable loss, by the philanthropically-minded employer. Although this was modestly considered an experimental undertaking, it is remarkable how little the continuing organization of the orchestra, sustained by Higginson for thirty-seven years, deviated from the formula outlined in the prospectus which had issued in the spring of 1881, Minerva-like, in full perfection from his fertile brain. The principal provisions were:

(1) conductor and musicians to be engaged at a contractual season salary
(2) virtually full-time seasonal employment of the musicians and the restriction of their outside engagements to those which are compatible with the priority of the orchestra
(3) low admission prices
(4) full season of weekly concerts
(5) permanent orchestra, for an indefinite period in the future
(6) music of the highest type
(7) conductor to be solely responsible for the artistic direction of the concerts

Pathbreaking as was this economic solution, the musical ideals of the community had been more or less well established by a combination of forces. The programs of the Harvard Musical Association were of high order though execution was deficient as compared to Theodore Thomas' models of disciplined performance. John S. Dwight, who founded his *Journal* in 1852, had waged critical battles for Bach, Mozart, and the classical composers, and was passionately interested in the elevation of taste. The city had genteel traditions to uphold, and was moreover a metropolis of more than 400,000, with a homogeneity of population in sharp contrast to polyglot New York. Further, the primacy of Boston culture was at stake. Dwight, in his *Journal* of September, 1880, lamented: "We have a Hall, an Organ, and an Art Museum. Now we want an orchestra. . . . We are falling behind New York. We will become provincial without it!" The audience was therefore willing and expectant, and from the very first concert enthusiastic. Some had feared that the "comparatively low price of admissions would give the audience a 'lyceum' cast, but such proved not the case. The assemblage at the first concerts was one representative of our foremost patrons of music and such as an oratorio, an Italian opera, or a Thomas concert could attract." [25] It is therefore evident that Higginson supplied merely the keystone—a favorable economic ideology and the resources—to a structure that was all but complete.

The conductor entrusted with the launching of this new enterprise was the thirty-one-year-old, currently popular German baritone and composer, Georg Henschel, whose appointment had been occasioned by his temporary presence in Boston. He had, for the moment at least, produced a sensation by his energetic conducting of his own *Overture* with the orchestra of the Harvard Musical Association, and it was he who was invited by Higginson to form the new orchestra, at a salary of $10,000 per season.

As might have been—and was—expected, the sudden catapulting of a young, untried, foreign artist into such a position of prominence evoked bitter complaints from the displaced and aggrieved old guard that had been so loyal to Zerrahn, Listemann, and other local conductors "who have devoted their lives to Boston music and now find themselves without orchestras." By no means an experienced and "routined" conductor, this vocalist was heavily burdened not only with the acquisition of a new accomplishment, but also with the problems of public relations. The critical press, annoyed at the adulation received by the "fair-haired" novitiate, found it comforting to remind the new order: "We have had other conductors in Boston, and good ones." The *Home Journal* editorialized: "While we hail the new star, let us not forget the others who have brightened our musical horizon for many years."

The benevolent intention of marketing music at a loss brought in its train the criticism that the cut-rate system was undercutting the unsubsidized concert activities, thereby giving the public false norms of the financial value of musical services. But the near monopoly in musical affairs that wealth and skill conferred upon the new orchestra was partly mitigated by Higginson's considerate policy of employing almost exclusively local musicians in order to avoid offense to those who had labored unselfishly for years in the unproductive vineyard. In the relentless pursuit of perfection by both management and conductors, such delicate gestures of sentiment were soon to become an obsolete virtue. The lesson was soon learned that, if it was to achieve, an orchestra could never be local, excepting in name; for, like a baseball team, which similarly evokes its due share of civic enthusiasm, it was bound to seek its players in the open market, without regard to regional sentiment.

Henschel's inexperience, his unconventional tempi in some of the classics, his vigorous, bombastic, "drum-major flourish," the constitution of some of his programs, and the inability of the band to submit itself to an authoritative beat—all drew forth major critical assaults. The musicians were frequently preoccupied with many other musical functions of a less noble sort, they played under other conductors, and the priority of the new orchestra could not be enforced. All members from percussion to concertmaster were paid alike: six dollars per concert, and three dollars per rehearsal, of which there were three. As gratifying as was Henschel's initial success during his three years' tenure, it was evident that the orchestra had not been much more than a loose and easy-going aggregation. Higginson demanded more.

When Viennese Wilhelm Gericke, Henschel's successor, replaced concertmaster Listemann with twenty-year-old Franz Kneisel of Bucharest and Berlin, and added to his ensemble almost a score of other European importations, there was no doubt among the jolted players and patrons that a new order was established, not only in the matter of personnel but also, as they were soon to discover, in methods of work and discipline. Prophetically enough, the editor of the *American Musician* advanced his considered opinion that "the Gericke firings would not have happened if the musicians had been unionized as they are in New York." Gericke culled out the dead-wood which, either because of technical deterioration, superannua-tion, or personal insubordination, became an impediment to the real-ization of his artistic ideals. Contractual provisions were tightened. Nonattendance and tardiness were subject to "liquidated damages, non-arrival of steam or horse cars not excusing delay in arrival." To make possible longer seasons and more enticing contracts for those who were to come from afar to cast their professional lot in a new home, tours as far west as St. Louis were undertaken, and spring Promenade series were introduced.

To him who succeeds, much is forgiven. The success of the orchestra in Philadelphia and in New York, as well as at home, was unequivocal. If Gericke's style of conducting was cold and without dramatic force, the playing was for the first time precise and well coached. Gericke had "made" the orchestra, but it had been a hard pull. He had to establish a personal discipline to which Americans were not accustomed; and the patrons sometimes literally walked out on his severely classic programs. He had conscientiously subjected himself to the most grueling duties, and he suffered unceasingly from the pangs of homesickness. When he had arrived in Boston, "his English lasted about fifteen seconds" and continued as a handicap in making friendships here. He was ready for a rest, and could not be induced to remain longer than five years. He departed from "cool and cultured Boston," according to L. C. Elson, "amid floral tributes and gyrations of hats and handkerchiefs" and an *auf wiedersehn.*

The pattern of turning to Europe, that almost inexhaustible arse-nal of musical talent, was now firmly set, and this time (1889) Hig-ginson enticed to his organization the First Conductor of the Leipzig Opera, Arthur Nikisch, then thirty-four years old, but already a mature conductor of more than ten years' experience. Nikisch was an adherent of the Liszt-Wagner-Bülow school of con-ducting which deliberately set itself off from the metronomic and brittle Mendelssohnian tradition established at the Gewandhaus. Gericke, the technician, was now to be replaced by Nikisch, the poet, who would enliven the strong and well-articulated skeleton of Gericke's making with the flesh and blood of full romantic vividness.

Contemporary critical reports leave us a rather accurate portrayal of this exotic figure, the first conductor in America to display the major symptoms of the "prima-donna." A man of distinguished appearance enhanced by sartorial elegance and a well-trimmed beard, he slowly bestrode the stage, his black forelock vibrating over his forehead. To many visual-minded auditors he was undoubtedly a great conductor even before he had raised his baton. His conducting from memory, daringly novel in that day; and the pulsating rhythms of his flashing white cuffs, and other personal idiosyncrasies, so different from the ramrod dignity of his predecessor, inevitably drew upon his head the epithet of "poseur." By his ability to get himself talked about, he may have been among the first, but certainly not the last, to be accused of diverting public interest from the music to the conductor thereof.

But Nikisch also commanded compensating nonvirtuoso traits which contributed much to his success. He never lost his temper; he was gently persuasive rather than dictatorial with his men and was loved and respected by them. His gestures, although emphatic, were restrained and consciously interpretative rather than effusive. Finally, he lacked that passion for precision of rendition and driving discipline which often harasses the players to the limits of their endurance.

But such a man could not expect to avoid controversy. There were many who warned that the spit and polish of the old Gericke machine was going to ruin. One lesser known critic, distinguished for his uninhibited language, pronounced the new conductor downright incompetent. Nikisch soon divided the city into two factions, those who missed the predictable fidelity which Gericke had cultivated for them, and those who revelled in the fire and drama and spontaneity of his successor.

Classicists described him as given to erratic tempi, uncontrolled rubatos, extremes in slow and rapid rhythms, exaggerated pianissimos and bombastic outbursts of mere sound and fury. He was at the same time subtly poetic and frankly bizarre, he modernized the classics, and "denuded Beethoven of all dignity." In his first season he caused a sensation by slowly declaiming the opening measures of Beethoven's Fifth, and picking up the tempo on the sixth measure.[26]

In the Schumann *Spring* Symphony, as one critic averred:

he sparkling violin passages are so heavily weighted by Nikisch with
ninute nuances in the form of frequent ritartandos and unexpected ac-
cents, that the flow of these rippling figures is completely arrested, and
hey nearly lose their sparkle.

Again:

he opening movement of the *Freischütz* overture was taken at so slow a
pace that the rhythm suffered and the quartet of horns sustained their
cones with difficulty, or in other words, the *melos* did not come out.[27]

Philip Hale, the most influential critic in Boston, bemoaned the

undue passion in comparatively passionless melody. It is seldom . . .
under Mr. Nikisch, that you have any theme given in frank simplicity;
that a *piano* is observed strictly for more than two or three consecutive
measures. Thus in a symphony of Mozart or Haydn, there is almost constant overstress . . . there is the absence of repose demanded by the
spirit of the work.[28]

Later, at the Gewandhaus, the Leipzig critics echoed similar
sentiments, commenting on the "new tempi" and the "prominence
given certain instruments when Nikisch conducts." He "drags certain passages in order to work up to greater climaxes." [29] He was
also considered a master of the powerful climax. A Berlin critic
reported that he took the four measures of the well-known C major
entrance of the *Finale* of Beethoven's Fifth in a tearing *crescendo*
from *pp* to *fff*, the effect of which was inexpressible in words.[30]

It is, however, quite understandable that some should enjoy as a
thrill what to a staid and composed temperament would be a shock.
Krehbiel, of New York, who heard Nikisch only periodically, in
contrast to such resident critics as Philip Hale, asserted that Nikisch
was of "the type that put an end to the music-box style of interpretation," who "with the utmost freedom in time changes, yet in a
general way adheres to the normal unit of measure." [31] One Boston
critic admitted that the

slow tempo at which he took the opening measures of *Fingal's Cave
Overture* was an innovation, but as it was in entire harmony with his
conception of the work he was certainly warranted in interpreting it
according to his idea instead of blindly following the traditional readings.[32]

His constant endeavor was to invent a new twist to an old phrase, and "never played a piece twice alike." The superb orchestra was trained to follow his every momentary impulse with the hope that "things would click" in public. Sometimes they did not!

Although there are many pitfalls in retroactive judgments, and although it is difficult to recreate the norms against which such contemporary criticisms were written, such concrete descriptions of the conductor's interpretation are a rather clear indication of the early romantic interpretative styles employed by Liszt and Wagner, and for which the classicist Weingartner so severely criticized Bülow.[33] Nikisch was representative of a period which is today obsolete. While personal readings still are common, the range between the Mendelssohnian time-beating and whimsical "Bülowisms" has been very much narrowed. Individual deviations have become much more subtle—an inevitable outgrowth of the very gradual but definite development of audience familiarity with orchestral repertoire, with which drastic liberties cannot be taken with impunity. The Wagner school, which searched out and emphasized the *melos* in contradistinction to mere rhythmic performance, produced and even encouraged great license with the dynamics of the written score. Its extreme sponsors evolved a kind of fluoroscopic school of interpretative conducting, in which all the intimate inner details of the score were revealed with clinical clarity. As a Leipzig critic remarked in 1908: "Those who wish to hear the click of the metronome do not like to listen to Nikisch' Beethoven." [34] It was an era of Sturm und Drang which was later to be transformed into a period of mastery and restraint. It is a significant chapter in the styles of conducting as well as in the history of aesthetic theory.

Speaking broadly, neither party in the Boston situation was happy, and Nikisch departed abruptly before his five-year contract expired, leaving behind him the two contending camps of adherents and adversaries. His last Boston concert provoked a hysterical ovation to which he responded in a short speech of gratitude and apology. Whether the critics drove him from Boston, as his friends assert; or whether he had contractual disputes with Mr. Higginson, as contended by others; or whether, as Pfohl,[35] his German biographer, avers, he was fatigued from railroad travel and unendurably

ARTURO TOSCANINI

As conductor of the Metropolitan Opera, the New York Philharmonic-Symphony, and the NBC Symphony Orchestra Arturo Toscanini is commonly regarded as having attained the greatest heights in conductorial perfection. (NBC Photo)

A REUNION IN BOSTON, 1951
Left to right: Pierre Monteux (San Francisco Symphony); the late Serge Koussevitzky (of the Boston Symphony), and Charles Munch (who had just succeeded him in Boston). (Lenscraft Photos. Courtesy of George E. Judd, Boston Symphony Orchestra)

impatient with the half-baked culture in the United States—all this is immaterial since such eventualities usually have multiple causes. In any case, he returned to Europe to enjoy a career of triumph and adulation of a magnitude attained by few. He held simultaneously the conductorship of the two finest orchestras in Germany, the Berlin Philharmonic and the Leipzig Gewandhaus, and served frequently as guest conductor at home and abroad, thereby achieving the picturesque sobriquet of "conductor-on-wheels."

In 1912, after several years of persistent rumors that he would return to Boston, he visited this country for a triumphal tour with the London Symphony Orchestra. In several concerts in New York, the houses were generally completely sold out. The first night, Monday, April 8, however, showed many of the boxes unoccupied. Some interpreted this as spite work of the old buccaneering days; others saw it as a boycott of Brahms, who was on the program. The real reason was, however, that the first concert conflicted with the "fashion night" at the "Met," whose patrons amply filled the seats of the remaining Nikisch appearances. The New York critics, who always had a good word for the unrestrained romanticist in his Boston days, again exhausted their expletives. But in Boston, Symphony Hall was not full, and Philip Hale, who now observed considerable mellowing in Nikisch' conductorial style, still entertained lingering doubts about it "as a steady diet."

After Boston's failure to induce Gericke to return, and after Theodore Thomas, then in Chicago, and Hans Richter, probably the most celebrated conductor in Europe at that moment, had declined, the choice as Nikisch' successor in 1893 was Emil Paur. He was likewise "on the romantic side," although he lacked the polish and personal magnetism of his predecessor. Intensely devoted to his art, he was less gregarious, refusing to be the social lion and roar for his money.

After five years of Paur's service, Boston turned again to the Viennese classicist for whom Higginson, himself a conservative, had never quite lost his attachment. Gericke remained for seven years. But the audience was no longer the same. After having been exposed to Nikisch and Paur, it listened to the old "efficiency" with new ears. It was not long before the critics found that "he had grown cold," that "he repressed the instruments." A dangerous apathy began to settle over the audiences. By 1903, one reviewer observed that the icy Gericke was "ceasing to draw." Although publicly Higginson maintained a fine standard of correctness toward Gericke by assuring him that he could remain in Boston, privately he was more than happy to see him depart. Philip Hale cites Higginson's personal communication in attesting to the points of friction between the conductor and the philanthropist. One of these was Gericke's refusal to accept guest conductors with whom Higginson had hoped to recoup some of the growing deficits. The possessive Gericke, on his part, feared deterioration of the orchestra in the hands of strange conductors.[36]

With the new century, the time was propitious to strike a more modern note. Boston had achieved a high reputation and earned the full praises of the few foreign conductors who had been permitted to preside on the podium. The orchestra was installed in a new home, Symphony Hall, of excellent acoustics, which was built in 1900. If, as many people complained, it monopolized the musical scene, and the usual miscellany of concerts and recitals were neglected, it was equally true that the drawing power of the orchestra alone called attention to the city as a musical center and in its own right attracted students and achieved prestige. It is not surprising, therefore, that the ambitious community should seek what it had never before obtained: a ranking conductor, who had already "arrived." Nikisch himself now amply fulfilled such qualifications, and there were the aforesaid persistent rumors of his return. However, the final choice was Dr. Karl Muck, Conductor of the Royal Opera in Berlin and distinguished Wagner interpreter, who served brilliantly in Boston from 1906 to 1914, with a four-year interlude filled by Max Fiedler.

Like Nikisch, Muck was undemonstrative and economical in gesture on the podium; but unlike his great compatriot, Muck was "ever faithful to the composer," and was pre-eminently the type of conductor who does most of his work behind the scenes and during the rehearsal. He was essentially scholarly, and again unlike Nikisch, Dr. Muck, though some considered him uninspired, nevertheless enjoyed the united approval and general enthusiasm of the Boston patrons and management. The story of his departure is interesting and important, since it demonstrates that even in Boston, where music was cultivated in an ivory tower and protected from the chilly winds of the competitive world, it could not remain "above the battle."

War was declared on Germany by the United States on April 6, 1917, after a slow but steady accretion of anti-German sentiment following the sinking of the *Lusitania* in the spring of 1915. However, America was hesitant in manifesting these hostile feelings in the concert hall, and for a number of reasons: she was proud of her tolerance and individual freedom, and was self-consciously broad-minded; not everybody was at first convinced of the wisdom of American entry into the war; German music constituted the central core of American repertoires, and it was inconceivable that it should be curtailed; and finally the philosophy of the neutrality of art was deep-seated in the aesthetic thinking of the era. Philip Hale, some weeks after the declaration of war, feelingly epitomized these sentiments: "Men of various nationalities and various sympathies, united in the purpose of maintaining the high reputation of the Boston Symphony orchestra, knew in rehearsals and concerts only one country, the great Republic of Art." [37]

The cruel fact, however, was incontrovertible: America was involved in a serious war. The dramatic story of this conductor-friend of the Kaiser, which was a blend of "spy scare," of superpatriotism, of sudden "dislike" of German music, and of obstinate bungling of public relations, has been related many times. [38]

Very briefly, the facts seem to be as follows: After some months of sniping at Dr. Muck and rumors, beginning at least as early as February, 1916, that Muck was disloyal and even supplied information to the enemy, the patriotic groups of Providence, R. I., where the orchestra was to appear in November, 1917, determined to make an issue of his patriotism by demanding that he conduct the *Star-Spangled Banner*. Higginson, never a person to be intimidated, refused to consider the request, which turned out to be an ineffable blunder for which Muck was innocently accused. However, in subsequent concerts, the national anthem was played, both in Boston and other cities, and this particular crisis had apparently blown over. Though the January and February (1918) visits to Philadelphia found "many boxes were vacant," and some critics complained of Muck's "torpid rendition of the *Star-Spangled Banner*," and though he had run into violent patriotic opposition in New York, it still came as a surprise when, in March, 1918, almost a year after the declaration of war, Dr. Muck was suddenly arrested and interned, for reasons never officially made public. It was informally alleged that the charges were of a personal nature, irrelevant to the prosecution of the war, but that he had preferred to accept political arrest to the prosecution of the "genuine" charge. After the armistice he returned to his native Germany where he pursued a long and successful career, and died in 1940 at the venerable age of eighty years.

More was implied in the event, however, than a mere routine shift in conductors; for the momentous social and artistic changes trailing Muck's departure constituted a veritable crisis in Boston, and indeed throughout America. Mr. Higginson, the sole source of security for thirty-seven years, was now old, and his finances so shaken that at his death (1919) it had become impossible for him to provide for any endowment of the orchestra, with the exception, of course, of his music library. Mr. E. B. Dane donned Higginson's mantle and served as the "good angel" to save the orchestra for several years. But the best evidence that a financial reorganization was imminent came in the fall of 1923 with the revelation that the average annual deficit since Higginson's retirement had been about $100,000 and now exceeded the capacity of the philanthropists to overcome. Like other cities, Boston would have to devise a plan for a broader base of support. At that time her list of three hundred guarantors for the current season was published, and with it a general plea for all citizens to join in the cause!

Another symptom of the new era was the shift of artistic orientation from Germany to France. Of course, there had always been French music and French musicians, usually in the woodwind section, although it was German music which had evoked the sympathy of the Boston orchestra as well as that of every other orchestra in the United States. During and immediately after the war, it was obviously impossible to look for Muck's successor in the accustomed places. Although sentimental leanings were strong toward France,

Sir Henry Wood, Rachmaninoff, and Toscanini were approached. Rachmaninoff declined (for the second time since 1912) and negotiations with Toscanini collapsed before they could be terminated one way or the other. After a year's visit by Henri Rabaud, the trustees selected Pierre Monteux who had behind him varied experience with opera, ballet, and orchestra, and who was destined to serve the orchestra during the most critical postwar period of 1919–25.

The most severe shock resulting from the impact of the changing postwar world was the musicians' strike of 1920, which grew out of the issue of unionization. Seen in present-day perspective, it was inevitable that the Boston orchestra, like every other enterprise, would sooner or later encounter the issues of management and labor relations. The scale of wages of the rank and file in the orchestra was admittedly not so favorable as formerly. The musicians, however, had accepted as compensation the prestige of membership in the most noted orchestra in the country. But the postwar rise in cost of living was now beginning to overtake the musicians, and they accordingly submitted a request for wage readjustments. Supported by the local musicians' union in these demands, they were only following the accepted labor practices. Boston, conservative and isolated, was merely grappling with a question already settled in other communities.

The union had a strong bargaining position. Musicians were scarce, not only because the European supply was largely cut off, but also because of increasing demands for musicians in the new symphony orchestras then being founded in the western cities, and the new symphonic ensembles installed in the palatial motion picture theatres. Consonant with the principles firmly enunciated by Mr. Higginson many times before, the present board refused to bargain collectively, i.e., to recognize the union. Harassed by deficits, it further declined to consider the needed wage increases. The concertmaster, Frederic Fradkin, sympathized with the reform and joined the union. As a direct outcome of this gesture, the conductor and the concertmaster engaged in an altercation backstage previous to a concert on March 5, 1920. The concertmaster retaliated during the concert by refusing to rise with the orchestra in acknowledgment of the applause, which the conductor desired to share with his men.

On his dismissal for insubordination, thirty-six musicians failed to appear for the Saturday evening concert.

This was not the first "strike" in the history of the major orchestras—Walter Damrosch had suffered a brief walkout in 1893—and, of course, it was by no means the first labor dispute in musical circles—but it was by all odds the most disastrous to the orchestra and costly to the men involved. Although Boston, alone of all the orchestras, was not unionized, there were still in the country a sufficiently large number of open-shop industries to create an understandable expectation that the Boston orchestra might remain indefinitely an exception to the general rule. The strike was broken, but the orchestra lost one-third of its personnel, mostly in the German strings, and Monteux was faced with a task, similar to that of Gericke forty years previously, of building an orchestra almost anew and in an atmosphere of bitter hostility. The consensus of opinion is that he succeeded quite as well as his illustrious forebear. But if he had led the orchestra out of the wilderness, he was not permitted to lead it into the promised land. Monteux had gained the admiration of many people in Boston, but his New York critics and audiences remained cool toward his undemonstrative manner and his French programs.

The harvesting of the fruits of the arduous spade-work and the establishment of the Boston orchestra on a new level of brilliance was to be reserved for Serge Koussevitzky, the Russian virtuoso on the bass viol. Koussevitzky had had a varied career, not only as soloist in the music centers of Europe (he had been announced for tours in the United States although he had never carried out the projects), but also as conductor and publisher in enterprises which his personal means handsomely supported. Known to the American musical press many years before the Russian revolution, Kussewitzki (as the name was spelled before the adoption of the French orthography) was by 1917 considered the most famous conductor of his native land, and was accordingly elected to head the Russian "Orchestra of the State." Political events, however, prevented the actual realization of this plan and in 1920 he left the Soviet Union, settling in France where his Concerts Koussevitzky attracted immediate attention. His nationality, his political severance from the "despised" Soviets, his personal bearing, and, of course, the advance critical

notices of his concert activities—all made him the logical candidate
for a community in which the world-renowned orchestra was the
center of musical and social life.

During the period of its grievous collapse, the Boston orchestra
had suffered in national prestige while Stokowski was bewitching
his public in Philadelphia and New York. Koussevitzky was to recapture its old glory, and re-establish the rivalry between Boston
and Philadelphia, annually fought out in the arena of Carnegie Hall.

It could not be expected that there would be unanimity on his
interpretations of the classics and on his choice of modern works.
Although some felt the magnetism of his interpretations, others
decried his exaggerations in tempo and romantic leanings. "When
slow movements are played slower, Koussevitzky will play them"
ran the parody on the popular automobile ad. However, before
many seasons of his American career had elapsed, Koussevitzky was,
by common consent, included in the trinity of America's Great with
Stokowski and Toscanini. His regime in Boston reached a new high
in personal adulation, and before its close he had become a "living
legend," one of the many outward symbols of which are the four
honorary doctorates conferred upon him by as many different universities, and several biographies both reverential and critical.[39]

It was during his tenure, beginning in 1924, that the dead hand
of the past relaxed its hold and the union question was finally settled.
For Higginson, unionization had been a menace to the vital principle
of artistic supremacy which alone could permit the prosecution of
musical ideals, unhampered by rules and regulations of the union
order. The philanthropist had repeatedly threatened to abandon the
orchestra on that issue. But the Boston orchestra had long ceased to
be a personal enterprise—an elongated shadow of its owner and
benefactor. Even its exceptional musical excellence could no longer
justify its exemption from the ordinary process of collective negotiation which had become standard practice in orchestral and industrial contracts.

Evolutionary changes in our economic order were conspiring to
render untenable the privileged position of the Boston orchestra.
With the union in full control over broadcasting and recording,
which had become indispensable sources of revenue; with the cur-

rent custom of guest conductors and soloists; and with the appearances of the orchestra on its tour, it was relatively easy by means of the boycott for the union to engage in a pincer movement that made ultimate surrender the only alternative to annihilation. Simply stated, it was impossible for a nonunion orchestra to live in a unionized world. When, finally, James Caesar Petrillo succeeded to the headship of the Federation of Musicians in 1940, he menacingly announced a fight to the finish. Capitulation was only a question of time and appropriate circumstance. Bruno Walter and Chavez were forbidden by Petrillo to appear as guests; Howard Hanson had to cancel his engagement to direct his own symphony; Zimbalist, Szigeti, and Serkin could not accept invitations to perform with the orchestra. Financially, too, the orchestra was very vulnerable. Deficits were growing; concert halls were threatened with blacklisting for harboring the orchestra on tour; radio and recording were banned. Finally, after extended negotiations and some minor concessions on the part of the union, agreements were signed in December, 1942.

Another important venture during the Koussevitzky regime was the inauguration of the Berkshire Festival and its attendant functions. The devastation of Europe had thrown America upon its own resources in summer entertainment, in the training of orchestral musicians and conductors and in their continuous employment. The associated enterprises of the Berkshire Music Center at Tanglewood helped to satisfy these demands by instituting a series of festival concerts, establishing a school for players, conductors, and composers, and incidentally rounding the year's contract for the members of the orchestra.

Amid the flurry of his seventy-fifth birthday anniversary, his twenty-fifth in the United States, Koussevitzky announced his retirement, retaining however some participation in the Berkshire enterprise. Rumors had been persistent for some years that Mitropoulos, whose American debut he had sponsored, would inherit his mantle. Instead, to the surprise of many, it reposed in 1950 on the shoulders of Charles Munch, a French Alsatian, who had been an active conductor in Paris for twenty years, and had more recently visited the States with the Orchestre National of Paris.

Koussevitzky's farewell was a civic occasion and eulogies were extravagant. He was "the greatest all-round conductor of the day." He not only performed his concerts, and "never walked out" as did other conductors at times, but he also stimulated the creative minds of the time; he was a musical benefactor, and "as a citizen of Boston, lived an irreproachable private life." [40] His friends established an anniversary fund for the benefit of the orchestra so that, as the celebrant noted in a letter, the orchestra "to which I have devoted my best efforts for a quarter of a century shall never flounder or fail through lack of adequate financial support." Koussevitzky died on June 4, 1951.

REPERTOIRE Three different features characterize the Boston repertoire and distinguish it from those of all other orchestras in this country. First of all: Boston has been the most conspicuous and consistent proponent of American music. Although there has been some inevitable fluctuation in the intensity of this zeal, the cultivation of American music seemed to be little affected by the turnover in conductors, by passing historical circumstance, or economic conditions of the orchestra. Whether it was the three per cent under Henschel and Gericke in the eighties, or the ten to twelve per cent under Koussevitzky in recent decades—the quotas almost always exceeded those of every other orchestra. Only during World War I, when Chicago and St. Louis were affected by political considerations, did an ephemeral rival in Americanism intrude.

If the reasons for this nativistic enthusiasm do not lie in passing circumstance, they must be sought in the abiding conditions of that region. New England in general and Boston in particular have always been imbued with old American attitudes, and it was there that American arts flowered. Early American literature, painting, and architecture, as well as music, had their life and being in New England and not in polyglot New York. Most of the prominent early composers—Foote, Chadwick, William Mason, Converse, MacDowell, Paine, Mrs. Beach—spent part or all of their musical careers in and around that city. Harvard University, in nearby Cambridge, established the first chair of music in 1875, and through its students and graduates set the tone for musical activities. The New England

Conservatory of Music, founded in 1867, and the Boston Conservatory were among the first of their kind in the United States. The Boston publishers Oliver Ditson and especially Arthur P. Schmidt recognized and encouraged American composers by publishing their works.

Changing taste, the normal decline of interest in older composers, and the termination of individual careers, have, however, caused a complete mutation in the character and personnel of the American list. The original New England portfolio of compositions presented by Henschel and Gericke has been displaced by a broadly national group that encompasses not only the native-born from various parts of the country (Harris, Hanson, Copland, Barber, Carpenter, etc.) but also Americans by adoption (Berezowsky, Loeffler, Bloch). The flavor and concept of American music has also been modified. Formerly dominated by German models, it now carries the imprint of French instruction. To the ever-present motive of loyalty to native composers has consequently been added, in the case of contemporary music, the interest in modernism. The length of his tenure and his zeal for the music of his adopted country enabled Koussevitzky to contribute more substantially to the recognition of American composers than any other conductor. His abundant and discriminating selection of American works has been memorialized on frequent occasions.

A second persistent trait of the Boston repertoire has been the scanty attention to Wagner. In the early days, during the first burst of American enthusiasm, it was well below the average, and since the beginning of the century Boston has presented only one-third to one-half of the national average. The passion for Wagner, grown to a flame in the heat of controversy by Bergmann, Thomas, Damrosch, and Seidl in New York and Chicago, never exceeded a simmer in Boston. However, similar effects are often attributable to diverse causes. Boston's early conductors, Lieder-singer Henschel and the Viennese Gericke, could hardly have been expected to carry the torch for the German revolutionary. Henschel was an intimate friend of Brahms. Though by profession a singer, he was not an operatic performer who might have been instilled with fervor for

the new school. Gericke, who occupied the podium in two installments for a total of thirteen years, was a stern classicist, molded in
bourgeois Vienna where the anti-Wagnerian Hanslick had presided
over the taste of that conservative city. The critical atmosphere of
Boston was to some extent a duplicate of that of Vienna. Higginson,
who had received his musical training in the Imperial city, was himself an aesthetic conservative, as was John S. Dwight, editor of the
recently defunct *Dwight's Journal of Music*. Both were outspoken
anti-Wagnerian critics of influence. In commenting on an early
Thomas program in Boston (1869), Dwight reacted as follows: "The
Tannhäuser Overture led off. . . . Never did we hear it so well
played—Never did we enjoy the work so little."

On one occasion, Georg Henschel had protested against
Dwight's antagonistic attitude toward Wagner. In reply, Dwight
wrote a letter of explanation and apology which allows us to reconstruct the era (he was opposed to all moderns, including Chadwick!)
and the state of mind of those who found Wagner so intolerable.

Your informant must have wholly misunderstood my half playful and
(I admit) quite extravagant remark. I have not and could not have had
the slightest wish to prevent your making a memorial concert of Wagner
music, and I should be the last man in the world to vote for any pro-
hibitory committee or board of censorship. You have the right to make
your own program according to your own feeling of the occasion, and
I admired the earnestness and energy with which you set about it. What
I said (either to, or in the hearing of, Mr. Dannreuther) had no reference
to this concert or this orchestra, but was in continuance of some conversation . . . in which I expressed the depressing effect which so much
of the more modern ambitious modern music had upon my mind—so
many big words, which by their enormous orchestration, crowded harmonies, sheer intensity of sound, and restless swarming motion without
progress, seem to seek to carry the listeners by storm, by a roaring whirlwind of sound, instead of going to the heart by the simpler and divine
way of the still small voice. And then it occurred to me that it might
even justify a high court—a world's court of censorship—composed of the
greatest, clearing the musical atmosphere of many heavy clouds and of
much murky musical malaria. It was a sudden freak of thought, and of
course an utterly impractical extravaganza. But when I meet a red-hot
Wagnerite, I am sometimes tempted in a humorous way to say the worst
I can upon the other side.[41]

In justice to the memory of these two Boston citizens, however, it must be added that Higginson never abused his power by exerting pressure on conductors or public to enforce his private predilections, and that Dwight liberally opened his *Journal* to educational and critical articles on the new musical trends—a magnanimous example of objective journalism worthy of emulation today.

It could plausibly have been anticipated that Karl Muck would reverse the Wagner trend. When he arrived in Boston, he had already attained secure prestige as a Wagner interpreter in Bayreuth itself. Furthermore, Wagner was by then a universally accepted composer whose orchestral innovations had already been succeeded by still newer trends. However, Muck brought with him a distaste, common among exponents of the Wagner music-drama, for tearing the Wagner fragments bleeding from the context. To be sure, Wagner himself did so in the interest of certain public contingencies, as did Muck and other disciples. But the conductors' disinclination to torture the supposedly integrated unit by forcibly extracting from it sketchy morsels was not conducive to a liberal proportion of Wagner in the orchestral repertoire.

The third characteristic of the Boston repertoire is its tendency toward "progressivism." Not that such impulses touched every one of its distinguished conductors. Gericke never did cross the musical threshold of late-nineteenth century "modernism." Muck, though more hospitable and eclectic, nevertheless was not particularly enamored of contemporary trends. Nikisch displayed, of course, ample signs of romanticism. But it was with Koussevitzky that a new era of aggressive modernism set in. In fact, the reputation of his liberal predilections had preceded his arrival in Boston, with the result that his advent was contemplated with such dread by a number of important subscribers as to cause anxiety in management circles. As in the case of Seidl (New York) and Nikisch, his unconventional interpretation of the standard classics was received with lifted aesthetic eyebrows.

The conductors, as usual, impressed their individual stamp on local conditions, as far as those conditions either permitted or encouraged. When Henschel inaugurated the concert series, he was not a seasoned conductor—perhaps not a conductor at all!—with definite traditions and preformed policies. He was not averse to musical titbits which could be instantly enjoyed by the audience, and generally designed his program with appetizing desserts at the end. Some of these pleasant numbers have vanished into the first stage of oblivion—the popular programs—and some have been almost entirely forgotten: the overtures of Auber, Boïeldieu, Cherubini, Gade, Nicolai, several of Mendelssohn, and the symphonies of Raff and Gade, while certain other compositions of Mendelssohn, Schubert, and Saint-Saëns sound a little too obvious to present-day ears.

On the strenuous side, it was the controversial Brahms, friend and counselor of Henschel, with whom he exercised his audiences. It is difficult for present listeners to realize how austere and enigmatic, how protracted and discontinuous these abstract tonal creations sounded in an age when the programmatic Raff, the melodious Schubert, and the straightforward Beethoven were the regular fare. With his eight per cent devoted to Brahms, Henschel was greatly in advance of the New York orchestras who were playing only two to five per cent. Under such conditions, the leave-taking of the audience between the Brahms symphonic movements assumes added plausibility.

For rigidity of discipline, however, it was Gericke who was the real molder of the orchestra, both in the realm of cultivated taste and in personal administration of the orchestra. He lopped off the frills and concentrated on rigorous symphonic literature. The complaints of the audience, martyrs to aesthetic standards, got scant attention from one who had a mission to fulfill. L. C. Elson, the Boston reviewer, deplored the "rut of Haydn, Mozart, Beethoven, and Brahms to which Gericke clung with Viennese persistence." [42] The repertoire was anchored to the Austro-German traditions which accounted for nearly eighty per cent of it. The Gericke programs therefore lacked the sprightliness to which Henschel had previously accustomed the ears of the patrons, who reminisced nostalgically, "Henschel may not have been as good a conductor, but he is certainly a better program maker." [43] To Gericke, a mixture of such styles was a desecration, and thus it was that the segregated popular programs were instituted to assume the responsibility of the lighter fare.

Max Fiedler and Emil Paur, cultivating less artistic ruthlessness, offered a pleasant interlude for certain segments of the audience by alleviating the severity of the programs. Especially indulgent, Fiedler was very willing to unbend with Wagner excerpts; but physically he retained the stiff German rigidity, taking his bow by bending double exactly in the middle, straightening out, throwing shoulders back, with a military click of his heels.

The programs of the French incumbents Rabaud and Monteux were clearly products of the international crisis. The repertoire of 1918–24 was not the reflection of the conductors, but rather both the conductors and programs were the reflection of the anti-German and pro-Ally political and social climate of the day. While the German classics still bulked large, they had been severely curbed, and the French, swept up by the political tempest, rose to an unprecedented height of one-fourth of the repertoire, featuring some composers, like Saint-Saëns, who never again would be rewarded so generously with the favor of serious taste. Monteux, to be sure, had already startled his audiences with Stravinsky's *Sacre du Printemps*, but he was limited by time and circumstance in fully unfolding his liberal propensities.

During his twenty-five-year regime, Koussevitzky had ample opportunity to acquire, and in turn to abandon, various affections. In his early tenure, the mystical Scriabin was his *compositeur de résistance,* of whom he had more recently tired. Sibelius, Prokofieff, and Shostakovitch rate consistently high, and the latter two help to swell the Russian contingent to a new height of almost one-fourth of the total Boston repertoire. In the postwar period, both Sibelius and Shostakovitch slumped heavily, although for obviously different reasons.

Many composers and compositions were given experimental hearings and later dropped. Koussevitzky was most articulate in his policy that symphony concerts must not only entertain and elevate the public, and familiarize it with current trends in composition, but also serve as a training school for a selected group of contemporary composers, who might hear their works performed and profit by the experience. Since the orchestra is an expensive instrument, it can be used for such experiments only when assured of reasonable financial security, an understanding audience, traditions of artistic supremacy, and a conductor of discernment. Koussevitzky, with all his modernism, never strained this tolerance by indulging in the capricious excesses of Stokowski, but was nevertheless perpetually in the vanguard of current musical trends.

The Chicago Symphony Orchestra (1891)

Unlike the Eastern cities, Chicago was, in the period of the eighties, not a city of great cultural traditions. It was rather a vibrant and odorous industrial town, famous for its Armour and Swift stockyards, its Pullman sleepers and McCormick reapers, and thus performed much of the dirty work for the growing nation. But the captains of these industries, having attained wealth and leisure, were apparently now determined to emulate the patterns of the East by embellishing the crasser aspects of life with the veneer and polish of the polite arts.

From the standpoint of mere census enumeration Chicago with its million population in 1890 was large enough to support an orchestra; but its musical experience was almost entirely limited to the traveling orchestras, opera troupes, and concert artists that toured the West. In 1890 Chicago was merely an aspirant to rather than a participant in "culture."

Theodore Thomas [44] himself had paved the way for the Chicago orchestra—a service which he had also rendered to the orchestras in Boston, Philadelphia, Cincinnati, St. Louis, and other cities. Wherever he went with his traveling troupe, he thrilled audiences with the discipline and precision of his performance, an accomplishment made possible only because he had a permanent body of men who considered the orchestra their chief and specialized employment. After the failure of both Carl Bergmann and Henry Ahner, former members of the old Germania orchestra, to organize local orchestras, Hans Balatka, in 1860, enjoyed the first real but transient success. His group aroused some enthusiasm for a period of about six years, then gradually disappeared from the scene after Thomas had made his first of many Chicago appearances in 1869. It was obvious to all that he hopelessly outclassed the local contingent. His playing of *Träumerei*, strings muted, *pp*, in contrast to Balatka's "straight" reading was one of the sensations of that early season. Even the most untutored of his listeners could understand the difference. During the next two decades he paid many visits to the city, regaled his followers with nine seasons of summer night concerts at popular prices, and thereby practically killed off all indigenous efforts.

But by the end of that time, the now fifty-three-year-old migratory Thomas had become a tired man. His yearning for a permanent orchestra, on the order of that of Major Higginson of Boston, had never been gratified. Instead, he had been stalked by repeated financial and personal failures: the Philadelphia Centennial concerts, the Cincinnati Musical College, the American Opera Company—each of which would make a story in itself. Minor adversities had deepened his depression: The House of Steinway, which had generously supported him for years, was now also tired, and financial aid, which had been forthcoming from other friends, was inadequate; his age rendered it impossible to endure, much less enjoy, the tours that he had undertaken philosophically for twenty years; and finally his own personal temperament was far from adaptable. As he matured, he found it less possible to maintain even a semblance of the graceful cooperation essential to success in public undertakings.

If one wished to prolong the melancholy recital of mishaps and the overwhelming weight of circumstance that can shape destiny, one might continue. After the collapse of the American Opera Company (1885–87), which had toured the United States with opera in English, Thomas did attempt a comeback and returned to concert work in New York. But his absence had shaken his former grip. The New York audience had gone opera-mad; Seidl had captivated New York; Boston had entered the field with its own fine orchestra and was competing with New York, thereby closing that profitable outlet for Thomas; and finally, interstate transportation rules had been tightened so that traveling troupes were no longer eligible for the reduced fares that had previously made touring profitable.

It was at this juncture, in 1889, that Charles Norman Fay, a Chicago friend, had broached to him the possibility of coming to Chicago if guarantees could be raised for a permanent orchestra

ng the nineteenth cen-
, the band concert was
pular form of musical
rtainment. Mr. Har-
B. Dodworth was the
of the eminent line of
d directors in Amer-
vhich included Patrick
nore and John Philip
sa. The "band" concert
uded symphonic and
ratic numbers, and con-
ted an important stage
the development of
erican musical taste.
Dodworth was a vio-
t in the New York
lharmonic orchestra,
his programs can
dly be distinguished
n those of the Philhar-
iic. The youthful The-
re Thomas was fea-
d in the programs as
in soloist, probably
b piano accompani-
t.

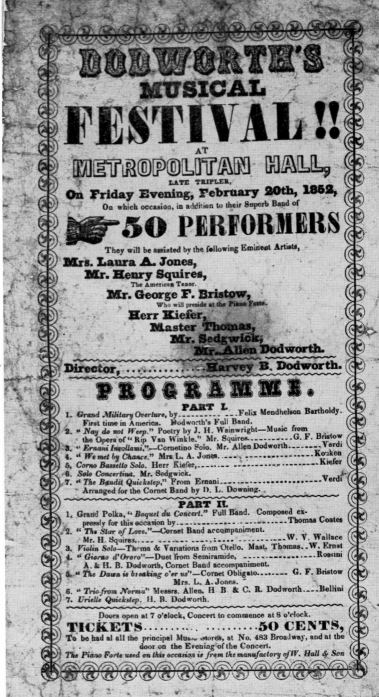

THE EARLIEST AVAILABLE PICTURE OF THE CHICAGO SYMPHONY ORCHESTRA — ABOUT 1898. *Theodore Thomas is shown conducting the orchestra in the auditorium. (Courtesy of the Chicago Symphony Orchestra)*

THEODORE THOMAS

Theodore Thomas may be called the "father of the permanent orchestra." He founded his own full-time orchestra in 1863, purveyed the finest music in New York and on tour as far west as San Francisco, and excited an interest in symphonic orchestras in the major cities of the United States. (Culver Service)

Thomas' quickened spirit replied with his oft-quoted retort: "I would go to Hell if they gave me a permanent orchestra."

In retrospect, Chicago seems to have been somewhat less than ready for such a metropolitan venture. Thousand-dollar pledges, by fifty persons, for only three years, was not big money even in those days and did not betoken complete appreciation of the responsibilities of the venture. After this short pump priming, its backers expected the orchestra to be self-supporting and even profitable as the Thomas summer concerts had been for ten years. But there were no suburbs where extra concerts could be given to alleviate deficits; although there was some intense musical interest in Chicago, there was no ready audience of sufficient dimensions in size and taste, as there had been in Boston, whose patronage would insure success. In sum, it was an uncomfortably small margin of safety to cover the unknown hazards of possible cooling of interest, or to offset a decline in financial competence of guarantors, and it was a long gamble that necessary additional sponsors could be found.

All these and many other impediments were actually encountered and eventually overcome. But at the moment, there was an element of strength and confidence in the original list of guarantors who, in addition to Fay, a business executive, included the most noted industrial and commercial names of old Chicago: Pullman, Armour, Marshall Field, Ryerson, McCormick, Potter, Blackstone, Wacker, Sprague, and many others.

Nor was Chicago rich in the requisite professional resources from which to build an orchestra. The city actually engaged not only a conductor, but an entire orchestra, for Thomas imported about sixty men from New York as the nucleus for the new group, to be supplemented by only about twenty-four chosen from the local supply—a circumstance which caused some disturbance in union ranks for a time. In one respect, however, Chicago was well equipped, so they thought: the new Auditorium, designed by the celebrated Louis Sullivan, built primarily to house the opera, had been dedicated in 1889 and possessed fine acoustics and a seating capacity of 4,800.

Thus Theodore Thomas in 1891 founded the first orchestra still surviving in the Middle West, but during the first ten years its survival was many times in doubt. Discouragements "came not single spies but in battalions": the programs were more erudite than the patrons who had enjoyed the annual light summer series had been led to expect; during the first eleven seasons the annual deficits averaged $33,000, which the guarantors were never quite able to liquidate; the post-Fair depression had caused a miscalculation of returns; some of the original patrons gradually faded from the picture, and new ones had to be recruited. Finally, Chicago was learning what everyone already knew in the East: Mr. Thomas was a difficult personality who made no concessions to the press and very few to the public.

Nevertheless, Thomas could not be tempted to Boston, where he was tendered the conductorship in 1893, just as he could not be diverted from his adopted country by an offer from the London Philharmonic in 1880. However, as the deficits gradually declined, the talk of abandoning the project was no longer heard. Chicago began to notice its new décor and to compare itself with Boston and Leipzig, the only other cities where subscription pairs were heard in excess of the number (twenty) offered in the metropolis of the West. In five years, Thomas was ready to display his achievement before his old New York audience. He had retained many friends in the East, who presented him with a baroque silver bowl, on which were engraved the profiles of Thomas together with the masters whom he had interpreted: Beethoven, Wagner, Brahms, and Berlioz.

To Thomas one of the most serious obstacles to the development of the Chicago orchestra was the Auditorium. It was simply too large. Since it could almost never be filled, the empty seats were depressing. Since patrons "could always get a seat," very few felt the necessity of purchasing season tickets. Its gigantic spaces required a volume of music which could be drawn only from a much larger group. But players cost money, which was not available. The audience was too far from the orchestra to achieve rapport. Rentals were high. Rehearsals often had to be held in other buildings. Everything was wrong. These torments, together with the merciless newspaper criticisms and the uncongenial climate, caused his position to become so unbearable that in 1899 he declared his determination to resign. The trustees likewise were becoming fatigued and concluded that they could not continue indefinitely the annual payments of $30,000 or more to support an orchestra. They saw clearly the only two alternatives: either abandon the orchestra or put it on a firm and permanent financial foundation. Was Thomas about to hatch another magnificent failure?

It was at this crisis that a truly farsighted solution was achieved. The trustees resolved to endow the orchestra by building a permanent home which would be a source of income and security. A public campaign for subscriptions was instituted which netted pledges ranging from ten cents to $25,000. The orchestra's present home, capacity about 2,500 persons, was completed and ready for dedication in December, 1904.

Officially everyone was pleased and enthusiastic with the new music hall. Thomas, who remembered the cavernous old Auditorium, was quoted as approving: "We are now in the same room as the audience." [45]

Privately, however, there were many criticisms, for the stage was shallow and the acoustics seemed inferior to the Auditorium. Both of these defects resulted from last-minute modifications of architectural details, occasioned by an event of such seriousness that any protest against them could not then have been entertained. The Iroquois Theatre fire of December 30, 1903, in which 602 persons had perished, so shocked the community that drastic enforcement of new fire laws took precedence over every other aesthetic, architectural, or acoustical consideration. In any case, there was much discussion of what "might have been" and, whatever the truth of these speculations, it is perfectly plausible to understand that, for Thomas' Chicago audiences, acoustical habituation to the smaller hall was more difficult than had been anticipated. However, it is probably too much to agree with the somewhat exaggerated feeling of one of the members of the orchestra ("my own instrument never did sound right in the new surroundings") that it was "grief and disappointment in the new Hall which shortened the life of Thomas."

Actually, Mr. Thomas did not survive the first concert in Orchestra Hall by more than a few weeks. His passing (January, 1905) was an occasion of world-wide mourning, and in the press of the day there was a remarkable volume of reminiscences on the qualities of the man who had given such a firm foundation to music in the United States.[46]

Musically, Thomas was a self-made man who had "learned with his public." He acquired his repertoire and his skill, and even his style of conducting, in public, and in thus fashioning himself, he was indispensably aided by his temperament. He was a man of iron will, with an inflexible determination to have things his own way. He could never compromise with charlatanism and was content with only the best possible musical product. In his conducting he took infinite pains to create effects; he was a conscientious, even severe, disciplinarian, but never cruel or abusive to his men. Some of his men recall even today his solicitude for their personal comfort, their financial and family affairs.

He was not a Karl Muck, thoroughly schooled in all the details of orchestral technique, much less a Nikisch or a Seidl who revelled in personal interpretation. He was rather a conservative, ever "faithful to the score." His claim to be the only conductor who executed the Bach embellishments according to traditional specifications was typical. There were many who admired the elegance and fidelity of Thomas, but also those critics, like Henry Krehbiel, for whom "polish was not enough" and who preferred the flexible individualistic readings of Herr Seidl.[47] Thomas was frugal in gesture and conducted with a beat that the audience could follow as easily as could the men in the orchestra. He had a "good back."

Although he gave his heart to the classics, it cannot be said that he avoided "modern" works. He sponsored Wagner from the very first concert of his career (1862) and in 1899 introduced Strauss' *Heldenleben* to America. In those days such an achievement was much more of a technical and aesthetic triumph than a corresponding innovation would be today, and for two reasons: most orchestras and conductors were not so firmly established as to permit such liberties with the audience, and the technical competence of the musicians was far below the standards achieved by the specialists of today. As one former Thomas musician expressed it, "the average music school orchestra today has a better bassoonist than we had in our professional orchestra fifty years ago." Thomas could not have dreamed of Stokowski's boast, made thirty years later, that every man in the first violin section was competent to act as concertmaster. The 5/4 rhythm in the Tschaikowsky *Pathétique* was a major technical hurdle, as difficult to negotiate, for the orchestra as a whole, as are the intricate rhythms of a Stravinsky score today. The story is told that, in order to absorb the feeling of the complexities of the 5-beat measure, Mr. Thomas—who usually spoke German to the overwhelmingly Teutonic membership—recommended that the familiar phrase, *"Ein Glass Bier für mich,"* exactly one measure in length, be repeated silently by the thirsty musicians while practicing the movement.

Thomas died at the height of his career, the very moment when his life ambition, a permanent orchestra permanently housed, materialized. In recognition of his achievement, the trustees renamed the Chicago Orchestra the "Theodore Thomas Orchestra," so that its founder might be forever identified with that body. Upon later reconsideration, however, this commendable gesture was found to be more sentimental than practicable. The name of Theodore Thomas, for a living and growing city orchestra, was too personal an association to carry the same significance to a new generation as it had to the past. The orchestra was, after all, a civic enterprise, supported by the citizens of Chicago who were to reap any prestige or advertising value which it might yield. There was likewise the distinct possibility that another orchestra might assume a title using the name of the city, to the detriment of the older and legitimate organization. Hence, the present name was adopted in February, 1913, in which the reference to Theodore Thomas is perpetuated in the subtitle: "Founded by Theodore Thomas."

Since Thomas died in midseason, it was obviously necessary to replace him immediately. The provisional choice fell upon a member of the viola section, the thirty-two-year-old Frederick Stock, who had served Thomas as assistant conductor for some time. Although Chicago emulated the Boston system of searching in Europe for worthy leaders, the appointment of Stock became permanent when Mottl, Weingartner, and Richter, among the most noted European conductors, had been considered. The youthful Stock, who had been a fellow-student in Cologne of Mengelberg and of Felix Borowski, the Chicago composer, pedagogue, and critic, was in fact much better prepared, academically, than was Thomas. In contrast to the literal Thomas, he continued to shock many of his men by his liberal excisions and editings of the scores, though for some years he was still a virtual apprentice in the art of practical conducting. However, he was recognized as a musical scholar, maintained fine diplomatic relations with the public, and elicited a firm loyalty from his men, who quite understandably preferred him to some more mature stranger who might have been imported to "reorganize" the orchestra.

Stock's long regime was momentarily interrupted by the events associated with the first World War. He might easily have become a victim of war hysteria, but he extricated himself by prompt and discreet action. He had applied for American citizenship shortly after his arrival in 1895 but, in the manner characteristic of those peaceful and complacent days, had allowed it to lapse without applying for the final papers. By voluntarily retiring "for the duration" until his papers could be put in order, he appeased the patriots and avoided nationalistic demonstrations which might have irreparably inflamed public opinion against him. In the interim Eric DeLamarter, a Chicago composer and organist, was appointed assistant conductor, aided by a number of distinguished guest conductors.

As in the case of Muck in Boston and Kunwald in Cincinnati, it required over a year for hostile attitudes to come to a head against the prominent aliens. Although war had been declared by the United States against Germany in April, 1917, it was not until August, 1918 —three months before the armistice—that Stock retired, to be welcomed back with cheers, telegraphic felicitations, and floral tributes six months later. Three members of the orchestra, who had also been "retired" or "dismissed," shared in the amnesty and were reinstated. During his absence, the now naturalized conductor committed his sentiments to writing by composing the *March and Hymn to Democracy* to celebrate his return to the podium.

World War I had brought home to the United States full realization of its past dependence upon foreign countries for the skilled members of its musical forces. In order to assure its supply of routined musicians, the Chicago orchestra organized an apprentice ensemble, the Chicago Civic Orchestra, for the training of young musicians. The first conductors were Mr. Stock, himself, DeLamarter, and George Dasch, members of the Chicago orchestra. This organization presents periodic concerts of the standard repertoire, and its alumni have been sought by the major orchestras of the country. The almost immediate effect upon the Chicago orchestra was to improve its own personnel by retiring more promptly the superannuated members and replacing those less prepared with the best candidates from the ranks of the undergraduate orchestra. At about the same time, a similar organization was founded in New York: the American Orchestral Association, whose title was later (1930) changed to the National Orchestral Association.

In the postwar twenties the Chicago orchestra was symptomatically threatened with dissolution because of difficulties now commonly referred to as "union troubles." These so-called union troubles do not grow out of casual and capricious circumstances, but have deep roots in the social and economic soil of the era. With the cessation of the flow of European supply, good musicians were becoming scarce, and competition for them was increasing. After the first World War, the cost of living turned sharply upward; motion pictures, during that expansive period, began to hire orchestras of symphonic proportions, and new orchestras were being established in western cities which formerly possessed only a small amateur group or none at all. All these factors pointed toward a campaign for important revisions in players' contracts, which management, largely dominated by philanthropists, naturally was loath to grant. In 1923, 1928, and again in 1932 during the great depression, management, always harassed by deficit bookkeeping, repeatedly released alarming publicity indicating an impasse in negotiations, which were, however, as many times resumed when "both sides compromised." In 1928 the Chicago players had actually been notified that they were "free to seek employment elsewhere," and in 1932 they likewise received their "discharge notices" when James C. Petrillo (then president of the Chicago local), and the orchestral management delayed in reaching an agreement. Although it is inconceivable at present that the orchestra should thus have been disbanded, musicians today give testimony to their feeling of insecurity during that postwar transition period.

Long, continuous tenures with a single organization are as rare among orchestral leaders as they are among baseball managers and football coaches, for the problems of maintaining public acclaim are analogous. Stock's career was closed only by his death in the fall of 1942, after nearly thirty-eight years of service, which is a record second only to Walter Damrosch's interrupted forty-three years' association with the New York Symphony Society. Mr. Stock was never a sensational or colorful figure; he had no national reputation for stylistic or distinctive readings. He was rather a scholarly, reliable, and substantial interpreter admired by his audiences and respected by his men.

After an interim of guest conductors, Désiré Defauw, a Belgian conductor, was appointed in 1943. During his four-year term, he was remorselessly harassed by various critics, both for his programs and his alleged deficiencies. In 1947 he was succeeded by Artur Rodzinski, whose resignation-dismissal in New York had made headlines. Known as the "builder of orchestras," Rodzinski was hailed by the aforesaid critics of the previous regime as a good omen for the resuscitation of the "rundown" orchestra, only to suffer a similarly violent ejection in Chicago in midseason after demonstrations of independence which the management would not endure. After two seasons of guests, Rafael Kubelik, the scion of the late Czech violinist, was appointed to assume his duties in the fall of 1950.

REPERTOIRE   Of all the orchestras in the United States, the Chicago orchestra presents a repertoire which is one of the most diverse in character and catholic in taste. It neither rides inordinate hobbies nor displays any conspicuously unusual phobias. Its two conductors during its first half-century have never been blatantly "progressive" nor have they lagged noticeably in the recognition of newer trends.

Some reasons for this condition are apparent. For nearly thirty years, since his first full series of concerts initiated in Irving Hall, New York, October 24, 1863, Thomas conducted seasonal series for all types of occasions and for all levels of audience comprehension without serious deviation or interruption. At the time he mounted the podium in Chicago on October 17, 1891, he had behind him a broader disciplined experience, and was intimately familiar with a more extended repertoire, than any European conductor of comparable prestige ever accumulates in a lifetime. Then, as now, the schedule of the average American symphony orchestra, playing a season of twenty or more regular subscription concerts, gives the conductor a heavier and more relentless schedule than the prima donna conductors of foreign training and prestige ever encounter in Europe. If therefore, a broad, substantial, unspecialized repertoire was to be offered, no man, here or abroad, was better qualified than was Theodore Thomas.

As for the Chicago audiences, they had no fashionable traditions for the exotic and no urge for the *dernier cri* in artistic creativeness. In fact, in the early days, it is probable that they were below the average of the Eastern cities in respect to aesthetic sophistication and curiosity. Chicago was merely a prosperous Midwest city which sought enjoyment in good music, and considered an orchestra as standard equipment in a city of its size and pretensions. Since there were no radios or records, a large majority of the potential audience of the Thomas concerts had had little opportunity to get acquainted with serious repertoires, except those offered by itinerant orchestras, of which the Thomas private orchestra had been an illustrious example.

In 1891, when he moved to Chicago, Thomas was almost at the peak of his ambitious career and had built a reputation as a conductor who never compromised willingly with his audiences. His frank interspersal of his repertoire, especially during the first several years, with a number of popular programs which were condescendingly offered for the delectation of the audience is evidence of his own appraisal of its level of sophistication. He did not find in Chicago an atmosphere in which energetic prosecution of experimental music would thrive.

But from Thomas a moderate list of selected novelties could always be expected. Since neither Thomas nor Stock supported one-sided or distorted tastes, one looks in vain for a Henschel and his personal affinity for Brahms; a Viennese Gericke who allots eighty per cent of his repertoire to the conservative Austro-German composers; a Koussevitzky and his Sibelius; a Toscanini and his Beethoven; even less a Stokowski with his early uninhibited explorations in cacophony.

The standard repertoire appears in national proportions. For the period of the nineties, Beethoven is perhaps a little low, with twelve to fifteen per cent, and Brahms, with five to six per cent. Known as a friend of the neo-German school, Thomas momentarily gave vent to his early enthusiasm by raising Wagner to the dizzy heights of fifteen per cent, which is a high proportion for any composer with the exception of Beethoven. However, he quickly deflated the German titan to a more normal nine per cent before the end of the century. After having introduced Richard Strauss to America with the world première of the Symphony in F Minor, December 13, 1884, he also performed the American première of *Till Eulenspiegel, Ein Heldenleben*, and several lesser numbers.

Next to Boston, Chicago is generally cited as a champion of American music. In his day, however, Thomas had not only failed to make a reputation as a friend of American music, but was actually criticized for his apathy toward it. It can be said only that he played a moderate number of American "classics" (Paine, Chadwick, MacDowell, Converse, *et al.*). Thomas simply affirmed: "I played all there were."

However, the Chicago orchestra did allow itself the luxury of a few indulgences to offset the drab gray of the "well-balanced" repertoire. Of these, the most unexpected was the ephemeral devotion to the Russians Miaskowsky and Glazounoff. Professor of Composition at Moscow, Miaskowsky had already attained a reputation before the revolution. Whether through aesthetic maturation or ideological expediency, his style grew more amenable to the requirements of the Soviet government. His fertile pen had produced the astronomical number of twenty-six symphonies at his death in 1950. Philadelphia was the first to accord this industrious Russian an American hearing when it played the Fifth Symphony in January, 1926. Since that date other conductors have sampled of the bountiful tonal array, but none with the apparent appetite of Stock, who performed nine of the symphonies. The Sixth must have been consumed with unusual relish, for it was given nine performances. The

Twenty-first was composed for the fiftieth anniversary of the Chicago Symphony Orchestra and "dedicated to its illustrious conductor."

Chicago has been second to Philadelphia in the presentation of Bach, and long before Stokowski developed his infatuation for him, Stock was playing twice the national average. But with both Beethoven and Brahms Chicago has maintained a consistently lower place than other orchestras. D'Indy was a favorite of Stock, although in general the French composers have had scant attention. Although Chicago was one of the earliest to introduce and favor Prokofieff, for him, as well as for Stravinsky, there has been no enthusiasm in the last decade. Shostakovitch has never been favored, and toward Sibelius there has been a similar aloofness.

With the passing of Stock, there disappeared some of the conspicuous features of his long tenure. American music declined precipitously; Bach could not maintain his relatively high position; and Beethoven ascended, under Rodzinski and guest conductors, to a position reminiscent of the Thomas days.

The Cincinnati Symphony Orchestra (1895)

Cincinnati has for many years enjoyed the reputation of being a musical city. This Midwestern community with its heavy German population, and its then basic industries of meat and malt liquors, gave Theodore Thomas some of his most hospitable receptions and instituted with his aid the biennial May Festivals, which continue down to the present day. The first of these festivals, projected by Mr. Thomas and Mrs. Maria Nicholas Longworth, was staged in 1873, and exemplified Mr. Thomas' concentrated devotion to music in general and instrumental music in particular. The stern conductor insisted on two conditions: that the festival be divorced from beer, which had in previous saengerfest years been purveyed in the gigantic barroom under the mammoth stage; and, the granting of coordinate importance to instrumental and choral music.

If today this would seem only a decent and modest requirement, it was nothing short of revolutionary in 1873. Cincinnati, like any other American city with a sizable German population, cultivated choral music. These choral groups, under the name of Männerchor, Liedertafel, Liederkranz, and Sängerbund, were founded to cultivate conviviality quite as much as the Muses. It was left to such serious leaders as Thomas and Leopold Damrosch, however, to elevate them to the dignity which they since attained. In the earlier days these festivals took on all the airs of a civic function. In 1880, a Cincinnati correspondent reports:

There has been a grand and unprecedented street cleaning, and this has been followed by the efforts of the decorating committee who have made us resplendent with flags and bunting. We have unlimited company from all the neighboring states . . . and we have even more unlimited brag. . . . I understand that today there is scarcely a seat left for any performance of the week.[48]

Today, most of these organizations have succumbed to the pressures of competitive social attractions of the modern way of life. A century ago, however, the choral groups were the nursery of musical training and in many instances, notably in Minneapolis and St. Louis, were the literal ancestors of the present instrumental organizations.

Cincinnati was among the earliest cities to mobilize substantial philanthropic aid for musical activities. That the effort proved abortive is merely evidence that its citizens had not yet accumulated the necessary experience for the organization of musical activities in our American culture. In 1878, the College of Music of Cincinnati was founded by a group which included such names as George Ward Nichols (chairman), Springer, Longworth, Shillito, and a score of other financial and civic leaders. Theodore Thomas was offered, and accepted, the headship. If Thomas did not dream that this was destined to be the second of his "magnificent failures," his intimates did. The single-minded conductor had never been distinguished for his adeptness at administrative functions in a democratic society. In fact, *Dwight's Journal* editorialized with a decorous touch of understatement: "Among the many discriminating friends whom Thomas made as an orchestral conductor, there were not a few who hesitated to form an opinion as to his fitness for the directorship of an educational institution." [49] Within less than two years, he was back in New York. The Thomas-Nichols imbroglio produced a national sensation. In general, the musicians were supporting Thomas; businessmen who knew that Thomas was receiving a salary of $10,000 from the College, plus other perquisites, "could see the other side." One can only speculate on the developments if the Cincinnati philanthropists had recognized the principle of "artistic supremacy" and if Mr. Thomas had been possessed of a more compromising spirit. Thomas' subsequent association with Cincinnati was limited to the direction of the Music Festivals, which he maintained to the last—1904.

In mid-century, Cincinnati was one of the terminal points of the growing German immigration. From these issued several local orchestras which were organized in 1857 and afterward under F. L. Ritter, and George and Michael Brand. The venture of 1857 under Ritter, who is best remembered today for his *Music in America* and other literary works, was the short-lived Philharmonic Society, organized on the cooperative pattern of the New York Philharmonic. A more pretentious undertaking was that of a Mr. Hopkins, who in 1865 not only organized an orchestra and choral society and paid the musicians, but also built a small auditorium. A much larger hall was built in 1878, at the instance of Mr. Springer, who contributed $200,000, matched from other sources. It is the same hall originally intended for the music festivals, which is still in use today as the home of the Cincinnati Symphony Orchestra.

In 1895, the year of the founding of the present orchestra, Michael Brand was the leader of a small orchestra of about forty men. It was in that year that a number of women, including Mrs. William Howard Taft, envisaged a plan for a permanent orchestra, subsidized by private benefactions, and conducted by a musician of note. Cincinnati was thereby to take its place beside Boston and Chicago, which had already attained national recognition. The conductor was to be chosen from a list of three who were invited in the spring of 1895 to conduct three concerts each, with an orchestra of forty-eight men, largely recruited from the orchestra of the aforementioned Mr. Brand. Of the three guests—Henry Schradiek, Anton Seidl, and Frank Van der Stucken—Van der Stucken was proffered the permanent appointment.

As Van der Stucken was at that time conductor of the Arion

Society of New York, a position which paid a salary of $4,000, as well as church organist, and conductor of free lance orchestral concerts, it proved difficult to induce him to embark on a new project in the West. However, the attractiveness of orchestral prospects, together with that of the directorship of the College of Music, overcame his hesitation. With Van der Stucken as Dean of the Music Faculty, the Cincinnati College of Music was considered an important feeder for the orchestra. Under the changed circumstances, Van der Stucken was able to perform an effective job where Theodore Thomas, the first incumbent, had failed. The new director established standards of discipline and artistic achievement that made it a real distinction to win a diploma from the College. As a conductor, he excelled in chorus work. He was a disciplinarian, a picturesque gentleman of vigorous and uninhibited speech, though off stage an affable and convivial personality.

In order to strengthen his orchestra, the new conductor imported from New York and elsewhere the principal players, who were put on salary while the local men were paid by the concert. Such a course was not at all unusual, and invariably accompanied the founding of every major orchestra in the nation. But the inevitable threat of noncooperation of local musicians was averted when the success of the project became apparent.

Van der Stucken is popularly referred to as the first native-born American conductor of a major symphony orchestra. Born in Texas (1858), he was taken to Antwerp as a child of eight years, received his musical training in Europe, and had attained a certain distinction there before returning to America in 1884. It could be argued, however, that Walter Damrosch and Theodore Thomas, both of whom arrived in this country in childhood and received all their training in the United States and so exclusively confined their activity to this country, were more American than Van der Stucken, whose American activity was flanked by professional residence in Europe.

But the fiscal problem reared its ugly head. At the close of the season 1906–07, the Cincinnati orchestra was disbanded, the official reason given as "labor trouble." Van der Stucken departed and accepted engagements in the East as well as in Europe.

Since there was no intention of allowing the orchestra to languish, the following two years were employed in fortifying the system of financial guarantees. By the spring of 1909 pledges of $50,000 per year for five years allowed the management to put the whole orchestra on season contract, and to engage a young English conductor, twenty-seven-year-old Leopold Stokowski, who had since 1905 been organist in St. Bartholomew's Church in New York.

From his subsequent eminence, it is not surprising that Stokowski's incumbency was impressive, even though without benefit of the podium trappings that he conjured up in later years. Inexperienced as a conductor, he was quite conventional, employed the score and the stick. But he was enthusiastic and dynamic, knew his repertoire, and he precociously scolded his audience for restlessness. He was democratic, especially when the orchestra was on tour. The men, as well as the management, genuinely regretted his departure after a short three-year turn. With his contract still two years to run, he requested release, pleading "lack of cooperation." Another view of his abrupt departure saw an implied slight to him in the continued use of outside orchestras and conductors for the May Festival. That fall, Stokowski assumed direction of the Philadelphia Orchestra, where he was able to consummate his grandest ambitions.

His successor was Dr. Ernst Kunwald, who had held several posts in Europe, including that of conductor of the Berlin Philharmonic popular concerts. Kunwald was a master of detail and was noted for his fine memory. His regime was rudely interrupted by the war. His status of enemy alien, together with certain indiscretions on his part, led to his arrest and ultimate deportation. As in other cities, hostile public sentiment was, however, slow to crystallize. At first, the public, especially that part of the public concerned with music, was proud of its American broad-mindedness and, steeped in sympathy for German culture, conveniently distinguished the blameworthy German government from its innocent people. In May, 1917, a month after the American declaration of war, Kunwald could close the season with Haydn, Bach, and Beethoven, and was the recipient of a vote of confidence in the form of a floral offering.

But with the intensification of hostilities, news of battle casualties, and the mushrooming of war activities, sentiment was bound to take an unfavorable turn. Kunwald, who had been dutifully conducting the national anthem, was now accused of not acknowledging its applause. The Vienna-born musician had never kept his loyalty to Austria a secret, though he claimed always to have acted "correctly." If reminiscences of some of his players are to be trusted, he expressed, in his remarks to his audience, his willingness to remain in America and build up the "finest orchestra in the country" if the public wished it, though he frankly acknowledged that "my heart is with my country." His first resignation was not accepted. Arrested in December, 1917, he was interned in Fort Oglethorpe (official accusation never divulged), from where he was later deported. Guest conductors for the remainder of the season were: Walter Rothwell, Victor Herbert, Henry Hadley, Gabrilowitsch, and Eugène Ysaye.

The obvious political strategy was to turn to our allies for the next conductor, although many critics protested against the apparent indifference to American candidates. Ysaye, the Belgian violin virtuoso, who had turned down the New York Philharmonic in 1898 and now found himself a refugee from his devastated native country, was engaged at $25,000 on a five-year contract. He was a romantic figure of leonine proportions and imposingly groomed. The acknowledged "king" of violinists of the pre-Kreisler age, he played with abandon and enthralled those who enjoyed the free, unrestrained rubato style. But now his powers were on the decline. Suffering from several physical ailments, his virtuosity deserted him. Nor had he kept abreast of current trends. He, who had thrilled his audiences with the concertos of Vieuxtemps and Wieniawski, found that Stravinsky "made me dizzy; and all modern music was just that much noise." [50] In his conducting he became erratic, affected in manner, lackadaisical in discipline, and was neglectful of even the simplest administrative requirements in planning and executing the repertoire. In 1922 after "differences with the Board," he departed for his native country, where he died in 1931.

Wounds of war had healed sufficiently to allow a reversion to the country which before the war was the most reliable source of talent —Germany. The Cincinnati post was offered to Fritz Reiner, who was then conductor at the Royal Opera in Dresden, after a rumored rejection by Koussevitzky. Reiner, then thirty-four years old, was

THE FIRST CINCINNATI MAY FESTIVAL, 1873,
THEODORE THOMAS, CONDUCTOR

The period of music festivals and Saengerfeste was an epoch of expanding musical interests. Note the seating arrangement of the orchestra, with the cellos and double basses in the middle. (From a contemporary sketch. The Bettmann Archive)

DIMITRI MITROPOULOS

A Greek contribution to American music, Mitropoulos is shown conducting the New York Philharmonic-Symphony Orchestra. From 1937 to 1949, he directed the Minneapolis Symphony Orchestra. (Courtesy of New York Philharmonic-Symphony Orchestra)

almost unknown in America although the Dresden Opera had carried him to prominence in Europe. He spoke English rather fluently, and was obviously a thoroughly schooled musician.

Reiner left in 1931 to accept a post in the Curtis Institute, Philadelphia, and was followed by Eugene Goossens, one of the most versatile of present-day conductors. He had created a sensation in England in a brief career with his own specially assembled group. His enterprising and antiromantic repertoire included in 1921 Stravinsky's *Sacre du Printemps*, which made a profound impression on his Queen's Hall audience, and many other contemporary works. His experience embraced the opera, in which he was a protégé of Thomas Beecham, and the ballet, in which he conducted the Diaghileff troupe. Composer of over a half hundred compositions, his name has appeared on the programs of orchestras both in Europe and the United States. Goossens was not a glamorous conductor, and lacked therefore the popularity that derives from a colorful personality. He did his conducting "straight" without flourish or temperament, and he was rather democratic in his relations both with the public and his men. Because of his diversified experience, his repertoire was expanded to include the ballet and the opera.

In 1947, after sixteen years of association, both Mr. Goossens and Cincinnati were reconciled to a change. When Goossens announced his acceptance of the directorship of the orchestra in Sydney, Australia, there was considerable agitation to appoint the noted Frenchman, Paul Paray, who would presumably have placed the orchestra among the best in the nation. But, if Paray ever had any intention of accepting the offer, it was not evident in his prohibitive financial terms.

The choice settled on a young American, Thor Johnson, then a member of the Juilliard faculty in New York. A product of Koussevitzky's Tanglewood school and a student of European teachers, he had created a sufficiently favorable impression in guest appearances in Chicago, Philadelphia, and Cincinnati to merit the offer of a permanent post. Cincinnati thereby became the oldest major orchestra with an American conductor, with Detroit and Los Angeles the only major orchestras with an American director at that time.

The orchestra has inherited fine auditorium facilities. During its first two seasons, the concerts were given in Pike's Opera House. But from 1896 to 1911, the orchestra used the famous old Music Hall, built in 1878. With its capacity of 3,600 this auditorium proved too large—a problem also encountered by Theodore Thomas in Chicago. The hall could never be filled, tickets were never at a premium, and consequently morale was low. At this time, Mrs. Thomas J. Emery had undertaken the construction of an auditorium for the Ohio Mechanics Institute, which proved easily adapted to the needs of the orchestra from 1911 to 1936, when expanded needs turned them again to the historic Music Hall.

The orchestra has accumulated an endowment fund, heavy contributions to which were made from the estates of Cora Dow (1915), Mrs. Nicholas Longworth (1923), and Mrs. Victoria Hoover (1924). This capital amount is, of course, far from adequate to cancel the inevitable deficits of an active organization. Friends of the orchestra undertake to raise an annual maintenance fund to supplement the endowment. Among the most generous patrons of the orchestra have been Mr. and Mrs. Charles P. Taft, who not only quietly assumed the deficits of the orchestra during the twenties, but likewise were the motivating force in founding the Institute of Fine Arts for the permanent civic sponsorship of the arts.

REPERTOIRE   A unique reputation for diligent cultivation of the American composer had preceded the Texas-born Van der Stucken when he made his debut in a guest program in Cincinnati in 1895 and amply fulfilled this promise with an all-American program of Chadwick, Foote, Victor Herbert, Parker, and MacDowell. He had been enacting similar exploits in New York since 1884, and was reputed to have been the first to reverse the customary flow by carrying to Europe a sample of American creative music. He presented an all-American program on foreign soil at the Paris Exposition in 1889.

Away from the Eastern atmosphere, where the physical presence of the American composers and the nativistic journalism exerted their pressure, his Americanism quickly subsided. But he was still the aggressive, enterprising conductor, espousing liberally the music of Sibelius, three per cent, and Strauss, five per cent. But his somewhat excessive devotion to Liszt (seven per cent) and Saint-Saëns (six per cent) was not sufficient to avoid the accusation of modernism.

If Stokovski (in the then current orthography) had not yet evinced the symptoms of his later experimentalism, his regime did expose his romantic inclinations by allowing Tschaikowsky (fourteen per cent) to dispute the traditional throne of Beethoven's thirteen per cent. Brahms received the normal allowance, while Strauss' six per cent was at that time twice the national average. The potentialities of a blend of these romantic propensities with the classic Bach apparently had not yet occurred to the twenty-eight-year-old conductor.

Kunwald was almost completely enclosed in the Austro-German orbit, musically as well as politically. Like Gericke and Muck in Boston, Kunwald followed the broad and safe path leading from Haydn, through Mozart, Beethoven, Brahms and Schumann, to Wagner and Strauss, and accumulated a total Teutonic repertoire, for the immediate prewar years, of seventy per cent of the entire Cincinnati repertoire. His modernism hardly extended beyond Strauss, and almost completely avoided even such "novelties" as Debussy.

With Ysaye, the French influence had its day for the first time, and rose to the unprecedented total of over twenty per cent, the result of a coincidence of the temper of the war period and the predilections of the conductor. Saint-Saëns, d'Indy, Franck, and Berlioz prospered, and several of these tasted prominence for the last time.

With Reiner and Goossens came the inevitable postwar return to "normalcy." International tensions, which produced temporary affectations in the taste, were eased. The French contingent was deflated from a previous twenty-two per cent to nine per cent in the first five years of the Central-European Reiner, while the Austro-German group recovered some of its lost prestige. But the day of the German-saturated sophisticates, dictating an unchallenged Teutonic program was gone forever. The Mucks, Gerickes, and Kunwalds were not recalled, and the high priorities granted the German stalwarts before the war were not to be regained. But never has this reaction been sufficient to dislodge the Teutons from their position of dominance.

Goossens' impulsion in the British direction was not unexpected, and from an ignominious two per cent under the Teutonic Reiner, the British leaped to a respectable seven per cent within several years. American representation likewise gained under Goossens, who had spent an American apprenticeship of eight years as conductor of the Rochester Philharmonic. By 1945, for the first time since the days of Van der Stucken, Cincinnati competed with Boston itself for the premier position in the espousal of the American composers, among whom, of course, Goossens by this time could count himself.

The Philadelphia Orchestra (1900)

The musical ancestry of the Philadelphia Orchestra extends back almost into colonial days. This orchestra did not have the Minerva-like birth of the Boston or Chicago orchestras, whose sponsors called into being full-fashioned structures which immediately launched distinguished concert series. Neither can it show the unbroken, but precarious, duration of the New York Philharmonic, whose almost miraculous survival concealed the fundamental vicissitudes that it had undergone.

Officially, the Philadelphia Orchestra appeared on the scene late, after New York, Boston, Chicago, and even Cincinnati and St. Louis all had well-established institutions. This lag is sometimes ascribed to the survival of austere Quaker traditions that frowned on the pleasures of instrumental music and other pastimes that seemed incompatible with modest and industrious existence.[51] This theory may seem to gain support in the existence of blue laws which, prior to 1934, forbade Sunday concerts (and baseball) for an admission fee; but ignores the fact that, throughout almost 150 years, Philadelphia had been enjoying a continuous musical life quite commensurate with its size and commercial importance. It had a well-established opera series in the latter half of the nineteenth century, and harbored musicians of some note from its earliest days, among whom were Reinagle, Hopkinson, and Fry. The city was included in the tours of sensational soloists, Jenny Lind, Sontag, Patti, and of the leading orchestras, such as the Theodore Thomas, Jullien, Musard, and Germania groups. Manufacturing and publishing were in thriving condition. As early as 1854, we read in a letter from a Philadelphia correspondent:

Although this is termed the Quaker City, and you know that Quakers are opposed to music, yet so much attention is paid to it, and so much interest is felt, that those engaged in the pianoforte business cannot get instruments enough to satisfy half the demand. . . . Musical entertainments pay remarkably well. Jullien gave four concerts to crowded houses.[52]

While it is true that the Society of Friends discouraged levity and was hostile toward musical indulgence, it must be remembered that by no means were all Philadelphians affiliated with that faith, and that Quakers were characteristically tolerant toward divergent beliefs.

The records of public concerts in Philadelphia begin as early as 1757 when a series of programs was offered, admission one dollar, one of which George Washington attended. James Bremner, organist, composer, and teacher, settled in Philadelphia in 1763 and organized a concert program in 1765 that included a Stamitz overture, a Geminiani concerto, and overtures by Martini and Arne. In the post-Revolutionary period similar programs were instituted by John Bentley and Alexander Reinagle, who included in their repertoire the compositions of Corelli, Mozart, Haydn, Stamitz, and K. P. E. Bach. During the period of the Constitutional Convention, George Washington again indicates by entries in his diary his attendance at the Reinagle concert.

The most important single local antecedent to the present orchestra during the first half of the last century was the establishment of the Musical Fund Society in 1820. Its origin dates back to a concert given in 1815 for the benefit of the poor, which yielded over $1,000. From this success sprang the idea of a series of concerts "for the relief and support of decayed musicians and their families and the cultivation of skill and diffusion of taste in music." [53] These two objectives, formulated on similar English models, were admirably pursued during the active period of the society from 1820 to 1857, and somewhat more sporadically even up to the present time. This society enlisted the aid of the nonprofessional but music-loving public, whose subscriptions furnished a broad base and a solid foundation for the "Fund" with which to implement their idealistic purposes. Their auditorium, Musical Fund Hall at Eighth and Locust Streets, erected in 1824, had a capacity of 2,000, was available for opera and miscellaneous public purposes, and constituted an important source of revenue to the society. However, during the period of unprecedented economic prosperity in that city after 1850, interest in the Musical Fund Orchestra waned while the more sumptuous opera gained adherents. Therefore, with the construction in 1855 of the Academy of Music, an auditorium with a capacity of 3,000, the Musical Fund Society went into partial eclipse.

The Academy, an appellation of prestige at the time, was so named after the New York Academy of Music at Fourteenth Street and Irving Place, then the home of both the opera and the New York Philharmonic Orchestra. The new hall in Philadelphia was advantageously located in the then "quiet" section of the city at Broad and Locust. This Renaissance structure, which still serves the Philadelphia Orchestra today, was built on the plan of La Scala in Milan, Italy. It is famous for its excellent acoustics and is now the oldest concert hall in the United States in use by a major orchestra. In order to insure its preservation, a controlling block of stock was purchased in 1950 by the Orchestral Association.

Though opera gained ascendancy, a succession of ensembles kept an interest in orchestral music alive. The Germania Orchestra, a professional cooperative organization similar to the New York Philharmonic, founded in 1856, overlapped with the Musical Fund Society Orchestra for nearly forty years—until 1895—and constituted a kind of orchestral backdrop for the city's music activity. About half of its membership was later absorbed by the orchestra founded by Henry Gordon Thunder, a Philadelphia organist and composer, which became, in turn, the nucleus for the present Philadelphia Orchestra, founded in 1900.

However, these forerunners of the present orchestra were exclusively local affairs with no formal sponsorship and economic support, and were artistically tentative in taste and technical competence. Until Theodore Thomas was spirited to Chicago, Philadelphia had regularly enjoyed its quota of his concerts. After that period, the New York Symphony under Damrosch, and the Boston Symphony Orchestra under Gericke and Nikisch periodically satisfied the cravings of the more discriminating tastes with five to ten concerts per season. This expedient of borrowed plumes could hardly be a matter of pride to a city of over a million population, nor yield adequate aesthetic gratification to the growing number of cultivated amateurs. A large number of these avocational players had, in 1893, formed the Philadelphia Symphony Society, an amateur organization conducted by W. W. Gilchrist, and it was this group which supplied the organizational spark though not, of course, the professional personnel, that energized the new movement.

During the summer of 1899 Fritz Scheel, a German musician recently from San Francisco, conducted a series of concerts at Woodside Park. In these concerts, as well as subsequent ones, Scheel created a tremendously favorable impression. Here seemed to be the man and the occasion to kindle interest in a permanent orchestra. Mr. Dunglison, president of the Musical Fund Society, acting in consonance with the ideals of the society, called a meeting of civic leaders, secured 120 guarantors who raised $15,000 to which the Fund contributed $500, and announced the first six concerts of the Philadelphia Orchestra to begin November 16, 1900. Previously, Theodore Thomas and Walter Damrosch had had their supporters for the proposed new orchestra. In fact, Mrs. E. D. Gillespie, warm friend and patron of Thomas, and President of the Woman's Commission of the Philadelphia Centennial, was moved to boycott the new project with the failure of her candidate. Some progress had also been made toward inviting Walter Damrosch and his New York Symphony Society to transfer to Philadelphia, as Thomas had moved to Chicago. This plan engendered violent opposition and was soon dropped.

Scheel, who had been an assistant to Bülow in Germany, had conducted an orchestra at the Columbia Exposition in Chicago (1893) and a San Francisco orchestra in 1895–99. He possessed an extensive knowledge of repertoire, was a good judge of musical talent, achieved disciplined command of his men, and maintained high standards, if not an advanced taste. Such qualities, though admirable, are not of a sort to insure wide public participation after first enthusiasms have been dissipated. Scheel used to remark that he was thankful that the conductor always turned his back to the audience so that he could forget its vanishing size. In an auditorium with a capacity of 3,000, the orchestra, during its first years, frequently had to content itself with an audience of only 600.

Although Dr. Edward I. Keffer, an amateur violinist and dentist by profession, was the leading spirit at its founding, the Orchestral Association must attribute its subsequent stability to two converts to the cause, who had previously evinced no interest in orchestral music, but became most faithful workers in the vineyard: Alexander van Rensselaer, its president for thirty-five years (1900–35), and Edward Bok, editor of *The Ladies Home Journal*, who is generally conceded to have "saved" the orchestra, with an annual contribution of $100,000 from 1916 to 1920. He joined the board in 1913.[54]

The Woman's Committee, founded in 1904, when the infant orchestra was in financial straits, has also played a major role in the social and financial security of the orchestra. Its activities have for years been directed by Miss Frances A. Wister, a member of one of Philadelphia's oldest families, who still presides over the ritual of presenting, from the stage of the Academy on the last Friday matinée of the season, the traditional gold watch to memorialize a player's completion of twenty-five years of service to the orchestra.

During the first year of its existence, the orchestra was still composed of local musicians, who had joined the orchestra to supplement their professional income and to gratify their higher taste. As in every other city, it was soon discovered that no first-class orchestra could be forged out of local talent. It was necessary to tap a wider market, which, in keeping with those times, was, of course, Europe. For this purpose, Scheel was authorized to go abroad to recruit new members, a move against which the pathetic protests of the local musicians were entirely impotent. The assurance of the committee that "it would accept every Philadelphia musician who was competent" consoled only those few who could compete with the available European importations. Many local players were ruthlessly replaced, to the undoubted benefit of the artistry of the orchestra, but to the great personal grief of the less proficient. Like the other orchestras, this one had inevitably floated helplessly along in the stream of events. Initiating the laudable project of a Philadelphia symphony orchestra, the committee had announced its belief that

with a sufficient number of rehearsals, under a capable director, our home players will be able to render great orchestral compositions efficiently and acceptably.

But within less than two years

Fritz Scheel . . . changed the personnel list so it read like the roster of every court orchestra in Germany.[55]

Unable to endure the heavy demands made upon his varied services to the community, Scheel died in 1907, and was followed by Karl Pohlig, who had to his credit a considerable experience in Germany, Austria, and England, and was brought to Philadelphia direct from Stuttgart. His five-year regime in Philadelphia was undistinguished—a kind of interregnum between the lamented Scheel and the dazzling Stokowski. Temperamental friction hastened his relinquishment of his $12,000 job. Pohlig returned to Germany in 1912, received a life appointment as General Musical Director of the Court Opera in Braunschweig, where he died in 1928.

Scheel and Pohlig survived several real crises, and put the orchestra on a fairly secure musical footing, but were not able to enlist great wealth in support of the orchestra. It was left to Leopold Stokowski to exploit public support to the limit and to elevate the organization to a place rivaling the best in the world.

In Philadelphia, Stokowski quickly succeeded in riveting the attention of the public upon his work by his daring technical and administrative innovations and his unconventional programming. The management was kept in perpetual nervous suspense over his next demand, and his audience, in a dither of curiosity for the next surprise. He abandoned score and baton; he reseated the orchestra; he played incomprehensible music and scolded the audience for its indifference toward it. Experimentally, he permitted the violinists to bow independently; in 1929, he passed around the concertmaster position in alphabetical order. He virtually compressed evolutionary eras into the span of a few years.

But he elicited loyalty from patrons and civic bodies and capitalized upon every circumstance to gain notoriety for himself, for the orchestra, and for the community. His contemporaries among the orchestra personnel, patrons, and associates still recount anecdotes of his kaleidoscopic temperament: his modesty and conceit, his generosity and his cruelty, his permanent reforms as well as his experimental failures, his affability and his social aloofness, his wit and sarcasm, his "Polish accent" and his lapses into conventional English. Like so many other colorful figures, he was an enigma in that he had his enthusiasts as well as his detractors. But whether he is viewed as a poseur who impressed the ladies and inhibited the critics, or a musician of discernment and inspiration, a charlatan or a genius, he packed the house, and there were until recently occasional voices who proclaimed that the orchestra was still traveling on the prestige of his era.

One of his early predilections was the staging of monumental works, as for example: Schoenberg's *Gurrelieder*, Stravinsky's *Oedipus Rex*, and Prokofieff's *Pas d'Acier*. The first and most sensational of these was the Mahler Symphony No. 8, *The Symphony of a Thousand*, in the spring of 1916. Stokowski had attended the world première of this symphony in Munich in 1910, which had given him a sensation like that of "the first white man to behold Niagara Falls." Shortly after his arrival in Philadelphia, this thirty-year-old conductor launched his plans for what was then considered a fantastic project. It required an appropriation of about $15,000, which the board skeptically approved. The symphony was performed nine times in Philadelphia, and was transferred to New York for a single performance at a cost to the New York management of $12,000. The nine Philadelphia performances left $10,000 worth of orders unfilled, while ticket scalpers reaped the benefits of the short supply —a thing almost incredible to contemplate for a symphony concert!

The affair was both sensational and musically notable. It brought the professional elite to Philadelphia. Patrons gasped at the technical and administrative virtuosity of the youthful conductor, but were less unanimous on the aesthetic contribution of the work. Some critics condemned it as a circus performance of *Kapellmeistermusik*, sanctioned by newspapers and promotion-minded board members more bent on flamboyant publicity than sincere advancement of a noble cause. Whether or not such a cynical view is justified, there is no doubt that the event catapulted the city, the orchestra, and the young conductor into an intoxicating position of notoriety from which each and all distilled the last ounce of profit. The Philadelphia Chamber of Commerce was moved to pass a resolution of commendation, in which it ventured the opinion that the symphony orchestra "was a commercial asset to the city, rendering it thereby more attractive to visitors, a better home for its citizens and of greater value to the nation." [56] The orchestra was lifted from its sixteen-year-old status of a stepchild, during which "the story . . . is one of constant begging on the part of everybody connected with the institution," [57] to a position of strength from which it was able to launch two endowment campaigns netting nearly two million dollars within several years—a success sufficient to convert even a carping critic to the belief that the cause of music had been advanced. As for Mr. Stokowski, who engineered the project and had conducted the massive spectacle without a score, it marked him as "the" conductor of the decade, won him a doctorate from the University of Pennsylvania, and four years later, the Philadelphia award of $10,000 for having made the greatest contribution to civic affairs. It also precipitated the recurrent rumor that he would probably soon "go to a larger city"—all of which likewise redounded to the benefit of every one concerned. That this advantage should not slip away unexploited during the crucial five-year endowment campaign, the provision was agreed upon that "the contract of the present conductor, Leopold Stokowski, shall be extended to cover this period of five years."

The extended story of the performance of the Mahler Symphony No. 8 testifies to a unique circumstance: never before, and probably never since, has a permanent symphony orchestra and its activity been so thoroughly integrated with the life of a city. Never before had there been such a genius for publicity who extended the functional boundaries of a concert so far into nonmusical realms. It was a civic enterprise in which one thousand citizens cooperated in the actual performance, in which commercial and cultural interests were well mobilized, and in which, still more miraculously, each interest was completely gratified with the results.

The new conductor felt that the desirable improvements in orchestral performances, as well as their audience effect, could not be achieved with the conventional disposition of the personnel. To that end, Stokowski instituted a number of rearrangements in the seating of the orchestra, one of which has been extensively copied by other orchestras: the shift of the cellos to the front right, a position occupied traditionally by the second violins for more than seventy-five years.

A more drastic transformation, more melodramatic than valid, was that of the "upside-down" [58] orchestra, sprung upon the audience in 1939–40, in which the strings were ignominiously shunted to the rear of the stage, and the woodwinds, brass, and tympani moved to the front. This promotion of the winds was in part a recognition of their growing importance in modern instrumentation; but it was likewise conjectured that the strings, being weaker than the winds, would be reflected more effectively from the rear walls of the shell if they were located nearer to that surface. This seating plan gained no adherents whatsoever and was quickly and quietly abandoned. But it was an indication of Stokowski's growing curiosity concerning the problems of acoustics, electronics, recording, and broadcasting, which began to be apparent some ten years previously while he was experimenting with the Bell Telephone Company. In 1932 he was probing new types of recordings with the Victor Company in Camden; in 1933 he toyed with the transmission of sound by telephonic reproduction projected into the auditorium "with undistorted sonority giving a concert from an empty stage." In order to achieve "close understanding between engineer and conductor," he at one time (1933) placed the control engineer on the stage directly in front of the podium instead of in the sound booth.[59] In fact, in such quick succession did those devices trickle from their source, that the *Musical Courier* was provoked to editorialize in March, 1933, that "no musical season can properly be called complete, apparently, until it has been the occasion for at least one startling innovation by the ingenious Leopold Stokowski."

Mindful that the final test of music is its effect upon the ear of the listener, Stokowski undertook to reduce visual distractions by darkening the stage during the performance. Thus on October 19,

1926, the New York audience found a yellow insert in its program book which carried the following legend:

The conviction has been growing on me that orchestra and conductor should be unseen, so that on the part of the listener more attention will go to the ear and less to the eye. The experiment of an invisible orchestra is for the moment impossible—so I am trying to reach a similar result by reducing the light to a minimum necessary for the artists of the orchestra to see their music and their conductor. . . . Music is by its nature remote from the tangible and visible things of life. I am hoping to intensify its mystery and eloquence and beauty.

(*signed*) Leopold Stokowski

The stage was accordingly darkened, each music stand equipped with an individual desklight, and a dim yellow Pentacostal spotlight floated down from the ceiling to play directly on the head of the conductor. Public reaction to this starlit atmosphere can be imagined. For every critic who found the new arrangement "restful to the eye," two others observed how it "brought into dazzling prominence his mass of golden-colored hair," but that it "left the magnificent playing of the orchestra quite unaffected."

There is perhaps some validity to the notion that the sawings and scrapings and other gymnastic contortions of the players and conductor are merely so much machinery which should, in the interest of aesthetic purity, be mercifully concealed from the audience. However, even when music is not associated with any other art or activity, there is some psychological loss in transmission to the sense organs through an artificial and arbitrarily enforced segregation of the senses. Instead of interfering with one another's reception, the simultaneous appeal to various sense departments more commonly intensifies the stimulus. The sense of smell enriches taste, the eye reinforces the ear, one sense responding unselfishly in the service of the other. While conflict and distraction are, of course, perfectly possible, a well-modulated coordination of gestures of the conductor and the rhythmic movements of the players aid the listener in focusing his attention on the music and accentuate the various fragments and contrasts in the composition rather than conflict with their enjoyment. This belief, without its academic trappings of psychological theory, seems to have been naïvely sensed by audience and management alike, and constitutes one of several reasons why this interesting excursion was quickly abandoned.

Stokowski is most popularly associated with his batonless conducting introduced in 1930. Although Safonoff had dispensed with the baton thirty years previously, his manual technique had not been elevated into an art of its own, and it was to this art that Stokowski gave its climactic development. His arms, wrists, and hands to the very tips of his fingers became interpretive clues to musicians and audiences alike, and his digital choreography became itself the subject of discussion and admiration. The baton had become merely a "stick," a lifeless encumbrance, inadequate to transmit the refined and delicate nuances of an inspired soul.

Stokowski was the last of the concert-platform lecturers. He was rivaled only by Walter Damrosch, who was already retiring from such competition. Today chatting across the footlights, never extensively cultivated, is a lost art. Stokowski's own personal eccentricities were perhaps epitomized for his audiences in these podium talks. At any rate, the audiences seemed at the moment to acquire personalities of their own, too. They also became eccentric. They had often carried on conversations, coughed, shammed apathy and walked out, and finally they hissed. And "Stokie" rebuked them for hissing. The occasion was Schoenberg's *Five Orchestral Pieces.* "You have a right to make such noises," he told them, "we on our part have a right to play the things we believe in." [60] In the fall of 1929 he told the New York audience that there was a large waiting list for the Philadelphia concerts and that the subscribers who did not like the programs might give up their seats to accommodate others. He would often render didactic explanations of new works, as he did on the occasion of his presentation of Stravinsky's *Sacre du Printemps,* when he urged the audience to understand it: "It is not beautiful music, but expresses a state of nature." [61] At times he could be entertaining and witty. Thus, in the fall of 1926, when he was prominently mentioned as the conductor for the merger of the Philharmonic and the Symphony Orchestra of New York, he boasted to the audience, after receiving vociferous applause for a Bach program, "You think they play well? . . . Ah, you should hear my two New York orchestras!" [62] It was about the same period that he initiated a referendum on whether to abolish applause, which to him was "a relic of the dark ages." "The strange beating of the hands has no meaning," he declared at the concert of November 8, 1929.

Stokowski was now at his peak, and generally included with Toscanini, Koussevitzky, and Furtwängler in the quartet of the world's greatest living conductors. His salary reached a reported high of more than $100,000 a year.[63] But it was inevitable that such a dynamic character, full of color and showmanship, would have differences with his board. It is also normal that after fourteen years his fascination for the audience should have been to a certain extent dissipated, and the unity of his Board of Directors should be ruptured. After a leave of absence (1926–28), he gradually reduced his conducting load. From 1936 to 1940, he conducted only a few concerts, in the fall and spring.

In the fall of 1936, Eugene Ormandy, then conductor at Minneapolis, was appointed co-conductor. From the first he undertook most of the conducting and became Musical Director in 1938. After several "resignations" and reconciliations, Stokowski finally retired from his position as conductor-in-chief, to take effect at the close of the 1935–36 season, timed to synchronize—intentionally or not—almost exactly with the resignation of Toscanini from the New York Philharmonic-Symphony. In perfect conformity with his flamboyant career, he closed the season with a transcontinental tour which ended in a triumphant epilogue in Madison Square Garden on a Sunday evening in May, 1936, where he conducted a concert before 12,000 persons, only about two weeks after Toscanini's frenzied farewell in Carnegie Hall before an audience one-fourth that size.

With the passing of Stokowski, the orchestra lost some color in the eyes of many patrons. But at the same time, the growing musical maturity of the audience made such theatrical excitement much less necessary. Consequently the orchestra, under Eugene Ormandy, now settled into a period of quiet dignity and reserved distinction.

Running true to form, the orchestra suffered from persistent attacks of deficit budgeting. Although it has at times shown a nominal surplus, the cumulative losses outran the efforts of all philanthropic appeals. When the union, in the fall of 1948, demanded a higher scale, the bankrupt management threw the public into a mild panic by officially announcing the abandonment of the concerts. But, of course, the incredible could not happen. Two days later, the usual "compromise was reached." But it was becoming only too evident that the symphony orchestras of the land were left orphans by the death of the philanthropic parents who had originally brought them into life. Since 1947, the management had been appealing to the city fathers to adopt the child. Finally, in the fiftieth year of the orchestra's existence, the City Council voted $50,000—a sum equal to the annual amusement tax paid to the city by the orchestra—to purchase four free public concerts in Convention Hall. These were performed before an average audience of 15,000 citizens. Thus one more city has followed what seems to be the emerging pattern of financial relief of the harassed symphony orchestras.

On the eve of its semicentennial, the orchestra was able to fulfill a promise that it had made to itself as long ago as the heyday of the Stokowski era: an excursion across the water. But depression and war had conspired to cheat it out of a junket that it amply deserved. Under the sponsorship of a British impresario, it finally embarked on a tour of England in the spring of 1949, during which it regaled the enthusiastic audiences of ten cities with twenty-eight concerts within a period of about three weeks. This was the fifth American orchestra to have undertaken such a cross-cultural mission, the others having been the New York Symphony under Walter Damrosch, in 1920; the New York Philharmonic with Toscanini in 1930; Toscanini's NBC orchestra and Stokowski's Youth Orchestra to South America in 1940. The only blemish which marred the orchestra's visit in Britain is noted by the British critic, Ralph Hill:

The recent costly and badly organized adventure of bringing the Philadelphia orchestra over to England is a good example of the public's inability to pay fantastically high prices for seats, even for an exceptional occasion.[64]

REPERTOIRE   Fritz Scheel and Karl Pohlig had nourished the orchestra on the conventional Germanic fare, alike in essentials, differing only in such particulars as Pohlig's downright idolatry of Wagner, and the somewhat more balanced programs of Scheel. Pohlig neglected Beethoven in favor of the more popular Wagner and Tschaikowsky, and gave unusual weight to Goldmark when in other cities he had almost dwindled to the vanishing point.

If ever a conductor injected his personality into the repertoire, it was Leopold Stokowski. His incorrigible and restless experimentalism often made the Philadelphia repertoire a temporary shelter for composers who appealed to the conductor as worthy of at least one venturesome performance. It was thus that Carillo, the "microtone" specialist, Varèse, Ornstein, Brooks, and others received isolated hearings. This policy was, of course, a bone of contention with the Board of Directors, while audience reaction was a mixture of excitement, amusement, and resentment. In 1932 this "debatable" music was attached as a trailer to the regular program, so that the less stouthearted members of the audience could, if they desired, escape the hazards of its emotional eddies.

A more permanent contribution was the conductor's affection for the master of his first instrument: J. S. Bach. He arranged for orchestra several dozen titles: chorale-preludes, suites, preludes, fugues, and miscellaneous numbers, treading in the footsteps of Mendelssohn and Joachim in inaugurating another Bach revival. The propriety of making "gorgeous tone poems" out of classic models may be a matter of taste and aesthetic philosophy, but the enrichment in variety, scope, and volume of the Bach repertoire, which was less well known to orchestral habitués than to piano and organ students, was a grateful pedagogical service to the general cause of historical erudition. His all-Bach program, with a Bach encore (December, 1926), is probably as unique in repertoire annals as are the left-wing laboratory compositions that caused so much gossip. That Bach, aided by these arrangements, should top Tschaikowsky, Strauss, and Mozart, threaten Wagner, and approach within one or two percentage points of even Beethoven and Brahms with enthusiastic acclaim from both audience and management, is a worthy feat.

Stokowski seemed to have an affinity for compositions that lent themselves to rich sonorities and pliant melodic lines. Tschaikowsky, Rimsky-Korsakoff, Strauss, Sibelius, and Wagner all loomed large in his concert portfolio at some time or other. Philadelphia led all others in the volume of Rimsky-Korsakoff. But Stravinsky, Miaskowsky, Shostakovitch and many others he also welcomed with "first-time" performances. The American composer, by and large, did not profit from his explorations, and not even during World War I did American music exceed a modest six per cent. Responsibility for this inhospitality to native composers throughout the history of the orchestra probably derives from the conductor's disinclination toward American composers and from their relative scarcity in Philadelphia as compared to Boston, New York, and Chicago.

Under Ormandy the breath-taking experimental quality of the repertoire disappeared. The program structure became no less virile but more predictable. There were, of course, the normal fluctuations in favorites. Rachmaninoff had developed an especial friendship for the orchestra, and his proportion in 1935–40, several years before his death, was about three per cent, with a slight increase since that time. The vitality of Tschaikowsky remained, while that of Strauss, Sibelius, and Wagner all fell to previous levels. With the departure of Stokowski, Bach could not retain his extraordinary preferment, but was reduced by half, to little more than three per cent. The Austro-German group, never excessively high during the preceding twenty-five years, declined to a still substantial fifty per cent, of which thirty per cent is accounted for by those bulwarks of the repertoire, the three B's.

The Minneapolis Symphony Orchestra (1903)

The Minneapolis orchestra began as an adjunct to a choral society: the "Filharmonix" Choral Society which was founded in 1892 to gratify the musical propensities of the Germans and Scandinavians. In time, however, with expanded tastes, they felt the need for reliable orchestral accompaniment, which could be assured only by a well-organized permanent orchestral body to which members had a certain loyalty, and to which they were bound for rehearsal and concert time.

Emil Oberhoffer, German-born musician, then an organist in Minneapolis and conductor of the renamed Philharmonic club since 1901, undertook to assure himself such an orchestra by enlisting the interest of philanthropic citizens in this more costly project. The civic leader in this enterprise, a man to whom the musical community owes its greatest debt, was Elbert L. Carpenter, lumberman, amateur musician, and co-founder with Oberhoffer of the new orchestra. It was he who not only contributed of his own wealth but, still more significantly, organized the business and commercial interests in support of a type of project that had already gained acceptance in the Eastern cities. Thus in 1903 the Minneapolis Symphony Orchestra was officially founded, with Oberhoffer as its conductor, a membership of sixty men, and a guarantee fund of $10,000 annually for three years.

But Minneapolis was still a relatively small city with a population only slightly exceeding 200,000, the smallest city in the United States to be entertaining such metropolitan ambitions even when the "Twin Cities" are taken as a unit. Facilities were primitive; the orchestra could not even find a home. A wanderer in the city, it performed its early concerts in churches and other available auditoriums. This embarrassing condition was soon corrected by an unusual arrangement with the Northwestern National Life Insurance Company. In exchange for $5,000,000 in life insurance to be sold by the orchestra and its workers, the insurance company agreed to erect on its downtown property (Eleventh and Nicollet) an auditorium on the model of Symphony Hall of Boston, for the benefit of the orchestra, to be let at a nominal rental.

The orchestra prospered, its guarantees were increased, and the conductor, who adapted the programs to the gradually maturing tastes of its patrons, was popular. Having outgrown its vocal beginnings, the partnership with the choral organization, which had been sharing a considerable proportion of the concert offerings, was dissolved in 1907, leaving the orchestra as an autonomous body, sponsored by the newly-formed Minneapolis Orchestral Association, Mr. Carpenter president.

The Association was characterized by aggressive administration in that it not only offered the regular subscription concerts and Sunday "pop" concerts, but also initiated very early (1913) a series of children's concerts. These concerts are still affectionately remembered by the present middle-aged patrons whose early tastes were awakened by the illuminating explanations of Mr. Oberhoffer, his illustrations at the piano, and the orchestral fare of his musicians.

Nationally, the orchestra was most distinctive for its tours, which were begun in 1907 and confined principally to the Middle West and West. Other orchestras have occasionally made more spectacular junkets, but the Minneapolis orchestra was then, and is still today, the most consistent and the most extensive touring organization of all the orchestras in the country. Unlike the Thomas "Highway," which hit only the high spots, the Minneapolis Highway wove through the smaller cities, the university and college towns, at a time when fine orchestral music was to them a real and inspiring novelty. It was not yet the general custom to travel with the complete home personnel. With a complement of fifty instruments, about two-thirds normal size, perhaps the strings did not always balance the brasses in a Wagner excerpt. But the Minneapolis orchestra, with its conductor of such dignified bearing and graceful gestures as to seem the very epitome of musical genius, took his message to the grass roots quite as significantly as Theodore Thomas had to the metropolitan culture zones a half century earlier.

But there is rarely a virtue without some necessity. The circumstances which necessitated these magnanimous feats of tourism were somewhat analogous to the circumstances surrounding the early travel activities of Theodore Thomas—the need for a long and favorable contract with the musicians. This supplement to the home schedule is the key to the difference between merely indifferent talent and paucity of rehearsals, and competent musicians with adequate rehearsals. If one adds to this the natural inclination of the local business interests, who subsidized the orchestra to advertise their community, the motivation for orchestral tours is almost completely explained. In recent years a derivative financial benefit accrues to the orchestra in the increased sales of recordings, yielding greater royalties, as a consequence of the creation of widespread interest in the organization.

During its near half-century history of existence, the Minneapolis orchestra has inevitably experienced the same oscillations of fortune that beset other communities. Its continuance was threatened in the early twenties when, in response to postwar inflation, wage levels were rising and had to be met from meager resources. Another serious crisis occurred in 1929, when the very roof over its head was sold. The Northwestern National Life Insurance Company, having outgrown its quarters, disposed of its properties, including the "home" of the orchestra, to a realtor who promptly proceeded to raise the nominal rental that the orchestra had been enjoying to a prohibitive figure. Since the cost of housing is always a prominent item in any budget, public or private, this was no minor dilemma. However, here as elsewhere, adversity was turned to sweet uses.

It so happened that the housing crisis of the orchestra coincided with the construction (1929–30) of a new auditorium—the Cyrus Northrup Auditorium with a capacity of nearly 5,000—on the campus of the University of Minnesota. The idea struck root that the orchestra might be housed in that beautiful hall.

There were, of course, legal complications. The university was a tax-supported institution without authority to rent its hall to a private enterprise, or to divert any of its funds to such a purpose. There were, however, some extenuating factors. The orchestra was a cultural asset not only to the university and the city, but to the state as well. Educational institutions quite generally recognize such cultural obligations by setting up extracurricular music and lecture series, and reimbursing themselves through ticket sales, without encumbering the regularly appropriated academic funds. Why could not the university, it was asked, similarly engage the Minneapolis Symphony Orchestra for its total output? The university could sell the tickets and apply those funds to the expenses of the orchestra. The orchestra would still retain its autonomy. The Minneapolis Orchestral Association would continue to manage the orchestra, engage personnel, and solicit funds from philanthropic sources to cover the customary deficits.

This cooperative arrangement, which was facilitated by certain "connections" between the respective boards, was instituted in the fall of 1930. The manager of the orchestra today functions very much as does any other department head in his relations with the university administration, requisitioning funds, coordinating his activities with the department of convocations in order to avoid conflicts in the engaging of soloists, and scheduling the use of the auditorium to mesh with the many other activities of the university. Like any member of the university staff, the manager has even qualified for membership in the campus club. In recognition of the mutuality of this arrangement, members of the university are accorded reductions in season concert tickets in a manner similar to the reductions usually enjoyed by students and staff on athletic and other functions.

This unique plan has been of incalculable benefit to the orchestra. In fact, it is generally admitted by its spokesmen that the orchestra could not have survived the depression without this providential intervention. The large auditorium accommodates in a single sitting an audience that in Chicago, New York, or Boston would require a pair of services, while the administrative offices of the orchestra, its library, and its instrument room are also available at an economical "rental."

It solved still another problem—the rivalry with St. Paul. That city had for some years tried to lead a separate musical life. From 1908–15 the St. Paul Symphony Orchestra was conducted by Walter Henry Rothwell. After his departure, local demands were satisfied by engaging the Minneapolis orchestra for a series of St. Paul concerts. The auditorium of the state university was now, however, neutral territory, conveniently located for both cities, and large enough to absorb the St. Paul project.

The founder-conductor of the Minneapolis orchestra, like so many other conductors of a half-century or more ago, was a self-made man. A precocious pianist and violinist at the age of ten, and later a student of Philipp in Paris, Oberhoffer, like them learned his conducting "in public." His symphonic education virtually began with his appointment to the conductorship of the symphony orchestra. But he was a diligent student, industrious and eager in personal self-development as well as in the administration of the orchestra. A man of charm and a certain aloof dignity, aristocratic in bearing and demeanor, extremely gifted, he was relaxed in his gestures and had a "good back." In his interpretations, he constantly sought the melodic line, although he was not too meticulous in supplementary detail. If such discipline was not within the vision of the conductor, neither was it within the general competence of the pioneer orchestra.

In Minneapolis, as well as on tour, Oberhoffer was an educator who, like the young Thomas, started very much at the level of the audience and like many another conductor of yesterday "cut" the long compositions judiciously and expertly, adapting them to the length of the program and to the tolerance of the audience. His association with the orchestra endured for nineteen years—a record eclipsed only by Walter Damrosch, Stock, Stokowski, and Koussevitzky. In 1922 Oberhoffer was granted a year's leave of absence, after which he retired.

After a year of guest conductors—Bodanzky, Coates, Damrosch, Gabrilowitsch, Verbrugghen, and Bruno Walter—the Belgian violinist Henri Verbrugghen was appointed in the fall of 1923. Verbrugghen was a mature conductor and a veteran concertmaster of both French and British orchestras, with additional experience as choral and orchestral conductor in England and Australia. Well-schooled in orchestral routine, he introduced section rehearsals and established a discipline and precision hitherto unknown to that orchestra. However, as an interpreter he was more conscientious than inspired; his classic pedantry was unrelieved by vitality and warmth, and he failed to exhilarate his audiences. Such exhilaration was to be forthcoming in his successor.

In the fall of 1931, after having conducted only the initial concert of the season, Verbrugghen retired because of illness. An emergency call secured the thirty-two-year-old Eugene Ormandy. Ormandy's rise had been spectacular. In 1920 he had come to New York as a violinist for a recital tour that did not materialize. In desperation he joined the orchestra at the Capitol Theatre at a time when the larger theatres were establishing concert orchestras of symphonic caliber. He quickly rose to the position of concertmaster and conductor, was discovered by Arthur Judson and engaged for radio programs. After an appearance with the Philadelphia orchestra at Robin Hood Dell, in the summer of 1931, he substituted for the absent Toscanini in November, after which the reports of his success filtered through the nation.

It was at this moment that the Minneapolis post became vacant. Called as a guest, Ormandy remained as permanent conductor. His first appearance was dramatic: he conducted without stand or score, he rearranged the seating of the orchestra according to the "Stokowski shift"—cellos right-front, and won enthusiastic approbation of his program. He easily maintained his hold on the Minneapolis public for five years, when he resigned rather suddenly, succumbing to the irresistible attraction of an invitation to conduct the Philadelphia orchestra, contact with which he had maintained by annual guest appearances.

Very few orchestras are in a position to engage a mature and well-established conductor; but, like any other enterprise, they feel themselves fortunate when they discover a prospect on the rise. This time Minneapolis and Boston joined in an invitation to a guest conductor whose success in Europe left little doubt of his future usefulness. The Athenian, Dimitri Mitropoulos, made his American debut in Boston in 1936, followed immediately by a guest appearance in Minneapolis. Engaged by Minneapolis as permanent conductor in 1937, he remained with the orchestra until 1949. A tall, sinewy figure, gaunt and austere, he conducts without score or baton, mimicking the music with vibrating arms and fingers in an almost choreographic tremble. His players testify to his phenomenal memory, to his rehearsing the most modern composition, as well as infrequently used accompaniments, without benefit of score. He has maintained his pianistic skills and occasionally performs with his own orchestra in the simultaneous roles of conductor and soloist. For some years Mitropoulos had been serving as guest conductor with the New York Philharmonic. During the season of 1948–49, he absented himself for about half a season, sharing with Stokowski, as co-conductor, the responsibilities in New York. The permanent transfer was completed, and Mitropoulos was succeeded by Antal Dorati, formerly of Dallas, as full conductor in the fall of 1949.

REPERTOIRE Since the Minneapolis orchestra had its origins in a choral society, the first years of its existence are weighted with the choral performances of *Messiah*, Haydn's *Creation*, Mendelssohn's *Elijah*, and other oratorios. However, after four seasons, the chorus was abandoned and the repertoire presented the typical symphonic character.

Although Oberhoffer was of German extraction, his tenure is not marked by the near-monopoly of the Austro-Germans that characterized some of the other orchestras of that day. He was, after all, not a schooled conductor, whose long training had molded his tastes and frozen his allegiance in advance. During the early decades, the Sunday popular concerts constituted the larger part of the programs. The orchestra played to full houses in the days when the motion picture, the radio, and the automobile had not yet exacted their competitive toll from concert audiences. Even the subscription concerts did not demand from the audience a too sophisticated taste. Oberhoffer blended the solid fare of Brahms and Beethoven, approximately proportioned to the national average of that time, with relatively liberal quantities of Tschaikowsky and Wagner. As a gesture to regional national sentiment, Scandinavian composers—Alfven, Atterberg, Svendsen, Grieg—were given their day. These are not unusual names, but with the total repertoire much smaller than in the Eastern orchestras, they received greater relative emphasis. That Oberhoffer was not unmindful of current trends is attested by the appearance of such names as Sibelius, Stravinsky, Rachmaninoff, Borodin, Debussy, and Respighi, then relatively new to American concertgoers.

Verbrugghen will be remembered as a Beethoven exponent, who featured him to the extent of sixteen per cent, which was heavy enough to arouse "vox pop" protests from the audience. There were no other symptoms of top-heaviness. He dropped Sibelius, but enlarged the Handel contribution by the revival of *Messiah*.

Ormandy succeeded in glamorizing the programs from the very first concert, when the young unknown introduced the then novel number: Weinberger's Polka and Fugue from *Schwanda*. Ravel, Rachmaninoff, Debussy, Richard Strauss, Sibelius and other recent composers were welcomed with greater hospitality by both conductor and the well-prepared audience than by his predecessors, but without crowding out the classics. Emulating the trends in Philadelphia, where he was destined to transfer his activities, he shared in the Bach revival by offering in moderate quantity arrangements by himself, as well as those of Boessenroth (a member of the orchestra) and several other transcribers. Today, however, in reminiscing about "Gene," none of the experiences are remembered in Minneapolis with more relish than the popular concerts in which a score or more of Strauss *Wiener-Walzer* were tossed off with rhythmic elegance unmatched, in the minds of the patrons, before or since.

The repertoire of Mitropoulos is peppered with modernistic works that were passed in review without a second hearing. As in the case of Stokowski in Philadelphia, such performances often serve a pedagogical and clinical, rather than an aesthetic purpose, and are likely to inject controversy into public reactions. During this period, too, American music was at its lowest ebb as measured in purely quantitative terms. However, by including Barber, Copland, Block, Griffes, and Harris—to mention only a sample—Mitropoulos has given a hearing to a group of standard composers who amply satisfy the nativistic curiosity of most audiences.

The St. Louis Symphony Society (1907)

Like all other cities, St. Louis has seen a series of more or less sporadic musical organizations that have served as forerunners to the present orchestra. Prompted by the twin motives of professional livelihood and the cultivation of musical ideals, players began before the middle of the last century to form musical ensembles. The first local orchestra approaching balanced completeness was the Polyhymnia, consisting of thirty-five musicians—about the size of the eighteenth-century Haydn orchestra—which offered concerts from 1845 to 1852. Their avowed purpose was "the cultivation of musical art and the promotion of musical talent chiefly in the instrumental branch of the art, by common rehearsals and public performances." [65]

These beginnings were further stimulated by the visits of the excellent Germania orchestra, that small group of twenty-five immigrant Germans who implanted the desire for musical education in the principal cities east of the Mississippi between 1848 and 1854. In their first visit in May, 1853, this group of "instrumental solo performers" rendered the Beethoven Second Symphony complete, the first time it had ever been heard in St. Louis. This was followed a year later by a series of five concerts. The Theodore Thomas Orchestra of New York, on its many tours throughout the country, naturally included St. Louis on its famous "highway," making its first appearance on its first national tour (1869) as a "Grand Concert Organization of Forty Eminent Musicians, Comprising all the Celebrated Soloists of his Grand Orchestra." Thomas was destined, of course, to make many more appearances in the course of the next quarter-century.

But local musicians were beginning to capitalize on the growing musical interest of the rapidly expanding city. The most ambitious attempt at establishing a permanent musical organization occurred in 1860 when the newly founded St. Louis Philharmonic Society engaged Eduard de Sobolewski, who had previously held posts in Koenigsberg, Prussia, and in Milwaukee, at a contractual salary of $1,000 per season. Sobolewski (1808–72) had been a student of Weber and Zelter, and co-worker of Robert Schumann on his journal. Entering the United States in 1859, he was one of the thousands of professional German musicians to emigrate to this country to form the nucleus of a thriving American musical life.

The Philharmonic Society was formed "to advance the study and to promote the progress of music in St. Louis, and to encourage the reunion and social intercourse of the lovers of music in our city." It differed from previous organizations in that it combined choral and symphonic units. Its monthly concerts provided the first opportunity for the St. Louis population to hear the classics at regular intervals. The venture was financed by subscription memberships at fifty dollars per season, and performing dues of five dollars annually. In 1950 this society was in its ninetieth season; as a nonprofessional body, it presents several concerts per season.

The immediate antecedents to the St. Louis Symphony Orchestra are traceable to the year 1880, from which it officially dates its founding.[66] On September 1 of that year Joseph Otten, a Catholic organist and choral conductor, organized the St. Louis Choral Society, which presented one pair of concerts—its first—in the spring of the next year. Its choral offerings were of the highest type and included many of the works that are still standard: Handel's *Messiah*, Beethoven's *Mass in C*, Gounod's *Redemption*, and others. This group also collaborated at times with Theodore Thomas in local festival productions. Beginning with 1884–85, Robert S. Brookings, manufacturer, merchant, and philanthropist, recently better known as the benefactor of Washington University of St. Louis and the Brookings Institute of Washington, D. C., became president of the infant musical organization and established its finances on such a firm footing that the concerts broadened their scope by interspersing a few orchestral numbers among their choral works.

Almost contemporary with this well-managed choral group was the St. Louis Musical Union, an orchestra founded in 1881, which had likewise been rather well financed. The orchestra numbered fifty-four players and presented an average of six concerts per season in that city of 350,000. It was the merger of these two organizations in 1890, into the St. Louis Choral-Symphony Society, that constituted the next step in the direction of the present organization, and prophetically assigned to the orchestra a place equal with the chorus.

This organization ran true to form, however, in that mounting deficits soon threatened its survival. Mr. Otten, who did not relish retrenchment, resigned, and his place was taken by a young, temperamental musician, Alfred Ernst, imported from Germany in 1894 to guide the orchestra of fifty-two members. Ernst was an excellent pianist, a gifted musician, an aggressive leader, but a conductor "by the Grace of God." Contemporary accounts charge him with failure to study the score and depending on his musicians to follow his improvisations of the moment. With mediocre material, sparse funds, and rehearsals often weeks apart, there was produced something less than an artistic blend.

Nevertheless, the orchestra gained in flexibility and explored a progressive repertoire, although especially in the first years of his regime, the choral interests maintained a dominant position. Thus, in 1900–01, the chorus of two-hundred voices and the orchestra of fifty-five, presented three oratorios, three symphony concerts, two mixed popular concerts and two artist concerts. But under Ernst, orchestral music soon assumed new importance, and in 1905–06 he introduced a series of Sunday "pops" which for years to come were eagerly consumed by the general population of the city. However, finding it difficult to adjust himself to American ways, Ernst finally returned to Germany at the close of the 1906–07 season, to supervise the production of his operatic works. He died of wounds as a soldier in the German army of World War I.

The drift toward a bona fide symphony orchestra culminated in 1907 when the chorus was abandoned and Max Zach, violist of the Boston Symphony, was engaged by the newly organized St. Louis Symphony Orchestra. Zach had enjoyed a distinguished career of orchestral playing, having been brought to this country as a twenty-two-year-old lad by Gericke in 1886. He later became a member of the famous Adamowski String Quartet and conducted the Boston "Pops" from 1887 to 1897.

In accordance with the trend of the day, the members of the St. Louis orchestra were now placed on regular seasonal salary, the number of concerts was gradually increased, the orchestra enlarged, the repertoire modernized, and tours instituted. Zach also continued the Sunday afternoon "pops" series. They were given weekly throughout the season, exceeding the subscription pairs in number, and constituted a genuine contribution to the incipient musical culture of the community.

Fortunately, Zach could supply what Ernst lacked—discipline and precision. He himself had been tutored by the very paragon of the stern school of conducting, Wilhelm Gericke of Boston. But, like Gericke, Zach lacked the romantic impulse, the warmth and suppleness, demanded by the romantic repertoire. Players in his orchestra have remarked that Zach never did succeed in catching the required pliability of spirit to accompany faithfully such soloists as Rachmaninoff and Pablo Casals, who "bothered" him with their interpretative liberties.

Zach died in midseason, February, 1921. Among the guest conductors who finished the season was the noted pianist Rudolph Ganz, subsequently given a permanent appointment, after the Society had made an unsuccessful bid for Fritz Kreisler.

Ganz, who had had little orchestral experience, was a convert to that role. However, he conferred great glamour upon the organization, possessed fine social gifts, and was a personality of elegance, dignity, and refinement. But in general it cannot be said that he achieved extraordinary success, except in the children's concerts. In these he was so effective that his services were for some years in great demand by the New York Philharmonic and the San Francisco Symphony orchestras. He resigned in 1927 and soon rejoined the staff of Chicago Musical College, where he had previously been active.

After a frank attempt to revive a flagging public interest in the orchestra, through a four-year policy of guest conductors, Vladimir Golschmann, a young Frenchman of Russian parentage, was recommended by Damrosch and Koussevitzky as permanent conductor. He had been known in Paris as the "youngest conductor," having instituted the "Concerts Golschmann" in 1919 at the age of twenty-five. Like nearly all the conductors in Paris of the postwar period, including Koussevitzky and Monteux, he displayed pronounced modern tendencies.

With the advent of Golschmann in 1931, the Sunday "pop" series, which had for years loomed so large in the orchestra's schedule, were dropped, and only an occasional popular concert substituted. This was a result of the ominous competition of other forms of diversion which had developed since the war: palatial moving-picture theatres, radio, and other miscellaneous forms of commercial entertainment. In addition the public had, of course, been weaned from the light fare of the *William Tell* Overture and the *Peer Gynt* Suite, and had graduated into the subscription class where the symphony no longer held the terrors of earlier days.

In the fall of 1934, the orchestra moved to its new downtown home, the Kiel Municipal Auditorium, with a capacity of about 3,500, where it enjoyed reduced rent in exchange for several free public concerts. Its previous home, the Odeon, a smaller hall of about 2,000 seats, located on midtown Grand Avenue, had been destroyed by fire. The move to the new hall stimulated subscription sales and constituted a profitable arrangement.

The St. Louis Symphony, like some of the younger orchestras, has no endowment fund but depends almost exclusively on the annual "maintenance fund" to cancel the inevitable deficits. Consequently, the orchestra has passed through recurrent financial crises, which have earned for St. Louis the reputation of being apathetic toward its musical organization. Whether, in relation to its resources, these crises have been more virulent than in other cities, could be established only by marshaling the details of local circumstances. However, the orchestra has never been forced to suspend operations.

REPERTOIRE   Although Max Zach, the first conductor of the "new series," as it was then called, had gained his orchestral experience in Boston under the central European conductors loyal to their native art, he himself displayed more flexible tastes. The two poles of the classic sphere, Brahms and Beethoven, which had served for years as the axis of the Boston programs, here lost some of their importance. Zach's Beethoven proportion of eight per cent, and Brahms' six per cent, would be considered modest at that time. Instead, Zach featured the French (Saint-Saëns, Berlioz, Franck), the Russians (Rachmaninoff and Tschaikowsky), as well as Dvořák and Wagner. Such a musical offering was no doubt more suitable for an orchestra less emancipated from the box office than was Boston, and more tasty to his St. Louis patrons than to the audiences in his previous home.

If he did not import the austere programs from the East, he did carry in his portfolio the scores of American composers, many of them from his old haunts in New England. The names are familiar: Chadwick, Converse, Hill, Loeffler, Foote, MacDowell, Henry Hadley, Strube (German-born member of the Boston orchestra), David Stanley Smith (New Haven), together with a few additional local names in St. Louis: E. R. Kroeger, the leading musician of the city, and Samuel Bollinger. These made up a total of five to ten per cent of the repertoire—a percentage similar to Boston itself—during the first eight years of the Zach tenure. In 1917, with the necessity of asserting its nativistic faith, this city with its huge German population, enjoyed a repertoire of which twelve per cent—the highest of any orchestra—was of American origin. When the war fervor subsided, it was no longer necessary to profess one's Americanism in such stilted proportions. So, Rudolph Ganz, who had ascended the podium in 1921, deflated the quota to a more normal five per cent, which in turn shriveled to an "all time low" during four years of guest conductors—practically all from foreign lands.

The Parisian Golschmann surprisingly enough restored Beethoven and Brahms to their wonted place of prestige, but as compensation he favored the French during the first five-year period to the extent of a high fourteen per cent. This enthusiasm cooled a bit after a period of acclimatization in this country, and was replaced by a corresponding generosity to the American composer. In both cases, however, the composers selected were not the stereotyped members, but rather the less conventional advance guard. Between 1940 and 1950, the repertoire carried a definitely experimental tinge, with the inevitable number of single performances. By 1945–50, St. Louis was playing a reasonably liberal six per cent of American music. Proko-fieff, Shostakovitch—by now less controversial figures—also ranked high.

The San Francisco Symphony Orchestra (1911)

Coexistent with the vigilantes and the lurid Barbary Coast, there thrived in San Francisco at mid-century a musical life analogous to, if more rudimentary than, that of the cultivated cities of the East. After the trek of the forty-niners, this lusty village witnessed a sensational efflorescence of culture which was manifest in the building of theatres and in the consumption of elegant merchandise. Wealth moved with great ostentation. Clippers and steamers entered the harbor laden with the luxuries of Europe, and departed with millions in gold dust. In fact, it was a common saying that San Francisco was only one ship's passage behind the latest Parisian styles.

From the earliest days, the city was visited by the more intrepid itinerant musicians who had to sail "around the Horn" to reach this gold-infested American outpost, whose isolation was not finally broken until the completion of the first transcontinental railroad in 1869. In 1850, Henri Herz, the French pianist, who had lost his fortune in a Paris piano factory, included San Francisco in a long American tour designed to win it back again. Contrary to a persistent San Francisco legend, Jenny Lind did not appear in California, although two theatres were named after her. However, Catherine Hayes, the Irish songstress who was almost equally famous in her day, was toured to the West Coast by Barnum in 1852. Taking the cue from the hysterical worshippers of Jenny Lind in New York, the San Francisco fire department gave "Kate" Hayes a scarlet escort; and it was a $1,165 "top" that was paid the twenty-six-year-old soprano from Limerick for the auctioned seats, while the "Swedish Nightingale" could command a top premium of only $650, obtained in Providence, Rhode Island.

From 1854 onward, local ensembles began making their appearance in that teeming city of 40,000. Beginning in that year, Rudolph Herold, who has been termed the "father" of San Francisco's orchestral music, offered concerts intermittently for over twenty-five years. In 1880 Louis Homeier, aided by John Parrott (real estate and banking) as patron, organized an orchestra of forty men which had a life of several seasons. In the same decade, the young Gustave Hinrichs, later associated with Theodore Thomas in the melancholy venture of the American Opera Company, established a rival Philharmonic, which also enjoyed philanthropic assistance, and was later led by minor conductors. Hinrichs, after leaving San Francisco, gained some distinction as conductor of the Metropolitan Opera at the beginning of this century.

A more serious, but hardly more enduring enterprise, was that of Fritz Scheel, better remembered today as the founder of the Philadelphia Orchestra in 1900. This German conductor turned up in San Francisco in 1894 to entertain the patrons of the midwinter fair with the same kind of repertoire that he had offered at the Chicago World's Fair the previous year. He remained in San Francisco for most of the succeeding five years, offering variety concerts on the German beer garden style, as well as more formal performances with the Philharmonic, again subsidized by Parrott. Leaving San Francisco in 1899, he transferred to Woodside Park, Philadelphia, for a summer series where local sponsors discovered him and pressed him into service to form the Philadelphia Orchestra, over which he presided with eminent success until the year of his death in 1907.

By 1910 the Philharmonic Orchestra, in about thirty years of intermittent existence, had been led by various conductors and was aided financially by several persons of wealth. In addition, musical taste had been fostered by significant, though infrequent, visits of the two itinerant purveyors of good music: Theodore Thomas and Walter Damrosch. By the turn of the century, the growth of permanent symphony orchestras in the Eastern cities had instilled a desire for emulation in the rapidly growing metropolis of the Pacific Coast.

The occasion for its inception was the disastrous earthquake and fire of 1906. The problems of reconstruction caused civic leaders to take stock of their community needs and resources, and to formulate appropriate projects for future fulfillment. On this agenda was a symphony orchestra.[67]

Immediate conditions were, of course, unpropitious. The fire had destroyed all the theatres, including the Grand Opera House and the essential requirements for physical relief naturally sidetracked nearly all of the cultural amenities of life. But by 1909, with the determination to "foster music in all its forms and particularly to establish a symphony orchestra," the Musical Association of San Francisco was organized. The Association matured slowly. Not until the fall of 1911 was it assured sufficient funds to enable the sponsors to announce the actual establishment of a "permanent orchestral body along the lines of those maintained by the larger cities of Europe and the East," and to list the first season's schedule of six subscription concerts. Henry K. Hadley, American conductor and composer, was called as conductor, and on December 8, 1911, he presided over an orchestra of sixty musicians at the first concert in the new Cort Theatre—later known as the Curran—seating capacity 1,827. He offered the following cautious program:

Wagner: Prelude to *Die Meistersinger*
Tschaikowsky: Symphony No. 6
                        —Pause—
Haydn: Theme and Variations, from *Emperor Quartet*
Liszt: Symphonic Poem, *Les Préludes*

On the face of it, it seemed to the less sanguine observers that this orchestra differed in no significant respect from the numerous orchestral episodes of the abortive past. Some local critics rehearsed the failures of philanthropy in the orchestras of Scheel, Holmes, and Steindorff, and urged that a "permanent" orchestra could be secured only through a permanent form of financing. Apparently they were taking their cue from the Chicago experience, where the orchestra patrons had become tired of annual deficits and finally presented the orchestra with an endowment in the form of an auditorium and office building which is, to this very day, an indispensable source of predictable income. The San Francisco musicians were not permanently employed by the orchestra but were still dependent for their livelihood on their respective jobs in theatres and restaurants. It was, in short, still a pick-up orchestra, the "same" orchestra which had failed before. However, this orchestra did differ from previous embryonic endeavors in that its support was broad-based and did not depend on the whim of an individual benefactor; and the determination of its backers seemed to be more aggressive, as was evidenced in their formal organization, and in the importation of a conductor of some note at $10,000 per season.

The years of infancy of this new creature were attended by all the usual hazards. In the first place, basic financing did not proceed with the expected celerity. Even at the time of the first concert, survival of the orchestra seemed by no means assured, for it was observed in the prospectus that "the membership has now reached 300, but it is earnestly hoped that a membership of 500 may be obtained which would insure a permanent orchestra owned and controlled solely by the association."

Furthermore, professional resources were inadequate and physical facilities deficient. For its first concert, the orchestra had no nucleus of players, no chairs, no stands or equipment, and no library. Musicians had been hastily recruited from cafés, hotels, and theatres, while only a few first-desk men could be imported from New York. Because of previous commitments by the local musicians to their employers, concerts were scheduled on their free afternoons. Scores were borrowed from Seattle, where Hadley had previously conducted, and from the state university. Other scores were purchased on credit, and through the generosity of a well-wisher, the library of the recently disbanded Pittsburgh orchestra was acquired for a nominal expenditure. All these obstacles: limited library, inadequate rehearsals, the preoccupation of the men with more remunerative tasks in hotels, theatres, cafés, dance halls, and cabarets must be included in the reckoning of success and failure of these early enterprises. By the third season patronage became precarious, and a deficit, over and above the guarantees, became an ominous certainty. The *Argonaut* and the *Pacific Coast Musical Review* were also beginning to criticize the conductor for inadequate study of the scores and for deficient temperament and magnetism.

If it cannot be said that Hadley scored a popular and critical success in music, the debonair conductor, handsome, trim and "corseted" of figure, was quite congenial to the social group that sponsored him. During his sojourn in San Francisco, he composed the first of his three Midsummer High Jinks (1912) commissioned by the famous Bohemian Club, which had urged his original appointment. As early as 1900, he had composed his Overture *In Bohemia* for these same Bohemians, which, however, was not performed at that time because of his departure for Europe.

At this critical juncture in the development of San Francisco music, the city was visited by the Boston Symphony Orchestra, which had been invited on the occasion of the Panama-Pacific Exposition held there in 1915. This organization, under the precise and scholarly German, Dr. Karl Muck, presented a series of fourteen concerts in ten days, and for the first time awakened its Western audiences to a realization of quality performance. Plans were projected at once for the improvement of the local orchestra and for launching it on a national career. The orchestra personnel was increased from about sixty-five to eighty, and Alfred Hertz, then in the city, was secured to revitalize their ambitions.

The forty-three-year-old Hertz had enjoyed a distinguished career. For thirteen years (1902–15) he had been conductor of German opera at the Metropolitan Opera House where he had staged the first performance of *Parsifal* outside of Bayreuth on December 24, 1903, and had introduced Strauss's *Salome*, *Rosenkavalier* and other novelties to his American audience. He, too, had come as guest of the Exposition to conduct a Beethoven Festival during German-American week, at a time when this country was still neutral toward the year-old war. His conducting created a tremendous impression and it was with the greatest enthusiasm that he was selected for the renascent orchestra.

The fourteen-year tenure of Mr. Hertz was not a tranquil one. He was greeted with hostile agitation because of his German origin. This was quieted by his acquisition of citizenship in June, 1917, made possible by the fact that he had filed his first papers prior to the declaration of war. In the second year, he suffered some competition from other orchestras in that city of half a million. Among these, the People's Philharmonic Orchestra under Sokoloff, supported by a patron of means, was making a special bid for the popular field. In an effort to strengthen its competitive position, the San Francisco Symphony was reorganized in 1916 on a permanent basis, its members were employed full time and were, by contract stipulation, not permitted to play in any other orchestra without written consent of the conductor. Like every other city, San Francisco had yet to learn the difficult lesson that there was never room for two good orchestras. Alfred Hertz never knew a united San Francisco.

Financial struggles are, of course, never a novelty. Warnings were repeatedly issued declaring the organization in danger of collapse. Invidious comparisons with Los Angeles, where one opulent benefactor was able to accomplish more than four hundred patrons in San Francisco, were periodically drawn. President William Howard Taft, when breaking ground for the Fair in 1915, less than ten years after the quake disaster, had coined the rallying cry: "San Francisco knows how." But it was now feared that this challenge was destined to be countermanded. After fifteen years, apathy and friction reached the breaking point. Hertz resigned in the spring of 1930 with the din of a final salvo of frantic applause in his harassed ears, but manfully expressing the hope that a change of leadership might revive the flagging public interest. He retained many loyal followers and later had the consolation of frequent guest appearances.

However, the landscape was by no means all gray. Hertz was a picturesque figure known to many a man on the street for his distinctive "foxy grandpa" visage, and had more than succeeded in selling the orchestra to the public, especially in the popular concerts. Since 1922, these supplementary concerts had been bought by the Board of Supervisors of the city of San Francisco and presented in short annual series, either free or at popular prices in the huge Civic Auditorium, capacity 10,000.

To be sure, there had been detractors, both social and aesthetic. Certain groups continued their aloofness from the impecunious and sorely pressed orchestra, and critics commented on the heavy-handed German style of interpretation, stemming from the conductor's predilection for Wagnerian brasses that caused an unpleasant reverberation in the limited confines of the Curran Theatre. In their amiably franker moments, they referred to that auditorium as the "boiler factory." But, in the end, there was no question that the orchestra had become one of the accepted civic institutions.

Previous dissension and the ravages of the depression did not make its path a rosy one. Basil Cameron, an English conductor, recommended by Grainger and Beecham; Dobrowen, a momentary flash, and many other guests filled the interim of several seasons with a vanishing personnel. It was beyond the point of rallying to a periodic shot in the arm by a guest conductor, however. The vitality of the organization continued to ebb, and in 1934–35, the funds being completely exhausted, the symphony concerts were entirely suspended. Musical politics often run deep. Described as a "pawn of competing social cliques," the orchestra was fast sliding toward extinction, if indeed it had not already arrived there, when two new forces entered the scene to rescue the victim in good Western melodrama style!

In May, 1935, the electorate passed an amendment to the city charter exacting a half-cent tax for the benefit of the orchestra. In order to circumvent the constitutional prohibition of public moneys being diverted to private purposes, the act, which yielded about $40,000 provided for the appointment of an Art Commission that would "buy" the concerts from the symphony management, and resell them at popular prices to the public. This was then, and still is, an almost unique administrative invention for the support of symphony orchestras. What forces moved the public to vote taxes for such a musical luxury?

Through the agency of the Board of Supervisors and one of its members, J. Emmett Haydn, the city had actually been buying concerts since November, 1922, with moneys from a general publicity and welfare fund, and had thereby set a pattern that needed only to be modified in legal details. These concerts were performed in the Civic Auditorium and were well attended. The mayor and other officials favored the measure; the musicians' union, of course, supported it and enlisted the sympathetic support of the other crafts. Interested persons, including members of the symphony orchestra, carried on an energetic personal campaign, accosting the voters on the streets and in public conveyances, in an attempt to arouse them to the loss of prestige involved in the demise of their great civic asset. Finally, since there was no important voice raised against the proposition, it passed with a comfortable margin.

Although the passage of this measure injected a powerful excitant into the exhausted body of the orchestra, it alone would never have been sufficient to revive it. The new administrative board, reorganized to include a social segment not hitherto adequately represented, was a stronger tonic toward its convalescence. It also brought, after a short time, to the headship of the board, Mrs. Leonora Wood Armsby, from the "Peninsula," who has ever since been the genius of the governing body and the organizer of the community resources, and who, probably more than any other single force in the history of the symphony, is responsible for its present prosperity.

In the meantime, the housing problem of the orchestra had also been solved. For many years it had performed in the Curran, Tivoli, and Capitol theatres, all small auditoriums and often provided reluctantly by their owners because of competition with more profitable theatrical lessees. The urge to secure an adequate and exclusive home, which sooner or later besets the supporters of every orchestra, had likewise begun to attack the local promoters in San Francisco. Now, however, the city could boast of two auditoriums. The Civic Auditorium, a million-dollar coliseum-like structure, had been built for the Panama-Pacific Exposition to accommodate the many conventions and assemblages attracted to the city on that occasion. After the Fair this cavernous auditorium, conveniently located in the Civic Center but with acoustics something less than perfect, was bequeathed to the city. The smaller auditorium, the War Memorial Opera House, as its name implies, dedicated to the heroes of World War I, is also municipally owned (then the first municipally owned Opera House in the country), and seats 3,252. Likewise situated in the Civic Center, this gorgeous auditorium famous for its acoustics, was dedicated in 1932 and provided office space and all necessary facilities for the Symphony Orchestra and the San Francisco Opera, a practically ideal accommodation. Truly, wars and depressions furnish occasions for projects which we cannot afford in times of peace and "prosperity"!

The choice of the new conductor, Pierre Monteux, betokened an especially determined bid for national, and even international, status for the revivified orchestra. This resolve was echoed by the new conductor himself when he enunciated his objective "to restore the San Francisco orchestra to its former place among American ensembles, to give the public the best of classics and a suitable allotment of modern compositions." In his previous stewardship of the Boston Symphony Orchestra (1919–24), of the Diaghileff Ballet, of the Metropolitan Opera and the Concertgebouw orchestra of Amsterdam, and as guest of nearly every major orchestra in the country, he had achieved a reputation for scholarship, clinical virtuosity in score-reading and orchestral technique. If, because of the sobriety of his gestures, he lacks the glamour and demonstrative appeal of some of the prima donnas, he is still, according to the testimony of musicians throughout the country "a musician's conductor," and soloists attest to his flexibility and understanding. He has gained general affection by his restrained and equable temperament. His first concert was given in January, 1936, with an orchestra of eighty-six musicians. After nearly fifteen years, there is still a veritable "cult Monteux" and the public is as united as could be humanly expected. In March, 1945, the University of California awarded him the LL.D. degree.

To insure the audience of the future, the Musical Association established a novel affiliation with the students of the colleges of the Bay area. About 1938, student groups began to meet informally for advance study of symphony programs. The Association cooperated at first by supplying musicians to lead the discussions, and more recently by scheduling a third concert, duplicating the regular pairs, to which these forum members are admitted at a special rate. Youth Concerts, conducted formerly by Ernest Schelling and more recently by Rudoph Ganz, are likewise a part of the season's activities.

But audiences alone will not assure the perpetuation of the symphony orchestras. This can be done only by financial supplements from other than audience sources. Although tax support has contributed somewhat to its security, observers are concerned about the possible cross purposes and embarrassments of divided sponsorship of political and private agents. There is no question that the Musical Association would much prefer a direct subsidy, to be applied according to its own administrative discretion, to the indirect method of selling the services of the orchestra under circumstances which give it no voice in the control.

A second weakness in the San Francisco organization is the absence of summer activity. Music is everywhere a highly seasonal industry and, like all seasonal industries, has often attempted to straighten out and level off the hazardous fluctuations in employment. But although some off-season attempts have been made, San Francisco has no Ravinia Park, Lewisohn Stadium, Hollywood Bowl, Robin Hood Dell, Open Air Opera, Boston "Pops," Esplanade, Berkshire concerts, or Summer Opera. The continuity of employment offered by such summer activities not only extends the season for the musicians of the respective orchestras, but sometimes actually maintains the musical ensemble intact, and eliminates the necessity for the players to earn a livelihood by outside employment. These prospects tend to attract and hold good musicians and are therefore reflected in the quality of the orchestra and its accomplishments. The San Francisco Opera, in setting its schedule noncompetitively in the early fall, does inestimable service to the Symphony by employing a large segment of symphony personnel. Any circumstance which jeopardized the existence of the San Francisco Opera would to that extent jeopardize the quality of the Symphony Orchestra.

REPERTOIRE   During the first four years under Henry Hadley concerts were relatively infrequent, the days were troublesome, and programs were largely determined by available scores and funds. The balance listed toward the romantic side, with Wagner and Tschaikowsky matching Brahms and Beethoven with roughly ten per cent each. Saint-Saëns, Goldmark, and Dvořák, all popular in that day, were included, with Richard Strauss unexpectedly neglected. An American composer himself, Hadley nevertheless paid scant attention to his colleagues, though he performed about half a dozen of his own compositions, which is not, as conductors go, considered unseemly. In general, the repertoire was one that was not too taxing on a fresh orchestra; one that would be appropriate to an audience not too intent on strenuous edification; and one which a discreet conductor would consider safe and sane during the first tottering steps of an infant institution.

Hertz started in the classic manner with the staple Brahms and Beethoven. While he did not avoid Wagner, he gave him no undue prominence but rather paralleled his characteristic postwar decline in other orchestras. For the most part he pursued the general trends, drawing heavily on Tchaikowsky, Dvořák, and Strauss, and for diversity picked up some of the more contemporary figures, Respighi, Sibelius, Debussy, and Mahler. By no means distinguished for an urge to promote the Americans, he nevertheless made a nominal gesture of recognition toward native composers, especially those who were associated in some manner with the Pacific Coast: Ernest Bloch, who was director of the San Francisco Conservatory of Music, 1925–30; Albert Elkus, professor of music in various schools and colleges of the Bay area; Frederick Jacobi, Stillman Kelley, and others. Carpenter, Eichheim, Hanson, and La Violette are also represented.

With Monteux, the public was introduced to a more sophisticated inventory, commensurate with the growth in stature and security of the orchestra and the international eminence of the conductor. As could be anticipated, the French at once received delayed recognition with a proportion of fifteen to twenty per cent in 1935–45, by far the highest in the country. These comprise not only the conventional Chabrier, Berlioz, Chausson, and Ravel, but also the more militant Milhaud, Tailleferre, and Honegger. Monteux displays the typical Gallic apathy toward Sibelius and Tschaikowsky. Stravinsky, whom he virtually introduced to the world while conductor of Diaghileff's *Ballet Russe*, Hindemith, Prokofieff, Chavez, Villa-Lobos, and Bartok illustrate the conductor's contemporary outlook. A cross-section of American music is also given its day although, since Hertz, the American repertoire shows an almost complete turnover. In general, the repertoire is liberal and unhackneyed, but not sufficiently divergent from the general course to alarm the audiences unduly, though periodic protests against "modernism" have been raised.

The Cleveland Orchestra (1918)

For many years, Cleveland was the beneficiary of the musical achievements of larger centers. Cleveland was on the Theodore Thomas highway. Gericke and Nikisch of Boston followed, as did Damrosch and the New York Symphony. Earlier, Cleveland had entertained the Sängerfest in 1855, 1859, and 1874, as well as numerous miscellaneous soloists who toured the country.

Tentative efforts to establish an indigenous orchestra were made at various times by the musicians among the German immigrants who arrived in the city after 1848. Most of the organizations were necessarily so shortlived that a sample enumeration does them more than justice. In 1852, John Olker organized the Germania orchestra in that city of 20,000. The Caecelian orchestra followed in 1854; the Cleveland Philharmonic in 1881, and the Cleveland Symphony under Johann Beck in 1900.

Between 1901 and 1918 a concert schedule was made up of programs presented by the major American orchestras that included Cleveland in their tours. To administer and, if necessary, to subsidize the concert series of visiting orchestras, the Musical Arts Association was incorporated in 1902, content for the time with the borrowed finery of other cities. In 1913, however, Cleveland was stung with envy when visited by the orchestra from Minneapolis, a city half its size. With the encouragement of Mayor Newton D. Baker (later Secretary of War in the Wilson cabinet), the Cleveland Municipal Orchestra was organized for Sunday concerts at popular prices under the direction of Christian Tinner. But these lapsed during the war.

In 1918 Mrs. Adella Prentiss Hughes,[68] a Cleveland musician who has since been gratefully labeled "Mother of the Cleveland Symphony," attended the Ohio Music Teachers Convention in Cincinnati and heard a lecture by Nikolai Sokoloff, who was at the time conducting summer concerts in that city. Impressed, she secured him for a survey of public school music in her own city that fall. This was the first of a series of significant circumstances which terminated in the founding of the present orchestra.

Externally, the sequence of events seemed quite casual. As Pastor of St. Ann's Catholic Church, the Reverend J. H. Powers faced the not unusual necessity of raising funds for his parish. He himself was an amateur musician, and proposed to Sokoloff and to the Musical Arts Association the organization of a small orchestra for a benefit concert, with Father Powers (vocalist) as soloist. Fifty-seven men were recruited, and the concert presented December 11, 1918. So successful was the venture that twenty concerts of various types were given in Cleveland and seven outside the city during the season.

Sokoloff, born in Russia, had been a student at the Yale School of Music, a violin protégé of Charles Martin Loeffler, and a member of the Boston Symphony Orchestra from 1904 to 1907. For three years, beginning with 1914, he conducted the San Francisco People's Philharmonic, which attempted to supply the community with popular-priced concerts. In 1918 he was conducting summer concerts in Cincinnati when he was discovered by Mrs. Hughes.

The Cleveland orchestra began typically as a local band. The musicians, with the exception of the scarce oboe and English horn players, were recruited from local theatres, schools, and other sources. The defunct Municipal orchestra had left about three hundred scores and miscellaneous equipment, which Mrs. Hughes "picked up," while Sokoloff himself owned a small portfolio of scores. The concerts of the first season were presented in Gray's Armory (capacity 2,400), but in the following year were transferred to the newly erected Masonic Temple, which was only slightly smaller.

Under Sokoloff the orchestra participated in various community enterprises, offering children's concerts, sponsoring contests; and in 1927–28 it was joined by the Cleveland Playhouse, a dramatic troupe, for the presentation of Debussy's *Nuages et Fêtes* and other numbers. During the season 1921–22 the orchestra received $31,000 from the community chest, in payment for concerts in community centres.

The Musical Arts Association, a nonprofit corporation, continued to sponsor the concerts, administer the trust funds, and to acquire and hold its property. To one of the leading members of this association the orchestra is indebted for its present home. On the tenth anniversary of the orchestra, Mr. J. L. Severance, oil and steel magnate, announced a gift of $1,000,000 for an auditorium. Western Reserve University offered the site. These two gifts were supplemented by public contributions to an endowment and maintenance fund. The hall was dedicated in February, 1931, and named in memory of Mrs. Severance who had died since the announcement of the gift. Severance Hall is beautifully designed and situated, highly decorative in appointment, but seating only about 1,800 persons. It is among the smallest auditoriums in America to house a major orchestra.

After fifteen years of pioneer service, Sokoloff announced his retirement, to take effect at the end of the 1932–33 season. In a bid for greater national recognition, the conductorship was offered to Artur Rodzinski, who had come to this country as assistant to Stokowski in 1927 and was then enjoying a successful tenure in Los Angeles. He had gained a reputation for his organizing talent and succeeded in materially strengthening the ensemble. After ten years Rodzinski, who had in the meantime won notoriety as Toscanini's assistant for the training of the new NBC orchestra, graduated to the Philharmonic-Symphony of New York.

On Rodzinski's resignation, some critics lamented our subservience to Europe and pleaded for an American conductor. However, he was succeeded by Viennese-born Erich Leinsdorf, thirty-one-year-old operatic maestro, who had created a sensation at the Metropolitan Opera by his appointment as full conductor to that venerable institution at the age of twenty-six and by his public clashes with several operatic stars. Subject to the military draft, his service was brief. Much of his three-year regime was filled by guest conductors, one of whom, George Szell, was appointed permanent conductor in 1946.

REPERTOIRE   The infant years of the Cleveland orchestra, which was founded in the year of the Armistice, were influenced by the strong feelings and sentiments engendered during the war. The curtailment of such weighty composers as Strauss and Wagner, adversely affected by current political attitudes, produced a material shrinkage in the repertoire's German quota. The Austro-German proportion therefore hovered well below the fifty per cent mark throughout the first decade. The old Russians, with Tschaikowsky and Rimsky-Korsakoff, constituted about twenty per cent of the program time, and the French, also profiting from wartime sentiment, only slightly less.

A large fraction of its American repertoire was locally induced. Bloch, who was then on the threshold of his American career, was at that time a resident of Cleveland, and found a generous audience in the 1920's, but vanished under Szell. Loeffler, the former teacher of Sokoloff, had many renditions; Arthur Shepherd, assistant conductor, and later professor at Western Reserve University; Henry Eichheim, a fellow-student of the conductor; Carleton Cooley, a member of the orchestra; Herbert Elwell and Beryl Rubinstein, local composers—together with an occasional nationally-known American—comprised six to eight per cent of the Sokoloff repertoire.

This level of American participation was continued by his successor, Artur Rodzinski, but with increased national and diminished local emphasis. Though the war hysteria had cooled and Strauss was again admitted into fellowship, and though the Bach transcriptions prospered and the Mahler cult was born, the Germans did not recapture the position of lofty isolation held during the reign of the mid-European conductors. Rodzinski and other non-Teutons were now exalting the Russians and the French. Accordingly, Shostakovitch, Rachmaninoff, and Stravinsky were supplementing the pre-Revolutionary stand-bys to augment the Slavic strength.

The Rodzinski period was also marked by the inclusion of opera performances in the orchestral schedule. Victims of the war and other untoward factors, the provincial opera companies in Boston and Chicago had succumbed. Cleveland, as well as Cincinnati and Philadelphia, attempted to rekindle the depression patronage for the orchestras, to salvage operatic literature, and possibly also to gratify the professional passion of the conductors, by incorporating full operatic performances, as well as operas in concert form, in the regular season's offerings. The Cleveland project was made possible by the happy coincidence that, in 1918, the Musical Association had acquired for a nominal sum the entire collection of books, manuscripts, and scores comprising the library of the bankrupt Boston Opera Company. In five seasons, fifteen standard operas were staged. As in Philadelphia and Cincinnati, however, the opera has now been abandoned and the orchestra has returned to its basic métier.

The Los Angeles Philharmonic Orchestra (1919)

In 1880 Los Angeles was a small outpost community of 10,000 inhabitants, with a salubrious climate, but with no consciousness of its destiny which has since conferred on it such notoriety. However, the appearance of the characteristic symptoms of its mature personality were not to be delayed. The isolated frontier town was on the eve of a period of rapid growth on completion of the first of the several railroads which made Los Angeles a transcontinental terminal point. This all-important achievement was, in part, the work of William Andrews Clark, mining magnate and empire builder and father of William Andrews Clark, Jr., who subsequently became the founder and chief benefactor of the Los Angeles Philharmonic Orchestra.

It was also the eighties that witnessed the first musical stirrings under the patriarchal Adolf Willhartitz, who had already been active in St. Louis and who now organized an amateur orchestra of forty and a chorus of 120 for the production of light opera and the larger choral works.[69] The first exclusively orchestral body was not organized until 1893 when A. J. Stamm, also a German, pieced together an orchestra of thirty-five professional musicians. Lacking such instruments as the oboe and bassoon, they still performed works of Wagner, Rossini, Mendelssohn, Rubinstein, and other standard composers at their maiden concert.

The concertmaster of this aggregation was young Harley Hamilton, who lost no time in organizing his own group, the Los Angeles Symphony Society, in 1897. This orchestra, destined for a much longer life, was at first not much more richly endowed with finances and instruments than was its predecessor. However, with a little aid from such philanthropists as he could rally to his cause, and the personal purchase of the necessary scores, Mr. Hamilton persevered from the time of the first concert, which was given in a converted music hall, Spring Street between Second and Third, on February 1, 1898, until he retired sixteen years later. During this period he had laid a foundation of taste by introducing to Los Angeles the standard compositions of Brahms, Dvořák, Haydn, and a half-hundred other composers.

About the close of the century, the most prominent hotel in Los Angeles was the Alexandria, operated by Mr. Albert C. Bilicke. For entertainment and dinner music, he had imported from Vienna Adolf Tandler and several other instrumentalists who were creating a very favorable impression on some of the most influential people of the city. Although there were at least thirty candidates for the leadership of the Los Angeles Symphony Orchestra on the retirement of Hamilton in 1913, Mr. Tandler secured the appointment at $3,000 per season. Leaping from a modest dining salon to a concert stage, Tandler was fairly sensational. With an orchestra of ninety men, he often conducted without a score, instituted paired performances and children's concerts, and programmed many new compositions. Like many other conductors, he had his strong supporters who helped him enlist some philanthropic aid, as well as his detractors who remained unimpressed and unappreciative of his heroic attempts to simulate a great orchestra.

In the meantime, a significant new force was arising in the guise of a "Higginson" of the West: William Andrews Clark, Jr. The Tandler orchestra was merely a cooperative organization, which relied on local musicians and suffered from all the familiar infirmities attendant upon those circumstances. Mr. Clark recognized these provincial limitations and was determined to organize an orchestra on the contemporary Eastern pattern which would merit national recognition.

Clark was the educated and well-traveled offspring of the aforementioned empire builder, Senator Clark of Montana. He was by profession a lawyer, by avocation a violinist, and by inheritance the custodian of millions in mining and railroad wealth, fabulously augmented by the war prosperity of 1914–18. He came by his musical interests honestly, for he had studied the violin in Paris and Los Angeles, and had already organized in Los Angeles a chamber music group in which he played his instrument. From New York he had brought reminiscences of Anton Seidl, a frequent guest in his father's home, of whom he often spoke almost in terms of idolatry to his associates in Los Angeles.

Los Angeles had meanwhile become a progressive city of over half a million. All signs therefore pointed to its entrance into the national arena with a more aggressive policy for the cultivation of the arts as a civic asset. With a growth of national consciousness it seemed important to find a nationally recognized conductor, whose experience and reputation would lend immediate prestige. English-born Walter Henry Rothwell, then a resident of New York, had conducted opera both in the United States and Europe, and had been conductor of the St. Paul Symphony Orchestra from 1908 until 1915, when it was disbanded. Rothwell, therefore, qualified. He was empowered to employ a concertmaster and personnel—a few from strike-bound Boston—purchase the necessary scores, and make the general preparations for a symphony orchestra, whose inevitable deficits would be personally guaranteed by Mr. Clark. The ninety-piece orchestra opened the series of twelve pairs on October 24, 1919, in Trinity Auditorium.

The immediate effect of such grandiose planning on the old Los Angeles Symphony Orchestra was to induce practically all its members to desert it and contract with Clark for a place in the new organization. Tandler, with some small philanthropic support from a competitive social set still available to him, reorganized his own symphony in an intrepid endeavor to discard the cooperative system in favor of annual financing. After only a year's survival, however, friction developed with the musicians' union, which was the occasion, although hardly the real cause, of its demise.

From all indications, Rothwell was popular with the public. This former assistant to Gustav Mahler in Hamburg brought discipline, much needed at the time, to the new orchestra. Not the least significant circumstance in his success was his congeniality with his benefactor. "They made a good team." Mr. Clark attended rehearsals and frequently sat among the strings where Mr. Rothwell welcomed his presence and comment.

Mr. Clark's solicitude for the new venture was paternalistic and all-embracing. Even before the first concert of the season he raised the minimum weekly salary of his first contracts from thirty-five dollars to fifty dollars in order to offset the rapidly rising (postwar) cost of living. To each member of the orchestra he presented an insurance policy for the duration of his employment. Finding Trinity unsatisfactory, he purchased the lease of Clune's Auditorium, later known as the Philharmonic Auditorium, capacity about 2,600, which has since been the leased home of the orchestra. He shared with the conductor all the musical and aesthetic problems, and even stood with him on the podium for the conventional photographs. In order to lengthen the season for his musicians and thereby make his contracts more enticing to Eastern musicians, he encouraged, and materially assisted in, the establishment of the Hollywood Bowl summer concerts.[70] For three five-year periods, he underwrote the deficits of the orchestra, which cumulated to a total of almost $3,000,000.

But the creeping anxiety that a sole guarantor would eventually become indifferent or exhausted finally realized itself here, as it had elsewhere. Fashions were changing. Instead of the unstable equilibrium of the inverted pyramid, the one supporting the many, there had long ago set in a shift to broad-based support. Higginson, the American progenitor of the plutocratic system, had died in Boston in 1919, just as the Los Angeles Philharmonic was being born. In Philadelphia, Chicago, and other cities endowments or sustaining friends had assumed the responsibilities of the erstwhile "owner" of the orchestra. As long as "Will" Clark was willing, Los Angeles let him do it. But when he died in 1934, uncertain of the future of the orchestra, he had bequeathed his extensive collection of scores to the Los Angeles Public Library, and cut off without endowment the child that he had so long nurtured and reared.

Some months before his unexpected death he had, in fact, announced his definite and final withdrawal from the responsibilities that he had periodically reassumed with increasing reluctance. This had necessitated the reorganization of the board in line with the more popular method of financing. The new organization, the Southern California Symphony Association, solicited subscriptions of one dollar and up, and thus modestly set out to take its first un-assisted steps toward financial maturity in the fall of 1934, in the midst of the great depression.

Rothwell died suddenly in the spring of 1927. Emil Oberhoffer, who had conducted the Minneapolis Orchestra for nineteen years and had appeared in the Hollywood Bowl, was available to complete the season in the emergency. However, for the permanent office the Symphony board followed the usual procedure of searching in Europe for an available candidate, and imported Finnish Georg Schneevoigt who, however, remained for only two seasons. It was not a fortunate choice. Schneevoigt was lethargic and uninspired and never gained disciplinary control over his men. During his second season, illness necessitated the employment of several guest conductors, including Artur Rodzinski then assistant conductor under Stokowski in Philadelphia. With the resignation of Schneevoigt in 1929, Rodzinski took over the leadership and remained until the spring of 1933, when he was released to accept the call to Cleveland. This event coincided with the retirement of Mr. Clark.

From the standpoint of fiscal management, as well as conductorial opportunities, the Philharmonic was now on the threshold of a new era. The rise to power of the Nazi regime in January, 1933, had made the position of many German musicians untenable at home. Among the earliest of these to forfeit his position was Otto Klemperer, conductor of opera and orchestra, who had taken an active part in the politically indiscreet cultivation of contemporary and post-Wagnerian music. Already favorably known in the United States as guest conductor, Klemperer was eagerly sought in order to justify the faith of the orchestra in the new popular management. By standards both physical and musical, he was by far the most impressive figure yet to occupy the post as regular conductor. Six feet-four inches tall, he dispensed with the platform. Completely unhampered by baton, score, music stand, or podium, he bestrode the stage and gripped the attention of both musicians and audience with the sweep of his long arms. He was the first musical director of truly international stature and general musical maturity. For six seasons he was an outstanding popular success until at last failing health diminished his efficiency.

There followed, beginning in 1939, a procession of guest conductors: Coates, Stokowski, Walter, Wallenstein, Barbirolli, and others, until finally, among the many candidates, Alfred Wallenstein was appointed to the new leadership. Born in Chicago, he had spent most of his youth in Los Angeles, studied the cello with Julius Klengel in Leipzig, and had played under Stock and Toscanini before he gained recognition as an enterprising conductor of a radio orchestra.

The Philharmonic orchestra had been in great need of new orientation toward the growing complexities of the city's organization. Under the new regime, the number of paired concerts, which had fallen to as low as nine during the guest period, was increased; new financial resources, including the much discussed "racing fund," which dispenses its favors to all meritorious enterprises, were tapped; and a pension fund, initiated by a concert conducted by Toscanini, was established. The new conductor, to whom must be given a certain measure of credit for the financial and cultural renaissance (which was not achieved without some partisan conflict and revision in managerial personnel) is personally active in integrating the orchestra into the life of the community. Although children's concerts were no novelty, the children's series was strengthened by the purchase of programs by the city school system, and by various pedagogical and entertainment features designed to create an interested juvenile audience.

In addition to the tribulations that beset every orchestra and never are fully resolved, the Los Angeles Philharmonic is less fortunate than most major orchestras in that it has virtually no "home." The Philharmonic Auditorium is hardly acceptable as a final solution of the housing problem. Of its 2,600 seats, some hundreds are completely unsalable because the view of the stage is obstructed either by pillars or by the awkward angle of vision. The constant use of the auditorium for other functions likewise is a perennial obstacle in the planning of proper schedules, both for rehearsals and public concerts. A new home is ultimately envisioned. On a site already selected, west of the downtown section, according to the Greater Los Angeles Plan, a modern auditorium will be constructed, which will be more accessible than is the present building in the heart of the congested business area.

The welfare of the orchestra is to some extent influenced by unique local conditions. In addition to the prestige of the orchestra and the length of the season, the musician is attracted to Los Angeles by the seductive climate and by the prospect of employment in the studios of motion picture and radio. Employment conditions in the studios until recently have been extremely favorable, with shorter hours and a higher scale of pay. In fact, many musicians who have succeeded in securing posts in the studio orchestras are said to cast condescending glances on the hard-working orchestra player, with his strenuous rehearsal and concert regime, and the lower rate of compensation. Consequently, many excellent musicians are said to accept a chair in the symphony orchestra with one eye on the main chance in Hollywood, with a resulting higher turnover in orchestra membership than is healthy for continuous excellence of performance. The prosperity of the studios has therefore often operated adversely on the fortunes of the orchestra. Per contra, when there is a "depression" in the studios, the position of the orchestra is correspondingly favored.

Hollywood Bowl, a natural amphitheatre which now accommodates 20,000 persons, is also aligned with the fortunes of the Los Angeles Philharmonic. For its opening in the summer of 1922, Alfred Hertz, then conductor of the San Francisco orchestra, was willing to grapple with the hazards of outdoor performances, then not so generally accepted as now, which others had spurned. It was thought, quite rightly, that music out of doors, with ever so favorable acoustics, could not transmit the fine nuances nor convey the subtle emotional connotations to which audiences have become accustomed in the concert hall. And even if this difficulty were overcome, it was thought doubtful that mammoth audiences could be attracted to serious concerts.

It is of course true that throughout the United States outdoor activities of every type have been expanding; and musical activities have shared in this *al fresco* revolution. The prospects of music in Los Angeles have been enhanced by its equable climate and its reputation as ideal vacationland. According to a boast of one Californian,[71] the Lewisohn Stadium is plagued by its fire engines and showers, Ravinia Park by its heat and mosquitoes; while the rainless skies, top-coat temperatures, and insect-free atmosphere of Southern California allow the completest enjoyment of a Bowl concert.

REPERTOIRE The roll call of composers during the first years of the Los Angeles Philharmonic presents no conspicuous deviations from the general taste of the other concert-going communities of that time. Rothwell evinced no disposition to specialize, but rather possessed the temperament of a general practitioner. The "old reliables," Beethoven and Brahms, between them accounted for thirty per cent of the programs; Tschaikowsky competed with Wagner, each drawing off an additional ten per cent. Strauss (five per cent), Debussy (four per cent), Liszt, Mendelssohn, Dvořák and Saint-Säens pulled up next in the ranking of the regulars. Mahler was represented, but Bach had not yet been launched on his renaissance by Stokowski, and therefore had a barely discernible existence. The New England Americans were given a fair hearing by this English-born conductor who, having been educated on the continent, displayed no vestiges of his British origins.

It was during the brief incumbency of Schneevoigt that the centennial of Schubert's death was commemorated, which accounts for his extraordinary proportion of eight per cent. That Sibelius is not given a more favorable position by this Finnish conductor than his five points would indicate is, perhaps, partly to be explained by the fact that guest conductors during Schneevoigt's illness showed different enthusiasms.

With Rodzinski, the Austro-German groups reach an all-time low of thirty-eight per cent, brought about by the de-emphasis of Beethoven, and the actual omission of Liszt, Mendelssohn, and other dispensable Germans. The French came into their own with Debussy and Franck, and the Russians expanded with Tschaikowsky, Stravinsky, Rachmaninoff, and the emergent Prokofieff. It was Rodzinski's first responsible conductor's post in the United States—he had served as assistant conductor in Philadelphia—and he gave vent to his sentiments by lifting the American composer to a respectable six per cent, exceeded only by Chicago and Boston. It was in February, 1933, that he gained his American citizenship, and signalized the event by playing his first pair of concerts with an all-American program capped by the *Star-Spangled Banner*, a patriotic note that is indeed unusual in peacetime.

Klemperer had been known in Germany for his contemporary tastes. These he brought to this country in 1933 and displayed in his programming of Stravinsky, Hindemith, and Shostakovitch, the latter then on the threshold of his American career. With Bruno Walter, one of his successors in Los Angeles, he shared the espousal of Mahler. Except for his meager attention to American composers, this German emigré cultivated an advanced repertoire. From 1940, however, in part because of the growing composers' colony in the Los Angeles area, American representation grew apace to almost ten per cent, among the highest in the country. With so much public attention at that time riveted on the Good Neighbor policy, Latin American composers also crept into view: Chavez from Mexico (guest conductor), Mignone, Villa-Lobos and Guarnieri from Brazil. Of these, Villa-Lobos was soon destined to be heard in almost all major orchestras.

The colony of composers in Southern California are attracted, of course, by the studios, as well as by the climate, so salubrious for their declining years. Gershwin and Rachmaninoff, at the time of their passing, were living in that area, and Gershwin's death was marked by a special Gershwin program by the orchestra. Wallenstein has accorded the Americans an average, but well-selected, representation with relatively little emphasis on "local debts." In fact, the Wallenstein repertoire rides no hobbies, but has deflated previously exaggerated proportions, and lifted others to more normal statures. It presents a substantial and worthy assortment of standard and modern works relatively devoid of questionable experimentation. He seems to plan his repertoire to "give something to everybody."

The distribution of symphonic orchestras is much more widespread than might be inferred from the relatively short foregoing list. Many other cities have flourishing orchestras of shorter duration, or have suffered dark seasons which have interrupted significant developments. Because of these gaps in their history and the shifts from impermanent to permanent organization, the "legitimate" date of their founding cannot always be determined; for some managements have been disposed to push back that date as far as possible for the prestige which age confers. Because of the brevity and discontinuity in their history, as well as the shortness of season, it is impractical to analyze their repertoires, which, in general, are more standardized and less experimental than those of the well-established groups.

The Pittsburgh Symphony Orchestra

Among the oldest of these in-and-outers is the Pittsburgh orchestra, founded by the Art Society in 1896. Andrew Carnegie was listed among the contributors. During the first two years Frederick Archer, a local organist, was the conductor. In a bid for wider appeal, the management sought out Victor Herbert, already known for his light operas but who had gathered considerable experience in serious music as a member of the Thomas, Seidl, and the Metropolitan Opera orchestras in New York. If he built a reputation of brusqueness and highhandedness toward the men of his orchestra, he awakened great public interest in his programs and vivacious performances. The orchestra of seventy men, safely financed, toured the region, including New York. It was to all intents a "permanent" orchestra, correctly advertised as being "more than New York has." But the call of composition was too strong to resist, and Herbert retired in 1904 to devote himself exclusively to his métier.

During the next six years the orchestra was under the baton of Emil Paur, late of Boston and New York. But Paur's programs were "esoteric," the audience drifted away, and the guarantors became discouraged. In 1910 the orchestra was dissolved.

In the interval between its collapse and its regeneration in 1937 the city was provided with symphonic music by casual orchestras. In that year Otto Klemperer was "borrowed" from the Los Angeles orchestra to re-establish it as a major orchestra. Pittsburgh followed through with determination by securing Fritz Reiner, formerly conductor in Cincinnati. After having built up the orchestra to ninety men and the season to twenty-eight weeks in his ten years of service, in an economy move Reiner was threatened with curtailment of both personnel and season. Feeling that he could preserve his artistic integrity only by resigning, he did so in 1948 and the orchestra has since been under the baton of guests.

The Detroit Symphony Orchestra

While never of the highest musical excellence, the Detroit Orchestra has periodically furnished exciting copy for musical news. The orchestra had its undistinguished beginning in 1914 under Weston Gales, who had successfully sold himself to the city after an experimental concert the previous year. Its first bid for entry into the major class, however, was the appointment in 1918 of the distinguished pianist Ossip Gabrilowitsch as conductor. He reorganized the orchestra by importing new musicians, to the usual distress of the local union. With his wide personal following, Gabrilowitsch lifted the orchestra to great social heights and considerable musical excellence. After his death in 1935, he was succeeded by his associate conductor, Victor Kolar, the Italian Franco Ghione, and occasional guests. The city's previously high interest could not be maintained, and the orchestra became inactive in 1942–43. The year was bridged, however, by a radio series under distinguished guests, sponsored by a department store, and by a chamber orchestra under the direction of Bernhard Heiden, a young composer from Frankfort, Germany.

At this moment, a strong man took command. A Berlin-born industrial chemist, an amateur violinist in his own right, and fabulously successful as an industrial chemist, Henry H. Reichhold assumed sole responsibility for the revived orchestra. Having tasted of musical philanthropy on a small scale by guaranteeing the Heiden ensemble, he secured Karl Krueger, late of Kansas City, as musical director. He soon increased the personnel of the orchestra to 110 men, purchased the Wilson theatre, and undertook an aggressive and flamboyant campaign that featured the "world's largest orchestra." For a short period, Reichhold had dreams of building a musical empire independent of New York administrators, analogous to Henry Ford's several decades earlier. Included in this defiant project, in addition to the orchestra, were a musical journal, a concert bureau, radio and records, and finally a fling with the Carnegie "pops" of New York.

Many forces contributed to the collapse of the dazzling six-year scheme, the success of which would have been welcomed by many friends. It is idle to inquire whether the authoritarian nature of the sponsor, his imprudent public strategy, the alleged shortcomings of the conductor, the barbs of the critics, or the disputes with the orchestra personnel, contributed most to the unfortunate debacle. In 1950 Detroit was again without a symphony orchestra.

The Baltimore Symphony Orchestra

Baltimore has come to be known as the "cradle of municipal music." In 1914, when the city administration appropriated $8,000 for a municipal band, it occurred to some that a municipal orchestra would be equally feasible. Accordingly, Baltimore made history by founding an orchestra on a municipal appropriation, a method quite contrary to the philanthropic origins in other communities. But, like the municipal band, the orchestra was a local affair, limited in length of season and artistic horizon. The first conductor was Gustav Strube, formerly of the Boston orchestra, and at the time on the faculty of Peabody Conservatory. Although the city had stepped up its appropriations, they were never sufficient to guarantee an orchestra of a caliber worthy of the seventh city of the United States. As a result of long-smoldering difficulties, the orchestra disintegrated in 1942.

It was during this period that Peabody acquired as its new director Reginald Stewart, founder and conductor of the Toronto Philharmonic Orchestra. After the demise of the Baltimore orchestra, he submitted a plan for its reorganization which involved the coordination of conservatory and orchestral interests, and was promptly entrusted with its execution. He assumed the conductorship of the new orchestra at once. This type of operation had distinguished precedent in Leipzig exactly a century previously, when Felix Mendelssohn was the director of the conservatory, which he founded in 1843, and the conductor of the Gewandhaus orchestra between 1835 and 1848. New members were appointed to the Peabody faculty who would dovetail their services in the schedules of the two institutions. Still relying on the indispensable municipal grant, the orchestra solicits, as do all other orchestras, the funds of friends to balance its budget.

The Rochester Philharmonic Orchestra

The Rochester Philharmonic Orchestra was, until 1929, virtually the pit orchestra of the Eastman Theatre, a motion-picture house. Organized by George Eastman of Kodak fame, it presented the first of its periodic symphony concerts March 28, 1923 under the direction of Arthur Alexander. But with the double catastrophe of sound film and the depression, the basic employment of the orchestra in the theatre vanished. In this crisis the orchestra was taken over by the Rochester Music Association. A permanent nucleus of about forty-five players constituted the Civic Orchestra, which was supplemented to form a complete complement for symphonic purposes. Permanent conductors have been: Eugene Goossens (1924–31), José Iturbi (1936–44), and Erich Leinsdorf (1947–   ); and these have been supplemented by an extensive and notable guest list.

A distinctive feature of the Rochester orchestra is its collaboration with the Eastman School of Music, which is an integral part of the University of Rochester. Not only are the Philharmonic concerts given on the campus, but the orchestra participates in the American Festivals that have been instituted by Howard Hanson, director of the Eastman School, for the advancement of the American composer.

The Indianapolis Symphony Orchestra

The city of Indianapolis,[72] founded in 1821, experienced during the first half century of its existence a musical life that was normal for that period and the maturity of the community. Brass bands, choral groups, solo recitals, and occasional instrumental ensembles constituted the musical recreation of the epoch. After 1850 such activity was largely supported by the Germans who began to arrive in large numbers in various cities of the United States. The Indianapolis Männerchor is only one of the many German enterprises that has survived.

Among these Germans, incipient orchestral organizations soon appeared. In 1871, stirred by the fate of stricken Chicago, about forty musicians banded together for a charity concert, and continued to give light concerts as the Philharmonic Orchestra. Karl Schneider made an attempt in 1896 to establish a series with about sixty amateurs and professionals, occasionally importing aid from Cincinnati, but abandoned it in 1900. More enduring and significant was the project under the direction of Alexander Ernestinoff, which prospered between 1898 and 1914. Envisaging the possibilities of popular-priced music, Edward Birge, then director of public school music, organized the People's Concert Association in 1905 for the purpose of sponsoring choral performances, recitals, and concerts by visiting major orchestras from Chicago, Minneapolis, and Cincinnati. His scheme also embraced the indigenous orchestras which were successively conducted by Ernestinoff, Schneider, and Ferdinand Schaefer, a recent arrival from Germany in 1907.

The present symphony orchestra was founded in 1929, when local musicians found themselves displaced by sound-pictures or just plain victims of the depression. In this crisis Schaefer, a former member of the Leipzig Gewandhaus orchestra, again stepped forth to organize an ensemble which would supply serious musical entertainment, to preserve the musical skills endangered by enforced idleness, and to recoup their ebbing livelihood. But nearing three score and ten, Schaefer had already reached the customary retirement age when he assembled his sixty musicians for the initial concert. If the new orchestra was to prosper, the normal course would call for the engagement of a younger conductor. After a visit as guest conductor, November 17, 1936, Fabien Sevitzky, nephew of Boston's Koussevitzky and like him a double-bass virtuoso, was engaged. Sevitzky had come to this country in 1923 and, in deference to his more famous uncle, had shortened his name very early in his American career. The Indianapolis personnel was enlarged, the season offering increased from six single to ten pairs, season contracts became the rule, and the orchestra was thus placed on a permanent basis. Like his uncle, he dedicated his efforts to advancing the American cause and for some years attracted national attention by including an American composition on every subscription program.

The abandonment of the purely cooperative organization, which involved shopping for talent in a larger market, produced the same anguish in Indianapolis as it had in every other city. The fine sentiments that had nurtured and solidified the depression orchestra were rudely shaken by efficiency methods of the new order. "Indianapolis musicians have worked for seven years and have played rehearsals and concerts for as little as three dollars a concert. Yet they have now been denied the just fruits of their labors." So ran the petition of protest circulated during Sevitzky's second season. Of course, the protests remained impotent. In fact, the low return was undoubtedly the best evidence of the imminent collapse of a venture that could be saved only by the very reorganization which they deplored. In this respect Indianapolis was only traversing a stage which New York, Philadelphia, and the rest had already passed and long forgotten.

The orchestra waxed in strength and maturity, but did not escape the hazards that had befallen the older orchestras. It met its deficits, however, in a relatively novel way. Since 1931 the orchestra has been sponsored on a state-wide basis and is still administered by the Indiana State Symphony Society which solicits funds in the communities of the state. It was also one of the first to win a grant of tax funds for the outright purchase of concerts for public presentation. In 1943 the Indiana General Assembly passed an enabling act permitting the city to appropriate $50,000 from the school and civil budgets, this amount representing about one-fifth of the annual orchestra budget. These grants are never approved without a skirmish with the "anti-music lobby," which does not deem an orchestra an appropriate subject for public subvention, as well as with those civil departments that suffer inconvenient cuts in their budgets.

Washington, D. C.: The National Symphony Orchestra

In almost every country in the world, the political capital is at the same time the seat of cultural leadership of the nation. Paris, London, Vienna, Berlin, and Moscow are mature cities that incorporate all the pursuits of a cosmopolitan community: industry, transportation, commerce, education, and the arts. But the unique history of the United States has decreed another fate for its own capital city. It is, in a sense, a synthetic community, oriented almost exclusively around its political functions. Its industrial potential is negligible; its commerce is restricted by its unfavorable location; its essential population is transient and reserves its community pride for its "home towns." It follows that, with the exception of a few fine libraries and art galleries, the ingredients for a healthy cultural life hardly exist. Some of the libraries and museums that do embellish the landscape are to a large extent linked with the political functions of the city.

For some years the city imported concerts from New York and other neighboring cities.[73] When these were curtailed, Washington was threatened with musical famine. Faltering beginnings toward local sponsorship had, indeed, been made as early as 1902 when Reginald DeKoven conducted sporadic concerts under the name of the Washington Symphony Orchestra. Other conductors met with equally ephemeral success.

More serious efforts were made in the spring of 1930 when a group of resident musicians, driven by depression circumstances, banded together for cooperative concerts, and called Hans Kindler to lead them. A Dutch-American cellist, Kindler had previously occupied the first chair in the Philadelphia orchestra, had a modicum of conducting experience, and had been favorably known to Washington audiences.

Although the depression project was soon abandoned, Kindler picked up the challenge and made it his personal responsibility to lay the foundation for a permanent orchestra. The National Symphony Orchestra is almost literally his own creation. It was he who solicited funds, corralled the musicians, and took all the initiative and responsibility for aggressive action.

The founding of an orchestra is never an easy task. Even before the first concert (Nov. 2, 1931), seven important musicians had withdrawn because of schedules conflicting with their more secure and remunerative positions in the pit of the Fox Theatre. Promising players were often enticed by more favorable contracts to other cities. Since extra instruments, extra rehearsals, royalties, and rentals are expensive, programs had to be cut to the cloth of available materials. In fact, it was not until 1946 that Kindler felt safe in scheduling such numbers as Strauss' *Till Eulenspiegel* and *Heldenleben*.

Recurrent disputes with the union reached a climax in 1939 when the usual questions of imported musicians, salary scales, and length of season proved insoluble until John Steelman, Federal conciliator, offered the services of his staff for negotiation of outstanding differences.

In 1935 the orchestra was organized on a permanent basis. Musicians were given season contracts, tours were undertaken; in 1940 records were cut for the Victor company; and the fame of the Watergate concerts, the first of which had played to 10,000 persons in 1935, grew apace. When finally, in 1948, the Association had to undertake a deficit campaign to wipe out an accumulated debt of $50,000, one could safely conclude that the National Symphony Orchestra had "come of age"! Kindler, however, was ready to retire in 1949, and soon died. He was replaced by Howard Mitchell, associate conductor, the present incumbent.

The concert hall at the disposal of the orchestra during the twenty years of its existence is a rented home. It is not the worst-, nor yet the best-appointed concert hall. Seating 3,800 persons, Constitution Hall was designed primarily to house the many conventions that crowd the national capital. Its stage facilities are only moderately satisfactory; but more important, the busy schedule of the building often conflicts with its use for rehearsals and other functions related to satisfactory concert performance. The more sanguine friends of the orchestra hope for a new home, which, together with an endowment fund, would satisfy the ambitions of this, one of the youngest of the major orchestras of the country.

4

Life Spans of Composers in the Repertoire

IN THE HISTORY of the orchestral repertoire, the duration of the musical life of a composer's works presents about the same diversity as the duration of the personal life of individuals. There is a high early mortality, many live an average and uneventful life, and to only a few is granted a long and venerable career. The life of a composition as well as of a human being is determined by two factors, the environmental circumstances to which it is subjected in the course of its existence, and the initial vitality of the subject itself. These produce in both cases a characteristic biography or life history. The performance of a composition, which is obviously the principal reason for its existence, is the best evidence of both its initial vitality and of a favorable environment.

Since it is quite impossible to comprehend the multiplicity of details in the performance records of several scores of composers individually, these composers are classified into type-groups made up of those whose careers approximately coincide in length of time span, volume of repertoire, and historical pattern of popularity. Although aesthetic, musicological, and other considerations would often dictate alternative groupings, the historical analysis here contemplated is greatly facilitated by momentarily ignoring rival considerations. Accordingly, beginning with 1875 when symphony orchestras were on the eve of their expansionist period, most prominent composers are grouped into six major divisions:

(1) Six eminent composers who have maintained their pre-eminence: Beethoven, Brahms, Wagner, Tschaikowsky, Mozart, and Bach.
(2) A small group with high traditional prestige, who are maintaining a low but fairly stable popularity without significant fluctuations: Haydn, Handel, Weber, and Gluck.

(3) Composers in the ascending phases of their life cycles:
  (a) Apparently at or near their peak: Strauss, Sibelius, Franck, Stravinsky, Debussy, Rachmaninoff and Shostakovitch.
  (b) Recent composers: Mahler, Prokofieff, Schoenberg, Copland, Vaughan Williams, Hindemith, Milhaud, Bartok, and Walton.
(4) Composers who once enjoyed great vogue but whose life cycles have long been in the descending phase: Schumann, Schubert, Berlioz, Liszt, Mendelssohn, and Rubinstein.
(5) Composers who display a full life cycle in various stages of completion: Dvořák, Saint-Saëns, Smetana, Grieg, Goldmark, and MacDowell; Rimsky-Korsakoff, Elgar, d'Indy, Glazounoff, and Scriabin. Respighi, Bloch, Falla.
(6) Composers who were once quite prominent but are now totally forgotten: Spohr, Raff, Kalliwoda, Lindpaintner, Gade, and Hummel.

The Six Most Pre-eminent Composers

LUDWIG VAN BEETHOVEN   Beethoven has been the dominant figure in the history of orchestral music throughout the past and present century. Analysis of the repertoire solidly supports the prestige of his name, which has become synonymous with everything classic in music in the minds of both the connoisseur and the untutored layman. Although his music introduced novelties in form, instrumentation, and harmonic structure that startled some of the hearers who were accustomed to Mozart and Haydn, and shocked those patrons in France whose standards were measured in operatic terms, his world-wide eminence was never questioned even in his own lifetime. He is the clearest refutation of the cliché, commonly quoted in defense of modern trends, that "great" music requires a long apprenticeship on the part of the musical public before it can be appreciated. The Handel and Haydn Society of Boston, founded in 1815, placed with him an unfulfilled commission for an oratorio, and the London Philharmonic purchased directly from Beethoven himself several overtures and the Ninth Symphony. Britain, grown wealthy in its early industrial revolution, was then what America was soon to be: a country proud to adorn itself with the borrowed trappings of the aesthetically mature but less opulent continent, and to pay fabulously for it. Accordingly Beethoven, like Haydn, was invited to visit London to conduct his Ninth Symphony but was understandably prevented by his afflictions from realizing his ambition. In America there had been scattered performances of several Beethoven compositions since 1817,[1] and by 1842, only fifteen years after his death, the New York Philharmonic Society testified to his established fame by inaugurating its first series with what was then, as now, the world's most famous piece: Beethoven's Fifth. Today it is still a common practice to include all nine symphonies in the season's offerings.

This resplendent adulation, enduring for nearly 150 years, was never anticipated by Beethoven himself, though it could hardly be said that his temperament was marked by modesty or diffidence. In textbook homage, perhaps Bach exceeds him, but for actual performance popularity, the case of Beethoven is unique in its duration, volume, and general aesthetic luster. His career is not easily explained short of the eulogistic but inarticulate explanation that he simply wrote "good music."

On the other hand, Beethoven's margin of popularity over his competitors in the American repertoire has been constantly dwindling. Beginning with the founding of the New York Philharmonic in 1842, the Beethoven trend line may be conveniently divided into two periods, with the division point about 1890. The first period is characterized by a decline from the Olympian peak of over thirty per cent of the repertoire in 1842–45 to a position of less than fifteen per cent; the second period displays a gentler recession during which he at times rubs shoulders democratically with the rest of the composer population.

The first high popularity and his subsequent sharp decline in American orchestras may be ascribed to several factors. In this early period there was only one orchestra, the New York Philharmonic, later to be joined by the New York Symphony (1878) and the Boston orchestra (1881). The New York orchestras usually performed only four to six pairs of concerts annually, and the rehearsal periods were extremely limited. Repertoires were consequently small and lacked the variety of today. Nor was this circumstance psychologically too inappropriate. Hearing less music in those days, audiences still had much to learn from Beethoven, who was a relative novelty to them, although to conductors he was the very cornerstone of musical culture. And as the prolific Beethoven had produced nine symphonies of greatly diversified design, as well as overtures and other miscellaneous works, it was possible to maintain the necessary variety in numerous performances. During this period Haydn and Mozart, who had been equally and even more fertile, but whose melodic creations seemed more obvious and lighthearted, lost ground to the more dramatic Beethoven.

Such splendid isolation could not, of course, endure. Musicians and audiences were ultimately satiated, new geniuses appeared whose works were pressing for recognition, and new conductors—Henschel, Nikisch, Seidl, Muck, Safonoff, Stokowski, and Koussevitzky—were imported who were disciples of new romantic cults. Thus the combined gains of Wagner, Brahms, and Tschaikowsky were practically equivalent to the losses of Beethoven during the last two decades of the century.

These changes were further accelerated by the new conditions of orchestral organization. Paced by Boston and philanthropist Higginson, who imparted to other communities their new ambitions, seasons were lengthened, concerts became more numerous, and financial guarantees permitted compensation for rehearsals which were usually considered unprofitable, and therefore shunned, by cooperative orchestras. All of these forces were reflected in more experimental repertoires. Wagner became a public issue, Dvořák and Tschaikowsky gained extraordinary popular acclaim, and Strauss and Brahms enthusiastic partisans. The new romanticists as well as the older Thomas developed a new musical conscience and proclaimed their duty to keep their audiences abreast of current trends.

Although Beethoven was by no means smothered in these trends, his symphonies began to play a different aesthetic role in the repertoire. The battle for Beethoven and "complete symphonies" (rather than excerpts) had been won and it was now the Wagner-Strauss axis which was fighting for a place in the sun. But tastes slowly acquired are never lightly relinquished. Beethoven was no longer on the frontier of taste, but actually popular with the larger public who began to enjoy the pleasant relaxation of the familiar. It was his adaptability to both roles—the difficult and the exalted as well as the familiar and accepted—that perpetuated his name among the leaders of the repertoire. Beethoven is still holding his own; only Brahms, whose music gained adherents after a still greater struggle, also meets the challenge of the dual role.

The stability of the Beethoven offerings in recent decades is attested by the fact that he suffered no losses during World War I, when the works of other Germans, including Wagner, were very much reduced in the repertoire; and that there was no significant increase at the time of the centenary of his death (1927). Naturally great publicity was given this anniversary. The journals rehearsed the pathetic love life of the lonely bachelor, published photographs of a few of his many domiciles, pictured his ear trumpet and the spoon from which he took medicine during his last illness. They reassessed his place in the history of music, and exhumed his forgotten overtures and played practically all his compositions except the *Battle Symphony*, which had been ironically among his most popular numbers during his lifetime. Most orchestras, however, compensated for this orgy of Beethoveniana by sharply reducing their offerings the following season, thereby leaving the long-run trend unaffected.

During the war against fascism, the prestige of the familiar Third and Fifth of the liberty-loving Beethoven were hailed as the very apotheosis of freedom. Especially the Fifth, whose terse theme duplicated the rhythm of the Morse code letter "V," was frequently played to revitalize our faith in victory, and subsequently to celebrate its achievement.

The Fifth Symphony has for a century been conventionally accepted as the most famous symphonic composition ever written. It is compact in structure, displays a dash of sentiment in the second movement to alleviate the abrupt and strident opening, achieves a triumphal, dramatic, almost demagogic climax, and is of average length—all of which contribute to the explanation of its pre-eminence. Its nearest competitors are the Seventh and the Third. The sharp rise in national popularity of the Fifth after the beginning of the century is the result of its use by the conductors of the younger orchestras in converting the newer audiences to the enjoyment of their symphonic offerings.

The decline of the Ninth, from fourth place to a poor last place in the course of seventy years, is undoubtedly owing to the decline of choral music itself. In the earlier days most cities boasted flourishing amateur choral organizations, which eagerly collaborated with instrumental groups. But such organizations have almost disappeared. It is possible, also, that the Ninth Symphony, glorified by Schumann and Wagner, has lost some of its glamour for us, not only because of certain aesthetic misgivings, but also because it must share the sparse program time allotted to choral music with other works of interest and merit.

The various orchestras manifest different degrees of allegiance to Beethoven. Chance alone accounts for some of the minor differences. Temporary major variations in conductor and audience tastes are not however without significance. Verbrugghen was known for his partiality to Beethoven; W. Damrosch, Mahler, and others instituted Beethoven cycles. But no conductor of recent years has deviated so far from the general trend as did the conservative Toscanini during his tenure with the New York Philharmonic, where he offered Beethoven in twice the volume of the national average.

Although Beethoven's prime position is quite independent of a few such passionate enthusiasts, it has not remained unchallenged either by the inexorable rise of Brahms—the composer of the "Tenth" symphony—or by the occasional fanatic such as Safonoff with his Tschaikowsky, or the enterprising Thomas with his Wagner. At times Beethoven has even been conspicuously avoided. Chicago under Stock pursued other tastes, and Stransky, intent on balancing the budget, tickled the popular palate by nudging Beethoven just a little to one side to allow more room for Liszt, Wagner, Dvořák, and other more colorful favorites. At various times, and in some cities, Beethoven has consequently fallen below the general average of ten per cent of the repertoire and been topped by Wagner, Tschaikowsky, and Brahms for short intervals.

JOHANNES BRAHMS   The austere and often ponderous Brahms has been gradually inching his way into favor, and is today the only composer who is in a position to dispute the primacy of Beethoven. Catering to the more literate and thoughtful, Brahms' First has been carried on the crest of the sophisticated taste to the

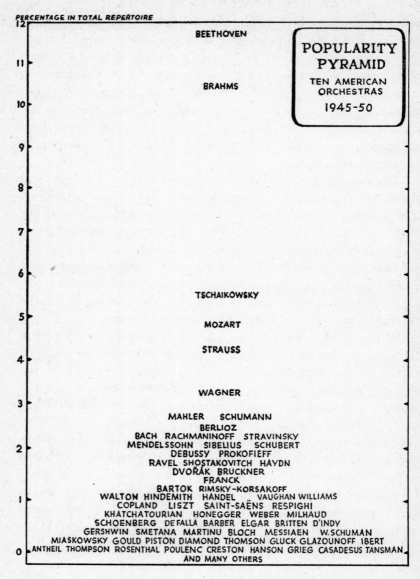

PERCENTAGE IN TOTAL REPERTOIRE

POPULARITY
PYRAMID
TEN AMERICAN
ORCHESTRAS
1945-50

BEETHOVEN

BRAHMS

TSCHAIKOWSKY

MOZART

STRAUSS

WAGNER

MAHLER   SCHUMANN
BERLIOZ
BACH RACHMANINOFF STRAVINSKY
MENDELSSOHN SIBELIUS SCHUBERT
DEBUSSY PROKOFIEFF
RAVEL SHOSTAKOVITCH HAYDN
DVOŘÁK BRUCKNER
FRANCK
BARTOK RIMSKY-KORSAKOFF
WALTON HINDEMITH HANDEL   VAUGHAN WILLIAMS
COPLAND LISZT SAINT-SAËNS RESPIGHI
KHATCHATOURIAN HONEGGER WEBER MILHAUD
SCHOENBERG DE FALLA BARBER ELGAR BRITTEN D'INDY
GERSHWIN SMETANA MARTINU BLOCH MESSIAEN W.SCHUMAN
MIASKOWSKY GOULD PISTON DIAMOND THOMSON GLUCK GLAZOUNOFF IBERT
ANTHEIL THOMPSON ROSENTHAL POULENC CRESTON HANSON GRIEG CASADESUS TANSMAN
AND MANY OTHERS

About forty per cent of the repertoire of the American orchestras is devoted to the top half-dozen composers, and about seventy per cent of the repertoire is built on the compositions of the twenty-three composers from Beethoven to Franck. The remaining thirty per cent is divided among several hundred composers.

188

kind of popular acclaim accorded formerly only to the symphonies of Beethoven. At least for the American audience, it vindicates, decades after it was made, the famous quip of Bülow who had dubbed it the "Tenth."

Brahms' ascent has been slow and his acceptance tentative. Heralded as the exponent of the classic tradition, he ran counter to the more sensational trends of the Berlioz-Liszt-Wagner-Strauss circle, whose audacious instrumentation, garish harmonies, and dynamic rhythms implemented the anecdotal and literary titles of their dramatic masterpieces. Their more extrovert qualities catapulted them over and beyond the sedate, contemplative, and unadorned Brahms, whose bag of symphonic tricks seemed to be limited to the variegated patterns of syncopation, his asymmetrical and polyrhythmical forms, his widely spread broken chords, his frequently interrupted melodic lines, and his chronic evasion of the obvious progression—traits which are responsible for the sense of elusiveness which many auditors still experience when listening to his symphonic works.

The violent personal controversy churned up among the followers of Brahms and Wagner in Germany did not touch America. For America was geographically remote and not bound by the academic and cultural traditions that gripped the European partisans. The German-American musicians who dominated the American scene had left their academic biases at home, or had never heard of them in the first place. Consequently both Brahms and Wagner were welcomed with equal enthusiasm without the rival emotional overtones that often characterized their reception in Berlin, Leipzig, and Vienna.

Brahms' American orchestral debut, with the Serenade No. 2, was made with the New York Philharmonic, February 1, 1862, Carl Bergmann, conductor. All readers of program notes will also recall the famous clash in 1877 between the elder Damrosch, victorious by one week, and Theodore Thomas, in their race to perform the première of Brahms' First in the United States. But the most potent initial force in giving Brahms an early major position in our repertoire was Georg Henschel, the first Boston conductor, who was his personal friend, and who had frequently sung to the accompaniment of the composer himself. In spite of the hostility of some critics toward his prosy compositions, the Boston conductors, Gericke, Nikisch, and Paur, continued to give Brahms about eight to ten per cent of the repertoire, certainly a very high percentage for any single composer. A diet so laden with what must have seemed to the audience like potatoes without salt—nourishing enough but tasteless—would in retrospect legitimize its protests against the conductors who unwisely served so unbalanced a ration.

It is amazing to observe in contemporary records the small spread in the relative popularity of the four symphonies. The First, Second, and Fourth cluster together rather closely and each represents during the ten-year period 1940–50 roughly about sixteen per cent of the total Brahms repertoire. The Third Symphony, the Haydn *Variations*, and the *Academic Festival* Overture follow in that order. The increasing prominence of the two piano concertos is at the expense of the diminishing attractiveness of the old favorites, especially those of Grieg, Rubinstein, and Saint-Saëns. The smaller numbers, the Serenades and Hungarian Dances, have practically disappeared from the serious repertoire.

What sustains Brahms in his competition with Beethoven is the almost uniform strength of four long symphonies, while Beethoven over the decades actually can offer only four or five of comparable popularity: the Third, Fifth, Seventh, and Eighth. The piano concertos compete very well with the Fourth and Fifth of Beethoven, while the single violin concerto is among the leaders.

It is hardly evident that both composers are being pressed to maintain their historical advantage against the collective assault of the "moderns." It is said that the younger members of the audience have reached a stage of surfeit with the thrice familiar Brahms classics. Eric Blom, prominent British critic, suggested that "it is almost as old-fashioned to enjoy Brahms as to be thrilled by a valentine." [2] Although that sentiment is by no means absent in the United States, there are evidently many "old-fashioned" people in our audiences.

RICHARD WAGNER In 1891 Mark Twain, who had joined the throng of American intellectuals at the Bayreuth Festival, reported in the New York *Sun* that in his humble opinion, the Wagner operas would be fine music if the singing could be left out.[3]

This facetious quip actually did epitomize the judgment of many a competent musical critic, and was pointedly prophetic of the destiny of many of Wagner's synthetic creations. Although Wagner entertained the theory that instrumental (absolute) music had exhausted its intrinsic potentialities, and that it could further realize itself only in an alliance with the other arts, the irony of fate would have it that Wagner has gained his most widespread prestige with symphonic excerpts from his operas with the "singing left out." His music thereby outlasted and contradicted the very theories which allegedly formed it!

Ever since Liszt declared that it was not necessary to know the drama to appreciate the music of Tannhäuser, there have been many critics who have maintained by one argument or another, that Wagner remains essentially a symphonic composer with the drama and vocal elements optional or even superfluous. In contradistinction to the Italian opera, which relegated the orchestra to a rhythmic accompaniment, a kind of tonal backdrop against which the vocal line was conspicuously featured, the Wagnerian music-drama elevated the orchestra to a status coordinate with the drama. Wagner took his technical cues from orchestral composers and strengthened the instrumental resources by following the most advanced models of Berlioz and Liszt in the chromatic melodic line, idiomatically developing each instrument to virtuoso proportions, featuring the brasses, and introducing polyphonic complexity.

Small wonder, then, that the orchestral "accompaniment" was to traditional ears a loud and noisy intrusion rather than a reinforcement of the vocal action; and that the "endless melody," which was preoccupied in furthering the dramatic action, was not recognized as a melody at all, and therefore easily dispensed with by the enriched orchestra. Like a symphonic poem, it was found that the orchestral "accompaniment" could stand alone as an autonomous composition; so that in time it constituted a major element in every repertoire of the symphony orchestras. It is true that, in opera performance, the Wagnerian orchestra was hidden under cover of the stage where it was less likely to obtrude and overpower in volume and interest. But this does not in any way weaken the aesthetic justification, once its symphonic virtues had been discovered, for lifting it from the pit and granting it a solo position on the stage commensurable with its symphonic content. The dramatic and vocal personnel of the musical drama, like the victims of the well-known Lord High Executioner, "never will be missed."

But operatic enthusiasts will flatly dispute the above symphonically biased assertions. Among these protestants would be included Wagner himself, who repeatedly refused permission to fragment his works. "In this he is right," says his disciple, Bülow, in a letter to Theodore Thomas, "for what is written for the stage, and in Germany is performed there, the composer does not wish to find its way to the concert Hall." [4] But even the unbending Wagner could make profitable compromises. He himself conducted orchestral excerpts in concert form in Berlin, Vienna, and other centers when financial necessity dictated and other circumstances made it prudent to do so. When Metropolitan conductor Anton Seidl found that the busy American daily schedule did not permit the staging of his operas in the uncut version, he unhesitatingly pruned them. While still in Germany, Seidl had explained the necessity of this procedure to the composer who, in an exchange of telegrams, gave his pointed assent in the laconic order *"Schiessen Sie los!"* [5]

The first performance of Wagner by the orchestras here under review occurred April 21, 1855, when the New York Philharmonic, under the direction of Carl Bergmann, presented the Overture to *Tannhäuser*. This progressive conductor, who had immigrated to the United States in 1850, joined the Germania orchestra as cellist, and later became its leader, had already offered a taste of Wagner to an American audience. In 1852 the Germania orchestra had performed the *Finale* from *Tannhäuser* in Boston, which the critic for *Dwight's Journal* (December 4, 1852) described as an "agreeable disappointment; it was less strange than we had been led to believe." In December, 1853, the same orchestra presented a "Wagner Night" in Boston "to gratify the public curiosity about Wagner."

With such devoted disciples as Bergmann and Thomas in America, Wagner at once became a fixture in the American repertoire. From the first concert he conducted in 1862, when he gave the

American première of the Overture to the *Flying Dutchman*, throughout his career on his famous "highway," Thomas made Wagner popular. As early as 1872 he scheduled a "Wagner Night" at the Central Park Garden Concerts, and the same evening launched the New York *Wagner-Verein,* which was committed to the promulgation of the cult and the construction of the Bayreuth Theatre.

The first real vogue for Wagner appeared in the early nineties when, amid an unprecedented controversy in both this country and Germany, he forged ahead to claim an average of ten per cent of the repertoire. Of the four orchestras existing at that time (the New York Philharmonic, the New York Symphony, Boston, and Chicago), the New York Symphony under Damrosch and the Chicago orchestra under Thomas were primarily responsible for his vogue. Wagner remained at this extraordinarily high level of popularity for several decades, in part because of the practice of feature concerts of individual composers, in part because of an occasional opera in concert form; and because Wagner's music was available to vocal soloists with orchestral "accompaniment."

With the upsurge of interest in Tschaikowsky and Brahms, the volume of Wagner was already shrinking before the patriotic onslaughts of World War I forced him into partial retirement. Although he returned when the stage was again safe for him, he never fully recovered. The long-time trend has been unmistakably downward (now at about three per cent) toward a gradual *"Wagner-dämmerung."* Such is the fickleness of taste that the "music of the future" sooner or later becomes the music of the past. Even so, the actual frequency in appearance of his name does not differ essentially from some who outrank him. In playing time devoted to him, his excerpts are usually shorter than the thirty-to-forty-minute symphonies of Brahms and Beethoven, which require an allotment of at least one-third of a ninety-minute program.

Although the trends are fairly uniform in all orchestras, fluctuations do of course appear and may be attributed to both personal and social factors. One of the most drastic of these forces was the first World War, which swept the Metropolitan Opera stage entirely clear of Wagner music-dramas and reduced the Wagnerian cascade to a mere trickle in the symphony programs. Although

Wagner was not then living, he was nevertheless the target of anti-German sentiment. The intensity of this totalitarian attitude toward the prosecution of the war differed among the cities. It affected least of all the New York Philharmonic under Stransky, an Austrian-Czech, who was periodically free from political suspicion and continued to cultivate a repertoire that would bring tangible returns at the box office. These benefits seemed not to have been endangered by orchestral excerpts from *Parsifal, Tannhäuser, Lohengrin,* and *Die Walküre* on the last program of the season 1917–18 and the *Bacchanale* from *Tannhäuser* on the program of December 15, 1918, approximately one month after the Armistice. Whatever other factors might have been operating, this is at least not inconsistent with the general policy, announced by some conductors, that only the music of living Germans (in effect the music of Richard Strauss) would be eliminated during the war period.

Of all the cities, Boston has remained most aloof from the Wagner cult, being consistently in the lowest rank throughout the history of the orchestras. On the other hand, Stokowski reveled in the grandiloquent phrases of the German postromanticist and pieced together what was perhaps the most comprehensive Wagner repertoire in America. The non-Teutonic Rodzinski, Golschmann, Monteux, Mitropoulos and Toscanini, like Koussevitzky, have paid only token respect to the music-dramatist, although Toscanini, like Muck, had gained distinction and acclaim for his direction of Wagner's music-dramas. This is not to imply that their non-Germanic cultural heritage alone precludes the cultivation of the German repertoire, but rather that most of these conductors appeared on the scene after the Wagner fever had waned, when the primitive excitement of controversy had spent itself, and a certain aesthetic satiety had already set in. After all, there were other causes to be espoused, among the French and Russian composers, which relegated Wagner to the category of a solved problem. He was still listened to with genuine satisfaction but did not enjoy the extra patronage which has its source in unsatisfied intellectual curiosity.

Of all the orchestral works of Wagner, the Overture to *Tannhäuser* was one of the earliest and the most frequently performed. It is the "William Tell" of the subscription repertoire. Almost every opera has supplied one or more excerpts that are now standard, and only a few of the earlier works, originally and specifically written for the orchestra, now survive. Prominent among them are, of course, the *Siegfried Idyll* (actually an adaptation of opera material) and the *Faust Overture*. But none has dropped as definitively to merited oblivion as has the *Centennial March*, written at the invitation of Theodore Thomas for the celebration of the birth of the American nation—the Philadelphia Exposition of 1876. This negotiation represents the most intimate point of contact of Richard Wagner with the American scene. A political revolutionary himself in his younger days, who had made inquiries into the possibilities of emigrating to the New World, he gave some grounds for hope that the occasion might inspire him. But never has the Muse failed so egregiously to heed the call of a suppliant artist. To some aestheticians it is undoubted confirmation of the theory that she cannot be bribed, not even with $5,000 cash in advance. For them it will go down in history as the most tragic example of the futility of commissioned music. For the disillusioned Thomas who had fought the valiant fight, who had hoped for another *Tannhäuser March*, or at least a *Kaisermarsch*, which would advance the causes of art and freedom, it was a bitter blow. The humiliating story has been repeatedly told.[6] Even the hero-worshipping Henry T. Finck, the New York critic, was pushed to the limit in explaining Wagner's failure and quotes the composer: "The best thing about that composition was the money I got for it." It is now, of course, a museum piece known only to the musical antiquarian. The American idolater may find consolation in the circumstance that the money was applied to ease the financially harassed artist and thus release his energy for greater things. Rose Fay Thomas states that it was applied on the debt of the Bayreuth Theatre, while Ernest Newman avers that it was used to finance a trip to Italy—all of which may reflect merely a problem of bookkeeping.

The second World War differed from the first in that none of its battles were fought on the concert stage. Although it propelled Wagner into a still more intense limelight, it had no appreciable effect on his already diminishing role in the American orchestra. We had, it appears, become accustomed to wars, were concentrating all our efforts on that disagreeable business, not allowing attitudes to run riot into sentimental bypaths. The recession in Wagner's popularity was therefore no greater than would normally be expected if the war had not occurred at all. That is not to say that Wagner was not again a subject of even more heated controversy. By some he was labeled the archvillain in German nationalism for supplying the artistic rationalization for the fantastic glorification of Teutonism that ultimately culminated in totalitarian Nazi ideology.[7] Wagner's granddaughter, Friedelind, now living in the United States, endeavored to clear him of this historical taint of the Nazi spirit.[8] But this issue cannot be arbitrated here.

PETER ILICH TSCHAIKOWSKY   In his essay on *Classicism* (1850) the literary critic Sainte-Beuve proclaimed an important psychological truth when he stated, *"Il n'est pas bon de paraître trop vite . . . classique à ses contemporains; on a grande chance alors de ne pas rester tel pour la posterité."* This observation applies to the fortunes of Tschaikowsky in the American orchestral repertoire. The tuneful symphonist, with his luscious harmonies and effortless progressions, found ready comprehension. Where Wagner aroused violent partisanship, and Brahms created puzzlement or apathy, Tschaikowsky kindled enthusiasm. In fact, decades ago, before a significant decline could have been noted, sophisticated critics doubted his sticking powers because enjoyment came too easily. He was the victim of critical slurs, and invidious comparisons: "Brahms is better than he sounds, and Tschaikowsky sounds better than he is." It is quite "the thing" to snub a composer whose music is enjoyed by the multitude.

Since the spring of 1876, when Tschaikowsky was introduced by Carl Bergmann in orchestral form with the Fantasie-Overture, *Romeo and Juliet,* his rise was brilliantly dramatic. Within twenty years he outpaced the pedestrian Brahms and was competing with Wagner, having garnered eight per cent of the composite repertoire. At times, this essentially European composer, with an exotic admixture of Russian flavors, outstripped both Wagner and Beethoven. He appealed to the general audience rather than to the connoisseur, and gave the conductors an outlet for their most romantic effusions.

Safonoff, of the New York Philharmonic, won his job on the strength of his exciting performance of the *Pathétique*. During his several years of tenure he filled an unprecedented twenty per cent of the repertoire with the works of his compatriot. Walter Damrosch and Stransky in New York; Stokowski in Cincinnati (fifteen per cent) and in Philadelphia (ten per cent, 1920–25); and Fiedler in Boston were also conspicuous among their colleagues at one time or another for their cultivation of the romantic Russian.

The composer's triumphant visit to the United States in 1891 was naturally both cause and result of his high popularity. At the invitation of Walter Damrosch, who presided over the dedicatory concerts of Carnegie Hall, he appeared as guest conductor on that solemn occasion, as well as for concerts in Philadelphia, Washington, and Baltimore.

The New York Symphony, the New York Philharmonic, and the St. Louis Symphony under Zach contributed palpably toward the building up of the peak of interest. After that time, his decline was rapid, reaching its lowest ebb (about five per cent) in the 1930's. From this low but still respectable position, however, a definite recovery seems to have been shaping, partly stimulated, no doubt, by the centenary of his birth (1940). Whether this revival—which has already given way to a slight recession—is permanent will depend on such factors as the urgency to cater to popular taste, a possible reversal of the derogatory attitude of the sophisticates toward an unashamed enjoyment of the lyrical genius, the fate of the piano and violin concertos among the soloists, together with, as always, the competition of other available music, old and modern.

Although a prolific composer, Tschaikowsky's representation has shaken down to a rather stable remnant which will probably remain, in spite of Sainte-Beuve, *"classique pour la posterité."* It includes the following items: Symphonies Five, Six, and Four, roughly in that order according to performances in recent years, the (First) piano and violin concertos, and the concert overtures *Romeo and Juliet* and *Francesca da Rimini.*

His well-worn Piano Concerto in B-flat Minor is probably the only standard concerto to have had its world première in America. Dedicated to Bülow, after the composer's famous altercation with Nicholas Rubinstein, the copy reached him shortly before the pianist was to leave on his American concert tour. It was first presented in Boston, October 25, 1875. Critical opinion was divided, although the *Finale* was encored. It has for years been the most popular of all piano concertos, in the "popular" sense of the term, having been abundantly recorded, and its principal theme cribbed for both song and dance. In fact, in symphonic circles, this concerto, with the Sixth Symphony, has achieved the status of a "warhorse."

Many other items are given periodic performances, but the works with which he gained his early successes—*Marche Slave, Overture 1812, Nutcracker Suite*—have slipped out of the subscription concerts to a more popular level.

WOLFGANG AMADEUS MOZART In 1800 Mozart, Handel, and Haydn were considered the ultimate in musical evolution. Their works were abundantly represented, together with such now forgotten names as Pleyel and Gyrowetz, on early American programs.

It was the "tutti frutti" nature of the conventional programs of the day, made up of music of all genres, which contributed much to the attainment of Mozart's exalted position. This circumstance tends to inflate the volume of the versatile composer, whose operatic arias, orchestral numbers, string quartets, and small ensembles magnified his "symphonic" importance. Since, however, Haydn, Cherubini, Rossini, Beethoven, as well as the many minor composers, were similarly prolific, his versatility alone cannot account for his great popularity in these early decades.

A glance at the London Philharmonic,[9] founded in 1813, will permit us to reconstruct the era of Mozart's pre-eminence much more confidently than an analysis of American orchestras which had no continuous series of programs at that time. Occupying practically twenty-five per cent of the London repertoire, he contributed more than any other single composer during the period of the infancy of that orchestra. However, neither in his symphonic works, nor in the operatic arias, could Mozart withstand the competition of the more romantic Beethoven and the more brilliant Rossini. By 1830 his star had faded to mingle with those of second magnitude.

Thus, by the time the New York Philharmonic was founded, the Mozart tradition had partially subsided. Against Rossini and Beethoven, he was beginning to sound obvious, and even a little trivial. Later, when the romantic influence had run its course, the delicate, unpretentious beauties of his music would come as a welcome relief to the thicker orchestration of Wagner and the labyrinthian polytonality of the later Strauss. Orchestral conductors, profiting by the increased technical proficiency of the instrumentalists, vied with one another in etching the clear, crisp Mozartian passages, which to Emperor Joseph II contained "too many notes," but by this time were generally described as "made up of not many notes, but just the right ones." Still later, Sir Thomas Beecham, Bruno Walter, and Richard Strauss were to make a specialty of Mozart.

As might be expected, time has dealt heavily with the six hundred miscellaneous compositions of this fantastically fertile genius. Never writing "for the future," Mozart himself would have been surprised to find that any of his compositions survived at all 150 years after they were so unostentatiously dashed off. In his own day he was known primarily as a pianist, improviser, and as a composer of operas. His instrumental works were almost exclusively "occasional" works, written not in spontaneous self-expression but for the hard-pressed, urgent, and definite purpose of pleasing his public, in the hope—too often pathetically unrealized—of a fitting financial testimonial. Shadowed by the glamour of Beethoven, Mozart nevertheless retained many admirers throughout the nineteenth century: E. T. A. Hoffmann, the conservative Spohr, Brahms, Tschaikowsky, and others revered his later symphonies. At the close of the century Mozart enjoyed a kind of mild renaissance, which prompted the usual archeological diggings, with the result that during recent decades many of the earlier symphonies are appearing for the first time in America.

Previous to 1900, the Mozart repertoire in the American orchestras was divided principally between the large number of operatic arias and overtures, and the late symphonies in G Minor, C Major, E-flat Major, and D Major (*Haffner*). The diminishing popularity of vocal numbers and the corresponding strengthening of the orchestra led to their gradual abandonment. In their place, however, were added violin and piano concertos, which had hitherto enjoyed only sparse performances, the serenades, and many newly unearthed symphonies—all of which produced a gentle but unmistakable rise in the Mozart slope.

Of the forty-one symphonies, the G Minor (K 550) has been the most frequently played throughout the history of the orchestras, while the C Major (*Jupiter*, K 551) runs a safe second. Several others receive more than periodic performances: K 385 in D Major (*Haffner*), K 543 in E-flat Major, K 338 in C Major, K 504 in D Major (*Prague*). In addition, the New York Philharmonic and the Boston orchestras have played K 201, K 425, K 200, and K 183, making a total of about a dozen symphonies that may be said to be in the current American repertoires. In terms of cold statistics, this may not seem to be a very impressive survival rate. However, if one considers that about half of the forty-one symphonies were immature and casual compositions, certainly not worthy of symphonic designation in the modern sense of that term, their durability is astounding. Add to these the overtures to half-a-dozen of the operas, a few serenades such as *Eine Kleine Nachtmusik*, several piano and violin concertos, and a host of minor numbers that are likely to turn up almost any time, and the result is a composite six per cent of the current repertoire, which shows no signs of declining, at present outpointing even Wagner and Bach.

JOHANN SEBASTIAN BACH   There is often a wide discrepancy between the academic prestige of a composer and his actual cultivation by conductors and performers. Mozart, Haydn, and Bach are among the most revered names in music, but their representation in actual performances is often relatively meager. Just as there are books that everybody talks about but nobody reads, there are composers that everybody reads about but few listen to. Allowing for the usual exaggeration in such a quip, fame is still a blend of many factors, some of them so purely adventitious that they have little relation to a composer's place in the repertoire.

Bach is, of course, supreme in the organ repertoire, and his clavier works possess incomparable aesthetic and pedagogical virtues. But he is a relatively unknown figure—grand but aloof—to the lay audi-

ence. He may be compared to a retired executive, scholar, or statesman whose past services are memorialized on every possible occasion, but who could not be expected to participate very actively in
current affairs. Johann Sebastian Bach is the "composer emeritus"
who is today best known by transcriptions and by his historical
influence.

To a musicologist steeped in textbook lore, and to many a practical musician, this judgment of Bach as an antiquarian will seem
harsh. To some aestheticians with a philosophical bent, the music of
Bach epitomizes the Eternal Pattern, an ill-defined concept, but one
that nevertheless affords a high degree of satisfaction. For a century
after his death he commanded only esoteric appreciation, but in
more recent decades he has had a slightly more substantial following.

This Bach renaissance is conventionally traced to the revival of
the *St. Matthew Passion*, which was performed under the direction
of the twenty-year-old Mendelssohn at the Singakademie in Berlin
in March, 1829, for the first time since the death of Bach and exactly
a century after its première in the St. Thomaskirche in Leipzig. According to Eduard Devrient, who sang *Christus* on that memorable
occasion the "new cult of Bach dates from March 11, 1829." [10]

Now, the sprouting of new aesthetic tastes does not differ in principle from the successful cultivation of fine vegetables. Remote as
they may seem, they have this in common, that neither can be conjured forth by the enthusiasm of the cultivator alone. Certain pre-
conditions must obtain before the fervor of the gardener can
translate the picture on the seed package into the luscious salad
bowl. There are no gaps in history. Bach's popularity did not leap
the century but its growth may be retraced in its successive steps.

Although the performance of the *St. Matthew Passion* delivered
a fresh impulse to the comprehension of Bach, he had really never
dropped from sight. The first issue of the *Allgemeine Musikalische
Zeitung* (1798), published by Breitkopf and Haertel, carried a copper engraving of his portrait. In 1800, in the same influential journal,
Bach was likened to Michelangelo and Newton, while Mozart, dead
seven years, was analogously coupled with Raphael. In 1803 he was
labeled "the greatest contrapuntist in the world"—a judgment not
noticeably at variance with that of the twentieth century. There was

naturally some disagreement: in a review of some of his works, a critic declared that they "contradict the frequently expressed opinion of the unlearned that Bach was the greatest mathematical music master, but nothing more." As early as 1804—five years before Mendelssohn was born—we read in the same journal:

In the musical world now is the time of the awakening of the Dead; and fortunately this resurrection includes only the Just. Seb. Bach, Handel and Emanuel Bach . . . and other great men of the past only ten years ago considered among the departed, of whom one spoke reverentially, but whose association we no longer enjoyed.

Beethoven, born only twenty years after Bach's death, had been thoroughly schooled in *The Well Tempered Clavier* which he included in his repertoire for the Viennese nobility, and he hailed with delight the (premature) announcement of a project to publish Bach complete. Mozart wrote to his father in 1782 that he was making a collection of the Bach fugues. Since commercial publication was not so general as it is today, the memory of Bach had been kept green by his pupils, who were scattered throughout Germany, and by his sons, who used the library which they had inherited. In April, 1828, one year before revival of the *Passion*, Spontini offered the Berlin première of the *Credo* from the B Minor Mass at one of his symphonic soirées. The Thomaskirche performed some of his motets and cantatas; and manuscript copies—a not unusual form of circulation in that day—of his works enjoyed a surprising circulation between the time of his death and the "renaissance" of 1829.[11] Indeed, a Leipzig critic, his civic pride apparently piqued at the publicity the Berlin papers gave the revival of the *Passion*, expressed his amazement at the fuss stirred up in that northern city, for "Bach had never been forgotten in Leipzig."

This is not to say that he had gained great popularity. Musical style had undergone great changes. Bach had expressed himself in a contrapuntal idiom that was dying, while the melodic style of writing had been gaining adherents even during his own lifetime. Sociological factors conspired to accelerate this tendency. The public theater was replacing the church as a source of musical delight, and the rising bourgeoisie, with its light secular tastes, turned away from complicated polyphony to rococo relaxation. Protestant religious services were themselves undergoing important alterations, rendering the older forms obsolete. Bach had simply experienced the personal tragedy of outliving the style that he himself had brought to perfection.

If Bach lost whatever popular audience he had ever had, he gained and retained professional adherents. In that sense Bach became the musician's musician. A new concept of the function of music, unknown to Mozart and to the rococo period, was being born. Rochlitz (a former pupil in the Thomasschule) the progressive editor of the *Allgemeine Musikalische Zeitung*, accordingly declared in 1802 that, though Bach was not popular, he was "elevating." In keeping with Schiller's system of aesthetics, which he apparently embraced, he declared (1803) that *"Kunst ist freilich ein Spiel, aber nicht Spielerei."* (Art is indeed a form of play, but not trivial).

Mendelssohn and Devrient undertook the performance of the *Passion* in an effort to enlarge the public following for the "half-forgotten" Bach—a project in which they were indispensably aided by a constellation of social and political forces. For the Bach revival in Protestant Prussia was as much a religious and political revival as a musical renaissance. Historical research, always an essential concomitant to a wave of nationalism such as inundated the Germany of that day, had dug up the German past and featured Bach as one of whom "all Germans should be proud." [12] Protestant zeal, which was shared by the Lutheran Mendelssohn, had adopted Bach as the father of its musical heritage. An editorial in the *Berliner Allgemeine Musik Zeitung* (1830) hailed the *Passion* as a counterirritant to irreligion. It is difficult for an American, who listens to the oratorios and operas essentially as concert performances, to realize the textual interest of the European audience. Berlioz was similarly astounded at a performance of the *Passion* in Berlin (1841):

One must witness the respect, the attention, and the piety with which a German audience listens to such a composition, to believe it. Everyone follows the words of the text with his eyes; not a movement in the house, not a murmur of approbation or blame, not the least applause; they are listening to a sermon, hearing the gospel sung; they are attending not a concert, but a divine service. [13]

Thus Bach was *not* French, *not* Catholic, but German and Protestant!

There were still other compelling factors. The growing popularity of the piano in the homes of the rising middle class naturally enhanced the significance of the music which served as such exemplary pedagogical training for that instrument. The increasing musical sophistication of musicians and public found an intellectual challenge in the complexities of the polyphonic idiom, so that a Bach fugue now became the apex of aesthetic achievement. Under the influence of literary musicians like Schumann, and the Idealist philosophers like Hegel, there was finally established an aesthetic ideology that elevated music into the moral sphere, designated it as Truth Incarnate, which relieved it of the eighteenth-century requirements of entertainment and relaxation. It became a member of the triune epiphenomenon comprising Religion, Philosophy, and Art. It was on this philosophical tide that Bach and Beethoven were lifted into the secure harbor of prestige and deification.

Even so, the present-day glorification of Bach has been slow to mature. Friedrich Zelter, who was the director of the Berlin Singakademie in 1829—a "pedagogical grandson" through Kirnberger, of Bach himself—and who had originally infected Mendelssohn with his own adoration for the contrapuntist, had been very doubtful of the wisdom of offering the *Passion* to the general public. Devrient relates that

Felix and I had frequent meetings to consider how the work could be shortened. . . . It necessarily contained much that belonged to a former age. . . . Most of the arias would have to be omitted . . . the part of the Evangelist would have to be shorn of all that was not essential to the recital of the Passion . . .

That some American critics also should consider the music of Bach partially antiquated is evidenced by the comment of such a Bach "idolater" as the Boston annotator William Apthorp, who complained in 1894 that Paur, the Boston conductor, had omitted only one of the seven movements of the Bach B Minor Suite:

With all that is great and immortal in the master's works, there are also some things in them which Time has thrown into obsolescence, and even the sincerest Bach lover . . . ought to wish these things wholly obsolete and buried for good and all.[14]

At that time historical scholarship had not yet begotten the fundamentalism of the purist. On the other hand, much more recently, the completely evolved purist appears in Bruno Walter, who does public penance for having violated the integrity of these two-hundred-year-old works.

I hereby confess that I transgressed in Munich against the *St. Matthew Passion*. For ten years . . . I performed Bach's works with cuts. This was unjustifiable.[15]

An interested observer of this reversal in aesthetic judgments can only speculate on the next shift in enthusiasm that will emerge from the still greater erudition of subsequent decades and centuries.

During the period of obscurity it was Bach's vocal works (motets and cantatas) and some clavier works (*Inventions* and *Well-Tempered Clavier*) that were kept alive. His instrumental ensembles, which should have been of all his works the most easily absorbed by the new orchestral bodies of the nineteenth century, were the last to be revived. The first performance of Bach in modern orchestral version was that of the Suite in D (then still referred to as "Overture") given by the Gewandhaus orchestra February 15, 1838. Mendelssohn was, of course, the conductor. Bach made his orchestral debut in London with the same composition, under the same conductor, with the London Philharmonic on June 24, 1844.

It was not until March 6, 1869, forty years after the initial performance in Leipzig, that the New York Philharmonic introduced the classic master in orchestral dress—the same suite—to its New York audience, Carl Bergmann conducting. In the meantime Theodore Thomas had already achieved the distinction of the initial Bach orchestral performance in America, with the Esser arrangements of the Toccata in F (January 7, 1865), the Passacaglia (April 8, 1865), and the familiar D Major Suite (October 26, 1867). Thomas' personal espousal of the new movement antedates even these orchestral performances. The Chaconne was in his violin solo repertoire at least as early as 1858, and the Mason-Thomas chamber concerts included arrangements of Bach as staple items from their

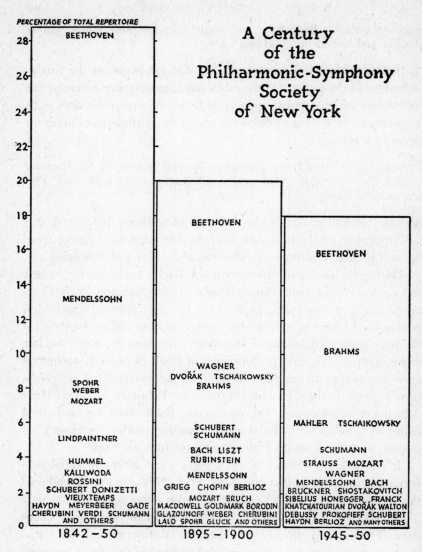

PERCENTAGE OF TOTAL REPERTOIRE

A Century
of the
Philharmonic-Symphony
Society
of New York

1842-50

- BEETHOVEN (28)
- MENDELSSOHN (13)
- SPOHR
- WEBER
- MOZART
- LINDPAINTNER
- HUMMEL
- KALLIWODA
- ROSSINI
- SCHUBERT DONIZETTI
- VIEUXTEMPS
- HAYDN MEYERBEER GADE
- CHERUBINI VERDI SCHUMANN
- AND OTHERS

1895-1900

- BEETHOVEN
- WAGNER
- DVOŘÁK TSCHAIKOWSKY
- BRAHMS
- SCHUBERT
- SCHUMANN
- BACH LISZT
- RUBINSTEIN
- MENDELSSOHN
- GRIEG CHOPIN BERLIOZ
- MOZART BRUCH
- MACDOWELL GOLDMARK BORODIN
- GLAZOUNOFF WEBER CHERUBINI
- LALO SPOHR GLUCK AND OTHERS

1945-50

- BEETHOVEN
- BRAHMS
- MAHLER TSCHAIKOWSKY
- SCHUMANN
- STRAUSS MOZART
- WAGNER
- MENDELSSOHN BACH
- BRUCKNER SHOSTAKOVITCH
- SIBELIUS HONEGGER FRANCK
- KHATCHATOURIAN DVOŘÁK WALTON
- DEBUSSY PROKOFIEFF SCHUBERT
- HAYDN BERLIOZ AND MANY OTHERS

Although the London Philharmonic Society, founded in 1813, has a longer history, the New York Philharmonic repertoire comprises more concerts, with a consequently fuller repertoire. Note the decline of Beethoven in relative importance, the increase in number of composers in the longer seasons of later years, and the "forgotten" names of the early years.

first season, in 1855. The very first appearance of Bach in any form on the New York Philharmonic programs (December 20, 1862) was a Prelude and Fugue for piano (which was not to be considered incongruous with orchestral concerts for many years to come), performed by J. N. Pattison, who had acquired his musical training in Germany.

The tardy recognition of Bach's orchestral works lies in the circumstance, among others, that vocal organizations, like Zelter's Singakademie, were then more prevalent, had more prestige, and were much more maturely developed, than was the orchestra. Consequently, Bach was not yet "discovered" as an orchestral composer. Nor were his instrumental works adapted even to the instrumental ensembles which did exist. Orchestral color and instrumentation, as today conceived, were of course unstandardized in the early eighteenth century. Suites and concertos were usually custom-made for the available combinations of instruments, many of which, like the high valveless trumpet and the viola d'amore, are now obsolete. As a result all Bach's works had to be edited and arranged in terms of the modern idiom.

Today, clavier, organ, vocal and other works have all been transcribed freely for the modern orchestra by Bach enthusiasts, and constitute a substantial portion—probably seventy-five per cent —of the current Bach "orchestral" repertoire. Although some of these transcriptions have had rather wide currency, most of them have been prepared by the conductor, or by a member of the orchestra whose local reputation had contributed a personal touch to the vogue of that music. Such manipulation should not be a new experience for Bach works, for the great composer himself, according to the exigencies of the day, frequently reshuffled his own creations and, at times, appropriated the themes of others. Zelter transcribed some of the clavier works for string quartet and renovated others in order to eradicate from the German Bach the "French froth" and thereby lay bare the "true elegance" of the master.[16]

Although to many scholars transcriptions are a species of aesthetic sin, Bach has been transcribed—and, of course, edited—ever since he came to the notice of German conductors. In the early years of the American repertoire the conductors availed themselves of transcriptions made by German musicians, J. J. Abert, Heinrich Esser, Bachrich, Raff, and Hellmesberger. Gericke, Seidl, and Mottl, conducting in the United States for a period, and Theodore Thomas and George Bristow likewise adapted Bach for their own purposes. Today such well-known composers and conductors, representing all leading nations, as Bantock, Elgar, Respighi, Schoenberg, Pick-Mangiagalli, Siloti, Tansman, Honegger, Weiner, Mitropoulos, Barbirolli, Stock, Stokowski, Ormandy, Boessenroth (Minneapolis Orchestra) and Caillet (Philadelphia Orchestra), Goossens, Sir Henry Wood ("Paul Klenovsky") have made Bach available in modern tonal flavors, have expanded his repertoire and nourished the taste for his music.

Of all composers and conductors who have added their increment to the orchestral renaissance of the Leipzig cantor, none has been as enthusiastic and influential as Stokowski during his quarter-century with the Philadelphia orchestra. Stokowski had begun his musical career as an organist in London, continued it in the organ loft of the St. Bartholomew Church of New York, and has never relinquished his devotion to the master of organ composition. He has added about two score titles to the Bach heritage. This personal influence is evident in the gradual rise of the Bach volume to an unprecedented seven per cent during Stokowski's tenure in Philadelphia, and its precipitous decline after his departure. A romantic rather than a classicist in stylistic predilections, Stokowski has often been vehemently criticized for the vibrant sensuousness of his transcriptions and for his supposed infidelity to the classic reserve of the original subject.

This of course strikes at the very root of the philosophy of transcriptions and inevitably raises a controversy whenever the old masters are included in the repertoire. Historical erudition seems to predispose some scholars to a museum-like preservation of the original artifact. Such a musico-archeological exponent recreates as far as possible the tonal balance of the archaic instrumentation. Theodore Thomas aspired to do just that.[17] But to those who know how easily Handel and Bach transcribed the work of others, and who wish to incorporate old composers as living elements in contemporary musical life by profiting from the acoustical and aesthetic developments of the intervening period, some modernization would seem defensible. One may even be permitted to question the consistency of such critics. The *St. Matthew Passion* was originally designed for three-dozen performers, restricted instrumentation, and boy sopranos. Today it is staged with a hundred-piece orchestra and a well-trained adult mixed chorus of five-hundred vocalists. It is probable that this commonly accepted "transcription" violates the expectations of the original composer more than does the transference of a fugue from an organ, with its orchestral potentialities in its manifold registration, to the modern orchestra itself. Perhaps, after all, it is true that the Bach organ attains its ultimate realization in the Stokowski orchestra. Stokowski, like Zelter and Mendelssohn, "modernized" Bach; and all of them may be at least entitled to the claim that their arrangements were popular and successful. Without these transcriptions, the great Passacaglia, the Fantasia and Fugue in G Minor, and a dozen other significant works would be an absolutely closed book to a large block of sincere music lovers.

The composite trend line for Sebastian Bach—which includes the transcriptions—displays a continuous and almost uninterrupted rise from the very occasional appearances before 1875 in the New York Philharmonic to about 3.5 per cent of the national repertoire in 1930–35. After that, he receded to about 2.3 per cent in 1945–50. Although this trend is more or less parallel in all orchestras, Philadelphia and Chicago cultivated him most energetically. In Philadelphia Bach achieved a peak of seven per cent in 1930–35, a quantitative recognition otherwise reserved for Wagner and the symphonists Brahms and Tschaikowsky. In retrospect, a recession would seem inevitable with the passing of devotees of the stature of Stokowski and Stock. The celebration of the 250th anniversary of Bach's birth (1935) and the bicentennial of his death (1950) could halt only temporarily his decline to a good two per cent of the composite repertoire.

The compositions most frequently programmed are the Suites, No. 3 and 2, the *Brandenburg* Concerto No. 3, *Pastorale* from the *Christmas Oratorio*, a large miscellaneous collection of preludes and fugues, choral preludes, and of course, the *St. Matthew Passion*. His relatively short numbers are not the stuff to create volume repertoire in a symphony orchestra. A statistical measure which is based on playing time may therefore not do complete justice to the frequency of his appearance.

Composers with Low and Stable Trends

FRANZ JOSEPH HAYDN   Of all the standard composers in the present American repertoire, the names of Handel and Haydn appear earliest in the annals of the American orchestras. Of their contemporaries, Pleyel (Haydn's greatest rival), Arne, Gyrowetz, Stamitz, Gossec, Gretry, Vanhal, Kozeluh, to say nothing of the scores of contemporary composer-performers who occupied a large segment of the colonial programs—all have vanished. With Sebastian Bach (whose name, of course, does not appear in the eighteenth-century American programs), Handel and Haydn display a life span of longest duration.

In the eighteenth century, colonial music was, in the main, an offspring of English musical life. The names on the musical programs, like the names of cities and streets, were brought in the bag and baggage of immigrants, the great bulk of whom came from England. It is amazing how quickly these conditions were reflected in the taste of this country. The reverence for both Handel and Haydn, who ruled public taste in England at the close of that century, is further incorporated in the name of one of America's oldest choral societies, founded in Boston in 1815.

It was not English music that dominated the colonies, but rather English tastes. England was at that time a prosperous industrial and colonial empire, whose wealth attracted the continental musicians very much as does America's in the twentieth century. Like her cotton, tea, and fruits, most of her composers and her music were importations. Thus Haydn's pardonable urge for economic security overcame any disinclination to travel when he accepted Salomon's invitations. It is understandable, therefore, that the continental aesthetic as well as material produce arrived in America in English bottoms.

As in England, the Haydn symphonies, or "Grand Overtures" as they were sometimes called, constituted one of the pillars of the informal American repertoires which enjoyed a transient existence in the theatres, gardens, and salons of the Eastern colonial seaboard. Most of these symphonies, which appeared as early as 1782 in New York (during the British occupation), in 1786 in Philadelphia, and some years later in Boston and Charleston, are unidentified except in a few instances through their sobriquets: *La Chasse* (No. 73) and *La Reine* (No. 85). They are representative of the compositions that fostered Haydn's reputation throughout Europe and finally led to his triumphant appearances in England with the Salomon orchestra in 1791–92, 1794–95. In the forty-piece orchestra during Haydn's first visit was the German oboist, Gottlieb Graupner, who subsequently emigrated to America and settled permanently in Boston, where he was influential in introducing the later symphonies, especially the *Surprise* and *Military*.

Some fifty years later, when the New York Philharmonic society was organized, the star of Haydn had been dimmed somewhat by the brilliance of the works of Beethoven. While three of the Beethoven symphonies were performed during the first Philharmonic season of three concerts, Haydn had to await the third and ninth seasons for the first two symphonic offerings. This marks his approximate pace down to the present day, almost always maintaining a sure and predictable position, but never crowding the leaders.

More precisely, this trend shows a recession between 1875 and 1900, when most of the present orchestras were founded, but then takes a definite upward turn which continues to the present day. In 1926, the editor of *Musical America* could state that Haydn was "no longer a musical mummy," but had now again come to life.

This ascent, unambiguous but by no means dramatic, roughly coincides with the centennial of his death (1909); the observance of the bicentennial of his birth (1932); the launching of a project for republication of his "complete" works (never completed) by Breitkopf and Haertel (1907), which gave the symphonies a new, chronological numbering; and a growing archeological and scholarly interest in his life and works. As a result of this historical interest, nearly a dozen of his earlier symphonies have been performed for the first time in America.

No musician need, of course, be reminded that these symphonies of "Papa" Haydn are possessed of the utmost lucidity and elegance, that they manifest both zest and charm, and an integrity absolutely unmarred by any affectation, exaggeration, or bombast. In all these qualities, they speak directly to the twentieth-century era. To project these characteristics requires the most disciplined effort of the best symphonic ensembles. From the standpoint of program building and audience appeal, the Haydn works furnish scintillating relief from the congested orchestration of the late romantics, and melodic relaxation from the modern percussive styles.

The new Breitkopf and Haertel catalogue has set the number of "authentic" symphonies at 104, many of the earlier ones being, of course, in the modern sense "symphonic" by condescension only. Of the total, about thirty have been performed, and about ten of them may be said to be active in the repertoires here under review. The most frequently played is the G Major (No. 88), with No. 100 (*Military*), 101 (*Clock*), 102 and 104 attaining considerable vogue. Less frequent renditions are enjoyed by Nos. 92 (*Oxford*), 94 (*Surprise*), 95, 97, and 99. Among the almost two score symphonies with single appearances is found the short "Toy" symphony, not dignified by inclusion in the conventional numbering. This "symphony" was performed by the New York Philharmonic under Rodzinski, February, 1945, in celebration of the birth of his son—testimony to the whimsical miscellany of factors that may determine the ingredients of concert programs.

GEORGE FREDERICK HANDEL   For more than a century after his death Handel's prestige was limited to choral and religious music. Just as Beethoven and his satellites dominated the nineteenth century, so Handel, with Purcell, Corelli, and Pergolesi, swayed the taste of the eighteenth. His traditions dominated English musical life, and to a certain extent that of the continent, and pointedly influenced both Haydn and Mendelssohn in their oratorio creations.

His strictly instrumental compositions, especially the Concerti Grossi, could not compete with the "grand" symphonies of Haydn, Mozart, and Beethoven, which had rendered obsolete the preclassical, unstandardized orchestra. The exclusively orchestral music, occasionally demanded in concert programs of the day consisted of overtures to his oratorios. Then, as now, Handel's greatest fame rested on *Messiah* which was presented (incomplete, seventeen out of fifty-seven numbers) for the first time in America in New York in 1770 —one year before its première in Germany.

This choral orientation toward Handel still prevailed during the first decades of the New York Philharmonic, on whose programs Handel's name was represented exclusively by arias, until an archeological interest uncovered his forgotten works in the same manner as was occurring with his contemporary, Sebastian Bach. Although it was not until the present century that the instrumental works were played with frequency, isolated performances dot the repertoires since October 21, 1868 when Thomas played the "celebrated music composed by Handel in the year 1749 for the *Royal Fire-works* . . . from the original score . . . for the first time in this country" in Castle Garden on his "Handel Night." [18] The London Philharmonic played its first Handel instrumental selection in 1872 —an Oboe concerto. This was followed in 1874 by a Concerto Grosso (No. 11). But the Germans, who claimed Handel as their own and restored the *umlaut*, which Handel had discarded, were perhaps more aggressive in this Handel renaissance than were the English, who had really never forgotten him.

From Germany were brought his various works in arrangements by Bachrich, Mottl, Kogler, and Franz Wüllner, and these were played frequently in Boston and Chicago; later came the arrangements of Harty, Beecham, Sir Henry Wood, and Elgar. Of all these, German or British, the arrangement of the *Water Music* by Hamilton Harty, late conductor of the Hallé orchestra of Manchester, is the best known. As in the case of Haydn, new compositions are being uncovered. In addition to the *Water Music*, the Concerti Grossi Nos. 5, 6, 10, and 12 are frequently performed, and two score other compositions occasionally. The *Messiah* is today infrequently included in orchestral series, but the abrupt rise in the Handel composite curve in the beginning of this century is to be explained by its annual performance by the Minneapolis orchestra during its first six seasons. Handel has been running a steady course at about the one per cent level, and occasionally weaving into our concerts today, as two centuries ago, delightful episodes of refreshing music.

KARL MARIA VON WEBER If Handel and Haydn made their debuts on the American platform in the eighteenth century in an English atmosphere, that atmosphere has long since been transformed, through the processes of migration, to a German domination of the musical world in the nineteenth. More than Beethoven or any other composer, it was Weber, an ancestor of the German opera, through whom Germany began to sense its musical destiny. And if one work must be selected which epitomizes this transformation, it is Weber's opera, *Der Freischütz*, which marked the emancipation of German music from Italian rule. The dawning faith of German nationalism was emotionally nourished by these operas, a social task which Wagner was to carry on more dramatically later in the century.

Even without these nationalistic political overtones, Weber's music possessed a brilliance that enthralled audiences. During the first fifteen years of the New York Philharmonic, Weber was among the leaders, with six to nine per cent of the repertoire, a total all the more remarkable because of the brevity of the compositions. The overtures to half-a-dozen operas, some chamber music, the *Conzertstück*, several arias, and later the whirling *Invitation to the Dance*, were all frequently played. Since that time the inevitable decline has set in. But the short, compact overtures to *Der Freischütz*, *Oberon*, and *Euryanthe* still open many a program. Weingartner, Berlioz, and Stokowski have arranged the *Invitation to the Dance* to startle the ear with a flash of virtuosity, but in the present decade this number has practically disappeared from the more formal subscription series. The old-fashioned *Conzertstück* still turns up at intervals. Weber probably will remain indefinitely one of the "immortals," his percentage hovering modestly around one-half of one per cent, which many a modern composer would be more than proud to claim.

CHRISTOPH WILLIBALD GLUCK Were it not for the historical significance of Gluck, his present position in the orchestral repertoire would scarcely be noted. It was he who started the chain reaction of romanticism through Weber, Berlioz, Liszt, and Wagner. For us he periodically adds the antique patina of a musical heirloom. Overtures to *Alceste* and *Iphigenia in Aulis* and excerpts from several operas, Mottl's synthetic Ballet Suite, extracted from various sources, and an occasional aria exhaust his present representation. Quantitatively, this is not impressive, but insofar as the well-constructed repertoire should recall for the intelligent listener the significant landmarks in our traditions, such tiny flashbacks serve an indispensable and pleasant educational function.

Composers in the Ascending Phase: Apparently at Peak

RICHARD STRAUSS The late Richard Strauss has been designated the greatest of recent composers, whose only possible rival is the much less versatile composer one year his junior, Sibelius. There is nothing in the American repertoire experience of these two contemporaries which is inconsistent with such high esteem. Both show a rapid ascent in popularity beginning in the 1890's; but Strauss has maintained a leading position of from four to five per cent of the national repertoire, except during the hiatus of World War I. Only recently has he shown a slight decline, as the less worthy of his numbers are being dropped from the repertoire.

Strauss unloosed his garish symphonic creations upon an 1890 audience that was still reeling from the onslaught of Wagner. It was just beginning to relax to the less strenuous strains of Tschaikowsky when the new sensation was launched. This post-Wagnerian romantic never aroused the bitter controversy provoked by his predecessor, but he did evoke just enough bewilderment, it seems, to become accepted in the orchestral and operatic repertoires without too much delay. If he offended many aesthetic tastes, he was also an astute showman in composition, and an exceedingly calculating negotiator. From all sides one heard variations on the theme that "Strauss makes money even when his music does not."

Like Berlioz, his romantic forebear, he often chose lawless and

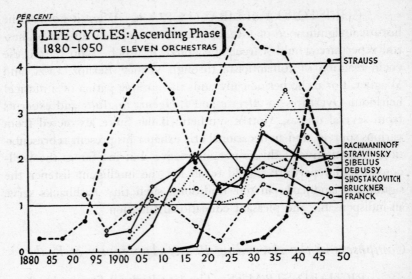

The rise of the best known composers during the past seventy years. Note the decline of Richard Strauss during World War I. His complete disappearance from the repertoire in the season 1917–18 is concealed because the plotting is done on a five-year average.

picturesque characters as the principal subjects for many of his symphonic poems and operas, and startled his listeners with tone pictures of grotesque form and splashing color. Musically, the early tone poems of "Richard II" (another Bülow quip) were an extrapolation of the trends begun by Wagner and Berlioz, with complex but enormously competent counterpoint, with snatches of beautiful melody, even reminiscent of the waltz king's coloration and dramatic content. There were those who loved to take a crack at the derivative nature of his work, who were convinced that the old boys had done it better. Said they:

If it must be Richard—then let it be Wagner
If Strauss . . . then Johann.

But people were rapidly attuning their ears, and Strauss was acclaimed.

It was not surprising that a composer, endowed with his commercial sagacity, should recognize the opportunities, both aesthetic and material, in a visit to America, of which he availed himself on two occasions. His first visit occurred in the early months of 1904. Appearing together with his wife, a singer, he conducted twenty-one concerts with almost as many orchestras. Most of his New York appearances were with the Hans Wetzler orchestra, a raw and untrained group (temporarily augmented to 110) with difficult rehearsal conditions. He conducted the New York Philharmonic in the final pair of concerts for the season in March, 1904. He had experienced some difficulty in concluding an agreement with Boston, where it has been said by some that his asking price was too high, and by others that Gericke was averse to vacating the podium for the distinguished guest. However, Strauss finally did conduct its Pension Fund concert. As a conductor he was described as undemonstrative, casual, and not in the least picturesque. A minor scandal occurred when he accepted an engagement to appear with the orchestra in the Wanamaker auditorium in New York, presumably for an appropriate consideration. Both in Europe and the United States, it was generally declared that he had degraded music by playing in the auditorium of a department store!

In 1921–22 he paid a second visit to the United States. World War I, which we entered in the spring of 1917, had played havoc with German music in general and Strauss in particular. Not only the sentimental aversion of many patrons toward German music, and the disinclination of managers to risk public demonstrations and boycotts, but the accumulating royalties of enemy aliens argued the prudence of a general policy of excluding the music of contemporary enemy composers. The result was that Strauss was totally expunged from American programs during the war years.

Strauss himself had shrewdly endeavored to evade exactly such an eventuality. He had refrained from signing the *Manifesto of German Intellectuals* defending the invasion of Belgium, to which ninety-three Germans of international prominence had affixed their signatures. He was presumably motivated either by the conviction of the priority of art over politics or, as a colleague insisted, he was "too clever to ignore his royalties in London, Paris, Moscow and New York." [19] In his own country, he counselled tolerance toward enemy musicians, excepting those who had actually vilified German Kultur.[20]

However, his restoration was not long in coming. In October, 1921, this erstwhile enemy was officially received as reconciliation ambassador by Mayor Hylan of New York only a few· days after the same official had waved a patriotic welcome to General Foch, the Generalissimo of Allied Forces. At his first concert in Carnegie Hall, America mixed politics and art beautifully by solemnly presenting the ex-enemy with a large wreath beribboned in the Black-White-Yellow of the new German Republic. Appearing in more than forty concerts in nineteen cities as far west as Kansas City, he was elaborately dined and feted everywhere. He complimented our orchestras, and demonstrated the authoritative readings of his works. Finally, as palpable evidence of the American appraisal of his achievements, he took with him to Germany an estimated $50,000.

As a composer, his maiden appearance on American programs occurred in December, 1884, when Theodore Thomas, conductor of the New York Philharmonic, who had met the youth in Munich, performed his Symphony in F Minor from manuscript, for its world première. But Thomas never repeated this number, written in the classic tradition. It was not until he adopted, and adapted, the romantic forms of the symphonic poem that Strauss found himself. His present strength in these concerts lies in *Death and Transfiguration* (introduced by Seidl, January 9, 1892), *Till Eulenspiegel* (by Thomas, November 15, 1895), and *Don Juan* (by Nikisch, October 30, 1891), the last-named an earlier work generally described by critics on the occasion of the composer's first American visit as "the most melodious and most easily accessible to the audience." The fact that these compositions, together with several others, have endured for more than a half-century not only as staples but as thoroughly stimulating musical experiences, must justify ranking their composer among the great. No recent or contemporary composer has attained this rank.

However, unlike Beethoven and Wagner, who grew in stature in their later works, and unlike Mendelssohn and Schumann, whose works continued to find favor with the public even though they showed no significant development, the later orchestral works of

Strauss have never enjoyed the critical esteem bestowed upon the products of his youth. The *Alpensymphonie*, the last of the larger symphonic works, for the première of which Stransky, Stokowski, and Kunwald contended, has had practically no repeats. In general his orchestral style has become more and more onomatopoetic (as in *Symphonia Domestica*), more polyphonic and polytonal, with an almost mechanical harmonic and contrapuntal complexity, a style for which Johann Quantz, the flutist of Frederick the Great, two centuries ago coined the term *"Augenmusik."*

In addition to his symphonic works, some orchestras, notably Philadelphia and Chicago, have featured excerpts from his operas. *The Dance of the Seven Veils* from *Salome*, and the *Waltzes* from *Rosenkavalier*, which were written in the style of his namesake, the waltz king, are very popular. Mitropoulos presented a concert version of *Elektra* in 1949–50.

Strauss has been so commonly accepted that no conductor can be said to ride him fanatically, or to avoid him unduly. Thomas and Stock in Chicago, Kunwald in Cincinnati, Hertz in San Francisco, Rodzinski, Stokowski, and Ormandy—these were somewhat conspicuous among their respective contemporaries for their hospitality toward Strauss.

During World War II Strauss suffered a decline because American and Russian composers were catapulted into the political limelight, rather than because of his identification with the enemy nations.

At home, in Germany, his Jewish librettist and his non-Aryan daughter-in-law placed him in an equivocal position. Nevertheless he straddled the issue of musico-political integrity with characteristic caution. As head of the *Musikkammer* he appeared to collaborate with the new regime, but soon resigned. In June, 1948, he was cleared by a de-Nazification board, after a two-year investigation.

Although his compositions will undoubtedly linger many years after his passing, he nevertheless will be remembered as the last of the German dynasty of musical titans which has held sway in the concert halls of the world for over a century. Strauss brings to a sputtering close the Golden Age of Teutonic music, an age whose grandeur has not yet found a new national home.

JAN SIBELIUS   There has developed in America and England a reverence for the creations of Sibelius which critics in Germany and France (and some critics in this country) have difficulty in comprehending. During the first few years of this century, Theodore Thomas and Van der Stucken, both unfettered in their taste and with a flair for musical reconnaissance, welcomed his presymphonic works, while the Second Symphony (the first one to be imported), had its first American appearance in Chicago on January 2, 1904. From these small beginnings Sibelius continued for several decades with a modest two per cent of our repertoire, but in the thirties he forged ahead to double this figure—not a phenomenal, but nevertheless a very tangible, growth. This most decisive rise in his career coincides suggestively with the increasing interest in, and sympathy with, "gallant little Finland," which had regained her independence from Russia after World War I and, alone among the sovereign nations and allies of Europe, recognized her international obligation by regular payments on her war debt to the United States. This impact of politics upon aesthetic taste, is nevertheless difficult to measure because of the presence of other factors with which it is blended.

Other circumstances also contrived to establish the Sibelius legend. For some reason, the northern geography of his homeland impressed itself upon some of the critics and wrapped his personality in a mystery of bleak grandeur that allegedly reflected itself in the tonal flavor of his compositions. It furnished some very fine metaphors, which commentators often find very useful and which the audience almost invariably takes to its heart. Actually, of course, such geographical determinism is entirely spurious, for Finland, like any other inhabited country, has a variety of weather, and with some discretion one could match almost any passage or movement of the Second Symphony (which was the special victim of this logical fallacy) with any desired meteorological phenomenon, and prove just about anything.

In 1914, when *Valse Triste* and *Finlandia* had attained a popular success, Sibelius visited America as guest of the Norfolk Festival in Connecticut, where he conducted several of his works and a new symphonic poem, *The Oceanides*, written for the occasion. In recognition of the distinguished guest, Yale University conferred upon him an honorary doctorate.

Although all orchestras shared to some extent in this popular rise of the Finnish symphonist, it was Koussevitzky and Stokowski who were the most energetic and consistent in their espousal of him. Koussevitzky gave him the "cycle treatment," 1932–33, as did Werner Janssen and his orchestra in Los Angeles. These cycles contributed materially to the six per cent level of Sibelius in that five-year period. The cordiality between the Master and the Maestro was reciprocated in an invitation to the Boston conductor, whose father-in-law was then living in Finland, to conduct the opening concert of the Sibelius Festival in Helsingfors on the occasion of the composer's seventieth birthday (1935). Stokowski had displayed evidence of his esteem when he gave the American première of the Fifth (1921) and the Sixth and Seventh (1926) symphonies. Philadelphia continued cultivation of Sibelius until 1940, when general enthusiasm for him began to subside.

As measured by the American repertoire, recognition has come late to the composer whom some have been pleased to call the "Beethoven of the North." In 1905, when Strauss occupied one of the major positions in the repertoire with a rank of four per cent, Sibelius was still struggling for a tentative hold on the program time. If slow growth presages a longer life, Sibelius should outlive his German rival, who has been touched by almost no adversity, except those attendant upon political involvements, and who has received every material and honorific consideration. But such good fortune is not apparent in his national proportion of two per cent, while Strauss enjoys more than twice that magnitude. Sibelius differs from his German colleague in another very material respect. Since Finland was Russian territory at the time when his compositions became available, and since America has no copyright treaty with Russia, Sibelius has no way of collecting on his genius from the country in which his compositions have been most admired.

The First, Second, and Fifth symphonies have become apparent fixtures in the American repertoire, while the Third, Fourth, and Sixth are rarely played. One unique distinction must be accorded Sibelius. He is the only twentieth-century composer who has written an established violin concerto (1903–05)—which was introduced to America in 1906 by Maud Powell. In this respect it shares a prestige analogous to Rachmaninoff's Second (1901), similarly the only standard piano concerto born in this century. Unlike Richard Strauss, who continued to compose almost up to his last breath, Sibelius' pen has been dry for a quarter of a century. The repeated promise of an Eighth Symphony was honored only in the breach. Although still vigorous for his eighty-five years, it now appears that his creative energy has been exhausted.

CÉSAR FRANCK   Franck has long been the leader of the French school of the symphony, if for no other reason than that his Symphony in D Minor is the only French symphony of unquestioned rank, except, of course, the century-old *Fantastic Symphony* of Berlioz. Comparison with those of Saint-Saëns, Chausson, and d'Indy only emphasizes this eminent isolation. Although much of the work of this fertile composer was mediocre, he has left two numbers which are still secure in the repertoire—the aforesaid symphony and the *Symphonic Variations* for piano and orchestra. The gradual fading of a dozen other compositions probably indicates that his present one and one-half per cent represents the peak of his popularity.

IGOR STRAVINSKY   With the passing of Richard Strauss and the retirement of the aged Sibelius, Stravinsky remains the "dean" of the celebrated active composers. His neoclassical works have influenced, via Nadia Boulanger and Fontainebleau, many of the modern American composers, and constitute the bulwark of his current repertoire. The *Firebird* and *Petrouchka* suites are almost as standard as the Brahms and Beethoven symphonies, although the sensational *Sacre du Printemps* (1913), one of the most revolutionary pieces of the last decades, seems less able to maintain itself. Many of his more recent compositions have had single performances, and as long as new works flow from his pen, Stravinsky may confidently expect a hearing for them. However, none has earned general acceptance and, unless the standard few develop a still stronger attraction, it seems probable that Stravinsky has reached a statistical peak. Monteux, Koussevitzky, Stokowski, Klemperer, and Rodzinski have been among his more fervent sponsors.

After his first American tour in 1925, he often appeared as guest conductor, and settled permanently in this country in 1940. Shortly afterward, he filed his application for citizenship and expressed his appreciation for that privilege in an arrangement of the *Star-Spangled Banner*, which customarily prefaced the symphony programs in those troublous times. In St. Louis he rehearsed the number, but the musicians did not react favorably to its unfamiliar dress. Only two weeks after Pearl Harbor it seemed unwise to tamper with people's patriotic emotions, however much the new orchestration "came from the heart." It was, however, presented in Boston in January, 1944, and was thus characterized by the *Christian Science Monitor:* "harmonies have been acidulated, note values altered, and even the melodic line reshaped."

CLAUDE DEBUSSY   Walter Damrosch and the New York Symphony Society early bestowed their favor on Debussy. During the first decade of this century, Damrosch presented two all-Debussy programs, supplemented by soloists and chorus. His was the first established orchestra to present the *Nocturnes* in 1905; and in the same year he gave the first of many performances of *L'Après-midi d'un Faune*, which featured the newly imported flute virtuoso Georges Barrère.

With these performances Debussy opened in the New York Symphony with about two per cent of the repertoire, and this per cent became stabilized, as the composite national average. Not even during World War I, when the French repertoire was appreciably augmented, did Debussy profit from its sympathetic rise. The most probable reason for this was that his moderate orchestral output had already been fully exploited. Since the beginning of the century, *L'Après-midi d'un Faune, Nocturnes, Images,* and *La Mer,* which constitute three-fourths of his orchestral legacy, together with some scattered offerings of solos and arrangements, comprise his contribution to the repertoire. He represents a significant break in the German front, both in the style of his orchestration, which is of open texture rather than tonally overladen, and in national emphasis.

ANTON BRUCKNER   Bruckner may be said to have developed a cult without a congregation. Like Mahler, he has had more prophets than followers, at least in his American experience. A Wagner devotee from the beginning of his career, Bruckner was fated to live in anti-Wagner Vienna. In the early years—in the seventies—this pious personage, so devout that he knelt in prayer backstage before every concert to gain the strength which he sorely needed, was so involved in partisanship that conductors hardly dared play him. That he could have had such unshakable faith in two diametrically antithetical characters as God and Wagner, for both of whom he suffered his quota of taunts, might seem astonishing. But this naïve, simple-minded peasant continued his heavy investments in faith and devotion, as well as in lengthy improvisational scores, though neither paid him high dividends.

In Leipzig, where his pupil Nikisch presided, and in New York, where Damrosch and Thomas were the reigning influences, his Wagnerian leanings did not constitute such an obstacle as in Vienna, the protected domain of the anti-Wagnerian critic, Eduard Hanslick. This famous arbiter of taste—personifying the nineteenth-century conception of a critic—would at times dip his pen in a blend of ink and gall, and splatter it abusively on the sponsors of the neo-German school. Consequently Bruckner's first real success did not occur until Arthur Nikisch brought out his Seventh Symphony in Leipzig in 1884. The following year Walter Damrosch introduced him to America with the Third Symphony. Theodore Thomas produced the Seventh in New York in 1886, and the Fourth in Chicago in 1897, and Gericke the Fifth in 1901 in Boston.

Bruckner, of course, has never been popular in this country, but rather the beneficiary of public curiosity. Famed for his dexterous extemporizations at the organ console, he seems to carry over this leisurely dawdling into his otherwise competent writing. Stories are told of his complete absorption in his public improvisations. On one occasion he consumed twice the allotted time so that the organ pumpers went on strike in fatigued despair. His symphonies often exceed the hour, and some one has unkindly observed that "in his *Adagios* the grass grows between the notes." Hanslick's verdict that

Bruckner is "interesting in detail but distasteful in toto," reflects the judgment of many an American listener as well.

All nine symphonies carrying opus numbers have been performed in the United States, though no one has ventured upon a cycle as did his devotee Nikisch of the Gewandhaus orchestra during the season 1920–21. Chicago has at some time performed all his symphonies; the New York Philharmonic, all but the First and Third; Boston, all but the First, Second and Sixth, and Cincinnati all but the First. The Seventh, Eighth, and Ninth are the most frequently played, if that adverb is appropriate to such occasional performances, and the First, Second, and Sixth the least. The 1930's and 1940's witnessed a favorable trend in the curve, owing largely to the coming of Bruno Walter, whose fidelity to both Bruckner and Mahler is well known, and secondarily to his cultivation by Koussevitzky in Boston.

SERGEI RACHMANINOFF   The personal influence of Rachmaninoff in the molding of his own repertoire trend was enormous. A concert soloist with a facile romantic style of composition and a picturesque and exploitable homeliness of figure, he found it very easy to arouse public interest in both himself and his music. Twice he had been offered the conductorship of the Boston Symphony Orchestra, and twice he refused that musical crown, preferring to dedicate himself to composition and concertizing. Characterized by a prodigality of melody, his music does not surprise the listener with strange progressions, nor harass him with unresolved dissonances. The erudite critic might justifiably recall the cases of Raff and Spohr who became "classic" almost too soon to endure. The Symphony No. 2 and the Piano Concerto No. 2 still hold their own and these, together with more isolated performances of the Third Piano Concerto, the *Rhapsodie on a Theme by Paganini*, and other compositions, have pushed his curve continuously upward since 1904, when his name first appeared in Boston. His death in 1943 has already affected the fortunes of his music adversely and reduced slightly the 2.75 proportion in the repertoire, which he enjoyed at that time.

DMITRI SHOSTAKOVITCH   If ever a composer was propelled into screaming prominence by political forces, Shostakovitch was that composer. It all began peacefully enough. The First Symphony was given its American première by the alert Stokowski in November, 1928; the Fifth was given a similarly successful concert audition ten years later, though Rodzinski and the NBC orchestra had anticipated it with a radio première a month earlier. During the decade of the thirties, all Russian arts aroused an increasingly benevolent interest on the part of many American intellectuals. In the case of Shostakovitch, this interest was certainly not diminished by the first of several spectacular repudiations by his government in January, 1936. By 1940 this precocious youth, through both merit and circumstance, had earned the proportion of about one per cent of the American repertoire—a percentage of not inconsiderable magnitude for a contemporary composer. Within about five years, animated by war hysteria, he composed the Sixth, Seventh, Eighth, and Ninth symphonies which were made available with almost commercial promptitude.

It was in the dramatic episode of the production and presentation of the Seventh Symphony that the political overtones were first generally perceived in America. Professedly written during the siege of Leningrad, where the Muses spoke in thundering cannonades and during which Communist Russia inadvertently became the active ally of capitalist America (December 7, 1941), this *Leningrad* Symphony became the symbol of the binding tie between the new and strange political bedfellows. Stokowski, who was then under contract with NBC, Rodzinski of Cleveland, and Koussevitzky all vied for the prize of the first American performance. Actually, the National Broadcasting Company had already secured the rights for Toscanini, who agreed to conduct its radio debut in July 1942. Not since the Metropolitan Opera placed *Parsifal* on the boards in 1903 had there been such a buzz of anticipation over an American première. Photographed at Kuibyshev, then the temporary Soviet capital, the score arrived in the United States in the form of one hundred feet of microfilm after a journey which included a flight to Teheran, auto transportation to Cairo, and the final leg by air to New York.

Less than two years later, the Eighth was given its American

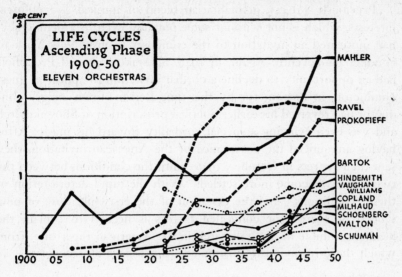

Among the more recent composers whose rise is pictured here are two Americans: Aaron Copland and William Schuman.

première, on April 2, 1944, by the New York Philharmonic, Rodzinski conducting. Political implications were again evident when this performance was prefaced by a grand eulogy of our Soviet ally, intoned by the Director of the Division of Soviet Supply of the Foreign Economic Administration. For the rights to this première the Columbia Broadcasting System, in this physically undamaged country, had paid to Shostakovitch, by now a highly publicized ex-firefighter of war-ruined Leningrad, the sum of $10,000.

This unprecedented enthusiasm for Shostakovitch not only reflected a kind of left-wing taste, but was augmented by press agentry on an almost planetary scale. It was nourished in America by an understandable sympathy for a ravished country, by the glamour of the name of the composer, and, ironically enough, by the normal capitalistic competition between two national radio chains and the Eastern orchestras. There was not then, nor is there today, a genuine aesthetic acceptance of the later symphonies, and even the First and Fifth have been criticized for tonal overexpansion and derivative eclecticism.

Previously (1942), a totalitarian blend of musical and political interests, which is not without some potency even in a democracy, had motivated an invitation to the composer to visit New York to conduct his Seventh. Again, in 1946, Shostakovitch and Prokofieff had an opportunity to decline a cordial invitation to appear as guest conductors in Boston; for by this time Boston's own emigré conductor had reversed his earlier political proscription of Shostakovitch and was even evincing a special cordiality toward his music. After having announced the acceptance of the American invitation, they sent their regrets in October, 1946 "until the conditions between the two nations become more settled." With the rapid deterioration of these "conditions," and the cessation of the erstwhile flow of new works, no search for concealed factors is needed to explain the headlong tumble of Shostakovitch in the American repertoire, from which there is obviously no immediate prospect of recovery.

Composers in the Ascending Phase: Recent Group

GUSTAV MAHLER   Gustav Mahler carried on the traditions of Teutonic length with which German composers have been periodically afflicted ever since Beethoven scored the fifty-five-minute *Eroica*. His music is abnormally protracted, it is imitative and often disjointed, and sometimes trite, and the choral supplements tend to restrict performance. With all their color and competent orchestration, his nine symphonies are certainly not strikingly novel and do not stir up the controversies—as did Wagner, Strauss, and Stravinsky—which inspire fanatics. In fact, they have often been labeled as *"Kapellmeistermusik"*—another neologism coined by Bülow to describe the unoriginal concoctions of the conductor-composer who secures his materials from the masterpieces which he conducts. Notable among Mahler's disciples, who would, of course, question such harsh judgments, is Bruno Walter who has loyally dedicated himself to the task of "uncovering the sources of exaltation flowing from his music."

Das Lied von der Erde, which is scaled down to more conventional proportions, employing only two solo voices, has won a place in the standard American repertoire; it has received its quota of performances ever since Stokowski gave the American première, December, 1916, in Philadelphia. All nine symphonies have been played by the major orchestras.

The most sensational production of any Mahler symphony was, of course, the performance under Stokowski of the Symphony No. 8, *Symphony of a Thousand*, in the Spring of 1916, which propelled the young conductor into national prominence, in spite of the mixed aesthetic feelings with which the production was received. Frederick Stock, of Chicago, followed with a performance the following year; the Cincinnati May Festivals of 1931 and 1939, and the Hollywood Bowl orchestra, with Ormandy, produced it during the Summer of 1948. As conductor of the New York Philharmonic, Stokowski repeated it in April, 1950. The ambitious task of presenting the complete cycle of the Mahler symphonies was undertaken by the Radio City Music Hall orchestra, Erno Rapee, conductor, which broadcast its program on successive Sundays during the season 1941–42. Because of the prohibitive length of most of the Mahler compositions, single movements are not uncommonly programmed, and long movements are cut—even as Mahler himself felt few compunctions in altering the works of any composer excepting Wagner. The curve of Mahler has been rising slightly and stands now at two and one-half per cent, with the New York Philharmonic, over which Mahler himself once presided, leading handsomely in the espousal of his music. The return of Bruno Walter was, of course, the most forceful personal factor in this renewed interest. Boston has been second to New York in hospitality toward Mahler.

SERGEI PROKOFIEFF   Prokofieff has not been supported by the political ballyhoo accorded his colleague Shostakovitch, and his rank in the repertoire is consequently considerably lower, with the present record at one per cent. Koussevitzky, a friend in pre-Revolution days, has taken the lead in championing this modern Russian, with Philadelphia and St. Louis very close seconds. During several visits to this country between 1918 and 1939, he performed his own piano concertos and conducted his symphonic works. His First Symphony, *Classical*, is by far the most frequently played, and has indeed become a "classic." The Suite from *The Love of Three*

Oranges, and the *Scythian Suite*, have also been given repeated hearings, and about twenty other numbers have been played. The Children's Fairy Tale, *Peter and the Wolf*, is enjoyed by adult sophisticates, but is not to be expected frequently on these subscription programs. His performance rank does scant justice to the reputation of the man whom many critics denominate one of the most distinguished composers in the whole musical world today—in view of which, the prognosis is excellent.

ARNOLD SCHOENBERG   As in the case of Prokofieff (*Classical* Symphony) and Hindemith (*Mathis der Maler*) and other innovators, the most accepted composition of Schoenberg is the one which does least violence to current styles. *Verklärte Nacht* (1899), written while he was still under the influence of Wagner and previous to his deflection into "atonal" bypaths,[21] has been consistently performed while practically none of a dozen other compositions have been played twice by the same orchestra. If the *avant-garde* has hailed him as the greatest contemporary genius, their verdict is not reflected in the active repertoire. For almost fifty years this celebrated musician and pedagogue has been more written about than played, and has produced nothing that has "caught on." Whether his music is a natural evolution from the chromaticism of *Tristan*, as is contended by the Schoenberg school, with the public taste in a deplorable cultural lag; or whether the composer was deceived by his own clever contrivance of an aesthetic theory which is simply too unpsychological to gain adherence, is another of those temporarily insoluble questions which we so glibly pass on to a supposedly omniscient posterity to decide. The moral distinction between admirable aesthetic integrity and mere doctrinaire obstinacy cannot easily be resolved.

Stokowski valiantly espoused the cause of this unconventional Viennese by presenting at least a half-dozen of his creations during the 1920's. For the performance of the controversial *Five Orchestral Pieces*, the conductor received as his reward a jumble of applause and hisses from his partially amused and partially offended audience. In London, Vienna, and Prague they were similarly greeted.

In July, 1951, Arnold Schoenberg died in Los Angeles.

AARON COPLAND Contrary to the uncompromising policy of Schoenberg, Copland was somewhat more amenable to the pressures of public taste. He has shifted styles, abandoned the brazen cacophony of his early experiments, and more recently displays evidence of a search for a congenial meeting ground, somewhat left-of-center, with his public.

As a twenty-four-year-old student of Nadia Boulanger—in fact the very first of a long migration of Americans to Fontainebleau—he made his orchestral debut with the New York Symphony, Walter Damrosch, conductor, in a performance of the Symphony for Organ and Orchestra, January 11, 1925, with Mlle. Boulanger as organist. It was especially the dissonant finale that reportedly moved Damrosch to the famous remark that "a man who could write such music at twenty-four might some day be capable of murder."

More important, of course, was the second performance of this number a month later under the baton of Koussevitzky in Boston. This was the very first of a long series of services not only to Copland, but also to American music, by the Boston conductor. It cannot be said that the audience received these "barbaric" and "brutal" cacophonies in a friendly spirit. Warren Story Smith, of the Boston *Post*, opined that "Copland not only looked into his heart, but also into the score of Stravinsky's *Sacre*," which had caused such a scandalous riot in Paris in May, 1913.

Since that debut, however, Copland has become the most universally performed American composer in the serious repertoire. Performances of *A Lincoln Portrait*, *Billy the Kid*, *Quiet City*, and *Appalachian Spring* have been rather widespread, although Copland, too, suffers from the affliction of single renditions. His overall national average is approximately one per cent.

RALPH VAUGHAN WILLIAMS Vaughan Williams is one of the few English composers to have a modest but secure place in the American repertoire. The programmatic *London* Symphony and the *Fantasia on a Theme by Thomas Tallis* were first performed by the New York Symphony under Damrosch and Coates in 1920 and 1922 respectively, and since then have been regularly heard. His other compositions appear less frequently, although John Barbirolli leaned rather heavily on him in New York in 1936–40.

PAUL HINDEMITH   Hindemith came to the attention of the public not only through his compositions but also because of his promotion of the idea of *Gebrauchsmusik*. Mindful of the dilemma in which musicians found themselves by composing in a social vacuum, without reference to particular purposes, he proposed that music should be frankly utilitarian and thereby again close the gap between composer and consumer that was created during the nineteenth century. This constituted an admission of bankruptcy of the romantic theory of self-expression, and was a step toward the recognition of composing as a useful craft.

Since his name first appeared in the season 1924–25 on the Philadelphia programs, about a dozen of his compositions have been performed, but none with the frequency of his *Mathis der Maler*, one of his later, though more conservative, works. With his percentage at less than one per cent, future historians may have occasion to comment on the tardiness with which modern music is absorbed into the standard repertoire, for Hindemith is unquestionably one of the most respected of modern composers.

DARIUS MILHAUD   Milhaud was one of the famous "Six" who sowed discords and reaped a whirlwind of notoriety in Paris during the riotous postwar twenties. He had absorbed various trends, including American jazz and the folk music of Brazil, where he had spent two years (1917–19) in the French Legation. Before 1940 his performances were scattered, but since his permanent residence in the United States, practically all the orchestras have programmed his compositions, although as yet almost none has been repeated. The less radical *Suite Provençale* has been most generally played.

BÉLA BARTÓK   Of a dozen compositions of this Hungarian nationalist that have been included in the American repertoire, none of the strictly orchestral numbers has any circulation. On the other hand, certain soloists have espoused his piano and violin concertos. A mild revival occurred at the time of his death in 1945, in part motivated by sentimental impulses of the friends of the composer, who had died penniless in New York. But whether, as many had hoped, there would develop a demand for his nationalistic creations, it is too early to predict. His Concerto for Orchestra, commissioned by Koussevitzky, is one of about ten of his compositions on American programs, with the Hungarian Ormandy particularly hospitable.

WILLIAM SCHUMAN   William Schuman owes his entry into the repertoire largely to the sponsorship of Koussevitzky, who has played at least a half-dozen of his works. His early *American Festival* Overture has been the most generally accepted.

WILLIAM WALTON   William Walton, the young Englishman, is generally considered the most conspicuous prospect for the mantle of Vaughan Williams. He is a fixture in the repertoire, and his orchestral compositions have enjoyed repeated performances in New York and Boston. A Suite from *Façade* (to poems by Edith Sitwell), the concertos for violin and viola, Overture *Portsmouth Point*, and *Belshazzar's Feast* (chorus and orchestra) have been performed by several orchestras.

CHARLES IVES   Charles Ives, the musical sage of Danbury, Connecticut, would normally not be counted in the family of active American composers who have earned a niche in the orchestral repertoire. But he has been the center of so much discussion among the musicians and critics of unconventional propensities, that his presence cannot be ignored. For six decades he has been a voice crying in the wilderness.

Not only has he utilized polytonal and multirhythmic devices which have by no means yet become conventional, but his groping for expression which reflects the regional tunes, the local color of church and public square, marks him as the first to construct a genuine homespun New England idiom. Being a man of independent means, he personifies that "lunatic fringe" which cares not for audience, royalties, or recognition. As a result he has no audience, has received no money, and gained no general recognition. But in his old age, he is being sought out by the new musical generation.

Although some of his music has been recorded, he has had exactly three performances by the major orchestras of the country, but none by a regular conductor. Associate Conductor Burgin of Boston (1948) and guest conductor Slonimsky in Los Angeles (1933), have played his *Three Places in New England;* and Leonard Bernstein conducted the Second Symphony with the New York Philharmonic in February, 1951. This number turned out to be surprisingly melodious and conservative.

The Third Symphony, composed in 1904, revised in 1911, won for the ailing composer the Pulitzer Prize in 1946. Ives is an asocial individualist who writes as he pleases; but unlike Schoenberg, who has likewise enlisted the support of the liberal group, Ives has never buttressed his musical style with a thoroughgoing aesthetic philosophy.

Composers in the Descending Phase

ROBERT SCHUMANN   In the early years of the New York Philharmonic Society, just after his death, Schumann enjoyed a vogue equivalent to that of Mozart, and was outstripped only by Beethoven himself. Under Theodore Thomas he sometimes exceeded ten per cent of the repertoire, but with the enrichment of the repertoire by the later romantics, he yielded ground. Today he occupies about two and one-half per cent of the composite repertoire.

Though there has been a contraction in volume, there has been no significant shift or replacement in the representative works. The four symphonies, the *Manfred* Overture and the thoroughly standard Piano Concerto, then as now, constitute the bulk of his legacy. In the meager cello literature, his concerto perseveres, while the season 1937–38 witnessed the revival of the Violin Concerto by Yehudi Menuhin. Inexpertly orchestrated, his symphonies have been "retouched" by Mahler, Weingartner, and Stock, whose versions take advantage of orchestral color unsuspected by the pianistically minded composer. In spite of the technical shortcomings in his nonidiomatic orchestral lines, Schumann has survived because of his

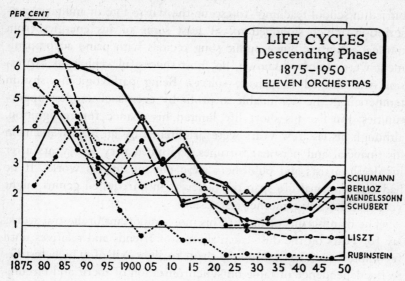

PER CENT

LIFE CYCLES
Descending Phase
1875–1950
ELEVEN ORCHESTRAS

SCHUMANN
BERLIOZ
MENDELSSOHN
SCHUBERT

LISZT

RUBINSTEIN

1875 80 85 90 95 1900 05 10 15 20 25 30 35 40 45 50

The old composers are constantly being crowded by the new entrants. Hence many of the famous names, while still being played in significant proportions, show a decline in relative *importance in the repertoire. Liszt and Rubinstein have neared the vanishing point.*

striking melodic motifs, buoyant rhythms, and vivid harmonizations, which keep him always well above the level of the commonplace.

FRANZ SCHUBERT   Overshadowed during his brief lifetime by Beethoven and Rossini, Schubert, who died at the age of thirty-one, achieved a posthumous renown in inverse proportion to his early failures. Numerous important factors militated against personal recognition. In the first place he was not a virtuoso on any instrument, being unable to do justice even to some of his own compositions. At a time when division of labor between executant and composer was not yet common, this avenue to public attention was closed to him. Although schooled in musical theory, his dramatic training was deficient, and in his early attempts to "sell" his operas, his lack of knowledge of stagecraft and his restricted range of musical expression killed all possibility of his being heard in the Rossini-mad Austrian capital. For several years of his life he was buried in school teaching—to escape the worse fate of military conscription—which siphoned off at least some of his energies from musical activities. Since public song recitals with piano accompaniment were almost unknown, his most successful vehicle of expression was limited to private soirées. Being pathologically shy in temperament, he was unable to profit by even such modest opportunities. Finally, his short life limited his chance for recognition, although his last few years were brightened by an improvement in his financial and personal fortunes. Within a very few years after his death, artists and publishers were picking up his works. If he had had a normal life span the believers in unrequited genius might very well have lost another test case.

The manuscripts of most of his more important orchestral works lay for years on the dust-laden shelves of friends and relatives until favorable coincidence brought them to light—all of which testifies to the dependence of fame on synchronization of merit and circumstance. The story of the recovery of the great C Major Symphony ten years after the composer's death—he would have been only forty-one—and its first performance by Mendelssohn and the Gewandhaus orchestra in 1839 is the hackneyed stock in trade of the program annotators. The devotion of Liszt in proclaiming the lyric genius of Schubert throughout Europe by a half-hundred transcriptions of his *Lieder* further spread his fame.

In America, Schubert's career was inaugurated with the rendition of the C Major Symphony by the New York Philharmonic in 1851 under Theodore Eisfeld, who had come to America in 1848. For some decades his proportion of the repertoire ranged from three to six per cent, until about the beginning of the new century, when the expansion of both repertoire and number of concerts seemed to settle Schubert on a safe plateau of about two per cent, which he still held in 1950.

A change in concert convention, effected early in this century, which restricts soloists to numbers of orchestral character, wiped out the two score *Lieder* which had previously enjoyed occasional performances in New York, Chicago, and other cities where vocalists were frequently featured in mixed programs.

Only two compositions may be said to have a firmly established place in today's repertoire—Symphonies No. 7 and No. 8. If Schumann had hailed the Seventh as a "masterpiece of heavenly length" the world has concurred in his judgment, but with some reservation as to the divine nature of its dimensions. At least Mendelssohn in 1840 and Mahler in 1910 (New York Philharmonic) played the fifty-minute symphony with cuts. Most critics would pronounce its redundancy as emanating not from any providential inspiration, but rather from the very human foible of a happy pen in the hand of an author who almost never perspired over a revised manuscript and whose first draft was usually his last. In the American repertoire it is played with almost the same frequency as the symphonies of Beethoven, Brahms, and the other masterpieces of hallowed tradition.

The *Unfinished* Symphony, more compact and utterly charming, was first performed in America by the Theodore Thomas orchestra in 1867. It is now often programmed in popular concerts. In recent years the Fifth in B-flat, a youthful work reminiscent of Mozart and Haydn, had gained some hearings, while many other works have been given isolated or infrequent performances. The Symphony in E, of which only a sketch exists, was orchestrated by Weingartner, and was given its American première by the Cleveland orchestra in the year of the centennial of the composer's death, (November) 1928.

In commemoration of this centennial, the Columbia Phonograph Company had announced a prize contest for the "completion" of the *Unfinished* Symphony. Although this work had been "completed" once before by one August Ludwig, a German critic and composer, and was thus performed by the Berlin Philharmonic in 1892, many connoisseurs were not convinced that the symphony required grafting of a third movement—to say nothing of the impertinence of such a project even if it were desirable. The conditions of the contest were therefore rescinded in favor of a more general stipulation that compositions should be conceived as an "apotheosis of the lyrical genius of Schubert." The $10,000 prize was won by Kurt Atterburg, well-known Swedish composer, with his Symphony No. 6, which was performed in Paris, Cologne, London, New

York, and Minneapolis. The competition was not without its scandal: in February, 1929, the *Musical Digest* brought out an article from the winning composer's pen entitled "How I Fooled the Music World" in which he admitted having plagiarized, although "without malicious intent," from various composers for the purpose of satirizing the would-be connoisseurs of the celebrant.

HECTOR BERLIOZ   Berlioz had his greatest run in the New York Symphony Society under Leopold Damrosch, who joined forces with his own Oratorio Society in giving complete and repeated performances of *Damnation of Faust, Romeo and Juliet,* as well as the larger orchestral works, *Harold in Italy* and the *Fantastic Symphony.* A few productions of such dimensions were quite sufficient to inflate the Berlioz contingent to ten or fifteen per cent of the total offerings in 1880, especially since his total season embraced only a half-dozen concerts. As choral music declined in importance and new financial support of the orchestra made inevitable an expansion of the series and consequently the repertoire, this arch-romanticist was reduced to the more conservative proportions of about two per cent. Although some of his once famous works are practically never played today, others have survived to retain their places in the approved library: *Fantastic Symphony,* the popular *Roman Carnival* Overture, *Harold in Italy,* for viola and orchestra, excerpts from the *Damnation of Faust* and from *Romeo and Juliet.* Historically he will be remembered as the founder of the virtuoso orchestra, insofar as such pat clichés are permitted, paving the way for Liszt, Wagner, and Strauss. When listening to the *Fantastic Symphony,* one would hardly suspect that it is separated from the Beethoven Ninth (1824) and the Schubert C Major (1828) by only a few years (1830). Although the continuity in musical heritage from Gluck and Beethoven has been reverently acknowledged by this composer, nevertheless his new twist in the permutations of melodic bits, the organic structure, the dramatic drive and the idiomatic exploitation of instruments and their juxtapositions, constitute a striking fulfilment of the past and a harbinger of the future.

FRANZ LISZT   Liszt can at times be passionately melodious or furiously bombastic. Both qualities will almost guarantee instant appreciation and a relatively early oblivion. In the 1860's Liszt was a "cause" to be espoused by pioneers such as Bergmann and Thomas. At the turn of the century, when ears had been attuned to more garish instrumentation, Liszt was an assured delight to any audience. He was therefore much played by Stransky, and any other conductor who was committed to enjoyable rather than to challenging programs. Today the record of all orchestras testifies to an ebbing interest. From five and six per cent in 1875, he has subsided to an average of one-half of one per cent of the 1950 repertoire. A few decades ago several of his Hungarian Rhapsodies were frequently played, but such transcriptions are now almost in ill repute. Ten or a dozen Symphonic Poems and the *Faust Symphony* had repeated performances in New York and Boston between 1860 and 1925; today only *Les Préludes* remains, with apologetic, infrequent renditions. The two Piano Concertos, especially the first in E-flat, will apparently guarantee for some time a mathematically discernible spot for the arch-virtuoso. Nevertheless, historically his place in orchestral composition is of especial significance; for, in the evolution of the Tone Poem, he stands between Berlioz and Richard Strauss, anticipated by the first, and rendered fairly obsolete by the second. He has provoked the observation from the ubiquitous wag, who is always ready to pounce with brilliant hindsight on a poor creature about whom society has changed its mind, that "Liszt's best work has been done by Wagner and Strauss."

FELIX MENDELSSOHN   When the orchestral scene opened in America, Mendelssohn was at the zenith of his career. He had initiated the Bach revival, was a brilliant virtuoso on piano and organ, a favorite conductor and composer in London, and had been conductor of the Leipzig Gewandhaus orchestra since 1835. He possessed all the qualifications, both primary and supplementary, for getting his things played: his inventions were melodious, he was a competent conductor and an educated and affable salon figure.

In the early years of the New York Philharmonic, the Mendelssohn repertoire was sufficiently extensive (about fifteen per cent at mid-century) to provide at least one title in practically every season, even in the short series of three or four concerts. The Third (*Scotch*) and Fourth (*Italian*) symphonies, several concert overtures, the two piano concertos, the violin concerto and the *Midsummer Night's Dream* music were all in very active performance in 1850. By 1900 many of these numbers had become "popular" and lost their hold in the subscription concerts. In this manner, the piano concertos were lost and the overtures were sharply reduced in frequency. Until 1900 the now virtually extinct overture, *The Lovely Melusine*, rivaled the still pleasurable music of *Midsummer Night's Dream* in frequency of performance in New York, Chicago, and Boston. Only the Violin Concerto has successfully resisted the normal aesthetic erosion and is still today one of the bulwarks of the violinist's repertoire. It is not only one of the three or four "old reliables," but it is also perhaps the oldest of the "reliables" in point of service actually on the boards. Composed in 1844, it was given its first American hearing in the programs of the New York Philharmonic, November 24, 1849, while the older Beethoven concerto was offered for the first time complete in that series on December 21, 1861, by the recently arrived Eduard Mollenhauer. Although in chronology it is antedated, of course, by those of Mozart and Beethoven, it was actually launched in the public domain about the same time as the Beethoven work. The latter had had few significant performances in Europe until Joachim and Vieuxtemps, about the middle of the century, gave it its currency.

During the last half-century, the Mendelssohn repertoire has been undergoing a general, and inevitable shrinkage. In 1900 his average stood between two and three per cent, but in the last few decades it has shriveled to half that size. Occasionally Mendelssohn, like any other composer, enjoys a brief spurt of popularity, perhaps only to give way to another composer for a similarly fleeting popular moment.

ANTON RUBINSTEIN   Rubinstein's pathetic ambition to become a great composer extended even to the neglect of his piano technique. Cheerfully would he have sacrificed the ephemeral fame of the concert artist for the more enduring role of a creator. In his own time he did enjoy the satisfaction of a certain prominence when, between 1880 and 1890, he occupied four per cent of the repertoire, a rank equal to that of Mozart, Mendelssohn, and Schubert. But his mimicry of German romanticism was not sufficiently sturdy to endure; and his *Ocean* Symphony, by far the most popular of all his orchestral works in its day, critics, resorting to an easy pun, thought too "watery" and unsubstantial for sustained musical fare. Conductors often took the liberty of fragmenting the hour-long work; but Paur played all seven movements in Boston, in December 1894, in memory of the composer whose death had just been announced. The Piano Concerto No. 4, played frequently and, during the last decades, almost exclusively by his pupil Josef Hofmann, is now much more likely to be performed by the conservatory graduate than by the concert artist. There is, of course, no guarantee that some capricious circumstance will not place his name on the program again for a very occasional performance, such as the golden anniversary of Hofmann's career, on which occasion the Third Concerto was sentimentally exhumed. But for all practical purposes this fertile creator has faded from view.

Composers with Full Life Cycles

Perhaps it requires a certain degree of audacity to forecast the completion of the life cycle of a composer, when ordinary experience testifies to the resiliency with which suspended animation may spring back into life. However, a large group of composers display that characteristic curve with a center peak, trailed by a slope that may not necessarily presage imminent oblivion, but does indicate that their appearances are thinning out.

There are many factors which enter into the determination of the "completion" of the life cycle. In some instances, the declining slope represents public satiety with a once accepted master. But often the decline simply runs concurrently with the composer's active, professional life. His prominence may be the result of a genial tendency to perform his compositions as they become available, with a certain experimental prodigality. In the course of time, the composer dies, this personal favoritism gives way to a sense of critical discrimination, relatively few compositions survive, and the trend is stabilized at a low frequency. Or his reputation may be a derivative one, stemming primarily from his eminence as performer, conductor, teacher, and pedagogue, or personal association with conductors who are in a strategic position to incorporate their interests in the going repertoire. With the termination of this preferential relation, or with the death of the composer or conductor, his compositions find themselves in the open market where they must compete on their supposed merits while the new generation of composers presses for recognition.

ANTONIN DVOŘÁK   The trend line of Dvořák shows to an uncommon degree the influence of personal factors. Although the maiden appearance of his music in these orchestras occurred in 1879–80 when the New York Symphony Society under the elder Damrosch played the *Slavonic Rhapsody, No. 2*, it was not until the early nineties, after Dvořák had established himself in New York as Director of the American Conservatory, that his popularity rose precipitously to ten per cent in the New York Philharmonic—a proportion commonly reserved for the masters. That was the decade of the world première of the *New World* Symphony, performed by Seidl with the composer himself in attendance (1893). It was the famous occasion on which the conductor revised the tempo of the slow movement, substituting with the composer's approval a slower tempo, which has since become the well known *Largo*.

Dvořák's prestige diminished somewhat after his return to Europe and his proportion of the repertoire took a sharp compensatory dip to two per cent. After 1911, however, his compatriot and pupil, Josef Stransky of the New York Philharmonic, renewed the public's enthusiasm for the piquant rhythms and colorful instrumental palette. The other orchestras, under more remote control, rendered Dvořák only "normal" acclaim. There followed a general and parallel decline in all the orchestras until the year 1941, when the centenary of his birth revived an interest in him. Chicago and Cleveland, the largest Czech communities outside of Prague, paced this trend; Cleveland and Cincinnati are the present leaders.

The *New World* Symphony is, of course, one of the standard

symphonies. In addition to it, the *Carnival* Overture, the *Scherzo Capriccioso* and the Cello Concerto comprise the core of the current Dvořák repertoire.

CAMILLE SAINT-SAËNS   Saint-Saëns seemed determined to create a masterpiece in almost every conceivable standard category of vocal and instrumental music, excepting the string quartet. He possessed a fantastic fluency in all idioms. He was a stylistic vagabond who roamed freely and without discomfiture in all musical realms. His music is impeccable in technique, idiomatic in expression, and utterly delightful. He wielded a "happy" pen. Such affable music has a certain stable following—it is still periodically performed—perhaps because no audience can too long endure the psychological strain of continuous cerebral challenge; everywhere there are listeners who hope to relax occasionally in a mildly emotional jag. Therein lies the indispensable programmatic function of Mendelssohn, Rimsky-Korsakoff, and Saint-Saëns.

Beginning, of course, with relatively nothing in 1875, Saint-Saëns climbed to a high point of over four per cent of the repertoire in 1900, lingered a few decades at that respectable height, and then descended simultaneously in all orchestras again to the vanishing point. He enjoyed a brief respite during World War I. If Allied music must be played, Saint-Saëns was perfectly safe and appropriate: a great patriot whose music was delectable to many who in those times might not easily absorb Debussy and Ravel. His patriotism often led to literary excesses, as in his call to banish *all* German music, not excepting Wagner and Beethoven. But he was more conservative than patriotic, for he was unfriendly even to the liberal wing of his own native music. Perhaps this octogenarian was under the strain of political pressure when he thus exposed himself as a hopeless reactionary who had outlived his time, and who was naïvely contriving to obstruct the inevitable.

He traveled widely in his heyday and was equally scintillating as piano and organ soloist, as conductor, composer, pamphleteer, and salon habitué. In October, 1906, he arrived in the United States, managed by the Knabe Piano Company, and appeared as pianist

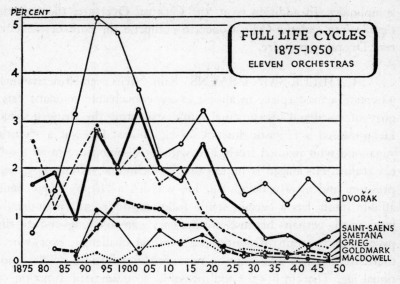

A number of important composers have "come and gone" during the last seventy-five years. The approximately complete life cycles of several of these, indicate their disappearance. Dvořák, however, is still quite active in the repertoire.

with the New York Symphony and other orchestras. In 1915, as a goodwill delegate from belligerent France, he visited the Panama-Pacific Exposition in San Francisco to which he had dedicated the *Hymn to California,* a gesture more appreciated for its sentiment than for its aesthetic excellence.

It is popular among many aesthetes of today to speak contemptuously of Saint-Saëns. If he epitomized a kind of musical mid-Victorianism with manners that were immaculately correct and highly stylized, this type of musical experience is held in great value by many. His Symphony No. 3, with organ, is still played, as are also the Piano Concertos No. 2 and No. 4 and the Violin Concerto No. 3. His Cello Concerto will probably never be permanently abandoned. His symphonic poems, including the *Danse Macabre,* have completed their popular run and are resurrected only infrequently, like the ghost in that eerie dance, only to fade away, at the light of a more modern day, into the oblivion from which they have temporarily emerged.

EDVARD GRIEG   Grieg has been kept barely alive on the subscription programs by his Piano Concerto. Originally in the standard repertoire of all pianists, it has been linked since 1915 with Percy Grainger, who made his American debut at that time, and who had spent the summer of 1907 under the composer's tutelage. This once popular work has been appearing with diminishing frequency on regular programs, and has now joined the concertos of Rubinstein and Saint-Saëns as the warhorses of student recitals. A brief revival was occasioned by the centennial of the composer's birth (1943) when several orchestras featured the number. His suites, symphonic dances, and other miniatures, which were pleasant enough in their day, now appear in only infinitesimal proportions. They have always been, and still are, standard items on lighter programs.

BEDŘICH SMETANA   Smetana, the first nationalist Czech composer, is known in this country today primarily by the Overture to *The Bartered Bride* and the Symphonic Poem, *The Moldau*, two numbers of overture length which do not accumulate an impressive volume. There is no symptom of their disappearance, and they will probably have periodic performances for some time. Stransky favored his fellow Czech with more than one per cent of his repertoire, but today the general average is considerably less than half that proportion. Recently George Szell, who had functioned for some years in Prague, introduced his American audiences to a revival of lesser-known works, including his own adaptation of Smetana's first String Quartet for modern orchestra.

EDWARD ALEXANDER MACDOWELL   For half a century it has been conventional to regard MacDowell as the most illustrious American composer. Traditional judgments change with reluctance, especially since the criteria of greatness are often nebulous and subjective. If reasonably objective criteria are desired, the volume of performance should partially serve that purpose. During the decennial period, 1940–50, only two offerings of MacDowell's music—in each case the Piano Concerto No. 2—have appeared in the regular paired series of the ten major orchestras under observation.

In Boston, which was more friendly to American composers than any other city, he made his first tentative beginnings in 1889 when the same concerto was played. At the time of his death, in 1904, he had reached two per cent of the repertoire. Of all Mac-Dowell's compositions, the *Indian* Suite, the Suite in A Minor, and especially the Second Concerto may be said to have enjoyed a public existence as measured by repeated performances. Single appearances have characterized a small number of others. However, among those orchestras which offer popular programs, the three named above, as well as transcriptions of several piano compositions, have had a fair following.

NICOLAS RIMSKY-KORSAKOFF   Rimsky-Korsakoff, that master of kaleidoscopic instrumental coloration, may now be said almost to have "descended" to the popular level. His strident and vividly exuberant style of orchestration has never been either puzzling or offensive. Beginning with about one per cent in 1900, he is again resting at the same mathematical spot after fifty years of satisfying exhilaration for musical patrons. He reached his pinnacle in the early twenties with about four per cent in the Philadelphia Orchestra under Stokowski, but never exceeded a national average of about two per cent. The insatiable Stokowski endeavored to enhance the exotic twang of the *Scheherazade* by means of an experiment in synesthesia. In January, 1926, he performed this oriental work with Wilfred's Clavilux, a "color organ" which projects its technicolor of abstract forms on a screen as "visual music." At least one critic thought that the music was sufficient unto itself.

In addition to that brilliant *1001 Nights*, the *Spanish Caprice* and the *Russian Easter* complete the standard repertoire of this most competent and disciplined, although not most original, member of the Russian nationalist "Five." The *Russian Easter* has become a "seasonal" piece annually played in this country with naïve disregard of the discrepancy between the Western and the Eastern calendars and the differences in tonal modalities in the divergent religions.

EDWARD ELGAR Elgar signalized the advent of England, "the land without music," into the circle of creative countries. He was the first of a line of modern British composers (Delius, Vaughan Williams, Walton, Britten, and others) to gain serious attention and even prominence in foreign countries, including Germany. This international acclaim was first earned in 1889 by his oratorio, the *Dream of Gerontius*, and the following year by the still highly esteemed *Enigma Variations*. His success was soon reflected in American repertoires. In 1907 he served the New York Symphony Society as guest conductor in a joint concert with the Oratorio Society. On the occasion of this visit, Yale University conferred on him the degree of Doctor of Music. Damrosch played a dozen of his compositions during and following World War I. Stock, with the Chicago Orchestra, followed the pattern of his predecessor, Thomas, who had given Elgar several "first times" in America, and gave him two and a half per cent of the repertoire. The Minneapolis Orchestra, in 1905 and 1906, presented the *Dream of Gerontius*.

After several decades of neglect, Elgar recovered some lost ground in the early thirties with the appearance of British conductors Barbirolli and Goossens. His death in 1934 also added some small stimulation to the public consciousness. His *Introduction and Allegro for Strings* and the *Cockaigne* Overture have been repeatedly performed; Menuhin played his Violin Concerto in the late forties. But were it not for his *Enigma Variations*, the late musician laureate of England would now have vanished from the American scene. In the popular mind he will live for some time in the stately march theme of *Pomp and Circumstance No. 1*, to which lyrics have been added ("Land of Hope and Glory"), thus making it both accessible and memorable to the masses and thereby insuring a destiny similar to that of Sibelius' majestic *Finlandia*.

VINCENT D'INDY As founder of the Schola Cantorum in Paris, d'Indy wielded a great influence in the more conservative wing of French musical society. Already famous in France, he entered the American repertoire in 1899 with the still famous *Istar* Variations and the *Medea* Suite, played by Thomas and Gericke.

His music did not flourish, however, until his visit to Boston and New York in the season, 1905–06. His next rise occurred during World War I when French composers became the beneficiaries of current patriotic sentiment. Although he had been dropped in Boston by Karl Muck for his cutting insinuations on the "Germanization of American music," he was, of course, quickly restored by the French successors to the luckless German conductor. Interest in the famous pedagogue and composer mounted during his second visit, 1921–22, when he conducted his works in several cities. Although his tour was judged "successful," the austerity of his music was far from arousing the feverish excitement touched off by his erstwhile enemy, Richard Strauss, who was touring the country during the selfsame season.

The compositions which have endured throughout his life cycle are the *Istar* Variations, the *Symphony on a French Mountain Air*, Symphony No. 2, and, to lesser degree, *Wallenstein's Camp*. Stock in Chicago and the French conductors in Boston enlarged his repertoire by the inclusion of his other works, but none has gained general acceptance. At present his music has almost vanished from the repertoire.

ALEXANDER GLAZOUNOFF   Glazounoff, sometimes called the "Russian Mendelssohn," created a sensation in the 1880's. His music, influenced by both the German and Russian traditions of the day, soon swept him into international prominence, with the inevitable concomitants: honorary degrees from Oxford and Cambridge and a visit to the United States (1929). Both Chicago and Boston were hospitable to him at the turn of the century, but Stock especially perpetuated these sentiments during the next two decades by playing about twenty-five of his compositions. After a dip in his popularity, Albert Coates, born in Russia of English parentage and with a record of successful conducting there, contributed to an American revival, especially as guest conductor of the New York Symphony, 1920–23. Of his prolific output, his Violin Concerto, Symphonies No. 4, 5, and 6, the Symphonic Poem, *Stenka Razine*, have had the most constant appeal in the past. Today only the Concerto survives.

ALEXANDER SCRIABIN Alexander Scriabin was first introduced to an American audience by Van der Stucken of Cincinnati with a performance of the youthful *Reverie* in 1900. Much more significant, however, were the American premières by the Russian Symphony of New York of the First and Third (*Divine Poem*) Symphonies in 1907, and of the Fourth (*Poem of Ecstasy*) in the following year. The Third and Fourth achieved considerable vogue in the United States. His last and most pretentious work, *Prometheus, a Poem of Fire*, was designed to effect a mystic union of sound and color and was scored for orchestra, chorus, and color organ. The Russian Symphony and the Philadelphia Orchestra each gave it a complete performance. The dreamy theosophical creations of his fellow Russian also appealed to Koussevitzky who early befriended the composer, propagated his art, and remained loyal for some years after assuming his Boston post. More recently, however, his enthusiasm for Scriabin definitely waned, and he publicly declared himself satiated.

OTTORINO RESPIGHI The peak of Respighi's popularity coincides with his visits to the United States in the period 1925–30. Of all Italians, none has contributed so much toward the advancement of orchestral music in his country as has this composer, who had succeeded in blending the classic ideal of form with romantic freedom and colorful orchestration. But the first excitement died down, and many of his dozen or more compositions were given isolated performances. Only the *Pines of Rome*, with the *Fountains of Rome* as runner-up, can claim inclusion in the charmed circle of the "standard" repertoire.

ERNEST BLOCH If one includes among the Americans those foreign-born who have achieved a considerable portion of their prestige while living in this country, then the Swiss-born Ernest Bloch has been the most abundantly played of all American composers. A prize-winner since 1919, his most publicized success was the *Musical America* award for his Rhapsody, *America*, given its world première by the New York Philharmonic, December 20, 1928, under Walter Damrosch, guest conductor. Although his residence in Cleveland and San Francisco gave special local impetus to performances of his works, his compositions have appeared in all the orchestras. Among those programmed most frequently are the Concerto Grosso, *Schelomo* (Hebrew Rhapsody for Cello), *Israel* Symphony and *Three Jewish Poems*. In 1925–30 one and one-half per cent of the total repertoire was devoted to his music; by 1950 it had declined to one-third of one per cent.

MANUEL DE FALLA   The Philadelphia and Boston orchestras introduced Manuel de Falla to their audiences during the season 1921–22 in excerpts from the ballets *El Amor Brujo* and *The Three-Cornered Hat*, respectively. Since then, these selections have continued to constitute the principal representation of this, the most distinguished of Spanish composers. His other compositions, sometimes found on programs—excerpts from *La Vida Breve* and *Nights in the Gardens of Spain*—are hardly sufficient to raise his present position to even as much as one percentage point of the total repertoire.

ROY HARRIS   Ever since Koussevitzky encouraged him to write his first symphony, Harris has been productive in both musical and literary fields. Like Aaron Copland, his pupil, he has energetically advocated the American cause and defended the music presumably written "in the spirit of the modern age." Koussevitzky launched five of his six symphonies, of which the Third has had by far the most impressive career. In 1943, when the Soviet Union was linked with the United States, Harris dedicated the Fifth to that temporary ally; and at the latter's request, it was short-waved by the NBC orchestra to that country. Harris has been played by practically every major orchestra, but with the reduction of the flow of new compositions has come the inevitable decline.

The Forgotten Names

The judgment of time has been harsh on many once favorite composers. Formerly widely renowned not only for their compositions, but for many other significant contributions as educators, performers and conductors, they are now extinct specimens, interesting chiefly as exemplifying the ruthless processes of history. Some of these were not mere "morning glories" which flowered for the moment, but had achieved substantial places in competition with the "immortals" themselves before the ultimate segregation had begun. However, their compositions did not long survive the days of their personal activities; the author's physical death was the usual signal for his disappearance from the repertoire.

Of these buried names, Ludwig Spohr was the most eminent. He was considered the greatest musical personage of his time, popular as orchestral conductor and violin soloist, as composer of operas, concertos, symphonies, oratorios, and chamber music, outranking even Beethoven in the eyes of some discerning critics. Students from foreign countries, including U. C. Hill, founder of the New York Philharmonic, sought him out as teacher, and to every violin pedagogue he is still known today for his *Violinschule*. He enjoyed an extraordinary vogue in London where, in 1820, he startled the members of the London Philharmonic, who had invited him as guest, with the innovation of the baton, a conductor's device which had been known on the continent for some time. With the Symphony No. 4, the Overture to *Jessonda*, and the Violin Concerto No. 8, together with less popular works, he was liberally represented on the programs of the New York, Boston, and Chicago orchestras until the close of the century. The New York Philharmonic Society, which played him to the extent of ten per cent, 1850–55, now has a collection of Spohr scores, acquired a century ago, which constitute a mute monument to his vanished fame.

Joachim Raff, the teacher of MacDowell, was another composer whose efforts met with immediate success. Of his eleven symphonies, No. 3, *Im Walde*, was considered his most gratifying work. In 1896 Philip Hale still maintained that Raff was the composer of one beautiful symphony, *Im Walde* and in the eighties and nineties it enjoyed numerous performances. Today the Wagnerian second movement and its Mendelssohnian *Scherzo* sound shallow and derivative. During the season 1930–31 it was resurrected by Toscanini and more recently by the CBS orchestra, but has had no performances since. The programmatic Symphony No. 5, *Lenore*, was only less frequently presented, and its *March* movement never failed to arouse a popular audience. However, the appetite for melodious romanticism, with unsubtle programmatic coloring, seems to have been satiated, and Raff went out of the repertoire with the passing of that taste.

Peter Lindpaintner and Johann Kalliwoda are total strangers today to any but the musical archeologists. Lindpaintner was an excellent conductor, held in highest esteem both in England and Germany, and was considered for the post of the London Philharmonic in 1855 when Wagner was invited. The overtures to some of his operas were recognized as those of a disciplined musician. Kalliwoda, whose Fifth Symphony was praised by Schumann, who further showed his regard for Kalliwoda by dedicating to him his *Opus 4*, was in Germany a somewhat less popular composer, but still influential and respected. The first decade of the New York Philharmonic coincided with the waning careers of these two men, and they soon quietly passed into history.

Because of the scintillating brilliance of the passage work in his piano concertos, *Septet* and other ensembles, which were well adapted to the light action and hard tone of the Viennese piano, the music of J. Nepomuk Hummel was still enjoyed for many years after the piano construction had been reformed. During its early years, the New York Philharmonic played his music frequently, and as late as 1893 de Pachmann performed the B Minor Concerto with the New York Symphony Society.

Never among the leaders, the Mendelssohnian Niels Gade still had a substantial number of performances during the first thirty seasons of the New York Philharmonic and during the first decade of the Boston orchestra. His First and Fourth symphonies and several of his overtures were repeatedly performed.

5

National Sources of the Orchestral Repertoire

THE APHORISM that "music is a universal language" which knows no national boundaries is countered by the obvious fact that music history is peppered with references to the "national idioms" of Spain, Hungary, Bohemia, Norway, Russia, and nearly every other country that has ever made any contribution to that noble art. There is no question that musicians and composers, like businessmen, tourists or just plain citizens, often think nationally, cultivate biases in favor of their own regions, and utilize the resources of their own land and culture in their compositions, which then become objects of sentiment not shared by members of alien faiths.

This sense of nationalism is conventionally thought to have germinated during the nineteenth century, and in the field of music is usually associated with the Romantic movement. Like all pat generalizations, this one can be accepted only with reservations. However, especially on the continent, music has tended to attach itself to political and literary ideologies, and to rally around the center of dominance of the national culture. This is a kind of mild totalitarianism which a motley population in a relatively traditionless country such as the United States may find difficult to understand or appreciate.

There are many ways in which these emerging national sentiments are awakened and manifested. Possibly the most important is the creation of a *Wetlanschauung*, which is designed to confer upon the national group the sanction for its separate existence. Intellectual and political leaders of European peoples have mobilized regional legends, exalted local geography and language, and glorified the heroes of war, history, and the arts. All these ingredients are nebulously but inspiringly amalgamated into the folksoul, or national spirit, which endows national life and all its products, including the arts, with their native characteristics, and constitutes a sharp focus of national pride. Such concepts give the incipient nation a past history, a present status, and a future destiny, as well as a geographical and cultural boundary line which separates it from neighboring groups, who are either inferior and to be despised, hostile and to be feared, or at least different, from whom they are to be distinguished.

But an abstract ideology, powerful as it may be, is not always a potent tool to gratify the national pride of ordinary people. Something more tangible and easily grasped is required for the bulk of the population. Accordingly, after the old feudal aristocracy had been destroyed, most European nations, large and small, turned to the musical forms of the simple folk, their songs and dances, as well as their myths and legends, which were viewed as grass-root emanations of their national spirit. These were then appropriated as the basic elements of their new art forms. Musical "entomologists" from Glinka to Béla Bartók beat the bushes of the backwoods for rare specimens of peasant songs, dissected them for structure, and mounted them in imposing collections. These were either presented "straight" or more commonly incorporated and absorbed into standard forms of song, symphony, and opera, on which they bestowed a national flavor. Weber's *Der Freischütz* was an early product of this movement. When Dvořák came to the United States (1891) to preside for a few years over the American Conservatory, he had already been so completely indoctrinated in that school of thought that he was ready to apply it to polyglot America. To the great consternation of certain American critics, he asserted that America, too, could turn to its "primitive" peoples—the Negro—for its national music. To illustrate the procedure, he composed a string quartet and a symphony "in the spirit" of the Negro folktunes which, however, Americans have innocently enjoyed ever since without any reference to their supposed derivation.

Such musical ethnology naturally turned up a great repertoire of tunes, rhythms, dances, and folktales that, in the minds of their enthusiastic devotees, were the incarnation of the folksoul, which constituted the presumable source from which they originally derived. Folksong is alleged to be more spontaneous, fundamental, and therefore a more valid and genuine expression of national character than the artificial and adulterated high art forms of civilized music.

Ethnologists well know that these national forms, although often the objects of intense loyalty, differ from one another not because of any inherent racial predisposition, but because they developed in cultural isolation in response to innumerable local conditions and circumstances. Because in some instances their local origin was more apparent than real, they sometimes became the mistaken subject of patriotic fervor—as in the case of the gypsy tunes that Liszt and Brahms passed on in their "Hungarian" rhapsodies and dances. Occasionally these aboriginal motifs have had an appeal even to other nations as quaint and exotic themes. Indeed, it has been said that the best "Spanish" music has been written by Frenchmen: Debussy, Ravel, Lalo, Bizet, Chabrier, who did much to popularize the Spanish idiom. Spain furnished the rhythms, France the technical and professional equipment to incorporate them into more pretentious forms.

In addition to this primitive material, nations have also turned to their less remote literary and musical histories for inspiration. There are numerous occasions of such reinforcement of group ego. Military defeat and oppression, which ordinarily is productive of deeply wounded pride, commonly seeks compensation in its own national traditions. German nationalism, stung by the Napoleonic defeats, contributed its bit to the revival of Bach; and France, after her defeat of 1871, unwrapped many of her musical heirlooms (Rameau and Couperin) to reshape significantly her subsequent musical tastes. Hungary, Poland, Bohemia, and the smaller European nations evinced the same preoccupation with their glorious past to console them for the inglorious present.

A third manifestation of nationalistic feeling, which influences the repertoire of a nation, is the disposition toward loyal preferential cultivation of its own music, whatever its forms, to the relative exclusion of foreign art. This type of "protective tariff" has been practiced by all countries, including the United States. The Russian Music Society, founded in 1859 by Anton Rubinstein, the London Philharmonic Society, the French Société—all had written commitments favoring the cultivation of native works and binding them to a certain quota of performance, while conductors like Koussevitzky have voluntarily given generous opportunities to native American composers who would most certainly have been ignored had they carried foreign labels. In times of national crises such sentiments are, of course, intensified, when "Buy British," and "Buy American" become patriotic slogans which apply to art and ideas, no less than to material goods.

This unfolding of the national spirit is not to be construed as a succession of rational or chronological steps. Although a people may be maneuvered into a nationalistic frenzy by Hitlerian calculation, more usually there is a sincere, spontaneous, slowly ripening group consciousness of which the aforementioned elements are important components.

Although there is an abundant literature on the general subject of "national" music, there is certainly no clear consensus on how the term can be defined; for the varieties of music produced within the boundaries of a nation are numerous, to say nothing of the difficulty of identifying the "nation" itself. Those who view the national boundaries as temporary historical solutions of physical struggles between peoples are more likely to abandon the mystical notion of the *Volksgeist* and its musical emanations, and to turn in the direction of the simple and forthright declaration that French music, for example, is simply the music written by composers resident in France. A national music idiom, insofar as it exists, is like the national flag, language, or other symbols in that it whips up powerful sentiments through habits of association and of planned and persistent indoctrination. After all, the sense of nationality does not reside in the germ plasm, but is an overlaid state of mind acquired, unconsciously or consciously, by a kind of cultural osmosis. As cultural patterns change from time to time, national music will also display varied patterns, and its classification into nationalistic pigeon-holes will necessarily give rise to strange incongruities, as in the case of Debussy and Saint-Saëns. Both were intensely national in sentiment, but quite incompatible with each other personally and musically. Truly, nationalism is only "culture" deep.

Such detached and cold analysis does scant justice to the sentiments which in part determine the popularity of the national composers, but they are among the many nonaesthetic factors which ultimately condition the taste of the public. If the assumption is correct that nationality factors do influence repertoire selections, the extent to which they do so may be measured by identifying and tracing the national sources of the repertoire and by tracing the occasion and origins of these influences. Accordingly, it will be necessary to split up, prismlike, the American repertoire into its nationalistic bands and measure the width of each in the musical spectrum.

But the difficulty of setting up "true" political boundaries and the ease with which they are crossed by the mobile musician, make national classification of some composers almost impossible. The simplest criterion of nationality would be, of course, birthplace. This criterion has the advantage of being at least unambiguous, for it would seem self-evident that no composer could have been born in two places at the same time. But this, too, turns out to be an oversimplification that does not reckon with vacillating geographical boundaries. Dvořák was either Bohemian or Austrian according to the sentiments consulted. Everyone knows that Chopin was born in Poland, though Warsaw was then a second capital of Russia.

But the real inadequacy of birthplace as a criterion of nationality is exposed by the fact that most of the important things happen to a person *after* he has been born. A rigid adherence to birthplace would ignore the remainder of the composer's life during which, of course, his compositions were conceived. French opera was founded by the Italian Lully; Cherubini, Offenbach, and Meyerbeer composed their best work in France; Clementi lived in England, and Spontini in Germany. Theodore Thomas and Walter Damrosch came to America as children. Handel offers a genuine dilemma, for he was born in Germany, wrote his operas in the Italian style, settled in England at the age of twenty-seven, was naturalized in 1726, anglicized his name by dropping the umlaut (he was less successful in shaking off his thick accent), developed the oratorio into an English classic form, and was finally buried in Westminster Abbey. Loath to abandon such a "national" ornament, the Germans include him among the *Deutsche Tonkünstler* with the umlaut restored. Still more confusing is the case of Frederic Delius who was born in Yorkshire of German and Dutch parentage (for many years he called himself "Fritz"), was a wool salesman in Scandinavia, managed an orange grove in Florida, studied in Leipzig, paid a few brief return visits to his "native" England, spent forty-five years of his life in France, but was buried in England, according to his own last wish.

In general, unless there are strong reasons to the contrary, a composer is allocated for present purposes to the country in which he has produced his major works, and in whose culture he has shared and participated. For those reasons Handel is counted as British; Chopin as French; the conductors Theodore Thomas and Walter Damrosch, as American. Stravinsky, Schoenberg and others, who migrated with mature reputations to the United States, are assigned to their respective European origins.

Austro-Germany

In peace as well as in war, weaker countries are usually "invaded" by the stronger. Unless interfered with by political decree or other barriers, the ordinary exchange of material and spiritual goods will normally seek a competitive level. That simple generalization epitomizes the complete conquest of America by Austro-German music.

This dominance of Teutonic music can be ascribed to a combination of several factors. In her early history, the three hundred German principalities, competing with one another in splendor by aping the court of Versailles, cultivated music as one of the principal adornments of courtly life. They thereby decentralized and increased the demand for skilled performers and composers. Catholic and Protestant churches likewise patronized the musical arts and encouraged widespread appreciation. Most German cities maintained a small band of *Stadtmusikanten* which were called out on civic and festive occasions, expanding their occupational opportunities. After 1800, nationalistic sentiments further nourished competition with Italian music, ultimately reducing the latter's influence and inflating the pride of the Germans in their own musical achievements. These circumstances did not prevail to the same degree in

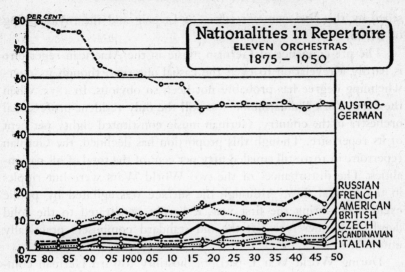

Although the dominance of German music in the American repertoire is well known, its near monopoly in the early years is not so obvious. It still accounts for more than half of all the music played today in American orchestras.

France, England, and Russia, and were therefore all the more effective toward raising the musical trademark "Made in Germany" to its high distinction.

For present purposes, Austria and Germany have been thrown together because they represent a cultural entity that could not be broken with impunity. Beethoven and Brahms, born in the North, and certainly considered German by everyone including themselves, passed practically their entire careers in Vienna. Though the Protestant North and the Catholic South are separable, there is no such distinction apparent in the national consciousness of the composers themselves, nor made by the world in general. One may note, however, a shift of musical supremacy from Catholic Vienna to the Protestant North in the course of the century—that is, to Leipzig, Berlin, and Weimar, and the intermediate city of Munich. Wagner, Mendelssohn, Schumann, Liszt, and Strauss represent the new generation succeeding Haydn, Mozart, Beethoven, and Schubert of the Vienna orbit. The dying imperialism of Vienna was partially superseded by the vital commercialism of Leipzig and the royal setting of Berlin.

The pre-eminence of German music in the American repertoire is hardly a revelation to even the casual observer, though its overwhelming degree has probably not been so obvious. In 1875, when the New York Philharmonic was still the only resident professional orchestra in the country, German music constituted eighty per cent of its repertoire. Though this proportion has declined, the German repertoire in 1950 still equaled fifty per cent of the total of all nationalities. The disturbances of the two World Wars were but ripples in the general flow. Although the surface was agitated by public excitement during the first war, it hardly penetrated to the solid depths, and therefore left the old standard composers practically untouched.

During World War I, patriotic hostility toward German composers was slow to develop in America because of our phlegmatic nationalistic sentiments and the geographic remoteness of the war. Since the American government itself had distinguished between the German people and its rulers, it was at first not quite clear what German music had to do with the war and its outcome. In fact, America, with its traditions of freedom, was rather sentimental and self-consciously proud of its professions of tolerance. In the spring of 1917, shortly after the American declaration of war, the Chicago orchestra closed the season with an all-German program consisting of Beethoven, Brahms, Strauss, and Wagner, to show the "folly of banning German music because we are at war." [1] Another critic averred that "intolerance of German music is, of course, absurd. . . . France bans Wagner, Strauss and the moderns, but France has been despoiled and she is proudly bitter. Her case is not ours." [2] It was not until January, 1918, almost one year after the declaration of war, that the Philharmonic of New York announced that it would not play contemporary German music (this was directed principally against Richard Strauss, who was accumulating royalties in this country). The following month Stransky took out first citizenship papers and in March, 1918, presented an all-Wagner program.

Anti-German sentiment was, however, slowly being kindled.

The sinking of the *Lusitania* in 1915, in which a Vanderbilt youth was among the one hundred American casualties (the family was active in Metropolitan Opera support) aroused much indignation. With the draft, casualties, and atrocity stories, a feeling of repugnance toward things German did eventually gain headway. It became not only a question of public sentiment, but also one of public safety against possible demonstrations and disturbances. Fritz Kreisler, a wounded Austrian soldier, who had been touring freely since 1915, had been forbidden by local authorities, in the fall of 1917, to appear in concerts in Pittsburgh and St. Louis because of possible incitement to riot. He thereupon tactfully announced the cancellation of all of his contracts.

Among our Allies, England likewise banned the playing of contemporary German music, to which the Germans flippantly retorted that they would like to "retaliate, were there any British music to boycott." Germany, where Puccini was very popular, had banned Italian opera since 1915.

This period witnessed the passing of the Teutonic near-monopoly on the position of conductor. The succession of Austro-German conductors had been an illustrious one. Henschel, Gericke, Nikisch, Muck, Paur, and Fiedler in Boston; Scheel and Pohlig in Philadelphia; Oberhoffer in Minneapolis; Bergmann, Seidl, Mahler, and Stransky, in New York; Stock in Chicago; Kunwald in Cincinnati; Zach in St. Louis; and Hertz in San Francisco had all had their origins and training in Central Europe. But for many reasons, both political and cultural, the great tradition had finally been dissipated, and only an isolated few—Fritz Reiner, Bruno Walter, and Otto Klemperer—were subsequently called to delay the complete passing of the glorious era.

France

Orchestral music had never reached the high development in France it had attained in Central Europe, and French conductors before World War I are not much more than names even to the informed American. In instrumental specialization, however, France had achieved a reputation for its woodwinds, and several of them, notably Georges Longy (oboe) in Boston (1898–1925), and Georges Barrère (flute) with the New York Symphony (1905–28) contributed greatly to American musical life in performance and teaching.

Aside from the war period, French music shows a stable twelve per cent of the total American repertoire. In the earlier years, the principal composers were Berlioz and Saint-Saëns. As they receded, Debussy, Franck, and still later Ravel and numerous moderns rose to compensate for the losses of the older generation.

For some time before the American entry into the first World War, France had made an effort to gain friends in this country. The eighty-year-old Saint-Saëns paid a visit in 1915, and other musical missions were knocking at our doors. In 1916 a committee of prominent New York financial leaders, which included Kahn, Vanderbilt, and Rockefeller, was formed to encourage the propagation of French music. With the declaration of war, April, 1917, that trend grew to flood tide, climaxing in 1918, when André Messager toured the United States with his celebrated Conservatoire orchestra.

The orchestras which led the patriotic procession in the United States were the Boston Symphony with Rabaud and Monteux, the New York Symphony with Walter Damrosch, who had already evinced a Francophile disposition some years previously, and Cincinnati, which, like Boston, had sacrificed its conductor to the war, and had placed the Belgian Ysaye on the podium.

The New York Philharmonic has been consistently timid in its espousal of French music; at the other extreme San Francisco, under Monteux, successor to Hertz, has accorded the French at least a short period of glory with twenty per cent of the repertoire during the first five years of his tenure.

Russia–Soviet Union

Beginning modestly with the prolific Anton Rubinstein, and later with the melodious Tschaikowsky and the sumptuous Rimsky-Korsakoff, the Russians have climbed to second place in the nationality competition in recent years, with twenty per cent of the repertoire. This resulted from the unusual popularity of several modern composers, Shostakovitch, Prokofieff, and Stravinsky, together with smaller increments of Rachmaninoff and Miaskowsky. This dramatic upsurge was not effected without a series of political interventions, of which Russia has been the beneficiary.

Early in the first World War, when Russia was the ally of Britain and France, any news from that mysterious country was good copy. More and more reports on Russian music began to seep into the columns of the American musical journals, and some of our symphony orchestras were only then discovering names which are today familiar and respected. Borodin, Glinka, Moussorgsky, and a dozen others were accorded belated recognition, and Glazounoff, Scriabin, Stravinsky, Miaskowsky followed. The Russian Revolution elicited considerable intellectual sympathy in America, which redounded to the profit of Prokofieff and Shostakovitch and was climaxed in the almost hysterical patriotic esteem of World War II.

Of all the nationalities, however, Russia has contributed most conspicuously to modern trends. The recent composers, together with a backlog of Tschaikowsky and Rimsky-Korsakoff, assure that country for a period, at least, a substantial representation. All orchestras have shared in this upswing during the war years, though Boston, with Koussevitzky, has outrun them all, and Minneapolis, with Mitropoulos, has been most indifferent.

Italy

The universal vogue of Italian musical terminology alone would be sufficient evidence of the early dominance of Italian music in Europe and America, analogous to the world-wide prevalence of the English language in the commercial world. This Italian control was bitterly resented by the German nationalists, who, as the volume of their own music accumulated, vented their protests by the use of a competitive German musical vocabulary. This chauvinistic precedent was not generally emulated, however, for the advantage of an international professional vocabulary is obvious, even though it must be Italian. It has been the eager refuge of many a guest conductor in a foreign land for whom that slender but expressive lexicon was the only verbal contact.

It was with opera, of course, that Italy had conquered the world;

until recently, her contribution to symphonic literature has been meager. As late as 1870 the Beethoven symphonies were unknown in Rome. Since Sgambati, who produced his first symphony in 1881 under German influence, is usually credited with being the first Italian symphonic composer, others have modeled after their Teutonic neighbors. Although the emergence of Italian symphonic patronage synchronizes with the careers of Respighi, Casella, Pizzetti, Malipiero, Tommasini, and others, the revival of the older schools—Vivaldi, Rossini, Boccherini, and Scarlatti—shares in the rising national fortunes in America. Of those responsible for that growth, none were so energetic in promulgating Italian tastes as Toscanini between 1926 and 1936—a devotion to his countrymen for which he has received some censure. In recent decades many of the gains of Italy's late renaissance have been cancelled, and she has returned to the insignificant position she previously held.

Great Britain

England, like the United States, has been an importer rather than a producer of music. Nevertheless, in recent decades she has gained a modest place in the American repertoire. Elgar, Delius, Handel, Vaughan Williams, and more recently William Walton, have been responsible for her appreciable position in the world's music. The New York Philharmonic and the Cincinnati orchestras were for a number of years under the direction of Barbirolli and Goossens, British-born conductors. In the thirties Barbirolli accorded the British six per cent of his program time while Goossens gave them four per cent. Philadelphia, St. Louis, and Minneapolis trailed with a more normal one per cent.

Latin America

Although economically and politically the United States is quite emancipated from its European ancestry, in cultural pursuits her line of sight has always been, and still is, over her shoulders Europeward. Such a psychological stance tends to exclude Latin America from her vision. Recently, however, orchestral institutions, organized similarly to those in Anglo-America, have arisen "south of the border." This has led to a flourishing musical life with the attendant production of composers and conductors. Mindful of common political, economic, and social interests in this hemisphere, the United States government has contributed its influence toward the cementing of cultural ties with her southern neighbors. In the threatening days of the 1940's both Toscanini and his NBC orchestra and Stokowski's Youth Orchestra toured the Latin American countries. The Latin American conductors Eleazor de Carvalho and Carlos Chavez have presided over various orchestras in the United States. Among the composers, Villa-Lobos of Brazil is the most noted and enjoys a statistically perceptible rank in the repertoire. Others, principally from Brazil and Mexico, are: Gomez, Guarnieri, Revueltas, Mignone, Pinto, Siqueira, Tavares, Braga and Fernandez. Although their contributions to the United States repertoire may be infinitesimal, they are comparable to the American contribution to the orchestras of Europe.

United States

When a new country does not possess the means for producing the goods that satisfy its consumer wants, it may import these goods from other nations. This the United States has done in the case of French wines, Irish linens, English china, Greek and Roman architecture, British political ideas—and German music. There is nothing humiliating in such a course, nor is it necessarily a symptom of national weakness. Quite to the contrary, cultural exchange between nations is a normal phenomenon which promotes amicable relations and contributes to the larger gratification of their citizens.

If such international exchange of goods and services is conventional and salutary, it is on the other hand no less normal for the rising young industries themselves to enter the competition in furnishing such goods and services, and to appeal to national loyalty to support that purpose. During the first half-century of the life of this country, this nativistic feeling had not yet been awakened in the realm of music. The colonists of the eastern seaboard had brought their tastes in their bag and baggage, and had re-established themselves here in their accustomed style and manner, so far as pioneer conditions would permit. In the concert halls of America, as in Europe, Haydn, Handel, Mozart, Pleyel, Gyrowetz, Vanhal, and Stamitz were the staples, later superseded or supplemented by Hummel, Kalliwoda, Beethoven, and a score of others without much thought of interpolating compositions by the few American composers who might have aspired to challenge their priority.

That the possibility of American compositions was condescendingly acknowledged at the time of the founding (1842) of the New York Philharmonic Society, can be deduced from the guarded commitment in Article VII of its by-laws:

If any grand orchestral compositions, such as overtures or symphonies, shall be presented to the Society, they being composed in this country, the Society shall perform one every season provided a committee of five appointed by the government shall have approved and recommended the composition.

There is no doubt that the conception of its function entertained by the Philharmonic Society was to propagate the taste for the great classics, and that any contemporary music worthy of such high purposes was hardly likely to emerge on the American frontier.

The earliest recorded protest, and by far the most vigorous, against the assumed supremacy of foreign music was voiced by the composer-critic William Henry Fry and the composer-violinist George Bristow, in the early 1850's. They were the first American-born operatic and orchestral composers of any pretension. Born in New York one year after the arrival of his immigrant father from England, Bristow was a leading member of the New York Philharmonic Society for the first forty years of its existence, and it accorded him single performances of three of his symphonies and two of his overtures at its regular public concerts. But the Philharmonic's ninety per cent German repertoire elicited from Bristow a protest against the "systematized effort to extinguish American music," and he punctuated his conscientious convictions by a brief withdrawal from the society (1854).

Neither Fry, who precipitated the controversy in a series of public addresses, nor Bristow, who echoed it, were of a temperament to belittle their own talents. Says Bristow:

Who are the men who told you that Americans cannot write up to the standard of the New York Philharmonic Society? They are the same style of illuminati that in the London Philharmonic, after attempting to rehearse it, kicked Beethoven's C Minor Symphony under their desks and pronounced the composer a fool or a madman.[3]

Fry, composer of operas and symphonies which were repeatedly performed in Philadelphia and New York, was still more frenetic in his indignant challenge:

I have no fear of having my symphonies played side by side with Beethoven's. . . . It is just what I ask. It has been done here repeatedly and I am satisfied with the result. . . . If you will cause a symphony of mine in four movements to be played by the New York Philharmonic . . . I will undertake to produce one in from four to six days, though some composers give four to six months to the task; and I have no objection to have a symphony so performed sandwiched between any two classical symphonies played on the same evening.[4]

In retrospect, it has seemed to some that these gestures were merely a misguided and quixotic outburst of wounded pride and frustrated ambition unworthy of a balanced personality. But it would be too much to state that they were exclusively so. The problem takes on another hue when viewed in its historical context. Fry and Bristow were the specialized manifestation of a comprehensive antiforeign sentiment that made itself felt in the arts as well as in the economic, political, and religious realms. They spoke not only for themselves, but for a large segment of the native American population, which constituted an understanding audience. It is doubtful whether even such self-willed temperaments as Fry and Bristow would have sallied forth so vehemently without a bracing atmosphere which could invigorate them with self-confidence.

During the period of the early 1850's, the United States was in the throes of a violent nativistic, anti-alien movement. The rate of immigration had greatly accelerated in the forties with the Irish wave following their potato famine in 1846, and the German wave that began with the disturbances of 1848 and endured through the next decade and beyond. This enormous increase in immigration alarmed many Americans who viewed it as a threat to their democratic institutions. They feared the destruction of American enterprise, the substitution of European culture, and even the control of the government by these alien forces. A pinpoint quotation of mere population data will tend to explain their unrest. For in 1850 New York City, which was the center of the nativistic movement, had a total population of about 500,000, of which 241,000 were foreign-born.[5] If one considers that almost one hundred per cent of the foreign-born were adults, and that about fifty per cent of the native-born were adults, it can be calculated quickly that the foreign-born adults (workers and potential voters) outnumbered the native-born adults roughly two to one! To this must be added their discrepant social ideologies and cultural traits, which were downright repulsive to many native Americans to a degree that is difficult to reconstruct in the modern cosmopolitan age. All the Irish, and some of the Germans, were Roman Catholic, which aroused great apprehension in a predominantly Protestant country. The Germans, many of whom were free-thinkers, drank beer, violated the Sabbath, cultivated and preserved their own language, newspapers, and schools, maintained these cultural traits with obnoxious pride, and were alarmingly successful in their infiltration of many occupations, of which music was only one of the most conspicuous instances.

Here was enough to offend every taste. Native-born workers, the professions, small business, and patriotic Americans in general resented mightily the transplantation of the institutions of monarchic Europe onto the free soil of America. While not lacking in a certain respect for the old world, aspiring American musicians found themselves overwhelmed by foreign traditions that threatened to stifle their own embryonic attempts to establish an indigenous culture. Said Bristow:

. . . From the commencement there has been on the part of the performing members and the direction of the Philharmonic Society little short of a conspiracy against the art of a country to which they have come for a living; and it is very bad taste for men to bite the hand that feeds them. If all their artistic affections are unalterably German, let them pack up and go back to Germany, and enjoy the police and the bayonets . . . where an artist is a serf to a nobleman.

Although both Bristow and Fry were no doubt interested in the success of their own compositions, their philosophy ran somewhat deeper, to promulgate a national school. Bristow, therefore, continues:

What is the Philharmonic Society in this country? Is it to play exclusively the works of German masters, especially if they be dead? . . . Or is it to stimulate original art on the spot?

America has made the political revolution which illumines the world, while Germany is still beshrowded with a pall of feudal darkness.

Musicians were not the only protestants. A similar sentiment of emancipation was expressed by Ralph Waldo Emerson in his famous Phi Beta Kappa address, "*The American Scholar*" (1837):

Our day of dependence, our long apprenticeship to the learning of other lands, draws to a close. The millions around us . . . cannot always be fed on the sere remains of foreign harvests.

And in his essay on *Self-Reliance* (1841), he announces a cultural declaration of independence:

Our houses are built with foreign taste; our shelves are garnished with foreign ornaments; our opinions, our tastes, our faculties lean and follow the Past and the Distant. . . . And why need we copy the Doric or the Gothic model? Beauty, convenience, grandeur of thought . . . are as near to us as to any, and if the American artist will study with hope and love the length of the day, the wants of the people, the habit and form of the government, he will create a house in which all these will find themselves fitted, and taste and sentiment will find themselves satisfied also.

The rebellion of Fry and Bristow could not, of course, escape without rebuttals. They drew return fire not only from the "government" of the Philharmonic, but also, from the universalists who viewed art, like humanity, as being "above all Nations." The running disputations were carried in the columns of various publications. Richard Storrs Willis, editor of the *Musical World and Times*, took strong issue with the nationalistic conception of music: "This is a wrong view of art—decidedly so. It is one-sided and contracted. Let us strive for art—universal art." He insisted, however, that Germany was the "land of real music."

This period saw the crest of the nativist movement. Its intensity was fated to subside with the approach of the great sectional conflict of 1861–64. Realistically, of course, music was one of the "infant industries"; but Bristow, Fry, and their colleagues, in the very nature of the case, were not in a position to slap a protective tariff on the competing importations as the manufacturers of material goods, with the aid of a friendly government, had successfully done. If one concedes the legitimacy of a campaign for an American school, Bristow's diagnosis was absolutely correct. It is interesting, if not profitable, to speculate whether the spark of American national music could have been shielded by any arbitrary method from the suffocating competition of European art, or whether the disparity between the merits of American and German music and the technical superiority of German executants would in any case have been sufficient to tip consumer demand toward the foreign product.

American musical interests have, however, never relinquished the militant nativist ideology, though their sentiments are now usually expressed in less virulent form. Recently, an American composer, much more successful than Fry or Bristow, paraphrased exactly their earlier lamentation and despairingly inquired: "What chance have we of producing an original native school of composers?" and then interjects the diplomatic reservation that

I have no quarrel with the masterpieces. I think I revere them and enjoy them as well as the next fellow. But when they are used, unwittingly perhaps, to stifle contemporary effort in our own country, then I am almost tempted to take the extreme view and say that we should be better off without them.[6]

Another distinguished American, a member of a celebrated line of native musicians and pedagogues, directed his barbs particularly against

the starvation diet in contemporary music . . . the fashion-enslaved, prestige-hypnotized minds that guide the rich and reactionary Philharmonic-Symphony . . . so totally devoid of any American loyalty to match the Italian loyalty (Toscanini) that is, after all, rather likeable in him.[7]

Before attempting an estimate on how well the American composer has actually competed in the American repertoire, it will be necessary to define a few terms and make a few basic assumptions. Reduced to question form:

(1) What is the definition of American music, and which composers should be included?

(2) What is the norm of "fair" competition with European composers?

Whether there exists a characteristic American idiom and, if so, what its earmarks may be, are not problems to be solved within the scope of the present study. However, the American repertoire has been frequently affected by the urge to develop a native musical dialect.

Of all the traits which American composers have explored—Negro tunes, Indian folksong, Puritan hymns, and jazz rhythms—the last-named has gained the greatest notoriety. Ragtime, its antecedent manifestation, had been successfully excluded from the genteel arts for two decades. Until then considered the aesthetic preoccupation of the proletariat, it became, after the first World War, a subject of controversy and even crashed the recondite pages of the *Musical Quarterly*. Critics began to inquire whether, after all, jazz might not be capable of serious emotions. Was not America overlooking a kind of musical resource whose significance Russia and other European countries had long ago discovered in their own more primitive social strata?

From the standpoint of the serious orchestral repertoire, the high point in the history of jazz in this country may be scored in the concert of Paul Whiteman's orchestra in Aeolian Hall, New York, February, 1924, when George Gershwin, late of Tin-Pan Alley, performed the première of his *Rhapsody in Blue*. The program opened with the *Livery Stable Blues*. Everybody of note was there, including Walter Damrosch, who forthwith commissioned the twenty-six-year-old artist to compose a piano concerto in the same genre. Damrosch gave it a hearing in 1925, as well as the same composer's *An American in Paris* in 1928.

Nearly every serious conductor professed a polite interest in the new trend of "symphonic jazz." It was the thing to do. Although Gershwin was not invited to Boston until January, 1932, when he performed his *Second Rhapsody* under the baton of Koussevitzky, all orchestras performed the Gershwin items at least once. But no major orchestra, except Philadelphia, from whom the world had learned to expect an occasional bizarre gesture, went so far as to invite the "king of jazz," Paul Whiteman, as guest conductor. In November, 1936, when much of the flurry had already subsided, Whiteman and his twenty-four-piece band merged with the Philadelphia Orchestra for the eighth subscription pair in which, of course, the *Rhapsody in Blue* was again featured.

The normal direction of migrant music now for once reversed itself, and jazz became an exportable item. Not only did Whiteman undertake a successful tour of Europe in 1926, but jazz bands became popular in England and France during the twenties. Looking for novelty to suit the mood of the restless postwar epoch, European composers were intrigued by the pungent rhythms and quickly, but briefly, absorbed them into their own styles. Auric, Milhaud, Stravinsky, Ravel, Tansman, "spiked" their music with the new intoxicating motifs, while Krenek created a sensation in Germany with the opera, *Jonny Spielt Auf*. A host of Americans were similarly imbued. Carpenter, Copland, Antheil, Gruenberg, Bennett, Gould, and others flirted with the new "national" idiom.

But in the perspective of 1950, it turned out to be a passing fad. Whether the strictures of this idiom were too confining, whether the strings, which are so important in the symphonic band, were not given enough to do, whether it was just plain fatigue from the overstimulating rhythms, or whether jazz itself gave rise to newer forms that made the original inspirations seem archaic, it is still true that interest soon played itself out.

If it is difficult to characterize American music, it is equally difficult to identify the American composer. The native-born American composer offers few dilemmas; for, after a training period in Europe, he returns to America to produce his most important works. However, since about 1920, many foreign-born composers have been making their home in the United States. This was a novel turn of events which could hardly have been predicted before the collapse of European economy. Before World War I, it was well known that *conductors* and *performers* were attracted to these shores by the liberal economic returns in this rich and resourceful country. In fact, it was the accepted practice to recruit orchestral musicians and to entice soloists and conductors with fabulous fees, which were justified by the public acclaim for the artists. It was, however, not so reasonable to expect *composers* to seek a home in this country where there existed no mechanism to reward them in comparable measure.

But composers behave very much as do persons of more humble callings: when their environment threatens them, they assemble their paraphernalia and migrate to a safer place where they may ply their profession. Therefore, after each of the two World Wars and the intervening Russian revolution, the general depression and the persecution in Germany, emigration was greatly accelerated. In addition to the "push" from decayed Europe, there was the "pull" of Hollywood, as well as of the music schools and universities that were prepared to employ these composers, to say nothing of the "free air" and other liberal inducements of democracy.

Not all of these adopted sons have the same valid claim on the formal American appellation. Counted as Americans, for present purposes, are only those foreign-born who have made a substantial portion of their contribution while living in America.

It might at first glance seem simpler to label as American all music composed in America. This would, indeed, be very simple if some composers did not migrate in mid-career. Since, for practical purposes, it is composers, not musical titles, which are classified, all works of a given composer must go into the same pigeonhole. A second solution would be to count as American all music composed by musicians now permanently domiciled in the United States. This would result in the classification of Stravinsky's *Firebird Suite* as foreign in 1920, and as American in 1950. But it does not seem fair to inflate spuriously the "American" contribution to the repertoire by a heavy listing of compositions that were composed in Europe, attained prestige for their authors in Europe, and then by the happy accident of migration counted posthumously "American." [8]

For the purpose of this tabulation, therefore, composers who have produced their major works in Europe, whose career was well established there, are assigned to their native country: Hindemith, Stravinsky, Alban Berg, Rachmaninoff, Bartók, Schoenberg, and others. Those born in Europe, but who have migrated to this country young enough to establish their careers in the United States, are called American. A sample list, with ages of arrival: Berezowsky (21), Loeffler (21), Wagenaar (27), Bloch (36), Fuleihan (15), the conductors Theodore Thomas (10) and Walter Damrosch (9). Composers like Tansman, Prokofieff and Dvořák, who spent only a few years in this country and subsequently returned to Europe to continue their careers where they had initiated them, are, of course, counted as foreign.

Previous to 1900, the American contingent in the symphonic repertoire was small. In its regular concerts, the New York Philharmonic Society accorded single performances to Paine (1890) and Chadwick (1895) and two to MacDowell (1894, 1897), in addition to the aforementioned Bristow. More hospitable was the Chicago orchestra under Thomas. This foreign-born conductor, who had acquired all his training in America, extended commissions to John Knowles Paine on the occasion of the Philadelphia and Chicago Expositions, offered all-American programs at these expositions in 1876 and 1893,[9] and performed diverse works of Paine, Chadwick, MacDowell, Foote, Gleason, H. W. Parker, and other Americans during the regular seasons of the Chicago orchestra beginning in 1891. His American programs at the Philadelphia Centennial, July, 1876, and the Chicago Summer Concerts of August, 1882, were the first of their kind by an established American orchestra.

The Texas-born Van der Stucken, who had received all his training abroad, gained a reputation in the late eighties (1885–87) for his free-lance "novelty" concerts in New York, among which he likewise included American programs.

Boston was, of course, the early musical capital of the United States. The pioneer work of Lowell Mason in the public schools of Boston, the Boston Symphony Orchestra, the New England Conservatory of Music, Harvard University, which established the first chair of music in 1875—all were fertilized by a proud regional tradition, and reinforced one another in producing an indigenous musical culture that survives to the present day. With its prewar Teutonic conductors consecrated to the classics, Boston was, and still is, also the most enthusiastic exponent of native works. To be sure, the

THEODORE THOMAS'
UNRIVALLED
SUMMER NIGHTS CONCERTS.
On WEDNESDAY EVENING, July 19, 1876.
FIFTY-FOURTH
SUMMER NIGHTS CONCERT.
AMERICAN NIGHT.
When the programme will consist of works by American composers exclusively.

SOLOISTS.
MR. ALFRED H. PEASE,
The young American Pianist and Composer.
MESSRS. SCHMITZ, PIEPER, KUSTENMACHER, and ELLER,
Horn Quartette.

PROGRAMME.
PART I.
A SYMPHONIC POEM—A Day in the Country . . . W. H. FRY.
A DAY IN THE COUNTRY.
The Symphony opens with an *Adagio* movement, descriptive of a summer morning. Hymn of nature, the rising sun, "the cock's shrill clarion and the echoing horn." The next is an *Allegro*, musically painting the festivities of the villagers; the lads and ladies in their best array are about to join the dance. An *Andante amoroso* describes the jealous pangs of a disappointed swain. Then come the rustic dance, the rude and grotesque steps of the peasants, to the music of oboes and guitars, pictured in *Allegro*. The sun is setting as a recruiting party arrives, the soldiers join the dance, and more rude and boisterous the mirth as the Symphony concludes with a *Finale Stretto*.

CONCERTO FOR PIANO AND ORCHESTRA—E flat . . A. H. PEASE.
1. Allegro con fuoco.   2. Andante con moto.   3. Allegro vivace alla Marcia.
(Mr. A. H. PEASE.)

INTERMISSION.
PART II.
SYMPHONY—No. 1 . . . . J. K. PAINE.
   1. Allegro con brio.   3. Adagio.
   2. Scherzo—Allegro vivace.   4. Allegro vivace.

INTERMISSION.
PART III.
OVERTURE—Don Munio . . . . . . DUDLEY BUCK.
CONCERTSTUECK—For orchestra and horn quartette . . DUDLEY BUCK.
(Messrs. SCHMITZ, PIEPER, KUESTENMACHER, and ELLER.)
ALLEMANIA WALTZES . . . . . . MYRON A. WARD.
JAPANESE GALOP . . . . A. H. PEASE.

CONCERTS WILL COMMENCE AT 8 O'CLOCK.

This first all-American orchestral program by an established American orchestra was played in Philadelphia during the Centennial of 1876. Although the objective of the American orchestras was to perform the standard classics, Theodore Thomas presented a number of all-American programs in New York and Chicago.

native New England group of Paine, Chadwick, Foote, Converse, Gilbert, Whiting, and Buck, many of whom composed "with a German accent," has largely given way to a more modern national representation, but the adventurous policy of the Boston orchestra remains.

Since 1900, external circumstance and the growing maturity of our own musical resources have contrived to favor a general expansion of American participation in the repertoire. However, when viewed in relation to the total repertoire, the American contribution may still seem somewhat less than impressive. After two world wars, with the attendant inflation of national enthusiasm, the proportion of American music in the symphonic repertoire of all orchestras has attained in 1950 less than seven per cent. In the case of other nationalities, even such a percentage would allow several composers to show a significant position on the popularity pyramid, but American patronage is so diffused among innumerable composers that almost no one achieves a discernible fraction of the repertoire.

In the twenty-five-year period 1925–50 the names of 280 American composers appeared on the regular subscription programs of the ten oldest major symphony orchestras. Of these, 136, or fifty per cent, have been played by only one orchestra each, while only eighteen composers, or six per cent, have been heard in nine or ten orchestras. It is therefore apparent that most of the quota of American composers is consumed in purely token performances of local and regional interest. However, by volume of music, as measured in frequency of performances and length of compositions, this top six per cent of composers accounts for forty-five per cent of *all* American music played in that period. These eighteen composers not only appear in more orchestras, but are represented by more compositions, and are given repeated performances. If we arbitrarily establish a more liberal criterion of national prestige at a minimum of seven out of ten orchestras, we may conclude that thirty-four of the 280 American composers, or thirteen per cent, achieved national status at some time during the twenty-five-year period under review, and that they account for sixty per cent of all American music performed in that period by the ten major orchestras.

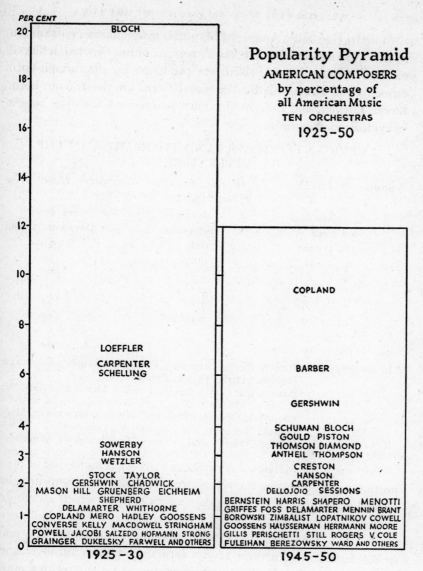

PER CENT

Popularity Pyramid
AMERICAN COMPOSERS
by percentage of
all American Music
TEN ORCHESTRAS
1925–50

20— BLOCH

18—

16—

14—

12—

10— COPLAND

8—

LOEFFLER

CARPENTER   BARBER
6— SCHELLING

GERSHWIN

4—   SCHUMAN BLOCH
                         GOULD PISTON
SOWERBY   THOMSON DIAMOND
3— HANSON   ANTHEIL THOMPSON
WETZLER   CRESTON
                         HANSON
STOCK TAYLOR   CARPENTER
2— GERSHWIN CHADWICK   DELLOJOIO SESSIONS
MASON HILL GRUENBERG EICHHEIM   BERNSTEIN HARRIS SHAPERO MENOTTI
SHEPHERD   GRIFFES FOSS DELAMARTER MENNIN BRANT
DELAMARTER WHITHORNE   BOROWSKI ZIMBALIST LOPATNIKOV COWELL
1— COPLAND MERO HADLEY GOOSSENS GOOSSENS HAUSSERMAN HERRMANN MOORE
CONVERSE KELLY MACDOWELL STRINGHAM GILLIS PERISCHETTI STILL ROGERS V. COLE
POWELL JACOBI SALZEDO HOFMANN STRONG FULEIHAN BEREZOWSKY WARD AND OTHERS
0— GRAINGER DUKELSKY FARWELL AND OTHERS

    1925–30   **1945–50**

*The turnover in American compositions in the repertoire is so rapid
that there is not yet an established, standard, American repertoire in the
accepted sense of the term. The repertoire life of American compositions is still very short. If this continues, the ranking of American
composers will show further violent changes in the next decade. As
American are counted those composers who were born in America or
who have done at least a considerable portion of their composing in
this country.*

277

The foreign-born American has made a significant contribution to the American portion. Of the American music that has achieved national recognition, one-third was produced by the foreign-born element, and two-thirds by the native-born. Of the foreign-born, Bloch, Loeffler, and Berezowsky must be credited with the largest individual contributions.

AMERICAN COMPOSERS AND THEIR MUSIC IN THE REPERTOIRE

Number of Orchestras in Which American Composers Have Been Heard: 1925–50

COMPOSERS		NUMBER	PER CENT
NO.	PER CENT	ORCHESTRAS	AMERICAN MUSIC
136	49	only 1	9.0
45	16	only 2	7.0
48	17	3 or 4	12.0
17	6	5 or 6	11.0
16	6	7 or 8*	16.0
18	6	9 or 10*	45.0
total	280	100	100.0

* In 10 orchestras: Barber, Bloch, Carpenter, Copland, Diamond, Gershwin, Hanson, Harris, Taylor, Piston

 9 " Berezowsky, Gould, Griffes, Loeffler, Mason, Schelling, W Schuman, Whithorne

 8 " Chadwick, Creston, Eichheim, Goossens, Gruenberg, Mac Dowell, Sowerby, Still, Wetzler, V. Thomson

 7 " Fuleihan, MacDonald, Menotti, R. Thompson, Wagenaar

Although the individual American composer is minuscule in proportion to the giants of the repertoire, the American group may be viewed as forming a little kingdom of its own in which a definit hierarchy quite naturally emerges. It is true, this ranking is not very stable. The tendency to perform principally contemporary an living American composers results naturally in quick turnover an brief life spans. By the time these pages are read, their relative positions may have undergone further alterations.

In their hospitality to American music, Boston and Chicago have been the most generous. But this statement, like every other statistical generalization, must be tempered by analysis and interpretation If the strictly local contingent of their American repertoire i measured for the quarter century 1925–50, nearly forty per cent of the American music performed by the Chicago orchestra is contributed by composers of the local metropolitan area. If more subtle personal ties were considered, this percentage would probably be increased. To be sure, some of the Chicago music did enjoy performances outside of that city, but not much of it; for the Chicago contingent of American composers represented only 5.7 per cent of the total American music played by the remaining nine orchestras. The Chicago orchestra's reputation for generous patronage of American music is therefore to a significant extent—i.e., at least forty per cent—attributable to the fact that Chicago is a rather important musical center, with a number of local composers.

Boston similarly illustrates the fundamentally regional definition of Americanism, though in somewhat lesser degree. "Local" compositions in Greater Boston comprise thirty per cent of the volume of American music, while these same "Boston-American" compositions constitute nine per cent of the American music of all other orchestras.

One may conclude, therefore, that if certain orchestras seem to be apathetic toward "American" music, it is at least partially indicative of the lesser prominence of their cities as musical centers without the opportunity to fatten their American averages on local composers. That a simple unanalyzed enumeration is inadequate can be shown by the hypothetical case of an orchestra that apportions, say, fifteen per cent of its repertoire to local composers, and another orchestra that devotes five per cent of its total repertoire to a well-screened nationally recognized American repertoire. The "fifteen per cent orchestra" would carry off the prestige of being the most generous in the cultivation of "American" music, although in the larger perspective this prestige would be spurious because based exclusively on regional patronage. As a matter of fact, that is exactly what has occurred. During the decade of 1935–45 San Francisco, Los Angeles, and Cleveland topped Chicago in their cultivation of a well-selected nationally American repertoire, exclusive of purely local patronage.

The foregoing argument does not imply that "local" renditions are necessarily a financial and musical waste. Since most reputations begin on the local level, this sort of experimentation is important—to say nothing of the calculated benefits of such performances to both composer and orchestral society. Furthermore, man does not live by masterpieces alone, and "lesser" works, even immature ones, furnish the critical perceptive background so necessary for the appreciation of "greater" works. It is the nature of human judgments, and of individual and national aesthetic development, that requires many to be called before the few are chosen.

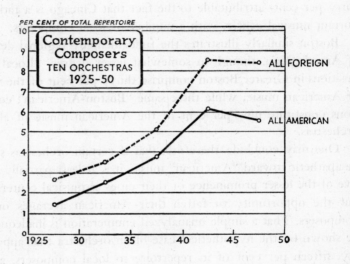

The volume of American music in the repertoire of the symphony orchestras does not quite equal the volume by foreign contemporaries.

As has been stated, ever since the days of Fry and Bristow, conductors of American orchestras, nearly all of foreign birth and training, have often been charged with unduly preferential treatment of foreign composers, and disloyal, unjustified neglect of American composers. Does the admittedly small percentage of American music constitute unfair discrimination? It is not a simple matter to appraise the justice of that charge. Obviously, some measurable standard of comparison must be established before the question can even be discussed.

In spite of an occasional argument to the contrary, one could hardly claim the total orchestral repertoire as the monopolistic province of the American composer. Furthermore, the established repertoire, foreign though it be, has become so firmly rooted for good or ill in the expectations of the audience that it would imperil the very musical institution itself to make drastic encroachments upon it.

There is, therefore, everything to be said for a preliminary hypothesis that the American composer could not assert the right to compete on equal terms with the staples of Beethoven, Bach, Strauss, and Wagner, and that the volume of repertoire accorded to such established masters should not be used as a criterion against which the competitive success of the American composer should be measured. It is rather with the foreign *contemporary* composer, who is in an analogous competitive position, that the comparison must be made. Therefore, in order to exclude the inappropriate comparison with the standard classics, the more or less arbitrary birth date of 1890 was set for the selection of comparable American and foreign composers.

It requires some temerity to set a norm for equitable treatment for these two groups—the American and the contemporary foreign composers. How is one to weigh such imponderables as the quality of music, the aesthetic traditions of the audience which must be respected, and the national pride to be indulged? Should the American quota be equal to, or exceed, the most favored single nationality? Or should it match all Europeans put together?

On the basis of the 50–50 criterion (i.e. Americans equal all other nationalities put together), it can be stated that the American composer competed rather unsuccessfully during the twenty-five years from 1925 to 1950. All contemporary music shared a substantial growth during this period, but foreign music enjoyed a somewhat more rapid acceleration in patronage. Of foreign contemporaries, perhaps Shostakovitch and Prokofieff, for reasons both political and aesthetic, constitute such special cases that even they may be considered by some as "unfair" competition. If one agrees to their

Contemporary Composers in Repertoire

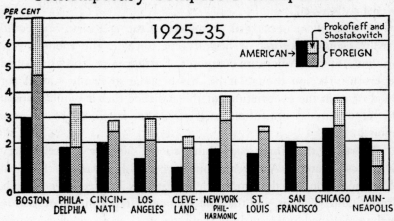

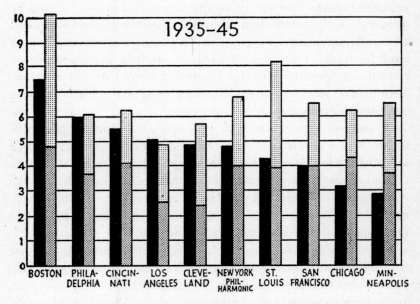

American composers were played in an amount approximately equal to all foreign contemporaries combined if Prokofieff and Shostakovitch are omitted.

elimination, there is no question that American music, in all but two of the orchestras, did enjoy a patronage as great as, or greater than, all other foreign contemporaries put together, as measured by proportion of total playing time.

The increase in American music during the decade 1935–45 may be ascribed to several factors, of which war enthusiasm is naturally the first to come to mind. Undoubtedly national patriotism directs attention to all national resources, material and nonmaterial, and contributes to a desire for self-sufficiency as well as the cultivation of national pride. There is, too, the obvious fact that the American composers were ten years older in the second decade and had had an opportunity to mature and develop their music. Again, European sources were drying up, and therefore offered diminished competition to American works. Undoubtedly, the conductors who were abandoning their European homes, were beginning to consider America as a more permanent abode. They were even eliminating their European vacations, which in the old days always included a "search for new scores"—a standard part of management's fall advertising blurb up to a quarter of a century ago. In short, orientation toward things American was more pronounced, thereby creating a favorable psychology for the adoption of American works. Of course, not all orchestras were equally zealous in following this trend. Boston, as usual, was the more enterprising, while Chicago and Minneapolis seemed to be the least affected.

If there was any hope that American composers would finally overtake their foreign contemporaries, such hope received a jolt during the five postwar years, 1945–50. The statistical reason for this condition can be very simply attributed to the oft-reiterated quick turnover in American performances, which has its corollary in their short musical life spans and their regional concentration. Few American composers achieve national representation. More of their foreign contemporaries do. While ten per cent of the foreign contemporary composers born since 1890, representing seventy-five per cent of the foreign music played, appeared in nine or ten orchestras, only six per cent of the contemporary Americans, representing forty per cent of all American music played, appeared in nine or ten orchestras. A recital of the names of the contemporary foreign composers will easily clarify these data. Appearing in nine or ten orchestras were the following in order of volume: Shostakovitch, Prokofieff, Hindemith, Milhaud, Honegger, Tansman, Walton, Khachaturian, Weinberger, Ibert, Britten, Chavez, and Kabalevsky—nearly all well-authenticated composers.

It is only logical to expect that foreign composers, who are included in the American repertoire, would have come to international notice, thus assuring them wide representation in America. A few of them have no doubt profited by their permanent migration to the United States. However, most of their performances consist of their older works composed on the European scene. Most of the "single-orchestra" foreigners are either the choices of guest conductors from abroad, or represent certain favorites of permanent conductors who had close professional ties abroad previous to assumption of their duties in this country. This, of course, includes practically ninety per cent of active conductors. There is hardly a permanent foreign-born conductor in this country, from Toscanini down to the youngest, who has not at some time or other provoked the critical jibe, "He plays the pieces of his [fill in the nationality] friends."

The "problem" of all contemporary music is not only a problem of nationalism, the foreign-born conductor, and the imponderables of merit and quality, but also a problem of "modernism." The relative force of these factors cannot be readily estimated because they are inseparable: it is almost impossible to play American music without at the same time playing "modern" music.

This dilemma of the modern composer is not of his own making, but is the product of the social circumstances into which he has been born. As compared with the composer of Mozart's day, he is beset with many discouragements. In addition to normal competition with one another, modern composers must compete with a long accumulation of hallowed works that are entrenched in prestige; and musical archeology is constantly adding to the already glutted supply. Consequently the modern composer encounters a saturated market that is inhospitable to the new entrant, and places on him the burden of aesthetic proof for crashing the established repertoire. Instead of being able to take it for granted that his music will be played, the young composer sees the conductors reaping special rewards for their enterprising courage in bestowing their attention upon him.

In these forbidding circumstances, the American composer cannot emulate the successful works of the past, adding a slight increment of individuality for pleasing effect, as Bach, Mozart, and even Beethoven and Wagner did at the beginning of their careers. The established masters are now so familiar to the audience that "derivative" qualities are easily detected and generally disparaged.

Finally, the romantic principle of composing for the future, as the old masters *unintentionally* did, is so well established that compositions too readily understood are critically received. Thus, the assignment of writing nonderivative, yet interesting, music of certain durability imposes a strain on the modern composer that was not felt in 1800. Small wonder that he often oversteps the bounds of comprehensibility and makes unappreciated flights into the unknown in a desperate effort at a distinctive contribution.

The problem of the historical shift from the concert of 150 years ago when nearly all music was "new," to the present time when nearly all music is "old," is a larger sociological and psychological problem. A standard of equity for new music cannot be established in a vacuum, but must be appraised in terms of the economic status of the orchestra, the social function of the orchestra, the constitution of the membership of the audience, and all the other forces which comprise life itself, in terms of which the diverse, and often incompatible, wishes and desires seek satisfaction. These are the subjects of the following chapters.

6

The Orchestra, Concert Folkways, and Social Life

The Function of the Orchestra in Community and Nation

THE SYMPHONY concert is not exclusively, nor in one sense primarily, a musical event. For, so complex and inseparable are human interests, that every social occurrence is a blended experience of varied and simultaneous motives. A concert is comparable, perhaps, to a dinner party, where the interest in food may be subordinated to business contacts, social prestige, ceremonial display, or mere convivial association. No hostess would be flattered to be assured merely that the food was nutritious, nor even that it was tastily served; for such an affair has well-accepted ramifications into many other avenues of social intercourse. A symphony concert is similarly a pluralistic event, which may supply an outlet for fashion, prestige, civic pride, heightened national consciousness, as well as musical delight. It is therefore no disparagement, but a psychological and sociological truth, that music is often secondary to nonmusical considerations.

Since music, too, is laden with these derivative functions, which vary considerably in character and proportion from person to person, the quality and meaning of "enjoyment" of a concert displays a wide range of variation in different epochs. When, for example, we reflect on the strenuous content of our recent and contemporary symphony programs, the awe in which the masterpieces are held, the reluctance with which the audience pits its taste and judgment against that of the critic and conductor, and the frankly tentative and reserved judgments of the critics themselves, it is difficult for the modern patron to realize that in the classic period, often called the "golden age," music was generally considered a matter of sheer pleasure, a forthright delectation of the senses, without any pretense of satisfactions of a more edifying nature. It is quite evident from Mozart's letters that he contemplated very little beyond the pleasure of the moment and harbored no conceit about the sacredness of his scores. In 1787 he writes of his having attended a ball where

I saw with the greatest pleasure all these people flying about with such delight to the music of my *Figaro* transformed into quadrilles and waltzes; for here nothing is talked about but *Figaro*, nothing played but *Figaro*, nothing whistled or sung but *Figaro*, no opera as crowded as *Figaro*—very flattering to me certainly.

His solicitous father shared this desire for instantaneous success, counseling him

to imitate the natural and popular style which everyone easily understands.

As if in reply to this recipe for success, the devoted son reassures his father at the time of the rehearsals of *Idomeneo* in Munich:

As for what is called popular taste, do not be uneasy, for in my opera there is music for every class, except the long-eared.

In speaking of his concertos, he almost apologizes for the esoteric passages:

These concertos are a happy medium between what is too easy and what is too difficult; they are very brilliant, pleasing to the ear, natural without being vapid. There are passages here and there from which connoisseurs alone can derive satisfaction, but these passages are written in such a way that the less learned cannot fail to be pleased, though without knowing why.[1]

Charles Burney, a scholar and friend of artists, statesmen, and musicians (including Handel and Haydn), writing his monumental history of music during the same period, voices the same straightforward and mundane conception, characteristic of the period of The Enlightenment:

Music is an innocent luxury unnecessary, indeed, to our existence, but a great improvement and gratification of the sense of hearing.[2]

Although much of Mozart's music is still played and enjoyed today, his guileless conception of its function has suffered eclipse, for the typical aesthetician of the romantic nineteenth century (descended, however, from eighteenth century antecedents) held in scorn the theory that music is made merely for pleasure. In fact, it need not even be beautiful. In reviewing Sibelius' Second Symphony, the late Richard Aldrich, then of the New York *Times*, expressed that notion as follows:

There is absolutely nothing in this symphony that is written to please the ear as many wish to be pleased. There is much that sounds chaotic and disordered; but it is evident to the listener who can take a larger measure of it, that it is all very definitely related, the coherent expression of a consistent idea. It is not too much to say that this Second Symphony of Sibelius is one of the strongest compositions in the symphonic form that have been heard in a considerable period.[3]

Such a sanction for what was then cerebral cacophony would have been inconceivable to Haydn, Mozart, Beethoven, and their contemporaries. Mozart, Handel, and Bach had great difficulty in producing music in sufficient volume and at a rate to satisfy the honest appetite for novelty on the part of their audiences, while today a novelty is something the modern audience is expected to endure for the sake of possible habituation and future delight. To explain this complete reversal in the conception of the psychological function of the repertoire, in the criterion of aesthetic judgment, and in the relation between the artist and his public, one must examine the intervening period: the nineteenth century and its Romantic revolt.

The shift is largely attributable to the complete sociological metamorphosis of the audience and of the social status of the musician. During the previous century, the pre-Napoleonic era, the musician had been an employee, who performed a skilled service according to contractual obligations—analogous to the twentieth-century staff musicians in a radio or motion picture studio, allowing, of course, for the divergent requirements of the period and the much greater sense of social stratification than now prevails. His secular audience consisted primarily of the nobility, many of whom were themselves adequate performers, and who sometimes arrogated to themselves the privilege of joining the orchestra. Some even utilized their leisure moments for composing. In fact, as late as 1905 Breitkopf and Haertel published a catalogue of compositions by

German royalty, including Kaiser Wilhelm—which serves to recall the piquant warning attributed to Brahms that "one should never criticize the compositions of royalty, for you never know who may have written them."

Composers were craftsmen who composed to order and who, like the architect, the portrait painter and the cook, expected their work to be appreciated forthwith. It would not have occurred to Bach, Mozart, Haydn, and the other *Kapellmeister* of the day to ignore the interest of the current generation by writing *Zukunfts-musik*, nor could they have had the temerity to expect their socially superior patrons to sit through repeated hearings of a suite or symphony on the chance that they or their descendents might possibly enjoy it at some future time. The liveried Haydn admitted that he experimented, but such experimentation was mild and inoffensive, and therefore tolerated and even enjoyed by the prince whom he was paid to serve.

By the turn of the eighteenth century, a social and political transformation had occurred with rather dramatic suddenness, as historical events go. In the history of music this consisted in the catastrophic bankruptcy, and consequent decline in power, of the musician's two richest employers: the church and the court. To gratify those who feel that they must pinpoint evolving historical events, one may suggest that it was the bombardment of Vienna in 1809, sheltering at once the aged Haydn, the middle-aged Beethoven, and the twelve-year-old Schubert, which actually and symbolically gave the *coup de grâce* to the feudal era and marked the transition from the old order to the new. The musician lost his job and became a free-lance composer and an itinerant performer, with all the risks appertaining thereto.

His audience was no longer the closed group of cultivated nobles and their leisurely satellites, before whom the composer was honored to display his accomplishments. Instead, the nineteenth century performer now served the emerging middle-class audience, the third estate, in a commercialized concert to which anyone had access who was able and willing to pay the price of admission. In this new pecuniary social order, the bourgeois audience was not sophisticated, nor well-schooled; but it was ready to be impressed by the virtuosity

and the eccentricities of a Paganini, a Liszt, and a host of other virtuosi who mushroomed from that soil. Instead, therefore, of an
attitude of reverence and awe on the part of the musician toward
his noble audience, it was now the audience which sat in bewilderment before the musician. The artist, in fact, held his audience—his
new patrons—in disdain for its crude and undeveloped aesthetic
tastes. In art the customer was never right. The mass of anonymous
urbanites, newly hatched under the wings of the industrial revolution, issued from office and shop, from banks and colleges, from the
professions and public services. Occupied, as they were, full time in
gaining a livelihood from the new competitive world, they were by
no means a leisure class, they felt keenly their inadequacies in the
arts, and acquired a veritable inferiority complex in their presence.
They suffer from this debilitating affliction to this very day. They
eagerly emulated the standards of the decaying, but still glamorous,
aristocracy by cultivating and supporting the arts, and stood ready
to be instructed.

Now, if the audience generated by the bourgeois social revolution thus drew away from the artist, the artist on his part also drew
away from the audience. Being no longer in the immediate employ
of a master whom he was being paid to serve, he developed a sense
of autonomy and self-expression in standards of composition as well
as in interpretation and execution. The artist even erected an ivory
tower where he could commune with his aesthetic conscience and
protect himself from any insinuation of being responsible to the
audience.

The evolutionary development of the musical arts abetted the
artist in his new independence. Orchestral instruments were being
improved, orchestras were being enlarged, and composition was becoming more difficult and esoteric. Beethoven's orchestral scores
looked "so black" that they literally sounded the death-knell of the
amateur player-cooks who had infested the mixed ensembles
during the courtly era. Music was now becoming a learned profession which a lifetime was too short to master. Art was really long,
and time fleeting. Liszt and Mendelssohn contributed enormously
to the enhancement of the prestige of the once lowly profession.
As a consequence of these social and technical revolutions, the

artistic gap between audience and musician, which had been negligible a generation or two before, was now widening; and the evident explanation was to be sought not only in musical terms, but still more significantly in terms of the social, economic, political, and technological changes unfolding during that period. It is only against such a social background that the problems of the contemporary "heavy" repertoire can be comprehended.

Synchronized with these social changes, philosophers, as is their wont and function, were drafting a system of thought designed to rationalize and buttress these overt historical trends, which were rendering music incomprehensible even to an intelligent audience. By an evolution too complex to rehearse at this point, music was elevated to the most exalted position among the arts; and in its unfettered creativeness, it approximated "pure spirit," universal and absolute Truth. Because of its mystical and supernatural characteristic, it possessed the power to exert a spiritual and ethical influence upon its auditors superior to that of any other medium. Such neo-Platonic doctrines of Hegel and Schopenhauer inevitably placed the great musician in a position of ethical leadership, conferred a certain sacrosanct validity on his "inspiration," and elevated him into the realms of near-infallibility. Music, the most exalted art, was not only a reflection of ultimate ideas and sentiments, but was actually a form of thinking in tones—an abstract, subtle, and direct communication superior to crude verbal symbols, independent of the physical actualities of the world, and therefore a "universal" language. The inspiration of the artist was thus of higher validity than the uninstructed taste of otherwise intelligent people. This was the ideology propagated by such philosophers as Schopenhauer, whose concepts dominated his disciple, Richard Wagner.

This dogma of artistic supremacy was imported to the United States from Germany in the baggage of musicians and conductors, and has set the standards for the musical repertoire to this very day. Indeed, in this country, where vertical mobility was much more rapid than in Europe, where class relations were elastic, where wealth was easier to come by, and the middle class musically unsophisticated, the musical gap was probably still wider than in the old country. Precisely because of this, the conductors assumed, and were given, greater latitude and freedom in America than in Europe. The programs in Boston and Chicago were much more radical —or "progressive"—than they ever were in London, Vienna, Leipzig, and Berlin, both in relation to the maturity of the audience and in absolute terms, as far as the latter can be measured.

The musical interpreters, Bergmann, Theodore Thomas, Gustav Mahler, Gericke, and the rest pressed the last ounce of vindication out of the mystical ideologies which upheld the didactic mission of music, and translated this conviction into an unrelenting policy, in the face of an indifferent, and even antagonistic, public. It is quite irrelevant whether it was Bergmann, Theodore Thomas, or Wagner himself—the essential remark has been attributed to all three—who replied to the protest, that they "do not like Wagner," with the determined resolve: "Then we will play him until they do." [4] The significant thing is that, consonant with the Romantic philosophy with which they were imbued, such a retort was symptomatic of a policy which nearly all symphony conductors relentlessly pursued. If Theodore Thomas seemed to be the most fervent missionary of them all, it was partly because, in those days, there was more proselytizing to be done. To him, a symphony program was a stern, humorless "sermon in tones." The function of a concert was not relaxation, but

what our overworked business and professional men most need in America is an elevating mental reaction which is not amusement.

He was convinced that music was a "powerful character building force" which, "by its uplifting influence" would transport one to a "higher plane." [5] The music journals of the day regularly carried long articles on the beneficent effect of music on personal character and national welfare. This identity between Beauty and Virtue was an old axiom dating to the Greeks, who were alleged to have brought this union to perfection. It was, of course, an abiding faith rather than an empirically derived discovery. But precisely because it was a mystic faith, it was more tenaciously and uncritically adhered to than if the generalization had been obtained from prolonged and painstaking empirical studies of human behavior.

The musical leaders were warmly supported in their ethical and didactic mode of thought and practice by critics, painters, authors, poets, and even psychologists. Henry T. Finck, critic and early Wagner biographer, knew of

no other art that so vividly arouses the unselfish feeling, the desire for sympathetic communion . . . one of the most important moral functions of music, that of weaning people from low and demoralizing pleasures . . . the best way to eradicate savage impulses. . . .

. . . If such performances of both sacred and secular music were more frequent, we should have less drunkenness, less wife-beating, less spending of winter gains, less winter pauperism.[6]

There seemed to be no area of human conduct which might not be susceptible to aesthetic influences. Western civilization itself was big with possibilities if the aesthetic front could be maintained unbroken. A biographer of Theodore Thomas wrote in 1927:

When before have we been aware of any such force at work on such a scale among us? Suppose it [the symphony orchestra program] to keep on for another generation, gathering head. It might produce in this country the greatest change ever known. . . . Two generations of it might change the whole American character; it might in the end scourge us of materialism. Is this fantastic? Not if what we believe about the power and the ethics of art has any foundation.[7]

Somewhat more vague, but in exactly the same vein, spoke John S. Dwight, the influential Boston critic, musical editor, and New England transcendentalist, who opined that "good music must have some intimate connection with the social destiny of man."[8]

William James, the philosopher-psychologist, warned that musical indulgence, however, could be overdone, by lapsing into an "inert sentimental condition" and thereby defeat the very ethical purpose of the arts. He therefore advised

never to suffer one's self to have an emotion at a concert without expressing it afterward in some active way. Let the expression be the least thing in the world—speaking genially to one's aunt, or giving up one's seat in the horsecar if nothing more heroic offers—but let it not fail to take place.[9]

Hanslick, too, deprecated the overzealous educational policies of the conductors. When, in 1880, Bülow closed a Beethoven cycle with a double performance of the Ninth, the famous critic deplored the "vigorous faith with which he propagated the Beethoven gospel by baptizing the converts, as it were, with a fire hose." [10]

In the nineteenth century, this general exaltation of the arts drew much of its strength from the deficiencies of the industrial era. Social critics like John Ruskin, William Morris, Walter Pater in England, and Ralph Waldo Emerson in America—each in his own way—were revolted by the misery and ugliness attendant on the growing pains of the new industrialism, and had a supercilious scorn for material science, which for them was the root of these evils. Said Emerson in his *Conduct of Life:*

Geologies, chemistries, astronomies, seem to make us wise, but they leave us where they found us. . . . All our science lacks the human side. . . . Science hates the name of love and moral purpose. . . . Beauty is the form under which the intellect prefers to study the world. All high Beauty has a moral element in it.

It is not at all obvious, nor even probable, that the industrial philanthropists, who liquidated the deficits incurred by Theodore Thomas, Gericke, Mahler, and Stokowski, necessarily shared these mystical convictions with the crusading conductors whom they sponsored. Some were indeed musical and philosophical dilettantes, while many of them were downright metaphysical illiterates and calculating businessmen to whom the ethical import of the Beethoven Third probably did not make much sense. However, in the meantime, the orchestra, with its conductor and esoteric programs, had achieved a certain prestige and glamour. Like fine churches, public buildings, and parks, it soon became an element in the complete apparatus of civic life which focused not unwelcome attention upon the community, and consequently deserved support. Such "tycoon" pride was characteristically expressed by the orator of the occasion at the dedication of Orchestra Hall, December 14, 1904:

Chicago has been the most public spirited city in the world. We are proud of our rapid growth in wealth and population, but we are not satisfied with the merely industrial growth of our city—we demand something more and something better. We look through the dust and smoke of Chicago as she is, to see the fair and noble form of our city as she will be, a center of influence, intellectual and artistic as well as industrial, a school for the nation, as Pericles declared Athens was the school for Greece.[11]

Intercity rivalry was a constant factor that stimulated audience, management, and conductors. Even the idealistic Thomas used this motif on his rebellious constituents in defense of his uncompromising stand on program construction:

The announcement of a symphony on the program was enough to keep many people from the concert. . . . When fault was found with the severity of the programs I would say: Do you wish our program to be inferior in standard to those of the Boston Orchestra? "No" was the answer . . .[12]

That an orchestra had merit as an investment that would redound to the economic benefit of a city was a frequent theme. It was agreed, however, that a city's musical life serves as an enticement to visitors and settlers, and the tours of the orchestra are considered favorable publicity. In one instance, the orchestra was declared to be a force in "helping to sell shoes" for the greatest shoe center in the country.[13]

There are many who are neither sensitive to the supposed ethical overtones of a symphony, nor concerned with the commercial potentialities of a fine civic orchestra, but whose private social ambitions are gratified by indulgence in such an honorific enterprise. These impulses manifest themselves in diverse ways: maintenance of boxes or other preferred locations in the auditorium; program listing as patron; socially exclusive erudition on matters artistic; all the subtle satisfactions accruing from the wide range of contact and intimacy with a fashionable concern, from the occasional ticket purchaser to the confidential relation with conductor and steering members of the board, with all its invidious prestige. The concert-hall box has now all but disappeared in the relentless democratization of audience and patrons. But it once reflected the highly prized perquisite of the social elite. The private corridor and the anteroom, which conferred a sense of aloof distinction, translated the symphony and opera into a social ritual more highly regarded than the aesthetic relaxation derived from the actual music, which, in fact, was often sacrificed.

Musical politics may run very deep, and orchestras have at times been a "football of society." With motives something less than sublime, various groups have often rallied around rival conductors, thus literally splitting the resources of the community to the detriment of higher values. On occasion, however, such competition has had its salutary moments. Witness the case of the prolonged feud between the followers of Damrosch and Thomas in New York, during which two orchestras challenged each other for supremacy. But in other less inspiring circumstances, two orchestras have been supported when nourishment was insufficient for one. That pioneer period has, in general, passed. Though factions will always exist, funds are not nowadays so plentiful as to permit the luxury of such wasteful competition.

Since 1893, when Walter Damrosch first organized them, many of the responsibilities for carrying on orchestral affairs have fallen to the ladies, whose efforts have proven indispensable to the solvency of the harassed orchestral institution. Largely for the benefit of the fashionable world, the matinee concerts (usually Friday afternoon) are maintained. Originally instituted by the New York Philharmonic as a public rehearsal which would offer bargain rates to students, musicians, or others who might wish to hear repeated performances,[14] these matinee programs have long since graduated into more or less exclusive afternoon affairs, constituting an integral part of the winter social season. In Boston and Philadelphia, where this "Friday Spell" exerts its full potency, this particular division of the audience into two segments has been profitable, for the house is sold out. However, in other cities, for various reasons, the Friday patronage, though involving a similar principle, has for some time been hardly sufficient in volume to persuade the management that the retention of the traditional weekday matinee was practicable. History may be repeating itself, for the economic aristocracy today, analogously to the feudal aristocracy of 150 years ago, is declining in power and is relaxing its control over our artistic institutions. Musically this may mean a popularization of the repertoire and a significant alteration in the role played by the orchestra in its community relations.

There remains another function of music in general, and the

orchestra and opera in particular, which has never struck such deep roots in the United States as it has in Europe: its contribution to national solidarity. The urge to integrate the various aspects of national life—religion, politics, family, industry, and the arts—is not an exhibition of any virtue or perversity inherent in man or nation. It is, sociologically speaking, induced by conditions of stress, national emergency, and tension, and does not flourish in times of peace, plenty, and repose. If this totalitarian phenomenon prevailed during the nineteenth and twentieth centuries in Europe, it is because Europe, unlike the United States, experienced an abundance of tension and relatively little repose. Nations are not "patriotic" when there is nothing to be patriotic about. Patriotism is rather a defense reaction, to protect the cherished values which are threatened, or *thought* to be threatened. If nationalism became the prevailing idea in the nineteenth century, it was not because of the vague, spontaneous, and unconditioned promptings of a "romantic impulse," but it stemmed rather from a definite crisis in the affairs of nations. Prussia suffered a humiliating defeat by Napoleon, Poland was dismembered by three powerful neighbors, Bohemia felt itself oppressed by the Hapsburgs, Norway was uncomfortably yoked to Sweden, and Finland to Russia. Although some of these culture groups were not to realize their nationalistic yearnings until 1918, their internal cultural cohesion was maintained throughout the preceding decades. This overwhelming preoccupation with their cultural autonomy is manifested in their musical preferences in creation and performance, as well as their political policies.

The usual European conception of musical nationalism is that of the folksong, in the largest sense, which becomes the basis of the more sophisticated forms in song, symphony, and opera. This conception was, indeed, a critical symptom of the growing national consciousness, for folksongs—the musical expression of the indigenous folk—could be despised only so long as royalty and nobility set the standard of taste. With that power destroyed, the center of gravity of economic, political, and aesthetic interests veered to the middle class, and to the rural regions which had previously been held in serfdom.

In addition to the important folksongs and folktunes, nationalism manifested itself symptomatically in subject matter of song and opera (e.g. Glinka, Weber); in the use of national dances (Smetana); in the revival of forgotten music and musicians from their historical past (Rameau, Bach, Purcell); in the pressure to perform native and contemporary works (Russia, France, Germany); the purging of foreign music and musicians (Germany, United States in World War I); and in the fabrication of an ideology which defines music as an emanation of the national spirit, or an economic class (Germany, Soviet Union).

If the United States has never been infected with the chauvinistic virus as severely as has Europe, it has at least not escaped exposure. For the United States is a mosaic of polyglot expatriates who have no common and glorious past that could be revived to flatter provincial pride. As a nation almost without a "history" in the venerable sense of the word, a nation that has never experienced a serious external crisis, there simply do not exist the first essentials for a good nationalistic debauch.

Two minor symptoms of nationalism did subsequently put in their appearance in the United States: the purging of German music during World War I, which has been a matter of apology ever since; and the inauguration of a kind of "protective tariff" for American works. But the wave of sentiment to "buy American" has never reached a high crest among the populace, and it remains today, as yesterday, the expression of small and interested pressure groups. It must be said, therefore, that the orchestral institutions and their repertoire are not, in the United States, a function of national solidarity. For the average consumer, they have remained essentially "above the battle."

Seating Plans

If we could reverse the passage of time, transport ourselves to the epoch when the oldest American orchestra was founded, and deposit ourselves on the movable benches in the Apollo Rooms for the New York Philharmonic concerts of 1842, we would witness a performance which differed as much from today's well-disciplined execution as the early practices in religion, government, housing,

Meignens Sinfonie.

Persons Represented.

A Meignen   D Der Haidrich   G Mehnuelin Bass   M Nanager
B Anno Sanguirico E Brass   to Utica — the Drum N Notari
C Den Cass   F Fiddles   I Peter Butler   O Smekschnitz
                                     Louis in the b   P Pini

Musical Fund Society Orchestra of Philadelphia about 1845—the earliest known sketch of an established American symphony orchestra in action. Note the leader, L. Meignen (A), in the concertmaster's position, standing on a raised platform. The soloist, the Italian buffa, Sanguirico
(B), occupies the center of the stage. Other personalities are identified in the longhand legend.
(From Madeira and Goepp.)

and costume differed from their modern counterparts. There would appear, of course, many fundamental resemblances to testify to the basic continuity from the order of that day to the present, but our transfigured visitor would be more conscious of the many mutations, through which have evolved the present institutions.

At the inaugural concert the musicians stood before their desks in the approved Leipzig Gewandhaus [15] manner—a pattern well-known in England and the United States too. A cartoon of about 1850 pictures the Musical Fund Orchestra of Philadelphia as standing; [16] the Chicago Philharmonic, under Hans Balatka,[17] in 1869, followed the same system; the Manchester (England) orchestra of 1840 is described by Richard Hoffman, the noted New York pianist of the Philharmonic days:

. . . I was taken and was allowed to be on the stage near my father whose chair I occupied while he was playing. The English orchestral players always stood while playing; they were not allowed the privilege of sitting and crossing their legs in the listless manner which so often offends the eye in our modern performances.[18]

The custom must have lingered some time in New York, for in 1853 a bewildered critic

cannot account for the necessity of the performers standing. Aside from being uncomfortable to them, this looks badly and impresses the spectators uncomfortably.[19]

The origins of this custom, which in Leipzig did not finally give way to general seating until 1905, are still obscure. Hanslick,[20] the student of Viennese musical history, averred that it had been necessitated by limited floor space, or possibly motivated by respect for royalty who were so frequently present. The "physical" logic of the standing position would have suggested the same practice. Players of wind and string instruments (excepting, of course, the cello), enjoy greater freedom of movement in the standing position than in the cramped seated posture. Accordingly, after the pattern set by Bülow of Meiningen, where all but the cellos stood, Gericke, Nikisch, and Paur in Boston and New York at times ordered their violins to stand, on the allegation that they thereby enhanced the volume of their tone.[21] In exceptional cases even today, for dramatic

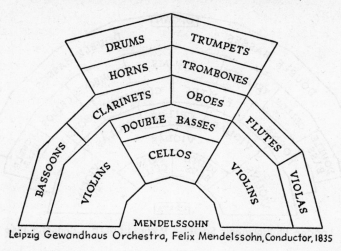

Leipzig Gewandhaus Orchestra, Felix Mendelssohn, Conductor, 1835

Mendelssohn was the first conductor to direct the Gewandhaus Orchestra with a baton from the podium. The players were ranged on steeply ter-raced risers. Note the central location of the double basses and cellos which, in spite of the addition of the time-beater, helped set the rhythm for the group. (Drawn from description in August Schmidt, Musikalische Reisemomente auf einer Wanderung durch Norddeutschland. *Hamburg: 1846.)*

reasons rather than for considerations of etiquette or physical con-venience, violins may still rise for the rendition of such numbers as Paganini's *Moto Perpetuo*, which features that instrument. Gericke theatrically performed Handel's *Largo* in Boston and New York in 1887, the violins ranged across the stage in standing position.

As orchestras grew in size and complexity, the necessity for coordination of the individual players increased correspondingly. Therefore, in addition to the desire for sheer comfort, the most compelling argument for the seated position, which Hanslick refers to as the "Viennese style," was the urgency for a mutually un-obstructed view of the conductor and fellow players. The old Gewandhaus orchestra had surmounted the obstacle of the standing position by steeply terraced risers.[22]

The seating plan, which has been fairly well standardized during the last century, rests on three major principles: (1) the relation of

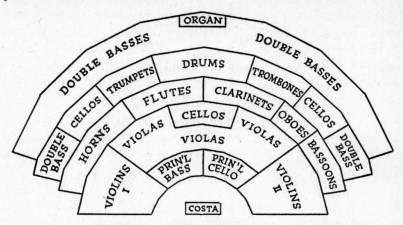

London Philharmonic Society, Michael Costa, Conductor, 1846

Costa was among the first to use a ground plan approximating the modern styles. Note, however, the divided cellos and double basses, and the location of the principal cello and double bass at the conductor's feet. This is a survival of the period when the bass parts set the rhythm and tempo of the playing, and took their position next to the conductor, who sat at the clavier. (Redrawn from Reginald Nettel, The Orchestra in England. *London: Jonathan Cape, 1946.)*

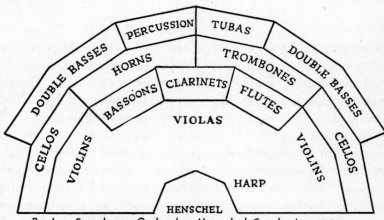

Boston Symphony Orchestra, Henschel, Conductor, 1881

Henschel followed the tradition of dividing the cellos and basses on the wings of the orchestra so that they could be plainly heard by the players. This seating of the basses persisted in America until about 1900, and was used by Theodore Thomas and Anton Seidl in Chicago and New York. (Compiled and drawn from various sources.)

the various choirs to one another and to the conductor for mutual visual and aural coordination and support; (2) acoustical effect upon the listener; and (3) the aesthetic and visual impression upon the audience. There is, of course, no precise unanimity of opinion as to which detailed pattern best promotes these ends, although the general plan, proposed by Berlioz in his notable treatise, is still basic today. That conductors were disposed to experiment drastically is evident from a critical comment on the disposition of instruments of the New York Philharmonic. In 1853, the previously cited New York critic was

surprised to see the tenors (violas) sent almost to the top (highest riser) of the orchestra—choked between the brass and the double-basses. To our thinking, the tenors, from their very character, must never be separated from the violins. . . . The celli were also scattered among the double-basses. . . . The celli must, like the tenors, form a compact body. . . . The double-basses ought to bring up the rear of the orchestra and only by rare exception be placed in the center.[23]

Berlioz in 1856 recommended the semicircular plan, which is in universal use today. The players are ranged in arcs, with the conductor stationed at the hub facing the orchestra, his back to the audience. Instead of standing in the midst of his players, facing half his orchestra and the audience, as did Jullien and many other conductors before 1850, he now stood aloof, more conspicuous and more responsible. First and second violins were divided to his left and right respectively, with the violas deployed in the middle; woodwinds behind the first violins and brass behind the violas; cellos and double basses in a double row in the rear, half of them on the right wing and half on the left; harp in the foreground close to the conductor, and percussion in the extreme rear.[24] This approximate arrangement has been preserved for us in a photograph of the newly founded Boston orchestra [25] under Henschel who, inexperienced in conducting, was probably happy to adopt the recommendation of the most authoritative text on orchestration of that day. However, the strangest detail of Henschel's seating for the first concert consisted in ranging the string sections (first and second violins and viola) in concentric semicircles around the podium. The first violins

Louis Antoine Jullien (1812–1860) was a popular French conductor who was active for some years in England and toured the United States in 1853–54. According to the custom which still prevailed in many orchestras, he faced the audience while conducting. Unfortunately no print of an American orchestra exists depicting this style of conducting. Here Jullien conducts a Promenade concert in London in 1849. The orchestra of sixty pieces which Jullien brought to America contained the finest instrumentalists available in Europe. (Drawing by Richard Doyle. Picture Post Library.)

occupied the first semicircle, the second violins the second semi-circle, and the violas, the third. Aside from the eccentricity of this system, the Boston habitués seemed to be most disturbed by the familiar faces peeking out of the most unaccustomed places. Well-known viola players sat apparently ready to play first violin, and some first violinists were stationed where one had been accustomed to look for the seconds. Since all the strings were thus divided, the complete orchestra was spread over the whole stage, the right half duplicating the left half.

Even before Berlioz had formulated his plan, the seating of the orchestra had already crystallized into recognizable form. Costa, the brilliant disciplinarian of the London Philharmonic, introduced a new ground plan as early as 1846,[26] while Mendelssohn in the same year was described by another observer [27] as having introduced in the Gewandhaus another system, in which the strings, woodwinds, and brass were ranged in separate tiers on a series of risers.

It is difficult today to understand the persistent tendency in all these arrangements to divide the cellos and double basses, half of each on opposite wings of the arc. Henschel, who had discussed the seating with his friend Brahms, had adopted the same pattern but soon abandoned it after having evoked this criticism, at the opening concert, of the "novel arrangement":

We think it a mistake to divide the cellos and the basses into two bodies, separated by the entire width of the stage. . . . The arrangement of the brasses at the back of the strings seems to be an improvement.[28]

Wagner, in his letter of advance instruction to Heckel of Mannheim, December 6, 1871, similarly requested that the double basses be stationed on the left and right wing-front of the orchestra; Seidl employed this arrangement in New York, and Thomas during the early years of the Chicago orchestra.[29] Probably no better explanation for the widespread practice of dispersing the basses has ever been found than the recommendation of Rousseau, who advises (under totally different circumstances) that:

the instruments of each section, except the basses, should be grouped together in the interest of unity and precision. The basses should be de-

Seating plan of the 110-piece Philadelphia Orchestra in 1950; the Principals of the sections are designated by asterisks. (Courtesy of The Philadelphia Orchestra Association.)

ployed around the two clavecins and throughout the orchestra, since *it is the bass which must control and support all the other parts, and every performer must be able to hear it equally well.*[30] [Author's Italics.]

One does wonder why this scheme, understandably necessary when the band was conducted from the clavier, held on so tenaciously into the period of the dominant, time-beating conductor.

Since about 1921, following the innovation of Sir Henry Wood and Stokowski, some conductors have moved the cellos to the right-front, occupying the area vacated by the second violins, which were placed inside the first violins. This conspicuous transfer is in recognition of the important thematic values of the cello voice, thus visibly dramatized in its new position. The second violins, on their part, are rendered somewhat stronger than previously since they are now turned out to the audience. On the other hand, they sacrifice the antiphonal emphasis which their separate location on the opposite side of the podium permitted in certain types of classical composition. A slight variation of the above, in which the violas occupy the old front location of the second violins, was introduced by Goossens and Koussevitzky in their respective orchestras—a seating which corresponds to the usual string quartet sequence.

A more drastic permutation of instruments, which today is more significant as historic testimony to the capricious experimentation of the young Stokowski [31] than as a lasting contribution to orchestral lore, was the reversal of the position of strings and wind choirs sprung on the audiences of Philadelphia, New York, Los Angeles, and San Francisco during the season of 1939–40, by its author, who was indulging his flare for acoustics and electronics. Nearly ten years previously, the conductor of the Milwaukee Symphony Orchestra [32] had anticipated this reshuffle on another theory—that the prominence of the strings was an anachronism in a period when modern instrumentation featured wind and percussion. These theoretical demands were satisfied by placing the woodwinds to the immediate front-right and retaining the strings at left.

Stokowski's "upside-down" orchestra not only was not imitated, but actually aroused universal aversion. It offended the visual habits of the audience, and was deemed unnecessary by musicians and critics, who reasoned that a good conductor had at his command

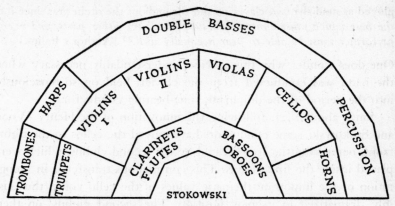

Leopold Stokowski's "Upside-Down" Orchestra, 1939—40

Stokowski's "Upside-Down" Orchestra was an acoustical experiment on the part of the resourceful conductor to strengthen the strings by placing them close to the reflecting surface of the rear walls. This seating plan was quickly abandoned.

many less circuitous ways of attaining balance. The pithy comment that, in this new order, the "front rows did not keep busy enough to put up a good show" epitomized the public verdict with more finality than any esoteric analysis.

In a "man's world" the symphony orchestras were naturally manned by men. But in retrospect, it is obvious that it was only a question of time before the feminist assault against the male monopoly would be made. Indeed, music was rapidly being accepted as a particularly congenial pursuit for the "weaker sex." Consequently the orchestra, like the barber shop, the halls of Congress, the army, and many another male sanctum, has experienced the infiltration of women. Although the harp was the entering wedge with which she gained early entry into the major orchestras, other instruments have subsequently been mastered, so that today very few orchestras still consider the orchestra as man's exclusive domain. As in so many other occupations, the process has been accelerated during the last two world wars when large numbers of men were diverted to more strenuous and urgent duties.

The issue of admitting women to orchestral posts had been repeatedly ventilated in the musical press, which adapted all the familiar antifeminist aphorisms to the special circumstances. Although women had been prominent as vocal and instrumental soloists, and though many all-women orchestras performed successfully, there was some resistance to mingling the sexes in the professional orchestras.

With a light repertoire, no travelling to do and no arduous rehearsals, they (all-women orchestras) might make a success as a unique feature in social engagements.

So writes an editor in 1895. There would be little prospect beyond that because of her alleged

physical incapacity to endure the strain of four or five hours a day rehearsal, followed by the prolonged tax of public performance . . . she cannot endure the strain of competition with men.[33]

A similar opinion was pronounced as late as 1925, after women had already found a place in some of the more important orchestras of the world. Sir Henry Wood, conductor of the London Queen's Hall Orchestra, claims to have been the first to admit women into a professional orchestra,[34] when in 1913 he "could not allow prejudice to prevail" and accepted six women in the string section. However, his colleague, Sir Thomas Beecham, who never fumbles an opportunity to express his sentiments in quotable style, takes diehard issue with the trend:

I do not like, and never will, the association of men and women in orchestras and other instrumental combinations. . . . My spirit is torn all the time between a natural inclination to let myself go and the depressing thought that I must behave like a gentleman. I have been unable to avoid noticing that the presence of a half-dozen goodlooking women in the orchestra is a distinctly distracting factor. As a member of the orchestra once said to me: "If she is attractive, I can't play with her; if she is not, then I won't." [35]

Semi-professional and amateur orchestras have long accepted women. However, it was a matter of public comment when Cleveland included four women in 1923. A sample tally taken during World War II yielded the following counts of women members in the principal American orchestras:

Baltimore	11	Indianapolis	13	New York	0
Boston	0	Kansas City	16	Philadelphia	5
Chicago	6	Los Angeles	12	Pittsburgh	18
Cincinnati	5	Minneapolis	5	St. Louis	5
Cleveland	4	Washington	16	San Francisco	8
Detroit	4	New Orleans	17	Seattle	21
Houston	26				

It is quite probable that the much discussed scarcity of good string players has been alleviated by the admission of women in what was formerly man's exclusive domain.

The Conductor

In 1842, the differentiation of the conductor from the general membership of the American orchestra had just begun. In Europe, on the other hand, such conductors as Habeneck (Paris), Costa (London), Spohr (Cassel), Weber (Dresden), and Mendelssohn (Leipzig) had already lifted this function to a high professional level before mid-century; but since no body of instrumentalists comparable to such orchestras existed in this country, the profession of conductor had not yet evolved beyond the rudimentary stages.

For the first several years, the New York Philharmonic directorship was "passed around," on the early pattern of the London Philharmonic, and had all the earmarks of being in part an honorific rather than a genuinely functional post. In fact, its constitution provided that the conductor should be chosen for each concert. Not only were no two concerts in succession conducted by the same person, but during the first season two or three musicians presided in that capacity within the same program. In 1842, the American orchestra was clearly at an intermediate stage where the person superintending the performance was no longer a *Kapellmeister*-composer of the eighteenth-century type, nor yet a modern conductor clothed with authority and interpretive rights which were soon to be his. This incipient conductor was then only the "first among equals" who devoted his energies exclusively to time-beating to achieve a minimum coordination in a common task. Before many years had elapsed, both the orchestra and public sensed the benefits of conductor discipline, and the selection of the conductor gradually

LEOPOLD STOKOWSKI

The most glamorous of American conductors, from 1919 to 1936 Stokowski kept the Philadelphia audiences in a constant state of excitement and expectancy. He continued his innovations with the experimental seating arrangement below, in which the positions of the strings and wind choirs are reversed. He is shown conducting the Philadelphia Orchestra. (Courtesy of the Philadelphia Orchestra Association)

BENDER PHOTOGRAPH

Two sketches of the Gewandhaus Orchestra, Leipzig, about 1840. The members of the famous orchestra did not take seats until about 1905. (The Bettmann Archive)

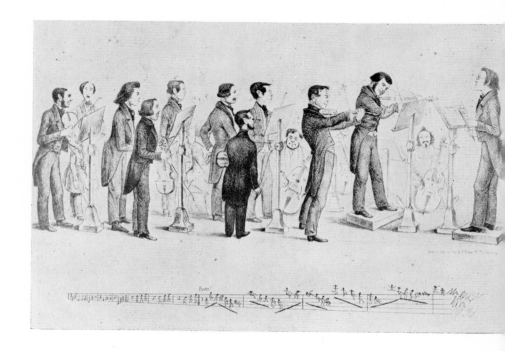

narrowed down until one man, Theodore Eisfeld, after having been repeatedly elected, was thereby transformed into a "permanent" conductor of the Philharmonic.

But within the next half-century the conductor was elevated from these embryological beginnings to a position of dominance never before known in the history of music. Thereby was inaugurated the era of the "prima donna" or "virtuoso" conductor, who welded the orchestra into his personal instrument and, equally significantly, became an arbiter of taste in the community.

The most powerful stimulant to the generation of this musical executive proceeded inevitably from the intrinsic nature of concerted music itself. The requirements of coordination of an increasing number of musicians, some of whom cherish their own aesthetic notions and are therefore "prima donnas" in their own right, would almost predestine the emergence of a kind of dictator who would impose his single will to guarantee the integration of the many. With the proliferating complexity of the score, which prohibits general familiarity on the part of the rank and file of the ensemble, the generalship of a conductor acquires both indispensability and prestige. It is easy to understand how this strategic function might be inflated, as in any other human relationship, by certain conspicuous personality traits which many conductors have not been loath to cultivate in both professional and public relationships. They thereby converted the baton into a wand, and the podium into a pedestal enshrouded in awe and fascination.

In the remote period of orchestral infancy, some of the more imaginative musicians had already correctly sensed the needs of more forthright control over a disjointed musical ensemble. Thus Mozart wrote to his father, after having observed the celebrated Mannheim orchestra in action:

I wish you could see the subordination that prevails there, the authority that Cannabich exercises. . . . Cannabich, who is the best Director I have ever seen, is both beloved and feared by his subordinates. . . . This can never be the case in Salzburg unless the Prince will place confidence in either you or me and give us full powers which are indispensable to a conductor of music. . . . In Salzburg everyone is master—so no one is master. If I were to undertake it, I should insist upon exercising entire authority. The Grand Chamberlain must have nothing to say as to musical matters, or any point relating to music.[36]

There have been conductors, both operatic and orchestral, who had actually achieved what Mozart so pathetically desired. Among the early conductors, there were a conspicuous few who possessed the executive abilities as well as the professional opportunities to enforce such discipline. Lully, at the Court of Louis XIV, with the aid of his famous "baton" and an ambition which was both shrewd and inflexible, set the standard and style of French opera for a century and more; Habeneck, the founder of the Concerts du Conservatoire (1828), conducting from the first violin part, with violin under arm or chin, succeeded, after several seasons of rehearsals, in disclosing for the first time, according to Wagner's testimony, the real beauties of Beethoven's Ninth; Michael Costa, the "drill sergeant" of the London Philharmonic (1848–54), paraphrased Mozart's complaint and anticipated the ideology of the whole fraternity of modern American conductors when he declared his conviction "that no orchestra can go well unless the entire control is placed in the hands of him who is the only responsible person for the accurate performance." [37]

But the tradition inaugurated by such pioneers was a long time becoming a general convention. Until the middle of the nineteenth century and later, with a few exceptions, discipline meant not much more than the mere synchronizing of parts, and the insuring of a minimum degree of amalgamation and unity by means of sparse rehearsals. That even this elementary requirement was no mean achievement in those days of tentative orchestral morale, when players were often incompetent, lazy, or even insolent, usually of low social estate and almost never well remunerated, is amply evident from the charges itemized by Berlioz in the first important modern treatise on instrumentation and conducting (1856):

. . . players of stringed instruments rarely give themselves the trouble to play a tremolo; many double bass players . . . from idleness . . . or from fear of difficulties . . . simplify their part; flute players often transpose entire passages an octave higher to gain ascendancy over the clarinets and oboes. . . . It occurs everywhere (I do not say in some orchestras) . . . that violinists do not count their bars rest, and always from idleness rely on others doing it . . . scarcely half of them come in again at the right moment.[38]

Individual show-offs could not resist the temptation to embellish their parts for grandstand effect or from mischievous impulses. Mendelssohn, with all his personal popularity, prestige, and aristocratic station, could not bend the London orchestra entirely to his will in manner of performance and choice of repertoire; Berlioz was not able to make his flutists in Stuttgart stick to the printed notes, nor to refrain from decorating their parts with trills and ornament.[39] These conductors would all have commiserated with Hamlet, who admonished his players: "And let those who play the clowns speak no more than is set down for them."

To a large extent such liberties derived from the undeveloped prestige of the composer as much as from the immature conception of the conductor. This prestige and authority was soon to materialize.

The romantic notion of the function of the conductor as transcending disciplined time-beating was firmly established by Hans von Bülow, Liszt, and Wagner, the first two as practicing conductors, and the third as both conductor and codifier of principles. Together they revolutionized the art of conducting by superposing on the practiced mechanical execution, which they now demanded from their players as a matter of course, an interpretative flexibility which reinforced the conductor's position. After the appearance of Berlioz' *L'Art du Chef d'Orchestre* (1856) and Wagner's brochure *Über das Dirigieren* (1869), the orchestra was bound to become a unified instrument, and a vehicle of the conductor's personal musicianship. The difference between these pioneer tracts is essentially that Wagner began where Berlioz left off. If Berlioz emphasized technical proficiency, Wagner took this for granted and made the conductor a full-fledged interpreter, seeking the "melos" in whatever voice or section it was to be found. No Nikisch would have risen from the pages of Berlioz' *Chef d'Orchestre*. That both Wagner and his audience recognized this shift toward romantic emphasis is clear from the report of Amy Fay, an American music student in Germany, who later became the sister-in-law of Theodore

Thomas. She sets down her observations of Wagner conducting his *Faust* Overture in May, 1871:

He didn't beat time simply, as most conductors do, but he had all sorts of little ways to indicate what he wished. It was very difficult to follow him, and they had to "keep their eyes on him" as B used to say. He held them down during the first part, so as to give the uncertainty and speculativeness of Faust's character. Then, as Mephistopheles comes in, he gradually let them loose with a terrible crescendo, and made you feel as if Hell suddenly gaped at your feet. Then, when Gretchen appeared all was deliciously melody and sweetness. . . . The effect was tremendous. . . . When he conducts he is almost beside himself with excitement. . . . He really seems to be improvising on the orchestra. . . . Wagner controlled the orchestra as if it were a single instrument and he was playing on it.[40]

An English critic made similar comments on the individualistic manner of Wagner's conducting during his one-year tenure in London:

So many quickenings and slackenings of tempo we never heard in a Haydn symphony before. . . . Mendelssohn's Fingal's Cave overture was taken slower than necessary at the beginning and faster than possible at the end. It was rather a zig-zag of a performance, but wonderfully vigorous and animated.

Professionally, Bülow established himself as the first virtuoso conductor when he startled Europe with the brilliant renditions of the traveling Meiningen orchestra in 1880–85. Bülow had all the virtues and vices subsequently associated with that species: talent for discipline and skillful rehearsing, conducting from memory, picturesque histrionic presence, personal readings, speeches from the stage, and public idolatry. Nothing new has been added since that day in America excepting, of course, the element of munificent emolument. With the establishment of the system of guest conducting which has flourished in Europe as well as in the United States since about the turn of the century, the virtuoso conductor achieves his highest pinnacle. In fact, the interpreter has gained almost higher priority than the music itself. We have come a long way from the timid and apologetic interruptions of Spohr who, in conducting the London Philharmonic in 1820, reports that "I took the liberty, when the execution did not satisfy me, to stop and in a very polite but earnest manner to remark on the manner of execution." [41] Compare this to the modern paragon of musicianship, the stern authority who wields over his troupe the power of hiring and firing as a constant threat to the incompetent and a spur to the indifferent.

The enhanced prestige of the conductor is further reflected in his position vis-à-vis the orchestra. Berlioz had expressly mentioned that the conductor should turn his back to the audience and face the orchestra. Costa and Spohr had already done so, but the practice was not yet universally accepted. Devrient, who had shared with Mendelssohn the responsibility of reviving the *St. Matthew Passion* in 1829, described how Mendelssohn took his position between the choruses, his back on one, his eye on the other and on the orchestra "since it was not proper at that time to turn the back to the audience." [42] Such a position was still a survival of the informal eighteenth century arrangement in which the conductor stood, or sat at the clavier, in the midst of his men and, with bobbing head and stamping foot, somehow assumed enough initiative to carry them along. As late as 1843, a picture in the London *Illustrated News* shows the conductor in the midst of his men, with baton, facing the audience but actually out of sight of some of his own men.[43] Jullien, who visited America in the fifties, stood similarly in the midst of his players facing the audience. In London, the "conducting" was actually shared between the first violinist "leader," who set the tempo, and the "conductor" who presided at the clavier with the score. This dual system was shaken, though not finally abolished, by Spohr in 1820 when he assumed entire charge of the rehearsal and concert, and shocked the assemblage with the employment of the baton to keep time.[44] Mendelssohn, who took the leadership of the Gewandhaus orchestra in 1835, followed the example set by Spohr and others in assuming personal direction of the orchestra, which had previously been in the hands of the concertmaster; and he, too, took his position, baton in hand, in front of the band.

Although the conductor had now taken his position at the head of the orchestra, it was not yet agreed that he should beat out every measure. This continuous windmill of gyrations was judged to be disturbing and offensive to the listener, and a physical and aural barrier to the unhampered enjoyment of the music. Devrient and Mendelssohn, in preparing the *Passion* music:

had many discussions about the best way to conduct. The continued beating throughout the movement, that must necessarily become mechanical, vexed me, and does so still [1869]. . . . It always seemed to me that the conductor ought to beat time only when the difficulty of certain passages, or unsteadiness of the performers, renders it necessary. Surely the aim of every conductor should be to influence without obtruding himself. Felix determined on this occasion to show me how this could be done, and he succeeded to perfection. I recall these circumstances with peculiar satisfaction, as in late years the extraordinary gesticulations of the conductors have been made a feature in musical performances.[45]

Devrient further refers with admiration to "the confidence with which he [Mendelssohn] would drop his baton during the longer movements when he knew they were safe." Richard Hoffman, the New York pianist, who as a youth had attended the Birmingham Festival of 1846 at which Mendelssohn conducted, confirms this *laissez-faire* conception of the conductor:

Mendelssohn would seldom beat more than the first sixteen or twenty-four bars of an overture or movement of a symphony; he would then lay down his baton and listen, often applauding with the audience. He would take it up again when he wished a *crescendo* or *rallentando* or any other effect not noted in the parts.[46]

Schumann, early in his career, actually found the conductor a distraction. In 1835, reviewing a concert conducted by Mendelssohn during the first year of his incumbency at the Gewandhaus, this progressive critic declared that:

Personally, I was distracted by the baton in the Overture as well as in the Symphony, and I agreed with Florestan who was of the opinion that in the Symphony the orchestra should stand as a republic over which no higher authority was to be recognized.[47]

Apparently Schumann miscalculated the trend when he failed to welcome this innovation and preferred the manner of Matthäi, the concertmaster, who had previously led the orchestra from the violin desk.

Mendelssohn, Bülow, Wagner, and Liszt soon made another advance in that they succeeded in compelling adequate rehearsals in advance of public performance. To impose upon the orchestra or chorus one's own private interpretation by means of a grueling series of rehearsals would have seemed impudent to all but a few aggressive musical authoritarians. But conditions were ripening for such an eventuality. The orchestral personnel was becoming more numerous, entrance cues less routine, and tonal balance more difficult to maintain. Rubato and other earmarks of romanticism were being developed which not only made coordination more and more difficult but also rendered the conflicting individual improvisational inspirations increasingly impractical. Conductors, given some authority as a consequence of such merely practical concessions, were emboldened to arrogate to themselves still more. Even the conservative Eduard Hanslick, who characterized "that insufferable tempo rubato as musical seasickness," was left not altogether unmoved by Wagner's rendition of Beethoven, on the occasion of the latter's 1872 visit in Vienna:

The new element in Wagner's interpretation of the *Eroica* consists, in brief, in a frequent modification of the tempo within the same movement. . . . Wagner's fluctuating measure, however, produces a thrilling effect especially in the Finale. . . . At other points, so it seems to us, Wagner goes too far with his "modifications." For example, when he opens the first movement in rapid tempo, and takes up the second motiv (45th measure) in a strikingly slower rhythm, whereby the auditor is confused by the shift from a barely established tempo, and the "heroic" character of the symphony is diverted into the sentimental.[48]

If not all the conductors indulged in the whimsicalities of a Bülow or Wagner, the pattern of conductorial supremacy was nevertheless set by the time of the founding of the Boston Symphony, at which time the scope of his authority was still further enlarged to include choice of repertoire and other functions then enjoyed by few conductors. The continental conductor was usually a member of the court and was by no means emancipated, as was indicated in Brahms' facetious reply to Henschel who had consulted him on the seating of his new Boston orchestra:

Your experiments in regard to the placing of the orchestra look very good to me. I should almost give preference to the first of the two drawings on account of the horns; the violas, however, seem to give trouble up to now. By far the best feature in both arrangements is the fact that no committee will be sitting in front of them. There is not a Kapellmeister on the whole of our continent who would not envy you for that.[49]

This evolutionary culmination, which made of the conductor an arbiter of taste and a performer on the collective instrument, attained its peak in America. Although it is plausibly argued that the music should have priority over the conductor, nevertheless, it is inevitable that, as the repertoire becomes more and more familiar, interest should shift to the manner and quality of presentation. Instead of an ever new repertoire, without rehearsals, as in the days of Mozart and Beethoven, the interest today lies in an *old* repertoire with *new* interpreters.

With the inauguration of the era of the virtuoso conductor, who was now not only a metronomic pace-setter, but also a subtle interpreter of moods and nuances, the baton seemed to some conductors to be just an expressionless little wooden stick. Wagner and other romantic conductors had already resorted to eyes, shoulders, and head to communicate their subtle nuances. Now the fingers were likewise to be mobilized, until the conductor fairly squirmed and wriggled with sentiment and emotion. The well-worn cliché, a "musician to his fingertips," was at long last to be rendered incarnate, and if the stick was an encumbrance to free use of the fingers, then the stick would have to go. A reporter's impression of Stokowski, during the transitional period, was recorded in 1928–29, when that ever-inventive maestro was a guest in Los Angeles:

He carries his baton as he comes in. . . . Perhaps the most impressive part of Stokowski are his hands . . . there is not the slightest doubt that every bit of shading is transmitted to the players with their aid. . . . He is a two-handed conductor, for he shifts his baton at will from the right to the left. His fingers curl and extend. They close and open.[50]

For Stokowski, the baton had obviously become a vestigial organ, and in the course of normal evolutionary processes soon disappeared altogether.

More usual than the dropping of the baton has been the habit of dispensing with the printed score. Ever since Bülow coined the phrase that the conductor must "either have his head in the score or the score in his head," there has never been a lack of candidates for the latter achievement. Bülow himself not only conducted from memory but his orchestra at times followed his lead by playing from memory. About 1880 Hans Richter startled the London audience by conducting Beethoven and Wagner without score. Nikisch in Boston frequently dispensed with the score. Wagner, of course, conducted his own music from memory, for which he was criticized in London in 1855 by the uninitiated public, who "detected lapses of memory," as well as "incorrect tempi and phrasings." With the then limited repertoire, it was perhaps no great feat. In general, however, scoreless conducting has always excited admiration. Toscanini, whose eye affliction required it and whose photographic memory permitted it, has become a model for those who were not so gifted.

There is no unanimity of opinion on the desirability of the actual physical abandonment of the score in public performance, and many conductors very sensibly do not consider it worth the risk of tempting a capricious memory, of which any human being may be an occasional victim. Soloists, especially, may feel uneasy if the orchestral score is not available for ready reference in an emergency, for eminent soloists have been known to suffer lapses of memory and had recourse to the conductor's score. The lapses of conductors are usually not so evident to the listeners, although a bassoonist who is expecting his cue after a long rest may suffer from the unreliable "showoff." The fact that a conductor has not discarded the score does not, of course, indicate that he does not "have the score in his head."

Some noted conductors have had the propensity to lecture their audience during the concert, although unfamiliarity with the native language of the audience forever barred most imported conductors from such amiable indulgence in America. The occasions for such verbal embellishments were manifold. Bülow, creator of quips and sarcastic sallies, and dubbed the *Conzert-Redner* of the Meiningen orchestra, was the prototype of this batonical liberty, and would frequently blend his platform art with disquisitions on patriotism or other congenial topics. In America, Walter Damrosch and Stokowski, both of whom introduced many musical novelties, possessed the extrovert temperament and the linguistic facility to wax didactic in the presence of any audience.

Both these conductors were at times inspirational, but often just plain "folksy." Stokowski would often generate a schoolroom atmosphere, scolding his audience for the foibles of harassed people who had mistakenly expected an hour of aesthetic relaxation. Late arrivals, early departures, coughing during the rendition of a number, or any other evidence of apparent indifference or displeasure, likewise elicited from the Philadelphia leader rebukes of a kind not to be found in the linguistic repertoire of the more genial and aristocratic Damrosch. Both conductors, naturally, laid themselves open to jibes—sometimes not too gentle—of critics and laymen, friends and foes alike, who did not take kindly to the phenomenon of a conductor thus stepping out of his prescribed role. To those who were irked by such a dual role, it must be said in condonement that their remarks doubtless rendered tolerable compositions which otherwise would have engendered only bewilderment and hostility.

The virtual disappearance of this conductorial license is the result of the loss of free intimacy between the conductor and his audience; nor do the large anonymous audiences, on their part, feel the same personal interest in the conductor. Above all, the audience of today is more sophisticated and would even tend to resent the pedagogical talks which were given and accepted with such grace a generation ago.

The ideals of orchestral democracy, to which Schumann made nostalgic allusion, were not to retire before the advance of the dictatorial trend without struggle. In their abhorrence for all traditional authority and their exaltation of personal liberty and responsibility, which flares so magnificently in the heat of every revolution, the early Soviets resuscitated the idea of the old informal ensemble of equals, and abolished the rank of conductor by distributing his functions, committeewise, among the membership. The Pervyi Symfonitchesky Ansamble (First Symphonic Ensemble)—*Persymfans*, for short—was organized in Moscow in February, 1922, by a group of about ninety musicians, some of whom had been members of Koussevitzky's State Orchestra previous to his departure from Russia.

In performance the ensemble was seated in concentric circles, the front, or outer row, with its back to the audience. The players were therefore in a position to maintain rapport by watching one another, and giving and receiving discreet gestures of shoulders and eyes. Since overall coordination could not be wholly dispensed with, the concertmaster sat somewhat elevated in the center, and gave the essential signals. Each choir had its leader who presided over section rehearsals and who was a delegate on the general committee which conferred on interpretation. At the full rehearsal, a member of the group usually sat in the auditorium to judge the effects. The right of democratic comment on matters of interpretation was preserved by the membership. That this could lead to procedures strange to Western habits might well be expected. Egon Petri, who appeared with the Moscow orchestra, once related how the double bass player complained that he could not hear the left hand of the soloist, and suggested that he play a little louder.[51]

The quality of the performance seemed to have met with considerable approval, though Glazounoff, on a visit to the United States in 1929, reported that their symphonic performances were superior to their accompaniments for soloists. The organization survived long enough, though very precariously, to celebrate its tenth anniversary in 1932. Toward the end of its career, it was experiencing increasing difficulties because of the staggered work week and the conflicting engagements of musicians who held other posts.

Similar organizations were founded in Leningrad, Kiev, Leipzig, and other cities, while in America, the American Symphonic Ensemble, "modelled after the Moscow *Persymfans*," was founded in New York in the fall of 1928, with the announced purpose to "heighten the musicianship and personality of each performer . . . and to permit the listeners to focus attention on the music." With a change in name to the Conductorless Symphony Orchestra, it presented a diversified repertoire including modern works and accompaniments to many soloists. Like the Moscow organization, it was built on a profit-sharing basis, assigned interpretive problems to a committee, and left the coordination to the concertmaster, Paul Stassevitch. It survived two years.

The externals of conducting, which are so dramatically obvious to the lay audience, recede in importance before the principal function of the conductor: the interpretation of the composition before him. Essentially, of course, any performance should be viewed as a cooperative enterprise between the composer (through the medium of his work), the performers, and the conductor. This leads to obvious jurisdictional problems. When, in the eighteenth century, composer and conductor were identical, expression marks were unnecessary, infidelity to the score not censured—if, indeed, it was noticed—and repeat performances were accompanied by considerable license and circumstantial tamperings.

Today, with such high specialization in both composing and conducting, conductors do not ordinarily compose, and composers are often poor conductors of even their own creations. Consequently there has arisen a kind of competitive cooperation between composer and conductor for the rights of decision on controversial problems which arise in the process of transmuting the dead notes into live performance. This issue is all the more complex in that the older scores—analogously, for example, to the United States Constitution—were written in response to conditions some of which no longer obtain. Present interpretations are therefore by no means unambiguous.

Now, in a manner of speaking, both the American Constitution and the Beethoven symphonies have "survived"; but neither has escaped amendments, and there is a range of influential opinion on still further editing. The interpretation of Beethoven, who constantly revised his own manuscript, raises many problems not unlike the interpretations of the words of Thomas Jefferson or James Madison. There are the fundamentalists who ascribe a kind of clairvoyance, an infallibility, to the founding fathers, political and musical, whose wisdom must be shielded from the fallible interpretations of lesser men. There is, secondly, the leftish opinion, which is willing enough to take its point of departure from history, but which will not be ruled by its dead hand and is intent upon adapting the past to the interests, needs, and pleasures of the present. This latter conception of the function of the conductor has been formulated into a philosophy. In the words of Dr. Hugo Goldschmidt, a German musicologist:

The interpreter's work is no mere execution, comparable, let us say, to that of the builder who transmutes the architect's plans into material reality. His task is, rather, to seize the vital conception of the art work, to blend it with his own ego and the views of his period. . . . His artistry is a product of its mental culture. . . . Consequently we shall always approach the art productions of earlier times through the medium of our own spiritual and emotional nature. . . . We hear the works of the masters of former centuries . . . with other ears than our forefathers. . . . What we have experienced since their time, this it is which sounds in those works to our ears. . . . Consider the history of Handel's art. The eighteenth century . . . admired it in the form of arrangements by Hiller and Mozart. Our present musical interpretation— on Dr. Chrysander's initiative—has gone back to the historically authenticated form. . . . But it owes its success, not to a recognition that things must be so because Handel would have them so, but because they appeal more directly to our sense and feeling than do the arrangements of the eighteenth and nineteenth centuries.[52]

The founders of this liberal wing in the realm of conducting were Wagner, Liszt, and especially Bülow. They modified the instrumentation, tinkered with tempo and nuances, and projected their own personalities into their renditions. They expressed contempt for the brittle metronomic style of conducting, as represented by Berlioz and Mendelssohn, who indulged in relatively little interpretive discretion. Of this school of free thought, the most distinguished exponent was Arthur Nikisch, conductor of the Boston orchestra in the early nineties, who in forthright manner announced his own conception of the conductor as a "recreator of the masterpieces according to my own ideas." By no means a disciplinarian, he indulged freely in almost capricious rubato style. He was never able "to leave a phrase alone"; he embellished the score until it fairly vibrated with his personality. Popular in some quarters in this country, he created a sensation in Europe, in Berlin and Leipzig, though he caused many of the judicious to grieve. Today, this extreme libertarianism has become obsolete, and there is no doubt that

Wagner, Liszt, Bülow, and Nikisch would sound strange to our conventional ears.

This strain of conductors has been opposed by the more elegant, austere, and scholarly Weingartner, Thomas, Muck, and Toscanini, who profess to withhold their own subjective impulses in favor of the composer who, of course, is "always right." Although, of course, never literally adhered to, authenticity of performance, rather than personal taste, is for them the criterion of acceptability. The first obligation of the conductor is to seek diligently the composer's intention; the second, to be faithful to it.

The innocent bystander may ask: "What is meant by the 'intention' of the composer, and how recover it from one who has been dead a century?" How can we be sure of his actual performance manner, or the manner which he would employ *if* he were with us today? Practically the only clue to the composer's intentions are the lifeless black symbols on the printed page, together with fragmentary instructions and supplementary inferences from the evidences of the day. Because of certain very obvious changes in the size of orchestras, character and balance of instruments, area and acoustics of concert halls, listeners' habits, and innumerable other circumstances, many minor modifications have of necessity been made, especially in the older scores, merely to *restore* the conditions assumed by the composer. Beyond that, the "intentions of the composer" would presumably call for the literal observance of the available score details, without undue liberties in tempo, nuance, cuts, and other specifications.

It remains a real question, however, whether such literalism—in the case of Beethoven for example—is actually more faithful to what, at best, is an awkward and incomplete symbolization of the creator's intention, than is the "free" fantasy of a Bülow or a Nikisch. Indeed there is some evidence that Beethoven, himself, was not a calm interpreter, but rather indulged in exaggerated extremes of emotional expression and rubato style while performing before the Viennese nobility. Who can confidently assert that the relatively metronomic renditions of a Weingartner or Toscanini correspond more faithfully to the intentions of a Beethoven than the quixotic latitudes of rhythm of Bülow or Arthur Nikisch?

The veneration of the past results from the intense preoccupation with historical scholarship, and thus the "return to authority" —which may be termed "fundamentalism"—is a popular and convincing slogan met with periodically in religion, politics, art, and other disciplines of life. The Bible, the American Constitution, the Communist Manifesto, the capitalistic doctrines of Adam Smith— all have been looked upon as final authorities, digressions from which are branded as reprehensible. However, it is not a simple assignment, this "return to the past," for its intentions are not easily discerned. Even those who claim conformity to authority are merely conforming to *their conception* of that authority.

Changes in political, economic, and aesthetic tastes are very complicated and cannot be set down as mere willful or "mistaken" divergence from past hypothetical norms. Norms are themselves the product of innumerable factors, the needs and interests and pressures of the epoch, from which they emerge. At a time when the tempo of a Beethoven *scherzo* depended on the technical competency or the lackadaisical habits of an underpaid musician, when first chairs were gained by seniority, and violists were recruited from superannuated and decrepit violinists, the greatest needs felt by a conductor and composer like Berlioz were discipline, accuracy, ability, and determination to "stick to the notes." Only after these basic requirements were satisfied could romanticists like Nikisch poetize.

In the meantime, the audience, too, was educated to the accumulated repertoire, became familiar with the manner of interpretation, and habituated to certain styles of rendition. It thereby developed into a pressure group on the conductor and performer. Like the child who knows the fairy tale from memory and is disturbed and puzzled by "errors" in the recital of the plot, so the informed audience is offended by liberties that are too unexpected. One need only read responsible criticism to learn that the most noted conductors have been charged with such aesthetic arrogations, resulting either from inexperience with certain styles or from personal caprice. In other words, with a sophisticated audience—or at least in the face of sophisticated critics—today's conductor cannot escape a kind of scholastic censure if he introduces interpretative innovations in which he would have been allowed to revel seventy-five years ago.

We offer the hypothesis, therefore, that styles of conducting, like political ideologies, are conventions which fluctuate from period to period and group to group, contingent upon many factors: the nature and erudition of the audience, instrumental competence of players, psychological satiety of the listener, the level of public criticism, the assumed function of music, and the like. In the better sense of the word, there are fashions in conducting, as sure as there are fashions in play-acting and oratory. The floral designs in the oratory of Daniel Webster and William Jennings Bryan now seem stilted and affected, and have been replaced by the direct, unpretentious clipped style usually associated with the British debate. The impassioned speech of Sarah Bernhardt, splitting the atmosphere with strident voice and extravagant gesticulation, seems now ridiculous rather than thrilling.

The "return to authority," evoked by the growth in historical scholarship, has been further intensified by the antiquarian interest in eighteenth-century instruments. Harpsichord recitals, originally designed for drawing-room soirees of the nobility, are now presented in concert halls before a public whose ears are attuned to the Steinway Grand. Like true believers in an ancient faith, we insist on the harpsichord as an accompaniment to the recitatives of Bach's *St. Matthew Passion*, without consciousness of the anachronism of an orchestra of one hundred players, of modern instruments, the cavernous auditorium and the chorus of five hundred voices, to say nothing of the modern ears of the auditors. William Apthorp, Boston critic in the mid-nineties, conjectured:

the harpsichord was a noble instrument to the perception of people who had never dreamed of a Chickering or a Steinway. . . . Use it in the accompaniment of a great air of Handel, and you introduce at once an element of quaintness—just the one of all others most foreign to the spirit of composition.[53]

Mozart and Bach wrote not only for their instruments, but also for their audience. The audience of the eighteenth century, with its listening habits, its religious, political, and social association, is beyond recovery, thereby making the instrumental renaissance sociologically and psychologically incomplete and subject to grave misinterpretation. Toscanini, in performing the Haydn Symphony in G, once reduced the strings by half in order to recapture the "balance" of Haydn's day. This was no doubt interesting and instructive, in a museum sense, but balance is more than a count of instruments and is unsuccessful unless many other acoustical and technical matters are considered. Furtwängler, like Berlioz, Nikisch, and other romantic conductors, protests against this scholastic antiquarianism. He recently described his reactions to an "authentic" Berlin performance of the *St. Matthew Passion:*

The impression created by this most soulful masterpiece was one of unbelievable monotony. I was all the more astonished when, on the following day, I read in the press that we had finally witnessed a model performance of the *Passion*. The utilization of old instruments, the small choir . . . reflected the current scholarship on the original production of Bach himself. . . . Here was, to be sure, not sentimentalizing, but the true Bach had no opportunity to speak to the hungry soul. The performance showed more interest in historical fidelity than in exposing the fundamental spirit of the work for the living audience.[54]

It is not to be implied that such throwbacks may not produce legitimate aesthetic pleasures. It is intended only to emphasize the futility of the belief that we are hearing Bach or Haydn as they were intended to be heard, and that we are duplicating the musical experiences of their audience. There is no true, unconditioned perception. A mind conditioned to Wagner, Strauss, and Stravinsky is incapable of perceiving a primitive orchestra in the manner of Haydn's audience of 1791 in Hanover Square Rooms of London.

Perfect fidelity to the composer's intention obviously does not permit the reconstitution of only one element (the orchestra) without similarly reconstituting the others. Since it is, of course, impossible to reconstitute the ears of the modern audience by causing them to miraculously forget all its intervening experiences, perfect fidelity would suggest the maintenance of the *relation* between the orchestra and the ears which perceive it. This end is best served by utilizing the modern orchestra, which is matched to the ears of the audience. The aesthetic pleasure that we sense in listening to the reversions to the past has little resemblance to the pleasures felt by

Haydn's audience. To it, Haydn represented the comfortable upper limits of dissonance. In 1770, Burney suggested that

> some of the discords in modern music, unknown until this century, are what the ear can just bear. . . . But I am convinced that, provided the ear at length make amends, there are few dissonances too strong for it.[55]

The modern audience has, of course, "made amends," and Haydn is today far within the limits of tolerance. It is clear that the "intentions of the composer" is a far more complicated problem than the superficial revival of a few antique instruments.

The late Chief Justice Charles Evans Hughes once expressed himself in an epic phrase on the "intentions" of the Constitution. He shocked the absolutists by declaring that the "Constitution is what the judges say it is." Perhaps this is an intellectual problem which transcends the field of music, and is of concern to all those who are faced with the interpretation of social history in any form. It is therefore impossible to arbitrate with finality between the Beethoven of Nikisch and Toscanini, or the harpsichord and Stokowski versions of Bach. To some critics, the staging of the uncut version of the *Passion* stems from misguided ancestor-worship.[56] It is not a cynical belief in the utter lawlessness of human judgment, but rather the recognition of period norms that prompts one to paraphrase the statement of the noted jurist: "Bach is what the conductor says he is."

Management and Union

The American symphony orchestra, like the genius in the garret, has almost always led a precarious hand-to-mouth existence. There is not a single orchestra in this country whose history does not include a number of assorted financial crises which have either threatened, or in some cases suspended its existence. It is well known that today they all must pass the hat and none could endure without some form of philanthropy.

This is not necessarily an accusation against our present social order and its tepid hospitality toward that high art. Perhaps, in the nature of the case, symphony orchestras cannot be expected to run the gantlet of our economic system, and be obliged to pay their own way. One's verdict on that issue would depend on his conception of the social function of the symphony orchestra, and on his economic ideology, which might range all the way from the capitalist extreme of Higginson, who was prompted to "share his good fortune with the rest of society," to official socialistic sponsorship as a public necessity. These policies of financial support have all gained a measure of adherence in this country during the one hundred years of the existence of the symphony orchestra, and have all been accorded a brief or lengthy trial.

The present financial structure of the American symphony orchestra is a culmination of a succession of short-term, and often desperate, policies to recoup deficits and straighten out periodic emergencies. Many times these vicissitudes of fortune have been glibly "explained" as the aftermath of economic depression, withdrawal of guarantors, or human miscalculation of resources and events. But these are not truly isolated and chance dilemmas; they are the manifestation of fundamental changes in the social order and are the very stuff that life is made of. It is their cumulated potency that turns the course of affairs.

American orchestral history brings to light seven more or less distinguishable economic devices for their support, which show relatively little overlap, excepting that the last will be found to permeate all the others. These schemes are: (1) the cooperative plan; (2) plutocratic support by one or more guarantors; (3) private enterprise, the risk being carried by conductor or manager; (4) endowment, accumulated from various sources; (5) broad popular support of small donors, usually referred to as the "maintenance fund"; (6) municipal or state taxation; and (7) self-support or pay-as-you-go system.

The cooperative plan is a mutual organization whereby the risks are distributed over the entire membership of the orchestra. The membership forms a democratic or communistic body which is completely and solely responsible for its own policies and their implementation. It elects qualified members, determines rehearsal and concert periods, owns or rents its library and equipment, selects its own officers, engages conductor and soloists, sets the program, pays all incidental expenses of management—and finally divides the proceeds. The New York Philharmonic Society carried on under this system for sixty-seven years, from its inception in 1842 to 1909, when it was taken over by a group of guarantors. Much more recently, in 1929, a group of Indianapolis instrumentalists likewise organized a cooperative society when the depression and sound pictures deprived them of their individual livelihoods. This organization similarly succumbed to philanthropic support in 1937.

The New York Philharmonic Society illustrated all the weaknesses of this pattern of communistic organization. Its very objective contains the seeds of its own destruction. The objective of such an organization is not primarily to provide the finest music in the most artistic manner, but rather to create self-employment. One must admit that this motive is both innocent and laudable, and much can be accomplished in such a society of like-minded colleagues. But for the necessary discipline, such an organization is completely dependent on self-discipline; and what Anton Seidl, as the leader of this part-time organization in the late nineties, had to contend with even during its most profitable era is intimately revealed in the confession of a member of the orchestra:

Nearly all the members of the Philharmonic play at balls and dances during the greater part of the year. They then get together to play a half dozen doubled up programs during the year, rush through old scores during five hour rehearsals preceding a concert and are then expected to play their programs artistically. Take into additional consideration that some of them never play at all except at the few Philharmonic concerts, and the tale of woe and disheartening anguish is soon told. . . . Many sincere men play incessantly at balls, dances, dinners, and parties for six weeks night after night until early morn and then after a Philharmonic concert find themselves denominated in the papers as great artists after scratching through a symphony.[57]

Sooner or later civic pride and aspiration, as well as the growing sophistication of the audience, which such a society has itself created, will inevitably render it obsolete. An "outside" committee of civic-minded persons will take over, a new conductor will be "imported." Amid injured feelings, economic hardship, and pathetically impotent protests of displaced members, the rejuvenation of the group will proceed until an orchestra is fashioned of which "the city will be proud." That was the monotonous story, with only the slightest variation, in New York, Boston, Philadelphia, Chicago, Cincinnati, Indianapolis, and many other cities.

Under very exceptional circumstances, a cooperative orchestra has been known to cultivate high excellence. The Vienna Philharmonic, also founded in 1842, noted before World War I as one of the finest in Europe, was such a body, which selected its own conductors. However, its membership contained the pick of that musical metropolis, and was practically identical with the well-trained permanent orchestra of the Imperial Opera, which was the site of its major activities. Like every other cooperative, it was reluctant to spend much time on rehearsals, and it was once reported that Furtwängler had not been invited to conduct its concerts in the late twenties because of the severity of his discipline.

In order to overcome the fatal weakness of inadequate remuneration, which in turn sets off the chain reaction of missed performances by its otherwise employed personnel, inadequate rehearsal time, retention of incompetent but loyal personnel, irresolute and inoffensive conducting by a conductor who reigns only at the pleasure of his subjects, it is necessary to shift financial responsibility from the players to some one who can assure adequate subsistence. This means the substitution of an aggressive management for the dead-level drift, to the end that the orchestra be the player's first love rather than a last resort.

This was the aim of Theodore Thomas when, in 1863, he organized his own orchestra, had daily rehearsals, personally guaranteed wages and, in short, gave full employment to the orchestra, which he made his private enterprise. In order to take up the seasonal slack, it became the painful necessity of the orchestra to travel and to organize tours, even during the unpleasant winter months. This extremely distasteful circumstance, as well as periodic personal financial losses, soon taught Thomas that such a "permanent" orchestra had no real permanence at all and could make no artistic progress. He had forged an excellent instrument, had welcomed occasional financial lifts from William Steinway and other friends (in those days the piano manufacturers—Steinway, Knabe, Weber, etc.—actuated by business as well as artistic motives—were the im-

Symphony Society of New York.

Founded by DR. LEOPOLD DAMROSCH.

FOURTEENTH SEASON, 1891-1892.

The Directors beg to announce that during the coming season the Society will give, as usual, Six Afternoon and Six Evening Concerts at MUSIC HALL, under the direction of

Mr. Walter Damrosch.

An annual guarantee fund of fifty thousand dollars has been subscribed by the following gentlemen :

ANDREW CARNEGIE,	JOHN D. ROCKEFELLER,
THEO. A. HAVEMEYER,	WILLIAM D. SLOANE,
COLLIS P. HUNTINGTON,	H. McK. TWOMBLY,
JOHN S. KENNEDY,	CORNELIUS VANDERBILT,
D. O. MILLS,	GEORGE W. VANDERBILT,
J. PIERPONT MORGAN,	WILLIAM K. VANDERBILT,

DR. W. SEWARD WEBB.

for the purpose of making the orchestra of the society a permanent organization, the members of which shall be engaged by the year, and shall be constantly under the training and direction of the same conductor.

This generous support gives the orchestra a unique position in New York, and to strengthen it still more, several eminent musicians have been added to its membership. Special mention should be made of Adolph Brodsky, formerly of Leipzig, who is engaged as concert master and solo violinist ; Jules Conus, formerly with the Colonne orchestra of Paris, as second concert master and solo violinist ; and Anton Hekking, formerly with the Boston Symphony Orchestra, as first and solo violoncellist.

The programmes will include the following works :

BEETHOVEN : Symphonies VII & VIII.	SCHUBERT : Symphony in C.
BERLIOZ : Romeo and Juliet.	SGAMBATI : Symphony No. II. (new).
BRAHMS : Symphony No. IV.	TSCHAIKOWSKY : Symphony No. V.
BRAHMS : Violin Concerto.	TSCHAIKOWSKY "The Tempest."
GOLDMARK : Theme and Variations.	WAGNER : Kaiser March.
DVORAK : Serenade for Strings in E.	WAGNER : Siegfried's Death and Funeral Music.

The soloist for the first concert will be Adolph Brodsky, violinist, his first appearance in America. At the second concert the well known contralto, Frau Marie Ritter-Goetze, will appear. The celebrated pianist, Ignace J. Paderewski, has been engaged for the third concert. Other important engagements for the remaining concerts are pending.

This prospectus appeared during the "plutocratic epoch" of the history of the American symphony orchestra.

Notice

Prices of Subscription.

FOR SIX AFTERNOON CONCERTS.

Parquet,	$8.00
Dress Circle—First two rows,	7.00
" " Other rows,	6.00
Boxes, six seats,	60.00

FOR SIX EVENING CONCERTS.

Parquet	$9.00
Dress Circle—First two rows,	8.00
" " Other rows,	7.00
Boxes, six seats	66.00

All Boxes contain six seats.   No single seats in boxes will be sold.

The dates of the Concerts will be as follows:

AFTERNOON CONCERTS.

At 2 O'clock.

Friday, November 13, 1891.	Friday, January 15, 1892.	Friday, March 4, 1892.
Friday, December 4, 1891.	Friday, February 5, 1892.	Friday, April 1, 1892.

EVENING CONCERTS.

At 8:15 O'clock.

Saturday, November 14, 1891.	Saturday, January 16, 1892.	Saturday, March 5. 1892.
Saturday, December 5, 1891.	Saturday, February 6, 1892.	Saturday, April 2. 1892.

PROGRAMME FOR FIRST CONCERT.

SYMPHONY No. VII, in A,	*Beethoven.*
CONCERTO, for Violin with Orchestra.	*Brahms.*
MR. ADOLPH BRODSKY.	
"HAMLET."	*Tschaikowsky*

Note the names of the philanthropists who guaranteed the "permanency" of the orchestra.

333

presarios and musical philanthropists); but, after 1881, he not too secretly envied the Boston orchestra with its personally guaranteed philanthropic security. The double function of impresario and conductor was too great a load even for such a strong back as that of Theodore Thomas.

The regime inaugurated by Mr. Higginson in Boston was destined to be one of the most dramatically significant experiments in the whole history of the American symphony orchestra, for it became the ideal pattern emulated, or at least envied, by all major orchestras for several decades. This system which, for want of a more elegant nomenclature may be called "plutocratic," consists in a happy segregation of the artistic and financial functions, in that one or a few persons of affluence take over the responsibility of meeting the deficits, which are assumed to be temporarily or permanently inevitable. The conductor then assumes sole responsibility for all the professional details including the employment of a corps of musicians whose major duty is to the orchestra concerts and rehearsals.

Besides Higginson and, later, E. B. Dane of Boston, other philanthropists who virtually signed a blank check to the credit of the orchestra for a shorter or longer period were: H. H. Flagler (oil) for the New York Symphony, W. A. Clark (mines) of Los Angeles, and Edward Bok (publishing) of Philadelphia. There were others, equally important, who shared economic responsibility in a more fragmentary but still substantial degree: E. L. Carpenter of Minneapolis, Charles Norman Fay and others of Chicago, Mr. and Mrs. Charles Phelps Taft of Cincinnati, Robert S. Brookings of St. Louis. For the ideology that motivated their philanthropy we may turn to Mr. Higginson, who was never pretentious, yet certainly not inarticulate, either in private conference or public ceremony. Having seen state subsidies in Europe, he epitomized the American philosophy of paternalistic capitalism on the occasion of the dedication of Symphony Hall, the new home of his orchestra, in October, 1900:

It is fitting in a Republic that the citizens and not the Government in any form should do such work and bear such burdens. To the more fortunate people of our land belongs the privilege of providing the higher branches of education and art.[58]

Although this was not the same social conscience which prompted the pre-Napoleonic princes to employ musicians as they did their cooks and coachmen, it still provided comparable security and stability in this modern commercial era.

History, however, in the derisive manner which she so often affects toward man's most noble designs, began almost immediately to reveal cracks in this handsome edifice. However magnificently conceived, a foundation consisting of one or a few individuals turned out to be too narrow to provide a stable equilibrium. Something more predictable and reliable—a broader base—was needed than the periodic liquidation of each annual deficit by a capricious individual. Death, financial adversity, or simple fatigue in the pursuit of what was once an exciting adventure, constantly threatened to wreck the structure in which the welfare of so many persons, and so much community pride, was involved. Some of the early philanthropists and energetic promoters had been sustained by their personal musical accomplishments: Higginson had been a student of piano in Vienna, Clark was a proficient violinist, and Flagler a pianist. Carpenter, Mrs. Leonora Wood Armsby (San Francisco), and Mrs. Adella Prentiss Hughes (Cleveland), were schooled musicians. But other projects were beginning to compete with music for the attention of potential donors: international peace, public libraries, medicine, research, and education. If that were not enough, the handwriting on the wall, which prophesied the liquidation of their huge personal fortunes, could already be deciphered. The era of buccaneering capitalists, who amassed their millions with no questions asked and no federal taxes to siphon them off, was soon to pass, as had the epoch of the proud nobility. Then, as now, their passing endangered the institutions which they had founded and sustained.

It was now beginning to dawn on public-spirited persons that, instead of the annual temporary relief of large direct gifts, a grant of investment capital, rooted in the industrial wealth of the nation, would be the source of a more continuous, automatic, and predictable flow of benefits. The earliest instance of this new direction was an endowment by Joseph Pulitzer who, in 1911, left, among the many other benevolences he created, a bequest of almost

$1,000,000 to the New York Philharmonic. In Cincinnati, Miss Cora Dow (1915) and Mrs. Nicholas Longworth (1923) left substantial bequests, and Mr. and Mrs. Charles Phelps Taft contributed $1,000,000 on condition that another two and a half millions be raised as an endowment. In Chicago and Cleveland, endowments took another, but equally profitable, form. A popular subscription made it possible to build and present a "home" (Orchestra Hall) to the Chicago orchestra, which, in addition, yields an income of rents which has contributed to its financial stability. Cleveland, in Severance Hall, also possesses a beautiful auditorium, the gift of the late J. L. Severance, which houses the offices of the orchestra as well.

But in a changing world, endowments also have their frailties. Although designed to cover future obligations, they actually never did so. The reasons are very simple: the progressive decline in purchasing value of the dollar and the shrinking interest yields, while obligations of all kinds have been expanding at a fantastic rate. Augmentation of dwindling endowment funds from dried-up sources is obviously a vain hope, and outright gifts of large dimension have long gone out of fashion with a more equable distribution of the national income. As a result, instead of a few large gifts, the new arithmetic calls for a multitude of little ones.

There are many variations to this theme, but the tune is always the same: no principle of orchestral finance has today gained more general adherence than the principle of the "broad base." Individual "friends of the orchestra," business houses, and local industries who make it a routine rule to contribute to almost any worthy cause, are solicited for annual subscriptions. This places the orchestra in a category not unlike the beneficiaries of the community chest, so that even the oldest and the finest orchestras find these handouts indispensable to a balanced budget.

In setting forth the cheerless recital of deficit financing, one may unintentionally produce an exaggerated impression of the plight of the orchestras. They obviously do enjoy some earned income of their own. In 1948 the Cincinnati orchestra rendered a public accounting to its subscribers, which may be briefly illustrated by limiting the bookkeeping to the best seats in the house:

Cost of production, as proportionately allocated to best seat		$7.05
Admission charge	$3.60	51%
Part of deficit made up by endowments	2.04	29
Part which must be made up by "friends"	1.41	20
	$7.05	100%

In other words, the customer purchased $1.00 worth of music for $.51. Although any estimate of an orchestra's degree of self-support is almost meaningless without a close analysis of its accounting system, one may still assert that most orchestras are seventy-five to ninety per cent self-supporting in terms of ticket sales, endowments and other fixed income. However, it is this last ten to twenty per cent, gifts by "sustaining members," that spells the difference between mediocrity and excellence. The largest single *earned* income is derived from ticket sales, supplemented by recordings and radio sponsorship, which in the last decade have constituted a providential intervention. However, the last-named sources vary enormously from orchestra to orchestra, for in general it is only the larger and more eminent organizations that can command such outlets in significant volume. Nor can relief be sought in increased admission fees, for music differs from such luxuries as tobacco and liquor in that its elastic patronage fluctuates greatly with varying economic conditions and the fickleness of public interest.

A half-century ago, guarantors had quietly assumed, and often overtly expressed the conviction, that symphony orchestras would and could ultimately stand on their own feet; that after a period of pump-priming, or through the farsighted provision of an endowment of capital stock, the orchestra would become a self-supporting business enterprise. It had not yet dawned on them that a deficit was not an occasional and unfortunate episode, but rather a chronic affliction. Instead of being a "grocery store" which, when well managed, shows a balance between income and outgo, the orchestra was rather to be classed as an educational institution in which the fees can never be raised to the level of costs. Today, no one sees any prospect that it will ever be otherwise.

Many musicians have deplored the fact that music is a victim of the economic processes, and its values distorted by those nefarious forces.[59] But in a manner of speaking the symphony orchestra cannot, of course, escape the economic processes. As long as the conductor receives his fee, the musicians their contractual salaries, the printer of the scores his profits, the owner of the hall his rentals, the custodian his wage, they are all enmeshed in its pressures. It is only a question as to how the costs will be distributed.

In a rigidly *laissez-faire* economy, those services and industries which do not attract sufficient support to sustain them, are simply left to perish unless they are willing to adapt the quality and volume of their services to the public demand. But insofar as any service or industry is affected with the public interest, such service is protected against destructive competition by society in its collective capacity. Therefore, after all other means of economic support have either failed or become obsolete, there remains finally, in default of private and voluntary aid, recourse to public taxation for the support of what to many citizens is a public cultural asset, and consequently a responsibility of the community. Libraries, museums, parks and zoos are educational undertakings which are a source of prestige and delight to the citizenry, and a symphony orchestra could appropriately be added to the list, so the argument runs. A few cities, notably Baltimore, San Francisco, St. Louis, Indianapolis, Philadelphia, and a number of smaller cities [60] have lent assistance in a direct or indirect manner, in exchange for which the orchestra often presents a series of concerts either without admission or at popular prices. Since most of these grants assume some service in return, they cannot be considered genuine subsidies, but rather earned income. But they all have the same purpose and effect—to alleviate the struggle for existence.

Subsidies by public taxation are still sufficiently infrequent in number and small in value to render the issue a controversial one among managers and public alike. Such a provision sometimes puts the symphony orchestra in competition with the fire department, street maintenance departments, public hospitals, grade schools, and all other municipal undertakings for a share in the tax resources. Taxpayers, whose streets need repair, have at times protested against the public subsidizing of this "luxury of the leisure class."

There are likewise those, especially among the spokesmen for orchestras that can limp along under the present system, who have expressed their apprehension that public assistance would, of necessity, be followed by its shadow, public corruption. Not only would politicians ultimately insist on the right of "nominating the fourth horn," but the character of the programs would deteriorate to the level of the strongest pressure groups. For whatever material gain music might thus achieve, it is feared she would bargain her very soul, her priceless artistic virtue.

It is countered by the proponents of the public system that, while political aggression is a melancholy fact, it is still true that our cultural institutions have, by and large, kept free of such venality, and that politicians have left them alone. Until recently, the accumulated experience was insufficient to venture confident predictions on the receptivity of the orchestras to public grants. It is, however, difficult to believe that any management, which now theoretically spurns such aid, would in the end choose to die a virtuous death rather than compromise a bit of its soul in exchange for material survival. This view is steadily gaining converts.[61]

In such dilemmas, it must be difficult for the well-wishers of the present-day orchestras to inhibit an anxious side glance at the dramatic theatre, which is a cultural institution of no less respectable ancestry. The theatre worries along without benefit of endowments, without philanthropic coverage of deficits, without radio or record sustenance. The theatre consists of a series of small enterprises, each of them entirely dependent upon the box office to recoup the investment which is usually furnished by a risk-taker. Therefore, it tends to scale its repertoire (to the great grief of many a judicious author) to that imperious circumstance. This necessity to appease the box office, according to some playwrights, has brought about the descent of the theatre from the realm of art to the level of "show business," with a businessman's criterion of success. It is not at all certain that the hand-to-mouth existence of some orchestras has not similarly resulted in a lighter, if not a deteriorated repertoire, as well as in a compromising collaboration with glamorous soloists to insure the success of "orchestral" concerts.

Artistic supremacy was a logical goal in the days of unfettered wealth, when fabulous fortunes were lavished upon private picture galleries, private yachts, private orchestras, and other "playthings of the rich." Today, when the "guarantors" consist of thousands of little men, from whom subsidies are coaxed in chicken-feed lots, reckless expenditures may not be practical. They may desire a *quid pro quo* in musical entertainment as well as an increment of prestige. In most instances today there is a "freedom within limits," a negotiated freedom with mutual dependence, in the dual administration, the degree of which varies from city to city and from year to year. The romantic concept of artistic supremacy, in the old sense, has given way to practical coordination. There is thus an inevitable relation between the economic security of the orchestra and the quality of the repertoire. In part to prevent the deterioration of the repertoire, and in part to prevent wholesale unemployment in a skilled occupation, the British government subsidizes directly or indirectly about ten symphony orchestras. The medium of distribution of government funds is the Arts Council, which was established in 1940.[62]

From the foregoing analysis, it is clear that the American symphony orchestra has always been, in the economic sense, a "parasitic" industry—in no way to be construed derogatorily—subsisting upon the surpluses earned by other industries which are then distributed through the medium of open-handed friends. It has long been observed that there are many cherished social values which will crumble if subjected to the rigors of the laws of commerce and exchange. Warnings have been repeatedly sounded against allowing serious music to become enmeshed in the natural economic processes and to become a victim of their criteria of survival. On the other hand, to expect an existence outside the social order may also appear to be a contradiction in terms. Certain forms of the arts have, perhaps, succeeded in establishing a *modus vivendi* within the commercial society, but not without encountering vital dilemmas. Conductors, opera and orchestra, have learned that prolonged financial embarrassments are not conducive to a good bargaining position in the maintenance of the integrity of the repertoire. Unsold season tickets are a constant temptation to sell "singles" with a seductive program. But it is a question whether strong *popular* support would be forthcoming for the financially weak *aristocratic* taste. By a program that is too esoteric, the orchestra may "aesthetisize" itself out of the market and endanger its existence more fatally than if it made some concessions to public taste.

THE MUSICIANS' UNION   At critical periods in the history of the symphony orchestra, management has often accusingly laid its plight at the door of the musicians who, because of their intractable demands, were charged with biting the hand that was feeding them. The salaries of the personnel, which amount to approximately half of the operating expenses, do constitute the largest single budget item.[63] Under the old cooperative system, these musicians had been satisfied with a mere trickle of pin money, but as the orchestra was transformed into a major occupation, they naturally endeavored to extract from it their major livelihood. Here was a fertile field for strife in which the musician naturally made strenuous attempts to strengthen his position.

Another source of friction was the growing authority and power of the conductor. Under the democratic cooperative system, he "ruled" at the pleasure of his subjects. Under the new regime, inaugurated by Higginson and followed by every other major orchestral administration, the responsible conductor held the power to hire, and the threat to fire for incompetence or insubordination, over every member of the band. In general, the musicians have now conceded this right to the musical director in the interest of musical efficiency, but the struggle has at times been a bitter one.

Both of these powers—business managers and musical directors—are, in a manner of speaking, the musician's natural enemies against whom the man in the ranks feels called upon to consolidate his forces for his own protection. Following the pattern set in the fields of industrial employment, unionization became the principal protective device which he adopted to insure his job and to improve his condition. The "competitive cooperation" which obtains between these contending parties is laden with many implications for the perpetuation of the orchestras, the competence of the membership, the effective artistry of its ensemble, and, not too indirectly, the nature of the repertoire.

The origins of the musicians' union in America may be traced to a small group of German musicians in New York who, in 1860, formed an association jestingly titled the Aschenbrödel Club, "for the cultivation of the art of music . . . and the relief of such members as shall be unfortunate." But before many years, a more serious atmosphere prevailed, and its members incorporated as the Musical Mutual Protective Union. Meanwhile Baltimore, St. Louis, and other cities established similar clubs, which, in 1886, consolidated as the National League of Musicians. Somewhat squeamish about considering themselves "laborers," the League resisted the urge to affiliate with the Knights of Labor and the American Federation of Labor until 1896, when a small number of Western locals attended the A.F. of L. convention in Indianapolis and laid the foundation for the American Federation of Musicians. The League soon capitulated and all locals finally entered the Federation. Its first president was Owen Miller of St. Louis. He was succeeded in 1900 by Joseph N. Weber of Cincinnati. In 1940 the presidential choice was J. C. Petrillo of Chicago.

The greatest source of competition for orchestra jobs in our undeveloped country up to the time of the first World War were the finished players from Germany and, to a lesser extent, from France and other European countries. It was not until the early eighties that the unions reacted energetically to this hazard, provoked by the members of the traveling bands and orchestras, particularly from Germany, who would often desert their native organization and seek work in the American theatre and concert orchestras. On the occasion of the World's Fair at Philadelphia (1876), Chicago (1893), and St. Louis (1904), as well as in ordinary years, hundreds of musicians of every grade entered this country while American musicians stood by powerless and unemployed. In order to secure well-trained talent, American conductors not only abetted this policy, but actively recruited especially competent players from Europe and imported them on contract for the best positions in their orchestras. To counteract this peril to their security, the American unions at first attempted to invoke the Alien Contract Labor Law enacted by Congress in 1885 for the primary purpose of preventing industrial employers from inducing immigration by making contracts abroad. Since the law, however, expressly exempted professional persons, it was not immediately clear how the

A Jullien concert in 1843. By this time the differentiation of the conductor from the general membership of the orchestra was well established in Europe but just beginning in the United States. (Picture Post Library)

The American orchestras have been through crises before. This is a sample of the civic interest in the Philadelphia Orchestra during the 1919 campaign. (Courtesy of the Philadelphia Orchestra Association)

musicians' unions could find relief in its provisions. As early as 1885 Theodore Thomas, who had obtained many members for his famous orchestra in Europe, secured an injunction from a Judge Potter against the Musical Mutual Protective Union of New York which was at that time trying to prevent the Belgian Felix Bour, oboist, from taking his place in Thomas' New York orchestra. In 1893, the same union dispatched a protest to President Cleveland on the interpretation of the law which "allowed bands and orchestras to enter this country . . . under the flimsy pretext of classing them as artists." [64] Even Arthur Nikisch, imported to conduct the Boston orchestra in 1889, and the opera composer Mascagni, who entered this country for a triumphant tour in 1902, were challenged, but merely evoked the expected ruling that they could legally enter to "pursue their calling." Taking no chance of being intercepted, Nikisch slyly landed in Boston after his arrival had been announced for New York.

As a deterrent to this foreign infiltration, the union had recourse to a contrivance of its own: the "six-months rule" concocted in 1882 by the New York local as a countermeasure against the engagement of Schreiner's German orchestra at Long Beach. It withheld union membership, and therefore employment, from a foreigner during the first half-year of residence in this country. However, when candidates for particular vacancies were clearly not available in the United States, the union usually waived this requirement. Such was the case in 1891 when Walter Damrosch, conductor of the New York Symphony Society, imported as his concertmaster the distinguished Russian violinist, Adolf Brodsky. It was this artist who had gained notoriety for his sensational première in Vienna (1882) of the now standard Tschaikowsky Concerto and occasioned one of the choicest examples of Hanslick's vitriolic style. Such a celebrity clearly merited the exemption accorded him.

Although many such instances of administrative tolerance could be cited, the unions could just as easily be aroused to drastic action. Two years after the Brodsky episode Damrosch, perhaps feeling himself secure, invited the much less famous Danish cellist, Anton Hegner, to take the first chair in the same orchestra. On Sunday evening December 17, 1893, shortly after his arrival in this country and without observing the "six-months rule," Hegner took his seat on the stage—a signal for the rest of the orchestra to walk off and desert their posts.[65] Pre-concert negotiations having failed, the union thus made its reply in the form of the first strike in American symphonic history. The musicians had, of course, acted under union orders. The chagrined Damrosch could only dismiss the audience with a few tactful and dignified remarks, of which he was always so eminently capable, and retire to the conductor's room.

This episode turned out to be a critical step in the establishment of the power of the union. Although Theodore Thomas had successfully defied the union in 1885 on the principle of restraint of trade, Damrosch had weakened his case by previously recognizing the six-months rule in successfully requesting its suspension in the Brodsky case. This time, however, the conductor for some reason chose to ignore the rule. After some weeks of negotiation, during which Hegner had twice illegally appeared with the orchestra, the showdown was set for the Sunday concert in question. The union had no choice but to follow through with the conventional fines for conductor and players: $20 for the first, and $10 for the second offense. There followed several days of uncertainty before Damrosch conceded defeat and paid the fine. The players, who had "acted under false assurances of the conductor" received remission of their fines.

There was some speculation that Damrosch after all may have enjoyed the last laugh. The strike automatically abrogated all contracts, which he then renegotiated on more favorable terms to himself. Some have even insisted that the whole strategy of the financially hard-pressed conductor was diabolically designed to that very end.[66]

Again, in 1905, the same Damrosch clashed with the union, and the rebuff assumed the still characteristic pattern. He was fined a "nominal" amount of $1,000 by Joseph N. Weber, president, for importing five French musicians for his recently reorganized orchestra —punitive action which was sustained at the May, 1906, convention of the American Federation of Musicians. Damrosch had proferred the usual claim that America could not supply his needs, while Weber had charged that the conductor had made no honest attempt to determine the availability of the supply in this country. The offending French musicians were, however, magnanimously permitted to join the union since "these men came to this country in good faith and were not responsible for their embarrassing predicament." [67]

On the more fundamental issue, the courts had always ruled since 1890 that musicians were "artists" and not laborers, and therefore not under the protection of the Contract Labor Law. In 1902 Alexander Bremer, then president of the New York Musicians Mutual Protective Union, directed another futile protest to President Theodore Roosevelt, in which he again insisted that musicians were "wage earners entitled to the protection of the law as were other wage earners." [68] On the same principle, in 1927, Joseph N. Weber submitted a brief to the United States Department of Labor anent an imported orchestra at the Carleton Hotel, Washington, D. C.[69]

The union interpretation really did not seem too inconsistent with the actual fact. Many of these musicians, either through incompetence or lack of broader opportunity, plied their music only as a part-time occupation, and simultaneously held cards as cobblers, stove-molders, saloon keepers, and what-have-you. In fact, Alexander Bremer was himself a minor official in the New York city government and his opponent in the election for the presidency of the M. M. P. U. in 1897 was a boss carpenter and violinist.[70] They were a versatile lot in those unspecialized days, and their varied talents undoubtedly dulled their devotion to a single art and facilitated the spread of the pattern of unionization of the "artist" with the artisan. Nor did those who were fortunate enough to gain their entire livelihood in music always scale the exalted heights of artistry, for there is nothing necessarily elevating or divinely inspiring in fiddling, night after night, in the squalid pits of cheap theatres, or in scraping through the popular rounds and dance tunes of the day. Such players quite justifiably felt themselves more akin to the hack worker than to the symphony artist, whose dignity might have inhibited crude protests.

But there were some symphony players who were conscious of a higher tradition, and who often winced a bit when "contemplating the fitness of the Bach and Beethoven interpreters, hod carriers, bricklayers and longshoremen forming a union to strengthen our position, while architects, painters, composers, actors and poets live a life of weary isolation." They feared that too close an affinity between symphony men and the run-of-the-mine theatre and dance musicians would aid the incompetent in rising, to jeopardize their own position and thereby depress the relative opportunities of the better-class musicians by placing all on one level.[71]

When it was not a question of importations from abroad, the local unions endeavored to protect their jobs from migrations from other cities. Because of the principle of local autonomy in the Federation, union cards are not normally transferable from one local to another. Hence there is always a union-imposed barrier to free migration which constitutes a vexatious restraint to the conductor or local management in strengthening his orchestra by bidding in the national market. Here too, however, amicable agreements are often made for the good of the order, although strife and friction were common, especially during the period of the founding of the permanent orchestras a half-century ago. When Theodore Thomas was engaged to organize the Chicago orchestra in 1891, he literally transferred almost his entire New York orchestra of sixty men to Chicago as the nucleus for the new body. In retort to union protests, Thomas insisted: "I shall select my players where I find them . . . New York . . . or Europe. . . . If there are good men in Chicago I will use them." [72] Van der Stucken in Cincinnati; Scheel in Philadelphia; Henschel and Gericke in Boston; Gabrilowitsch in Detroit; Rothwell in Los Angeles—all these conductors encountered this normal, but impotent, impulse on the part of the local musician to protect his job as it came in conflict with the principle of artistic supremacy as entertained by conductor, civic committee, and guarantors. On this front, too, the union lost its battle, for the modern orchestra had now reached a kind of "industrial stage" in which musical efficiency was the controlling law, and generally had priority over job security.

The displaced personnel of these early orchestras, and their public sympathizers, of which there were many, fought grimly and sometimes "split the community" in their pathetic efforts to protect the "local boys." The usual promise that "all competent musicians will be retained," was scant consolation to the mediocre majority. In extenuation of the demands of the perfectionist, most of the local orchestras had been mere "sandlot" affairs whose strength lay not in their musical ideals, but in social and professional companionship. In the cooperative manner, they usually divided the modest "take," which was never considered anything but a pleasant source of extra income, much less remunerative, but more exhilarating than the tedious theatre routine and humdrum teaching. But now the orchestra was to be organized from above, with the membership, and even the conductor himself, put in the role of salaried employees. At last, the conductor could choose his men rather than the men the conductor. Although the union has preserved certain safeguards against arbitrary and exploitive tactics, nothing is now more generally conceded than the essential and responsible right of the conductor in the selection of personnel.

With the problems of basic employment settled in principle, there is still the whole area of "working conditions" and their enforcement—including wage scales, hours, and the host of details—which are, of course, subject to continuous negotiation between union and management.

Although it was not until after World War I that negotiations on salaries and working conditions became momentous, periodic tiffs between union and orchestral management were not unknown before that. Early in 1904, while rehearsing the new and difficult score of *Symphonia Domestica* under Richard Strauss, who was then making his first tour of the United States, the members of the Wetzler orchestra of New York walked off the stage when the contractual rehearsal time had expired. This episode, which some have condemned as a rude and inhospitable gesture toward a distinguished foreigner, incidentally could not have befallen anyone with greater poetic justice, for no musician and composer had achieved a more deserved reputation for calculated negotiation with musicians and publishers than the fabulously successful Richard Strauss.

By 1920 the unions were entering into a period of increased bargaining power, and their demands for revision of salary scales, stimulated by the postwar inflationary spirals, threatened the very existence of some of the major orchestras. This bargaining power was enhanced by the relative scarcity of musicians during that post-war period. Not only was the competitive European supply cut off by more stringent immigration laws, but the fashion for symphony orchestras was spreading to the Middle West and the Pacific Coast where newly founded, or reinvigorated, organizations were bidding for the limited supply of competent players. During this period of Coolidge prosperity even moving-picture theatres were adding pit orchestras of symphonic proportions to the sumptuous décor of their cinema palaces. Clearly, it was a propitious time for unions to press their advantage. And this they did, to the great distress of the philanthropists whose economic surpluses, once the rich economic topsoil from which the arts had extracted their nutriment, were now being washed away by the slow but fatal erosion of the changing industrial climate.

Whether or not the contending parties fully realized the ruthless drift of events in which they were helplessly dragged along, there is nothing in the light of contemporary or subsequent developments which would suggest that either side was bluffing. H. H. Flagler, the guardian angel of the New York Symphony Society, was irked by the "continued attempt by hampering restrictions and purely commercial methods to destroy artistic projects," and warned that "if the worse element prevails I see but two courses open, (1) to give up altogether the maintenance of the symphony orchestras, or (2) to found nonunion orchestras." [73] In Chicago in the spring of 1923, the union threatened to strike "in the fall." These ominous soundings subsided only when "both sides compromised." This was the same orchestral management that, in 1928, had already notified the musicians that "they were free to seek employment elsewhere" when the differences were again patched up. Orchestras had folded up before. Cincinnati was dark from 1906 to 1908 when the management, even in those early days, met with "labor troubles."

As is usual in a democracy, both sides appealed for aid and comfort to the public conscience, each presenting its own case in the best possible light and that of its opponent in the worst. The "exorbitant and shortsighted demands of the union" were set off against the selfless generosity of the philanthropists, whose benefactions to society were made difficult, and even impossible, by the aggressive and myopic "commercial" motives of the players' union. As for the musician, he in turn considered himself worthy of his hire. He had a great investment in his long years of concentrated study and in the acquisition and maintenance of a costly instrument and delicate skills. The legitimately expected return on this investment was rendered precarious by the brevity of the concert season, the uncertainty of the yearly contracts, and the postwar inflation. All this obviously argued a sympathetic review of the player's plight.

This clash between the imperious demands of rising costs and the dissipation of available philanthropic resources assumed national proportions, and in the minds of some leaders required consultation on a national scale. In February, 1924, Clarence H. Mackay, who had recently become chairman of the board of the New York Philharmonic, invited the patrons of about a dozen major orchestras to New York for the specific purpose of discussing the now universally experienced mounting deficits. Many of the leading philanthropists were present: Van Rensselaer (Philadelphia), Hamill (Chicago), Carpenter (Minneapolis), Flagler (New York Symphony), together with Juilliard, Kahn, and Marshall Field, of the host orchestra. The managers, among whom were Judson (of New York and Philadelphia), Mrs. Hughes (Cleveland), Mrs. Caroline Estes Smith (Los Angeles), and others, joined in the deliberations. Some of their plans to reduce deficits had no durable significance, but the informal organization, expanded to meet developing needs, still exists and is convoked annually for the discussion of common problems.

There was one orchestra that did not avail itself of the opportunity to participate in the council on the pending crisis. Boston, which had operated the best of all major orchestras, and the only one on the open-shop principle, apparently felt no need for collaboration and, in fact, might even have pointed up the embarrassing anachronism of its position if it had taken part in the sessions. During all these decades, when union and management were learning to live together to promote their common ends, the Boston orchestra had been able to cultivate a splendid isolation from the inexorable trends.

There were several factors that contributed to the amazing self-reliance of the Boston organization. First, the paternalistic foresight of its owner had provided for a long and profitable season. Not only was the winter season of twenty-four pairs of concerts then the longest of any in the country, but the famous "pops," founded in 1885, and the Esplanade concerts, beginning in the late twenties, guaranteed to many a member almost full-year employment, and at a high wage scale. The Boston orchestra never stopped playing! Dignified supplementary income from teaching and summer resort contracts was facilitated by the universally acknowledged prestige of the orchestra. Consequently the musicians were somewhat less receptive to alarms of exploitation than they might have been under average circumstances. A large proportion had been imported expressly for membership in this orchestra and so felt a loyalty to it.

Over and above this whole scene, there hovered the ominously possessive philosophy of the guarantor, who, until 1918, assumed full personal responsibility for the economic security of the orchestra, and kept its membership dependent on the pleasure of owner and conductor. This watchfulness against any discontent must have been a powerful deterrent to overt expression of any latent restlessness. When, in 1903, murmurs of revolt became audible, Higginson rendered his usual obbligato in his typical unambiguous manner: "No one will interfere with my orchestra. If there is interference I will abolish it and declare publicly who is at fault and why it was done." [74] A much more serious crisis was weathered in 1920 when, as a result of a strike, the orchestral board dismissed the concertmaster and about thirty members of the orchestra in a desperate attempt to halt the inevitable.

But finally, when the scepter had dropped from the hands of the ruler, the orchestra lost its independence through a series of squeeze plays maneuvered by Mr. Petrillo: his refusal to allow Bruno Walter and Carlos Chavez to conduct the nonunion Boston orchestra; his threat to prevent Koussevitzky from accepting invitations from union orchestras; his threat to blacklist the auditoriums where Boston might appear. Most alarming of all was the imminent danger of interference with broadcasting and recording, which would have struck at the very subsistence of the orchestra. Finally, enmeshed in the larger world of affairs, the management could only capitulate in December, 1942, after having wrung from Petrillo certain minor concessions.

All symphony orchestras are now fully organized and, in that sense, the union "problem" may be written off as "solved." Harassed more than ever by deficit financing, management still resents many detailed restrictions imposed on its freedom to act in its own interests, and occasionally accuses the musician of not thinking beyond the tip of his bow. On the other hand, any idealism which the practitioner of the "queen of the arts" may have inherited from the nineteenth century, and any professional enthusiasm which formerly sustained him in the old cooperative days, must now be tempered by the realities of the competitive age. Although the symphony artist may at times still feel the discomfort of being yoked with the popular musician, they all present as solid a front as do the members of any other union.

The economic welfare of orchestra personnel has been severely affected by the technological revolution of the last decades. The incessant fear of displacement by the machine has gripped the modern musician as it has gripped the workers in every industry since the industrial revolution. The close of the last century witnessed the invention of the phonograph. In 1926 the Vitaphone made its debut in New York with Marion Talley, Elman, Zimbalist, and the New York Philharmonic. Alarmed, the American Federation of Musicians authorized a budget of a million dollars in 1930 to fight "canned music." In 1933, the American Society of Composers and Publishers published a brochure entitled *The Murder of Music* which endeavored to prove that the mechanization of music had had an adverse effect on the welfare of composers and performers. The charge, as made by the union, is simply that the musician is in danger of recording himself out of business. This crisis calls for a new pattern of emolument and a new principle of division of the income yield on musical recordings.

The new conditions touch on the symphony orchestra in several respects. Not only is the orchestra interested in tapping larger returns on its recordings—it has been suggested that the orchestra itself enter into a cooperative business in making and distributing recordings—but the decline in live music on the lower levels has robbed the symphony member of a large part of his supplementary livelihood and discouraged recruitment for the profession. The symphony orchestra draws its vitality from the broad base and general health and abundance of the profession at large. The struggle for survival in that respect is as critical as is the more fully publicized financial problem of the symphony orchestra.

The Audience and Its Folkways

It has always been the professed intention of modern orchestral leaders and sponsors to appeal, if not to the masses, at least to the middle class of limited financial resources. Hence, popular prices have played an important role in the policy of every orchestra. The basic audience of the subscription concerts of symphony orchestras is, of course, a small one compared to that of the commercial entertainments. A rough indication of this ratio may be gathered from the relative capacities of the concert halls and the moving-picture theatres. The New York Philharmonic, for example, estimates its annual attendance at between 250,000 and 300,000 in that city of seven million. In order to calculate the proportion of the New York City population which actually attends concerts more or less regularly, one would necessarily have to eliminate duplicates, compute suburban and out-of-town patronage, and make many other finer adjustments. If this were done, it would be impossible to conclude that more than two per cent of the eligible (adult) population habitually attends symphony concerts during the winter season.

This visible audience is, of course, significantly augmented by the uncounted listeners to radio and records, together with patrons of summer concerts, which may tap other strata of the population. There are no reliable estimates as to the extent of this dissemination of serious musical interests. There can, however, be no doubt that, in spite of the numerical limits to concert patronage, there has occurred a democratization in musical knowledge and appreciation not unlike the democratization in all other amenities of life. It is characteristic, especially of the United States, that the gap between the privileged and the common man has narrowed in every respect.

This transformation of the character and membership of the concert audience during the last 150 years has been one of the significant features in our concert life, for the audience is, of course, an essential ingredient of that life. From a small, closely knit band of aristocrats and nobles, socially more or less acquainted with one another, assembled periodically for a convivial gathering in which the musical program was only one attraction, the audience has been inflated into a large anonymous body, in which the consumption of music is the central event. While the noble European patrons looked down with some condescension on the socially inferior musician on the stage, the present bourgeois audience views the musician with respect and some awe. The parallel evolution of concert manners in part reflects this increasing prestige of the orchestra and conductor vis-à-vis the audience, as the latter has grown in intellectual stature and in its aesthetic grasp of more complex musical thought. As a result there has been a veritable social revolution in the nineteenth century, which is reflected in the general maturity of public decorum.

The primitive crudeness of the early American frontier folkways has been the subject of many a supercilious comment by urbane European travelers for two centuries. That such conduct should appear in the presence of serious music, which requires sophisticated attention and uncommon concentration, is only to be expected. Though many traveling virtuosi noted the diminutive aesthetic sense of the American frontier public, it should be remembered that the most elementary standards of deportment enforced nowadays in every motion picture theatre were by no means commonplace among the aristocrats of Europe. That Mozart was not accustomed to undivided attention from his audience was evident from a letter written to his father from Vienna in 1781:

I told you about the applause in the theatre, but I must add that what delighted and surprised me most was the amazing silence while I was playing.[75]

In the early days of the Gewandhaus concerts, organized by J. A. Hiller in 1781, conversation was freely carried on during the concert. When confusion became too unbearable, quiet was restored by the presiding merchant, who rapped for attention not with a gavel but, appropriately enough, on the keys of the piano.[76] In a letter to his family while conductor of the Leipzig Gewandhaus orchestra, Mendelssohn reported under date of October 6, 1835:

I wish you could have heard my *Calm Sea* with which the concert commenced. Both in the room and in the orchestra there was a quiet so that the finest tone could be heard.

Hanslick quotes instances of ill-mannered disturbances in various European centers, including Berlin and Vienna, "especially when women were present." [77] Drawings of scenes in the London orchestral concerts of the forties reveal similar informal behavior on the part of the fashionable patrons. Perhaps this period of immaturity was of longer duration in America, for with us it seems to have extended almost to the twentieth century. Dwight's *Journal* reports on the Thomas concerts in New York in 1875:

Not a week passes without some scathing rebuke from him [Thomas] to those illbred and ignorant people who keep up a continued buzzing during the performance of the music to the annoyance of all decent folk.[78]

That he must have been harassed by the same misconduct, even in his later Chicago days, can likewise be surmised from the following review of one of his concerts in 1896:

The chef d'oeuvre, of course, was Beethoven's *Eroica*, and in this the Thomas orchestra was at its best. It was received and followed with the closest attention and there was noticeably less conversation than on previous occasions. Perhaps this may be accounted for in the fact that few beyond the truly musical were present . . . because of bad weather.[79]

The New York Philharmonic tried to enlist public opinion as a corrective to the disturbances in their audiences. In their annual report of 1857, they declare:

We must necessarily insist upon musical good manners. The inattention and heedless talking and disturbance of but a limited number of our audience are proving a serious annoyance to our Philharmonic performances. The remedy for this, after all, lies rather with the audience itself than the society authorities. If each little neighborhood would take care of itself, and promptly frown down the few chance disturbers of its pleasures, perfect order would soon be secured. We hope this will be done. In foreign audiences it is effectively done.

The Metropolitan Opera House of New York, for all its aristocratic patronage, displayed no higher standard of propriety than prevailed in orchestral concerts. Henry T. Finck, the noted New York critic, relates:

Many of the stockholders have converted the anterooms of their boxes into luxurious parlors into which they retire and talk if the music bores them. But unfortunately there are some black sheep among them and their invited guests who do not make use of this privilege, but give the rest of the audience the benefit of their conversational accomplishments.[80]

Such improprieties on the part of the boxholders amounted to a minor scandal for many years. As late as 1915, Toscanini stopped the performance of *Euryanthe* as a reprimand to the disturbers of the peace, a remedy which Colonel Robert Ingersoll, who always sat in the pit, had recommended to Seidl in a public statement as early as 1890.

George Bernard Shaw, while serving as critic in London in the nineties, aptly analyzed the psychology of the chattering London audiences:

. . . the extreme smartness of these functions leaves the audience entirely preoccupied with the thoughts of being immensely in it.[81]

In the mid-twenties, Stokowski, Monteux, and Koussevitzky all had trouble quieting the New York audience at the beginning of the concert. Monteux would angrily rap the desk, while his successor, Koussevitzky, would quietly fold his arms and wait. Some conjectured that these visiting orchestras from Philadelphia and Boston attracted a similar "smart set," which had not quite accommodated itself to the restrained amenities of a symphony concert.

Whispering was not the only disturbance in the uncouth days. Late arrivals, early departures, premature donning of wraps during the last number, boisterous applause and demonstrations (especially for soloists), coughing, and other evidences of unappreciative restlessness were common vexations for orchestra and audience alike.

Many conductors have been distressed over such profane intrusions on occasions which were to them devout and exalting experiences. Various methods have been employed by them to train their audiences and render them "concert-broke." Bülow, the irrepressible eccentric, Walter Damrosch, Stokowski, have all been known to pause in mid-concert to discourse on social manners. Lamoureux, an excellent but uninhibited Paris conductor, resorted on one occasion to a more personal method of bringing home to a thoughtless culprit the sin of leaving the hall before the completion of the concert. Stopping the orchestra and fixing the victim in his gaze, he followed him with pointed baton until he had safely disappeared at the exit, after which the concert was quietly resumed.[82] Even Frederick Stock, the very model of tact and diplomacy would wave his handkerchief when coughing got out of hand. In 1910 he once suddenly halted his musicians during Smetana's *Moldau*, to allow the public to put on their wraps without musical accompaniment.

Barring the doors to latecomers brought many protests from patrons who, on their part, frequently complained of the inconsiderateness of the conductor who performed long opening compositions, thereby inflicting unfair punishment for what was after all only a thoughtless, or even unavoidable, tardiness. In Paris in 1899 one such tardy concert-goer, who arrived late for a performance of *Tristan und Isolde* by the Lamoureux Company, brought suit against the company for refusing to honor his ticket. The fact that the first act was more than an hour in length excited some sympathy for the victim. However, the French courts did not uphold the petition of the plaintiff. Recognizing that the ticket represented a bilateral contract, the courts held that, since the ticket carried a warning concerning the barring of latecomers, the plaintiff could claim no damages.[83] In Boston, the doors were not definitely closed to tardy patrons until 1922.

Audience reaction to a performance has taken many forms. Nothing would seem more in accordance with the laws of human nature than a spontaneous expression of appreciation for the enjoyment gained from a concert well done. The physiological tension, cumulated during the rendition of a number, may be discharged by almost any kind of overt manifestation: stamping of feet, cheers and calls, standing and waving of arms, and the more restrained handclapping. This whole range of public display of gratification, from sheer animal boisterousness to the most refined manual methods, is found in the history of concert and other performances. Clapping of hands, with occasional cheers, has now remained the only genteel manner in which an audience may vent its emotions.

However, there are those who have attempted to discourage even this simple demonstration as a violation of the solemnity of art. Untimely interruptions of a particularly brilliant passage in a vocal or instrumental solo, once considered the acme of flattery, and the inability of an audience to await the closing notes of the orchestral accompaniment to a concerto, have become a legitimate grievance in England, America, and the Continent that has long since been "corrected." The growing tendency to consider a symphony as one continuous number, which should not be interrupted by applause, first became a matter of editorial comment in American musical journalism about 1925. Some conductors, notably Stokowski, Toscanini, and Koussevitzky during the thirties, aroused controversy by their insistence on abolishing such interim applause. These new manners have not yet found complete acceptance among all audiences, and listeners are frequently beset by uncertainty unless the gestures of the conductor at the close of a movement are unambiguous. The contemporary public objection most commonly heard is that the uninterrupted symphony is a pretty long endurance test. This is balanced by the conductor's claim that applause breaks the spell and snaps the continuity of an integrated whole.

It should be observed that intermediary applause has long been deteriorating into the merely perfunctory. In the nineteenth century individual movements were considered units in themselves, individually applauded and individually encored. But in more recent times, no audience has considered the pause between movements as anything more than minor punctuation marks; applause at this point has become a vestigial convention without much meaning, often downright embarrassing in its listlessness. The conductors who wish to eliminate it are only pruning what has already withered away.

The *total* abolition of all applause, proposed by the whimsical Stokowski about 1930, had already been suggested 150 years earlier by his prototype, Friedrich Reichardt,[84] conductor of the Concerts Spirituels instituted in Berlin in 1783. He requested his audience to substitute *bravo* calls for the more childish hand-clapping. If the British-born Stokowski was a reader of the London *Musical Times*, he undoubtedly had noticed that similar suggestions to outlaw the "uncouth and barbaric noises" had been made by British critics in the twenties. Applause during the oratorios, a very popular concert form in that country, had long offended the delicate sensitivities of religious-minded folk. England's most noted critic, Ernest Newman, averred:

The day will come when audiences will not want to applaud after each movement. Later the day will come when they will not want to applaud at all, but will go out in rapt silence after a great performance of a great work.

Another critic, more facetious than fastidious, philosophized:

If you think of it, striking one palm against the other with a resounding smack is a queer way of expressing your delight; it suggests a monkey trick of primeval man.[85]

To which one may be permitted to counterphilosophize that there is not a single custom in food, dress, or behavior that excessive and uninhibited reflection cannot turn into the ridiculous.

Direct expression of displeasure is relatively rare among American concert audiences, for formal courtesy in public relations is one of the most firmly rooted folkways in a country which proudly professes the principles of social equality. This sense of diffident politeness on the part of the audience is significantly reinforced, however, by its feeling of inferiority and lack of self-confidence when confronted with the necessity of making aesthetic judgments. Hence, almost all music, even the most cacophonous, will generally receive at least token applause.

European audiences and musicians have often been much more forthright. George Bernard Shaw has described the catcalls from the balcony at the sight of a particularly execrable tenor. The excitability of the French audience at the première of Stravinsky's *Sacre* is well-known to program annotators. None of these instances can rival the perils of the *Lohengrin* rehearsals during the anti-

Wagner craze in Paris, when Lamoureux carried a pistol in his pocket against any possible eventuality.[86]

Occasions have been known, however, when segments of American audiences, temporarily acquiring a streak of bluntness and completely forgetting their manners, make their disapproval known in the brusque, old-fashioned, continental manner. Such nonconformist behavior could only have been encountered by the nonconformist, Stokowski, whose repertoire, speckled with musical curiosities, so frequently strained the aesthetic tolerance of his patrons. In the early twenties, Schoenberg's *Five Pieces for Orchestra* touched off a shower of forthright hisses, as it had in London. The indignant conductor turned to his audience and defensively pleaded freedom of expression for the artist. Those who agreed with him applauded; those who preferred freedom of expression for the audience made known their opinions by a contrary sign. Having apparently enjoyed their first taste of this new freedom, Stokowski's audience during the season 1928–29 expressed similar dissatisfaction with Villa-Lobos' *Choros No. 8*. On this occasion the conductor invited the disaffected members of the audience to leave "and smoke the classic cigarette." A few years later, in the fall of 1931, the audience tittered and became audibly restless during the rendition of Webern's ultra-modern *Symphonie*. The offended conductor stopped the orchestra and left the stage, but ultimately returned to repeat the number. Such isolated instances do not invalidate the generalization that the typical American audience observes all the good manners of the concert hall. Stokowski was, after all, at that time hardly a typical conductor, and any dereliction in observing the proprieties of the occasion was probably more an expression of a sporting impulse than a breakdown of social decorum.

The code of deportment that has evolved in the serious concert is somewhat relaxed in the "pop" concert. Because of the lighter repertoire, which is constructed for the avowed purpose of pleasure and relaxation, enthusiastic acceptance of the program is the rule. In the early days of the Boston "pops" a pleasant hum of chattering often disturbed the more serious listener and a program note sometimes requested silence for special solo numbers. Today in the Boston "pops," which are the oldest series of that genre in this country, general silence usually prevails during the actual rendition of a number, especially during solo renditions, although the conductor does not usually find it convenient to wait for the audience to calm down completely before raising his baton. He does not rap for attention, for under these informal circumstances, with the first-floor audience engaged in drinking and smoking, with waitresses slithering through the aisles as inconspicuously as possible, dead silence would be both unnecessary and impossible. Nevertheless, the principle is definitely accepted that the public is in reality an audience, and that it has its drinks with its music rather than its music with its drinks. The Carnegie "pops," instituted in 1946, come a shade closer to formal concert conditions since refreshment service during the concert is permitted only in the boxes.

The Program

"The Program's the Thing" for which the elaborate apparatus of the orchestra and its satellite institutions must justify their existence. It is the musical unit offered in the concert market to the consumer public. The repertoire, which is the aggregate of individual programs, is the critical point of contact with the auditors and the ultimate test of their success.

Although each program constitutes a small installment of the repertoire, each does also possess a life of its own and is usually built on identifiable principles. Conductors are often tagged by critics and populace as "good" or "poor" program builders, although such pat judgments are invariably related to the subjective standards of the observer; and the critics who launch them are often inarticulate as to the exact criteria employed in their formation. If there can be no universal standard for "good" program construction, there are, nevertheless, distinguishable patterns that have been followed, and perhaps a few basic principles that have at various times received some acceptance.

In former days, as an inheritance of the presymphonic period, when orchestral music had not yet gained its autonomous status, the prevailing type of program consisted of a miscellaneous collation

of numbers devoid of unity in the modern sense. The predominant
motif was, of course, variety. Such a conglomeration was the initial
program of the New York Philharmonic Society (December, 1842),
which consisted of the following numbers:

Beethoven	Symphony No. 5
Weber	Scene from *Oberon*
Hummel	Quintet for piano and strings
Weber	Overture to *Oberon*
Rossini	Duet from *Armida*
Beethoven	Scene from *Fidelio*
Mozart	Aria from *Belmont and Constanze*
Kalliwoda	New Overture in D

This juxtaposition of chamber music, operatic arias, and bona fide
orchestral numbers was not only usual for that day even in Europe,
but fifty years later in New York and Chicago such an intrepid
defender of the primacy of symphonic music as Theodore Thomas
was still finding it necessary to present a similar miscellany, which
included even unaccompanied piano solos. Although the present
"straight" orchestral program was already crystallizing in the minds
of the conductors, it was far from being spontaneously accepted by
the audiences.

One of the early customs, which seems strange today, was the
fragmentation of a concerto or symphony into its component movements, which were then interspersed with solo numbers. The purist
of today is conditioned to conceive of a symphony as a unified
whole to be interrupted not even by applause: "What the composer
hath joined together, let not man put asunder." But such dismem-
berment of multiple items was rather common as late as the 1830's
in Europe.[87] Chopin himself performed his Second Piano Concerto
in Warsaw at that time, dividing it into two segments separated by
a French horn solo. The span of attention necessary for a long and
continuous musical exposure is a matter of long habituation. Audiences of that time were accustomed to shorter selections. It will be
recalled that Beethoven recommended that his *Eroica*, playing somewhat less than an hour, be performed at the beginning of a concert
before the audience was too fatigued to endure it. By the time of
the founding of the New York Philharmonic this practice of frag-

mentation seems to have been practically abandoned, though in 1845 and again in 1846, Beethoven symphonies were sectioned for operatic entremets in the Musical Fund concerts in Philadelphia.[88]

Single movements of concertos were still extracted at a much later date in major orchestral concerts, not only without apparently causing offense, but actually with the approval of Finck, Hale, and other top American critics, who emphasized the separability of symphony and concerto movements in accordance with their individual merits and the expedience of the program. In 1894 Philip Hale,[89] the scholarly Boston critic, complained that a certain Boston Symphony concert was too long, and suggested that "the second and third movements of the [Beethoven Violin] Concerto could well have been omitted." About the same time César Thomson, in his appearance with the Boston orchestra in a New York concert, actually did play only the first movement of the Bruch Second Concerto. The *Finale* of the Beethoven Ninth has frequently been dropped, and in March, 1894, the Boston orchestra performed on its regular concerts only Movements III and II, in that order. Such violations of the supposed sanctity of a symphonic unit are practiced today only in "pop" concerts, although excerpts from operas and suites, as well as manifold other cuts, are executed without the protest of even the most fastidious.

Conductors of the American symphony orchestras have always conceived of themselves as educators rather than entertainers. Any differences among them lie in the intensity with which they have felt dedicated to their mission, and the degree to which they have compromised with the practical necessity of offering some relaxation to their audiences. Theodore Thomas, especially in his pre-Chicago period, knew at times how to effect such compromises and won many a patron with his delicate rendition of *Träumerei*, *pianissimo*, or with a vibrant Strauss waltz. But they knew also when to be obstinate. With a veritable Messiah complex, they were determined to preserve the integrity of Art and make no Mephistophelian compact with the vulgar appetites of the untutored masses. Henschel, undertaking a grave responsibility in founding the new Boston orchestra and prompted by an understandable desire to enlist the good will of his audience, announced it as his policy that only the first half of the program would adhere to the elevated didactic principle, and that the second half would be devoted to lighter numbers—Hungarian dances, rhapsodies, overtures—a kind of dessert to top off a nutritious meal. While Henschel placed the symphony in the middle of the program, as the main dish, flanked on either side with the apéritif and sweetmeats, the more severe Gericke, not wishing to break the spell, as he himself explained, placed the symphony almost uniformly at the end.

The Leipzig Gewandhaus, catering to an audience not nearly as mature as is popularly supposed, pursued a similar policy, but for slightly different reasons. The "heavy" symphony occupied the latter half of the program, which, like the final blessing in the church, some of the less faithful by an early departure might be permitted to forego.[90] But in spite of Gericke's zealous piety, the Bostonians, too, could occasionally be unfaithful, and even scoff mildly at the aesthetic creed of their conductor, as is pointedly evidenced by the uninterrupted procession that filed out to the music of Brahms' Second (Jan. 22, 1887).[91] They had similarly walked out between the movements of Brahms' First, November 16, 1885.

Some conductors strive for internal homogeneity of the program. They have a horror of disorderly hodge-podge thrown together for mere contrast and hedonistic surprise. To them, a program is knit together in a consistent unity, with an integrating idea, very much like the classification of artifacts in a museum. Such an intellectual approach to program building was entertained by Karl Muck, for example, who would avoid the juxtaposition of classic and romantic numbers as an intolerable incongruity, while less squeamish conductors might so join them in the interest of desirable variety.

In the late nineteenth century another form of "unity" was cultivated, namely, the "genre" program, which integrated the items on the program around a specific topic such as a composer, a nationalistic group, or a historical sequence. In the interest of popular appeal, rather than a more academic motivation, Theodore Thomas launched such concerts during his summer night Garden Series in New York and Chicago, and attracted the crowds with his Mendelssohn nights, Wagner nights, Schubert, Mozart, Scandinavian, and English programs—though these were not always topically entirely homogeneous. In July, 1876, this conductor, who had been at times attacked for his seeming aversion to American music, discreetly included an "American Night" at the Philadelphia Exposition. By the twentieth century the genre program had become a common practice in program design, of which Stokowski availed himself abundantly, and perhaps uniquely in a Bach program with a Bach encore (December, 1926). The composer cycle is an extension of this system to encompass a series of programs.

Such unified programs did not escape their critics, some of whom contended that inferior items were often included to satisfy mere titular requirements. At least one American composer injected a personal interpretation into what was developing into a common practice, and took offense at the segregated treatment of his nationality. He said so in a now famous letter to Felix Mottl, then conducting at the Metropolitan Opera, who had announced an all-American orchestral program in February, 1904:

I see by the morning papers that a so-called American composers' concert is advertised for tomorrow evening at the Metropolitan Opera House. I have for years taken a strong stand against such affairs and although I have not seen the program, fearing that there may be something of mine on it, I write to protest most earnestly and strongly against this lumping together of American composers. Unless we are worthy of being put on programs with other composers to stand or fall, leave us alone. By giving such a concert you tacitly admit that we are too inferior to stand comparison with composers of Europe. If my name is on the program and if it is too late to have new programs printed, I beg you to have a line put through the number, erasing it off the program. If necessary I will pay the expense of having it done. . . .

(*Signed*)   Edward MacDowell [92]

It is extremely doubtful whether such an unkind cut was intended by the noted Austrian visitor. MacDowell's resentment was, of course, a comprehensible reaction of a sensitive nature, sharing the prevalent frustration produced by the foreign domination of American musical life. Although we harbored no illusions as to the veneration for American music on the part of the proud exponents of the art in the land of Beethoven and Wagner, it must be said that genre programs had already gained such vogue that it was probably intended as a tribute to America to include them at all.

Mottl acquiesced, and substituted the *Rakozcy March* of Berlioz!

Critics of this earlier era occasionally commented on mere tonal and formal imbalance of programs. Thus William Apthorp, Boston critic, cited his own reaction during the nineties to both key and pitch relation:

I can remember an instance, not many years ago at our symphony concerts in Boston when Mozart's "Batti, batti" was sung immediately after an orchestral piece in C major. Now, "Batti, batti" is in F major; and no two keys are more closely related than F and C. Yet the difference in pitch of a fifth lower than the preceding piece somehow made the poor "Batti, batti"—one of the coyest, brightest inspirations Mozart ever put on paper—sound positively dull and heavy.[93]

Symptomatic of this type of standard, which may seem strange to modern post-Romantic ears are the prescriptions set down by L. C. Elson, one of Boston's most prominent musical pedagogues of that period. He enunciated the following canons of good program-building for "classical" programs: (1) contrasts of major and minor; (2) no two successive works in the same key; (3) no two similar works on the same program, e.g., Schubert and Mozart; (4) avoidance of abrupt transitions. He admitted that romantic programs almost automatically evaded these pitfalls.[94]

There are countless more or less external considerations which circumscribe the make-up of a program. Because of the rhythm of daily routine to which everyone is subjected, a certain predictability of length is essential, while the attentive powers of the audience set certain psychological restrictions on its maximum duration. The early English programs of the London Philharmonic often contained two symphonies in addition to minor works, a length against which Wagner, to mention only one conductor, complained during his one-year tenure in 1855. Most orchestras today set an approximate limit of about ninety minutes of playing time which, together with an intermission, establishes a norm of about one and three quarter hours for the total concert. Within these limits must be compressed selections of interest and variety; consequently any item of unusual length, no matter how meritorious, is handicapped in competition for acceptance, and particularly in radio presentations where time limits must be rigidly enforced.

The juxtaposition of selections must be controlled not only for unity and contrast or interest, but also in deference to the physical capacity of the players. Numbers involving unusual endurance of wind players, for example, are so placed as to afford adequate relief.

The day of the encore in the regular subscription concerts has almost passed, except in the case of an occasional soloist. But time was when the encore was a live issue and conductors of serious concerts sometimes encountered resistance in their attempt to educate audiences away from that survival of the "pop" concert. In 1896 Theodore Thomas, who was not known for any infirmity of purpose, caused a sensation in Chicago by refusing to grant an encore after three minutes of boisterous applause. In the same year the mild-mannered Walter Damrosch, usually given to condescending flattery rather than pedagogic censure toward his audiences, rebuked his listeners for their crude manners in drowning out with continued applause the orchestral number which followed a sensationally received piano concerto played by Joseffy.[95] Thomas, to whom the encore was an unmitigated evil, summarized, as succinctly as anyone, the conductor's point of view, when he stated that encores (1) break the predetermined continuity and balance of the program, (2) overextend its length, (3) tax the endurance of the players, (4) cause restlessness among those members of the audience who differ with the demonstrators, and (5) often disappoint the audience, since repetitions are not necessarily as effective as first renditions.[96] Popular programs, however, still maintain the encore since selections are shorter and most of Thomas' objections are less relevant. The encore issue has in recent times taken an additional turn. Formerly, it implied the repetition of the encored item. Today, with the acknowledged gap between the strenuous program and the general audience, the customarily lighter encore is often eagerly anticipated as a relief.

Above all these aesthetic policies, there hovers the shadow of sheer "public strategy" in program construction. This is an important consideration for every orchestra, though the old-fashioned philanthropic orchestra was relatively free from these pressures. In brief, it means that in order to gratify all segments of the heterogeneous audience certain requirements must be observed: the inclusion of standard and familiar items, of "box-office" numbers, of modern and unhackneyed compositions, experimental novelties to satisfy the intellectual patron and members of a cult, some pieces for light relief, and a certain minimum number of regional representatives. It is not easy to reconcile these conflicting demands with one another, or with the rules of prudent management. Deploring the hidden costs of many experimental novelties, an official of a Midwest orchestra appraised the cost of a certain novelty at more than $750, made up of the out-of-pocket expenses of rental, royalty, extra players and extra rehearsal, together with the loss of single admissions "which we would have had if a sure-fire number had been billed."

The symphonic repertoire has at times been invaded by the opera in concert form, usually sponsored by conductors whose career included operatic experience. Overtures and operatic excerpts have, of course, long been a program staple, and it would seem only a step to extend these fragments into a full length presentation. This expectation is all the more logical because the average American, exposed for the most part to foreign operas whose plots have little in common with his cultural background, often ignores the libretto in favor of the music. In other words, to the average American patron, a nineteenth-century opera is not much more than a dramatic concert in any case. The earliest of these denatured operatic performances was the concert version of *Parsifal* rendered by the Oratorio Society and the Symphony Society of New York in 1895 under the leadership of Walter Damrosch, who in 1908 presented Tschaikowsky's *Eugene Onegin* in similar manner.

Philadelphia, Cleveland, and Cincinnati, among others, have proceeded a step farther by presenting completely staged operas, either as an integral part of the regular series or supplementary to it. At times such performances have been found too costly for the orchestral management; in other cases the critics see in them a violation of the bounds of the orchestra's sphere, if not its competence. On the other hand, they undoubtedly serve a function in that they inject novelty into the repertoire, supply an outlet for the conductor who is trained in, and enamored of that musical genre, and afford their audiences the opportunity to indulge a taste which otherwise might remain ungratified.

To many a confirmed symphony addict, the soloist is an intruder who disturbs the proper enjoyment of pure orchestral music; but to the rank and file of box-office patrons the star has always been a glamorous attraction that compensated for many a dull moment of more abstract music. Although from the first program of the New York Philharmonic, many soloists were accompanied by the orchestra, such was by no means the universal rule. As the virtuosity of the orchestra increased, however, it waxed in pride and prestige; it was no longer a chance ensemble which was content to share in a mélange of musical offerings, but had matured into an autonomous entity, well qualified to furnish in its own right a full evening of inspiration and pleasure.

Not a small factor in the partial repudiation of the soloist was the emerging conception that the conductor himself was the "soloist" whose glamour might be dimmed by that of a competitor. It is still a moot question whether the soloist is a member *pro tem* of the orchestra subordinate to the conductor, or whether he is a genuine soloist with the conductor reduced to the role of the accompanist. Temperamental clashes arising out of this ambiguity in their jurisdictions are, of course, common. The more sensational features of the soloist still constitute an enormous attraction to an orchestral audience and are a good investment on the part of the management. Generally, however, solo contributions are restricted to numbers which are an integral element of the symphonic repertoire. For that reason vocalists, who in the early days were often featured, and just as often performed to piano accompaniment, are much less likely to be engaged by some of the orchestras now than formerly, while concertos are added with more thought to the requirements of the balanced orchestral repertoire. Some conductors, notably Toscanini, were notorious for the rarity of solo appearances on their programs. In his case, at least one obvious explanation is, of course, near at hand: no management would feel any inducement for adding an expensive soloist to a conductor who could fill the hall alone.

American patrons who suffer from an inferiority complex vis-à-vis Europe may be inclined to suspect a more elevated taste on the part of European audiences. But the conductors of the Gewandhaus orchestra, Rietz (1848–60) and Reinecke (1860–95), also considered themselves afflicted with the "solo evil." To the distress of the conductor, the soloist would often monopolize a concert by playing a number in both parts of the program. This occurred in Boston and Chicago as late as the 1890's.

In accordance with the educational function of the orchestral program, it has been customary to supplement the printed program with "program notes," which facilitate its understanding and enhance its appreciation. The present style of analytical notes is the culmination of an evolution which proceeded approximately through the following stages: (1) printed titles of musical selections, (2) printed words of vocal selections, (3) biographical data on the composer and other historical material, and (4) analytical notes presenting the formal structure of the musical composition. Scholarly fusion of the preceding rudimentary beginnings was made as far back as 1784 when Reichardt prepared notes for his Concerts Spirituels in Berlin.[97] The New Philharmonic Society of London, organized as a rival for the old Philharmonic, added analytical notes of scholarly merit to its programs in 1852, while the old Philharmonic instituted the practice in 1869. The New York Philharmonic offered notes on certain isolated compositions during the early years, and by the eighties these notes became more systematic. To modern patrons, these old annotations often sound crude and embryonic. Thus the last movement of the *Eroica* (second concert of the first New York season) "is a combination of French Revolutionary airs put together in a manner that no one save Beethoven could have imagined." The programmatic penchant is illustrated in the description of the *Dramatic Overture, Columbus,* of George F. Bristow.

The Andantino . . . depicts the vessels of the daring discoverer rocking idly at anchor . . . horns give signals to depart . . . tremolo movement in accompaniment indicates the bustle of preparation . . . an *allegro agitato* movement portraying the restless conspiracies of the enemies of Columbus during his protracted absence . . .

During the epoch when music still required a literary crutch to be comprehended by even the best audiences, the following program note was typical of the New York Philharmonic programs. The composer Rubinstein himself supplied the annotation for his Piano Concerto No. 3 on the program of November 16, 1889, Theodore Thomas, conductor:

In the first movement the Piano repeatedly requests admittance in the temple of the Orchestra. The Orchestra takes the matter into consideration and decides to test the capacities of the Piano. After frequent trials and consultations the Orchestra concludes that the Piano is not worthy to enter into the sanctuary. . . . In a later movement the decision of the Orchestra is again adverse. . . . Now the Piano loses its temper and challenges the Orchestra to imitate what the Piano can do and in the tumult of this attempt the concerto closes.

Instead of the crassly pictorial analysis, some annotators took a more mystic trend. Witness a few exuberant phrases, taken almost at random, from Wagner's analysis of Beethoven's Ninth, which have at times been lifted for American programs:

The first movement appears to represent a nobly conceived conflict between the soul and the power which ever opposes its strivings for earthly happiness. . . . Here and there we just perceive the sweet yet sorrowful smile of that happiness so much desired which seems now to invite us, but the attainment of which is prevented by our mighty and malicious enemy who spreads around us his gloomy wings. . . . How different is the effect of the opening strains of the third movement! Heavenly pure and soothing, they melt the wild energies of the anxious and despairing soul into soft and sorrowful sensations. . . . This is the last attempt to express by instrumental music alone, a certain finite and unalloyed joy; but the intractable element does not seem fitted for such restrictions: like the roaring sea, it foams up, sinks down again, and louder than ever the loud chaotic shriek of unsatisfied passion assails our ears. A human voice with the clearness and distinctness of language is now heard above the tumult of the instruments. . . .

If the first reaction of the modern reader is characteristically one of sophisticated disdain for such flamboyant romanticism, he should recall that such picturesque portrayals are well-matched today in the descriptions of the tone poems of Richard Strauss, even though many contemporary listeners may wish to ignore the story in order to apprehend the pure music. Modern scholarship, and the accumulated background of the audiences who are no longer listening to the classics for the first time, have conspired to cast program notes into different molds of historical and musicological stripe. Some of these have attained a certain distinction and permanency of value, e.g., those of Philip Hale, of Boston, and Krehbiel, of New York, and have enriched our musicological literature. This shift in the nature of program notes is an obvious adaptation to the fact that the current repertoire is predominantly old and familiar, and the crutch of programmatic and literary analysis is no longer essential to the audience's comprehension.

The Concert Series

Ever since the public concert system has been in existence, orchestral and ensemble concerts have been offered in series, given at more or less regular intervals during the season of the year. The Concerts Spirituels in Paris, Berlin, and Vienna; the London Philharmonic Concerts; the Gewandhaus concerts of Leipzig; the Société des Concerts du Conservatoire of Paris; the New York Philharmonic, and the Theodore Thomas concerts in the same city—all customarily purveyed their entertainment in "subscription series" rather than in single concerts. The reasons for such an arrangement arise from the character of the audience and, more particularly, from the requirements of artistic rendition.

A century and more ago, when concert halls were smaller, the audience was characteristically a more closely knit group than today. It consisted of the aristocracy and wealthy merchants who were known to each other and associated in the neighboring boxes, broke bread and sipped their beverages together during the intermissions, and even carried on their social intercourse during the rendition of musical numbers. A concert was a social institution of like-minded folk who periodically looked forward to gratifying their gregarious impulses.

As for the orchestra, the subscription system is necessary to its very existence. The great investment in time, money, and rehearsal energy required to build up an ensemble fit for public appearance by modern standards renders a single performance downright prohibitive. This proportion between overhead costs and concert sales does not obtain in amateur organizations, whose objective is self-cultivation rather than public approval, nor among those groups where rigorous artistic standards are, for any reason, not enforced. Hence, during the colonial days, the single performance of concerted groups, often instituted for an "occasion," was rather the rule than the exception. In the relentless evolution of things, however, these casual aggregations, with their informal standards, have been displaced by well-equipped and rigorously rehearsed groups for which a continuity of existence is the prime prerequisite. As a consequence, the series of subscription concerts, most of which are given today in weekly pairs, has become the backbone of symphonic organization.

The number of weekly pairs varies from city to city and has varied widely in the history of the individual orchestras, as may be gleaned from their respective histories. Most older orchestras offer a series of from twenty to twenty-eight weeks which includes shorter supplementary series of diverse nature. Minneapolis, of the older major orchestras, is the only one that limits its subscription series to single weekly concerts, for the very good reason—among others —that the University auditorium, which is its home, has almost twice the average capacity of the auditoriums in other cities.

Originally called "public rehearsal," the first of the pairs of concerts was instituted for quite another purpose than it now satisfies. The New York Philharmonic Society opened its rehearsal of its second annual series, as a privilege of its associate membership, and later invited the general public at a nominal admission charge. For most patrons the function of this preview of the program was a purely educational one, and they availed themselves of the opportunity for repeated hearings at a time when radio and recordings did not exist to fulfill that desire much more effectively. In addition to this educational facility, the public rehearsals which were held in the afternoon were advertised as especially appealing to "out-of-town patrons" and to "unaccompanied ladies."

In Boston the "public rehearsal" was planned by Mr. Higginson as a philanthropic concession to the less affluent population, but it did not long remain so. By the fifth season, the afternoon concerts had become so attractive to the wealthy class that the admission prices for the two series were equalized, and by 1915 the designation of "public rehearsal," by now a misnomer, was formally abolished. Today in all cities the afternoon concert is a "society" event. Unfortunately, in some of the smaller cities, this public is not now sufficiently numerous to maintain the solvency of matinee concerts. In view of such unprofitable luxury, some cities, e.g., Cincinnati and St. Louis, have shifted a portion of the Friday matinee concerts to Sunday afternoon in the hope of enticing another audience.

In addition to the basic repertoire of the subscription concerts, the major orchestras offer supplementary series which for the most part, cater to special segments of the population. One of the oldest and most firmly rooted in tradition is the Young People's and Children's series. Based on the reasonable theory that the children of today are the adults and potential subscribers of tomorrow, they are designed to "bend the twig" toward orchestral music, to nurture good taste, and so to assure an abiding interest in good music. To heighten this appeal, the conductors often empty upon the platform their bag of tricks: memory contests, quizzes, instrumental demonstrations, dramatic paradigms, lantern slides, anecdotes of famous composers, performance by an occasional *Wunderkind* and many pleasant variations on those themes. Extraordinary success in this specialty concert has been achieved by Walter Damrosch, Oberhoffer, Stock, Ganz, Schelling, Sokoloff, Stokowski, and Wallenstein. For some years after his retirement from the New York Symphony, Walter Damrosch, under the auspices of NBC, conducted the weekly radio broadcasts to the children of the nation. Although children's concerts had been tried before the beginning of the century, the radio carried the familiar salutation, "My dear children," to many areas which the major orchestras had never reached.

An intermediary link between the children's concerts and the regular subscription series is the "pop" program. Purveyed to those who may not have the musical maturity for the contemplation of masterpieces, the "pops" gratify the desire for less strenuous relaxation. The line of demarcation between the serious and the popular is perhaps not easily drawn and certainly is never permanent or of universal applicability. Beethoven's Fifth, the *Lohengrin* Prelude, and innumerable other compositions, which were formerly included exclusively on "serious" programs, are now listened to without special exertion. Thomas, as late as his Chicago days, included "popular" programs periodically in his regular series, and these were distinguished from the rest of the programs primarily by the absence of a complete symphony.

As the audiences became more cultivated and less allergic to "symphonies," conductors tended to specialize by segregating the popular items from the subscription series. Gericke instituted this reform in Boston in 1885, and Theodore Thomas for years adapted his repertoire to his New York audiences by catering to popular interest and the more sophisticated taste in separate series. In St. Louis and Minneapolis, under Zach and Oberhoffer, the Sunday afternoon "pops" usually overshadowed the serious concerts in patronage and frequency, and for some years constituted the bulwark of the season. Today popular concerts during the winter months are definitely on the wane and are scheduled only intermittently. The decline may be ascribed to three factors: (1) the competition of other recreational opportunities, such as motion pictures, sports, the automobile, all of which have enjoyed an unprecedented upswing during the last decades, (2) the demand on the part of those who have survived the "pops" age and have graduated to the serious concerts, and (3) the availability of popular music at convenient hours on radio programs.

Sunday concerts have been a fixture in most cities for many years. But there was a time when Boston, New York, and Philadelphia looked askance at such desecration of the Sabbath. Although Theodore Thomas, in the sixties, evaded the Blue Laws by an occasional "sacred" concert, it was not until 1891 when Walter Damrosch inaugurated his Sunday evening series that the interpretation of the laws was relaxed. His first offense, however, drew important protests, and the embarrassed board of directors declined to stand behind the conductor. Nevertheless, the concerts were soon resumed.

Another brush with the law occurred in 1907, when the Court

closed Carnegie Hall on two successive Sundays in December. But
a well-placed remonstrance reopened it immediately. After Sunday
concerts were held as "private musicales" open to "members" only,
Philadelphia legalized public concerts in 1934.

The Standard Repertoire

The "standard repertoire" is a concept which inevitably emerges
from the accumulated experience of both producers and audiences
of symphony concerts. It comprises the music that has survived
competitive selection, and is therefore a kind of social heritage
firmly grounded in human habit. Like every other social custom, it
is in a constant state of flux so that the central core cannot always
be clearly demarcated from the new experimental fringes, or from
the obsolescent remnants which are about to be sloughed off. Ab-
stractly, however, the standard repertoire can be simply defined.
Anything that is "standard" (1) is more or less enduring rather than
ephemeral, (2) transcends personal whims, (3) appears with more
or less predictable frequency, and (4) is approved by those who
profess the standard.

Realistically, the standard repertoire should be determined from
the records of the actual programs. For, if the concept of "standard"
has any meaning, it surely carries the assumption that we are abiding
by it. Compositions which never appear, or appear very irregularly,
could not lay claim to that term. To set up contemporary standards
we need only agree on a certain frequency of appearance and a
reasonable period of time which fairly represents the present era.
This cross-section of today, should include, of course, today's immediate roots in the past and a brief portent of the future.

The statistical array of standard works, if it is carefully com-
puted, will reflect local color. New York and Boston are, perhaps,
a little more adventurous than smaller orchestras in other regions.
Shorter seasons will present the standard repertoire in smaller installments, and their period of observation will therefore have to
be lengthened if orchestras with long and short seasons are combined.

To bear the stamp of national standard, the compositions will have to appear in a representative sample of all orchestras, and extend over a period of years sufficient to yield an adequate sample of the repertoires of orchestras with relatively short seasons. While most of the following standard works tabulated on that basis appeared with much greater frequency, the *minimum* frequency was set at two performances in at least eight of the ten orchestras in the period 1940–50 to allow for short seasons and chance variations. But even the marginal compositions which are heard in only five or more orchestras are of some interest.

COMPOSITIONS PLAYED AT LEAST TWICE IN PERIOD 1940–50, IN EACH OF EIGHT OR MORE ORCHESTRAS: 59 PIECES OF 19 COMPOSERS

Beethoven: Symphonies No. 1, 3, 4, 5, 6, 7, and 8; Overtures, *Leonore No. 3, Egmont, Coriolanus;* Concerto for Piano, No. 5; Violin Concerto.

Berlioz: *Symphonie Fantastique;* Overture, *Carnaval Romain.*

Brahms: Symphonies No. 1, 2, 3 and 4; Overture, *Academic Festival; Variations on a Theme by Haydn;* Concertos for Piano No. 1 and 2; Concerto for Violin.

Debussy: *L'Après-midi d'un Faune; La Mer; Iberia.*

Dvořák: Symphony No. 5.

Falla: Three Dances from *The Three-Cornered Hat.*

Franck: Symphony in D minor.

Mendelssohn: Concerto for Violin.

Mozart: Symphonies No. K550, K385, and K551.

Rachmaninoff: Concerto for Piano No. 2; *Rhapsody on a Theme of Paganini.*

Ravel: *Daphnis et Chloë* (Second Suite); *La Valse; Rhapsodie Espagnole.*

Schubert: Symphony No. 7.

Schumann: Concerto for Piano.

Shostakovitch: Symphony No. 5.

Stravinsky: Suite from *The Fire Bird.*

Strauss: *Death and Transfiguration; Don Juan; Don Quixote; Till Eulenspiegel.*

Tschaikowsky: Symphonies No. 4, 5, and 6; Concerto for Piano No. 1; Concerto for Violin; Overture, *Romeo and Juliet.*

Wagner: Preludes to *Meistersinger, Lohengrin,* and *Tristan; Love-Death* from *Parsifal.*

Weber: Overtures to *Der Freischütz, Euryanthe, Oberon.*

COMPOSITIONS PLAYED IN EACH OF FIVE, SIX, OR SEVEN ORCHESTRAS, AT
LEAST TWICE IN PERIOD 1940–50: 51 PIECES OF 31 COMPOSERS

Bach: *Brandenburg* Concerto No. 3.

Beethoven: Symphonies No. 2 and 9; Overture to *Fidelio;* Concertos for Piano No. 3 and 4.

Chausson: Symphony in B-flat.

Chopin: Concerto for Piano No. 1.

Debussy: *Fêtes* and *Nuages.*

Dvořák: Concerto for Cello.

Dukas: *The Sorcerer's Apprentice.*

Elgar: *Enigma Variations.*

Enesco: *Roumanian Rhapsody, No. 1.*

Handel: *Water Music.*

Haydn: Symphony No. 88.

Lalo: *Symphonie Espagnole* for Violin.

Mahler: Symphony No. 1.

Mendelssohn: Symphonies No. 3 (*Scotch*); No. 4 (*Italian*); *Midsummer Night's Dream* (Excerpts).

Moussorgsky: *Pictures at an Exhibition;* Prelude to *Khovantchina.*

Mozart: Symphony K543; Overture to *Figaro.*

Prokofieff: Symphony No. 5, *Classical* Symphony.

Rachmaninoff: Symphony No. 2; Concerto for Piano No. 3.

Ravel: *Bolero; Alborada del Gracioso.*

Respighi: *The Pines of Rome.*

Rimsky-Korsakoff: Overture, *The Russian Easter.*

Schubert: Symphony No. 8.

Schumann: Symphonies No. 1, 2, 3, and 4.

Shostakovitch: Symphony No. 1.

Sibelius: Symphonies No. 2, 5, and 7.

Smetana: Symphonic Poem, *The Moldau;* Overture to *The Bartered Bride.*

Strauss: Suite from *Der Rosenkavalier.*

Stravinsky: Suite from *Petrouchka.*

Tschaikowsky: *Francesca da Rimini.*

Vaughan Williams: *Fantasia on a Theme by Thomas Tallis.*

Wagner: Overture to *Flying Dutchman; Good Friday Spell* from *Parsifal;* Overture to *Tannhäuser; Siegfried Idyll.*

The younger orchestras such as Los Angeles and San Francisco, in some years of the 1940–50 decade, had only twelve to eighteen concerts as against the twenty-four or twenty-eight of Boston,

Chicago, New York, and Philadelphia. By actual count of total volume in that decade, the most productive orchestra played exactly double the volume of the least productive. In so limited a series of subscription concerts, an orchestra could hardly be expected to cover all the standard repertoire twice in ten years. Hence the required frequency has been set generously low. The four orchestras with the greatest volume of music show a failure to play only eleven out of the fifty-nine items at least twice in the ten years; while the four orchestras with the shortest seasons total forty-five such failures.

Some familiar favorites are missing from these lists. Bach is almost entirely absent, although a long list of twenty-six items were played repeatedly in one, two, or three orchestras. The composer is standard enough, but his patronage is distributed among several equally acceptable numbers. The *Brandenburg* Concertos were almost always represented but the choices were scattered among Numbers One, Two and Three. Preludes, Toccatas, Fugues, Suites, and the Passacaglia appeared often, but each orchestra has developed its own favorites in these various forms. Haydn and Mozart especially are underrepresented in the first list because of the variety of works presented by the different orchestras. Such a circumstance could never occur with César Franck, who wrote but one symphony and very few other acceptable works for the orchestra.

Whether or not there is any virtue in referring to these pieces as "standard," there is good evidence that they do represent the music to which the subscription audiences have been most constantly exposed for the past generation. The nineteen composers on the first list account for sixty per cent of the total current repertoire, and those on the two lists together more than seventy-five per cent of it. The standard names leave less than a quarter of the volume of present-day music for the hundreds of other composers of all ages and countries who hope for a hearing, including, of course, the three-hundred American composers who have failed to place a single composition in this "standard" list.

While the itemizing of the standard numbers may seem to some as having only museum interest, the important fact is that it can be done at all. It can therefore be said that the core of the orchestral repertoire is quite beyond the discretion or control of a single individual, whether conductor or manager. The list represents the power of "social heredity" absorbed and transmitted by musicians and audience in a collaborative enterprise.

7

Musical Taste and How It Is Formed

A CONCERT is made up of three indispensable human elements: the performer, the composer, and the audience—all embedded in a given social setting. But it is after all for the benefit and excitation of the audience that the complicated and costly structure of the symphony orchestra exists. Its repertoire is subject to a continuing plebiscite of the audience; and withdrawal or diminution of its patronage, for any one of many possible reasons, would endanger its very existence. Therefore any realistic analysis of the repertoire and prospects of the orchestra must be grounded in part in the human nature of that audience, and in the conception of the nature of beauty to which the audience adheres.

It may seem embarrassing to raise, and impertinent to attempt to answer, questions on the nature of beauty which have occupied the thought of mankind at least since the time of the Greeks. Many may, in fact, feel that such questions are irrelevant to the enjoyment of great music. But they are implicit in history, and their tentative solutions in every epoch are a part of the very process of living. Man not only acts, but he also reflects on his actions in order to make them plausible to himself and to his fellow man.

During the nineteenth century, when most of the standard repertoire of today had its beginnings, the problems of art and beauty were considered the province of philosophy and metaphysics, in keeping with the revived Platonic theories which dominated the arts of that romantic era. Beauty was Truth, unencumbered by the vicissitudes of mundane life. It was a kind of Universal, compelling on every perceptive intelligence. This view still has many disciples in art pedagogy and in the critics' fraternity, and explains the passionate enthusiasm and missionary fervor with which certain tastes are promulgated, the esteem in which the artist is held, the conception which some artists have of their own role, and the awe of the layman before a creative work.

However, with the development of the social, anthropological, and psychological sciences,[1] and their analysis of the diverse primitive and modern art forms, the tremendous variety of equally valid aesthetic standards could not but impress the conscientious and informed observer. The prestige that any given standard may command among its devotees takes on a rather provincial hue when examined in the light of the myriads of others that may be cherished with equal passion by their own adherents. In this great diversity of historically approved standards lies the reason for the supposed insolubility of the problem of beauty. Furthermore, new beauties are constantly being invented and old ones discarded. The solution is clearly not to be found exclusively in the nature of the beautiful objects themselves, nor exclusively in the human nature of the subject who enjoys them, but in the interaction or relation between both elements.

In view of the antiquity of the aesthetic problem, and the illimitable variety of data which might be mobilized for its solution, one century may seem a narrow base on which to build an edifice of artistic theory. But it is quite adequate for a generalization. A chemical experiment, for example, is interpreted not only in terms of the immediately observed data, but also in terms of all related experiments in the history of the subject. A novice, who has no knowledge of the history of the subject, and is unable to make comparative observations, could not be expected to extract intelligent conclusions from the experiment at hand. In a similar vein, this hundred-year cumulation of a small segment of art history is the occasion, but by no means the exclusive material, out of which the reflections of this chapter are fashioned. To some authorities, the taste of a century may not turn up striking mutations. But if taste can change a little in a short time, it can and does change even more in a longer period.

In explanation of these fluctuations in art tastes, it would be too simple and dogmatic merely to derogate as "decadent" those periods whose preferences differed significantly from the present, and to exalt those "golden" ages whose likings conformed to our own, only to have the next generation modulate, or even reverse, our judgments. A competent student of art history will easily demonstrate how such terms as Renaissance, Gothic, Baroque, Rococo, Romantic and other styles have some descriptive value, but are actually "loaded" abstractions which contain the retroactive judgments of another era, floated with conviction and great confidence, but signifying essentially a periodic re-evaluation of taste. It therefore has little meaning to state that, during his eclipse, critics were "mistaken" about Bach, and that his sons were "blind to his greatness"; that Brahms was long "undervalued" and Raff and Tschaikowsky "overrated"; or that "true" judgments cannot be ventured until after repeated hearings. The question is not intended to be facetious: Why should posterity always have the last word? Unless a given epoch exalts its own verdicts to a level of infallibility —as it often does—it must be acknowledged that every epoch, every age, is entitled to its own standards of judgment in matters aesthetic. The invidious distinctions so often drawn between epochs are psychologically and sociologically indefensible, and derive from a misconception of the nature of aesthetic "truth."

The standard of "truth" in matters aesthetic differs fundamentally from that of science. Aesthetic "truth" or appreciation is a psychologically *terminal* experience, a subjective and contemplative state of mind, in which every percipient differs from every other in slighter or greater degree according to his accumulated experience.[2] It is therefore essentially incommunicable except to the extent that the subjects' backgrounds are identical. Since aesthetic experiences are ends in themselves, and represent a state of personal fulfillment, they cannot be demonstrated as truthful or false by any external tests, for they reach their convincing termination in the subjective sense of gratification. Hence, aesthetic tastes cannot be "disputed," although their derivation may be traced and "accounted for."

In contrast, scientific opinion rests ultimately on a means-end scheme in which efficiency, or the test of adequate means for the achievement of a given end, is the criterion of "truth." Since the means toward the attainment of a given end are constantly subject to improvement, the scientific world permits of progress. Increased knowledge of physiology, and the analysis of meteorological phenomena represent improved means of accomplishing the socially approved purposes of curing disease and predicting the weather.

Since each stage in the development of science is more efficient than the preceding, one does not ordinarily conceive of a renaissance of the horse-and-buggy days. Revival of forgotten aesthetic stages is, however, not only possible but of frequent occurrence. This does not argue the "higher truth" of the revived music, literature, or the arts, but rather the flexibility and versatility of human habits. However, this adaptation to older art forms is never perfectly made. Modern man cannot view Greek sculpture with the eyes of a Greek, nor read Homer with the Hellenic mentality, nor listen to Bach with the ears of the Leipzig parishioners. If science is concerned with efficiency, it is, of course, absurd to speak of Catholic or Communist science. The results of the means-end tests are not dependent on one's ideologies; in fact they sometimes contradict them. There may, however, be Communist or Catholic art which speaks to the cultural interests of those groups, and is not easily interchangeable.

These distinctions have extremely important implications for the function of "experts" in the respective fields. In the area of science the basic assumption is the possibility, indeed the necessity, of absolute agreement between the experts. Consequently the judgment of the expert is compulsive on the less experienced layman. However, the aesthetic taste of the art "expert" does not possess that compulsive sanction. Art tastes are subjective rather than objective; they represent expectations and habits that arise from the experiences of the subject, and exist in terms of these experiences. Although technical workmanship, fidelity to tradition, stylistic details, and the like are objective and subject to "expert" opinion, these should not be confused with the actual aesthetic thrill derived therefrom, which ultimately remains a subjective personal possession. Therefore, according to Donald Tovey, British musicologist, when critics aver that "such and such a classic ought to inspire us with noble feelings because its sentiments are edifying and its form perfect, we may legitimately argue that it is useless to tell us that we ought to feel this and that, when as a matter of fact we feel quite otherwise." [3]

Since scientific "truths" are subject to the pragmatic tests of truth or falsity, scientific inventions have never engendered the messianic fervor which have accompanied artistic products. Simply because artistic convictions are not subject to empirical disproof, they thrive on, and accumulate, an authority which it is heresy to deny. Hence scientists, whose truths do not depend on belief or subjective conviction but on demonstrable objective evidence, can afford to be more tolerant than the exponents of nondemonstrable aesthetic or moral "truths." Intolerance rests on the psychological fact that aesthetic faith is not easily subject to contradiction, since it is self-contained within the subjective life of its interpreter and therefore engenders a sense of great introspective certainty.

Changes in aesthetic taste and judgment do not emanate solely from the dicta of aesthetes. They do not proceed from an exalted metaphysical realm, whence they are communicated to the chosen few who, like the apostles of old, feel called to share these privileged communications with the lay masses. The pattern of the repertoire, which constitutes musical taste, changing by small accretions, is formed by crosscurrents of many major and minor personal decisions and compromises made every time the program of a concert is selected or an annual series projected. The identity and strength of these forces differ from time to time and from place to place; but they are not capricious and whimsical—the patterns are too uniform for that. Nor are they automatic and preordained: the variations are too obvious for that. One can only conclude that musical opinions and tastes, like political and economic preferences, are forged in a matrix of social and psychological forces and, at any given time, represent a blend of both traditional factors and current experiences. One cannot come away from a study of a century of musical tastes without being struck by the perennial revision of human judgments, and the conviction that, under different circumstances, our tastes would have taken other channels with which we today would have been equally contented. And, unless human mentality reaches a saturation point, at which further development in forms, harmonies and rhythms cannot be absorbed or invented, society will continue to revise its most considered and hallowed judgments in the future, as it so obviously has in the past.

Of all the current theories designed to explain changes in aesthetic tastes, one of the most prevalent, and also the most suspiciously simple, is that art is a "reflection of the spirit of the age." According to this familiar principle, the stream of history is divided into broad periods, each of which is characterized by a "spirit" which pervades its totality and which binds it into a recognizable unit. There are many versions of this "spirit of the age," and not all exponents of this view would necessarily subscribe to the rather comprehensive formulation which avers that

Some very general trend in the evolution of mankind controls all forms of human expression and all the ways in which they act, be they politics, economy, thought or art.[4]

But no social scientist views society as a homogeneous entity in which an over-all "spirit" can be identified. Society is enormously more complex than the Hegelian *Zeitgeist* seems to assume. Instead of an integrated Society with a capital "S," society is rather a federation of various and diverse groups, each with its own interests and tastes, sometimes cooperating with one another, but quite frequently in mortal conflict. This unitarian view of Society, which has often been so congenial to totalitarian national aspirations as well, has lost much of its credibility in the more thoroughgoing, empirical methods of the twentieth century. This theory of an enveloping spirit has led to positing spurious relations between music, architecture, and other phases of life literally too numerous and too well-known to cite. The social approach to history is inconsistent with the synoptic notion of rolling into one the economic, technological, political, psychological, and other factors and labeling them with an intangible "spirit."

There is also the semantic objection, that an explanation of an event in terms of the "spirit" of that event is tautological. To explain rococo by the "spirit" of rococo, baroque by the "spirit" of baroque, is to explain something in terms of synonyms, which is no explanation at all. This is a grave methodological error that gives a satisfying sense of certainty for the simple reason that there is no possibility whatever of being contradicted. One reads the "spirit" from a few observed facts, and then reads it right back again into the unresistant period. "Spirituous" liquors analogously had their origin in similar verbalisms, but today modern chemistry and physiology have found more palpable explanations for the source of their potency.

It is noteworthy that this synthetic procedure is more successful when applied to bygone periods than to the present; living persons and the readily recognized multiplicity of circumstances make the omnibus phrase much less convincing. Past periods are more likely to be viewed as ways of action which have survived in the lore of scholars and in the visible remnants of the epoch. The distant perspective, which either magnifies or belittles fragments of history in accordance with our present biases, and purges them of inconvenient contradictions, portrays the past in exaggerated unity—a naïveté of which we are quickly disabused today by a vigorous election, a war, a religious or economic persecution, and all the ideological battles and the myriad other ugly symptoms of "man's inhumanity to man." For every theorist who posited an integrating "spirit," there has been another to underline the equally obvious "lags" and the "contradictions" in our social order.

This is not to say that there are no harmonies or adaptations in our social relations but such an oversimplified unity can be constructed only on the basis of a vague pseudo-psychological formula. It is a seductive intellectual enterprise, this pinnacling of all knowledge into an integrated whole; it represents scholarship run riot propelled by a questionable philosophy of history. One must therefore view with regret the borrowing by musicologists of such terms as "baroque" from its architectural origins, and its inflation and application to a broad span of geography and time, in a manner that cannot survive mature analysis. One cannot but deplore the defense of modern music by its alleged conformity to the "modern age," when many more specific arguments are at hand.

Some exponents of contemporary music, for example, lament the lackadaisical acceptance of the music of the "court age" instead of an energetic sponsorship of a type of music more "consonant with the machine age." But embarrassing questions must follow in the wake of this reasoning. How prove that the composer actually reflects the modern age? What *are* the earmarks of machine-age music? Is not the audience, which enjoys the allegedly anachronistic music, also a part of "the age" and therefore entitled to reflect it? May not the composer, who often leads a sequestered existence, actually be less representative of the significant forces and implications of the age than an intelligent, versatile, mobile man of affairs in the audience?

Although it has seemed to some students that this is the first time in musical history that the compositions of "the past" have so dominated the performance of the present, it is by no means a unique phenomenon. In fact, it is a historical commonplace that there has always been a lively borrowing and diffusion from other cultural epochs both in technology and in the arts. Literature, painting, and architecture reveal a clear "ancestor worship." Even the primitive and folk arts have been adopted eagerly and without mental conflicts by the most sophisticated cultures. The supposed incongruity of a capitalistic society enjoying ancient Greek art disturbed Karl Marx, who was also an advocate of the theory of the totalistic society and therefore felt that he had to reconcile this "contradiction." This he did by citing a person's normal enjoyment of an occasional childhood experience, which was equivalent to society's enjoyment of Greek culture, which represented the "social childhood" of our culture.[5]

The most irrefutable argument against the supposed incongruity between old music and the new times is simply that pleasure is undebatable. If a mature twentieth-century audience simultaneously enjoys the baroque Bach, the rococo Mozart, the romantic Schumann, the neo-classical Brahms, the Gallic Debussy, the Teutonic Wagner, the percussive Stravinsky, and the eclectic Shostakovitch, who is derivative of them all, how can one assert that it is enjoying them "by mistake" or that there are ethical and psychological reasons why it *should* enjoy something else. It is difficult to compose by fiat, but it is still more difficult to enjoy by fiat. Both processes are accomplished only by a process of conditioning, in a world whose systematic complexity we have not yet completely fathomed.

We therefore cannot resist the conclusion that musical taste is a system of very specific tonal habits, conditioned by the incessant flow of experiences of the individual person as a participating member of a complex culture group. A great range of experiences might conceivably contribute to the end-result of finding pleasure in many given types of music, much as some trivial incident might influence the degree of affection for or aversion toward another person. In order to understand more fully how the aesthetic quality of a musical composition is acquired, it will be necessary to ascertain its psychological components, and to explore how the standards of beauty become established.

Because of the human propensity to read into the object what is actually in our heads—"the elliptical fallacy"—it is often thought that the merit of a composition resides within it; and once that has been established by some kind of authority, there is a certain aesthetic obligation imposed on the auditor to put himself *en rapport* with the established masterpieces, and to attempt to "discover" for himself the beauties resident in those works of art that have been vouchsafed by "qualified" listeners.

However, psychologically and sociologically speaking, this is an unfortunate assumption. Beauty is not a transcendental entity waiting, perhaps in some outer sphere, to be incorporated into a composition by a sensitive composer; nor is it a quality resident *in* the object, or in the relationship between its parts, waiting to be discovered and enjoyed by an observer—any more than pain is resident in a red-hot stove, or the essence of patriotism in a multicolored flag. Beauty in music is not a fact but rather a human *experience*, a judgment that results from the *contact* between the particular arrangement of sounds and the particular background of the auditor. Beauty "happens" to an object. If there were no observer, there would be no beauty; if there are two simultaneous observers, the same object could be—and usually is—both beautiful and ugly simultaneously. Two or more persons, with approximately the same training, background, and fund of experiences, observing the same object, would necessarily be in approximate agreement as to its degree of "beauty." Hence, the cultural agreement on many masterpieces. Any object can be beautiful if it is matched with the appropriate observer who has the corresponding accumulation of experiences and store of habits. Thus it is false dichotomy to segregate the thinking subject from the object of thought. The real issue does not lie in the segregation of the two, but in the manner of their collaboration.[6]

When listening to a musical composition, we therefore do not hear only that composition, but rather a blend, or fusion, of the pattern of sounds in the immediate work plus the innumerable arrangements of tones that have been stored up in our own consciousness. It is against that background that the present experience is selectively perceived, defined, and evaluated. According to this principle of selective perception, we do not listen with our ears, but with our past experiences: sometimes called in academic psychology "apperceptive mass." Consequently, there are many things "out there" which we do not perceive; and there are many things which we think we "perceive" that are not "out there," but are "in our heads." No criterion has ever been established by which a concrete boundary line can be defined at which the irreducible minimum of raw music stops and the associative experiences of the listener begin. The psychoanalytic schools of thought would go far indeed in extending the scope of these associative experiences.

But audition is not only a matter of passive receptivity to tonal stimuli. It is also a process of fulfillment or denial of active expectations set up by the listener's past experiences. When the nineteenth-century audience first listened to Wagner with the expectations of hearing Beethoven's progressions and resolutions, they felt a degree of nervous frustration rather than aesthetic delight. In that sense it is inevitable that radically new forms of tonal organization will meet with delayed appreciation, until new habits of listening are formed. Every composer, depending on the degree to which he deviates from the past formal habits of his auditors, must retrain his audience in new listening habits and expectations before aesthetic pleasure can ensue. The successful composer thereby actually creates the public that later approves him.

It is evident, therefore, that a new composition may bear sufficient resemblance to the past—e.g. the early Beethoven to Mozart and Haydn—to be readily assimilable and appreciated by the audience. Or, in the case of the later Schoenberg and many other modern composers, the style may be so incongruous with current musical habits that the compositions become the subject of highly cerebral and clinical analysis, on another level of enjoyment, for the specialized auditor, devoid of any spontaneous lay audience appeal whatever. A small increment of novelty is essential; without it there is no interest to touch off attention and stimulate appreciation. It is for that reason that older compositions, having become too familiar through repeated hearings, are often greeted only with apathy or boredom. From this danger of satiety, the greatest masterpieces are not exempt. Its onset will vary according to the background of the auditor, the intervals between hearings during which one may "forget" a part of what has been stored up, and the degree of variety within the composition itself.

Such an analysis partially explains the differences in the contours of the performance curves of Tschaikowsky and Brahms. Tschaikowsky, a prolific composer, whose melodic turns were easily grasped, provoked little controversy, and harvested quick popularity. But he has been on the wane from sheer saccharine monotony. On the other hand, the polyrhythmic and compact Brahms, whose name was once the synonym for all that is intellectual and esoteric, has only recently been generally apprehended after a vigorous campaign on the part of conductors. Nevertheless, many can still listen with pleasure to Tschaikowsky—but not nearly so often. Others can no longer endure the deification of Brahms. The interest and sense of "novelty" in Mozart, Beethoven, Haydn, Debussy, Franck, and the rest can be maintained only by increasingly infrequent repetitions. The immortals can remain immortal only by not insisting on being too much alive. They may be resuscitated, or satiety may be delayed, by an additional increment, such as improvement in the quality of the performance, slightly unconventional interpretations, or such miscellaneous strategies as omitting repeats, and the addition of scholarship and formal analysis to the background of the listener, thereby diverting his attention to hitherto unnoticed detail.

There is, then, after repeated hearings, an optimum point of appreciation after which the law of diminishing aesthetic returns sets in, the attainment of which may be accelerated or delayed, but which in the long run is psychologically inevitable. With the introduction of newer technological mechanisms for the dissemination of tonal pleasures—records and radio—familiarity with these compositions will be increased and the approach of satiety hastened. Under such circumstances the repertoire may more quickly burn itself out than in the olden days of the New York Philharmonic, when it was literally impossible for even the assiduous concert-patron to hear Beethoven's Fifth more than once every couple of years! According to this principle of accelerated culture change, it is highly unlikely that there will ever be another "Beethoven" whose music will dominate the repertoire for over a century. Unless unforeseen circumstances intervene, life spans of composers will probably be shorter, particularly if the democratization of the audience, with the possible necessity of catering to less esoteric tastes, continues at its present pace.

Furthermore, audiences have undoubtedly undergone a temperamental change. Their disinclination to endure a long apprenticeship to an extremely novel tonal structure, which could formerly be overcome by the zeal of such missionaries as Theodore Thomas, does not augur well for a long life span for a composer. Half of the span of Brahms, for example, is an investment in endurance on the part of the audience in order that aesthetic pleasure may be reaped at the peak, which will gradually dissipate during the descending half of his musical life cycle.

It is not that modern twelve-tone scale is necessarily beyond the ultimate comprehension of the average music lover. But it is a new grammar which never comes easily no matter how spontaneously the composers profess to compose in it. If we cultivated it as assiduously and as long as the American audience did Brahms, it would probably fall into place, for it is probably impossible for Man to create anything to which he cannot become accustomed. But, without intense motivation and without belief in the infallibility of the composer, a modern audience is ill-disposed toward making the intellectual investment in an "esperanto" so long as the current language serves its aesthetic and social purposes.

There are those who may be offended at so prosaic a treatment of the arts, which suggests that good music is ephemeral and transient, and subject to the material vicissitudes of life. They would prefer to believe that Art secures its sanction from a higher realm, or that it at least possesses some distinctive objective trait to give it permanence and universality in its appeal to the discerning auditor. Such was the fervent faith of Leopold Damrosch, Theodore Thomas, Gericke, and Muck, who laid the foundation of the now traditional standards of taste. It is the long dominance of such a figure as Beethoven, more recently joined by Sebastian Bach, which appears to give plausibility to the faith in a universal Beauty. It is such phenomena which create the illusion of timeless beauty that transcends the ages, the passing of which is uncomfortable to contemplate. A well-developed historical sense, however, will awaken the realization that a century—or a thousand years—is but a moment in civilization. Bach and Beethoven are not "universal"; they merely have lasted a long time.

Such an argument is not at all nihilistic. It does not proclaim the nonexistence of standards. For it is an error to suppose that, if norms cannot be absolute or eternal, there can be no norms at all. But so intense is the quest for certainty that the difference between absolute and period norms is often overlooked. However, it is the only point of view that makes the incessant fluctuations in taste plausible and is, above all, consistent with the current conceptions of the workings and nature of the human mind.

Detailed studies such as these are therefore frankly postulated on the assumption that musical composition and its enjoyment is, in the largest sense, an acquired craft of Man, circumscribed by the interacting physical, biological, and social circumstances, and subject to all the psychological and sociological principles which underlie all other human behavior. Factual and quantitative studies have their place in any analysis of Man and his works, as a healthy counterbalance to the romantic terminology which so often surrounds the discussion of beauty and its production, endowing it with a spiritual entity that modern empirical thinking finds hard to assimilate. There is much mysticism in creativity; but no more than in the test tube. As self-evident as such a view might be, it is still true that to many persons it is neither desirable nor even possible to study the processes of musical composition and their social survival. Each composition, it has been asserted, is a unique product of a creative imagination, about which generalizations, by definition, would be excluded. Accordingly, musical preferences are subjective and personal; "there is no accounting for them."

Since no two compositions are identical, and since pleasure is by definition quite subjective and personal, such a view carries superficial credibility. But a second glance at the history of composition must convince an observer that "unique" is far too extreme a term. If a composition is actually unique, or as it approximates that description, it is to that extent alien to the stream of human thought, its language is not understood; it would evoke bewilderment rather than curiosity and aesthetic interest. The composer who flouts the current folkways of taste, and disregards the norms of consonance and form prevalent at the time, incurs the same risks of rejection as any other innovator in the political, social and economic, religious, or linguistic world. Not even the greatest innovators who have survived, have been so indiscreet. The deviant modern composers who rationalize their frequent failures to capture the approbation of public and critics by the complacent cliché that "all music was once new" and that the audience is "always about twenty-five years in lag behind the composer" do not take the penetrating view of history which would have warned them that not all good music of the past was *equally* new, and that the audiences of Haydn, Mozart, Beethoven, and even Wagner, were not a generation behind the composer. Haydn, who expressed appreciation for the tolerance of his benefactor, experimented well within the limits of that tolerance. The early works of Beethoven—with all the isolated points of departure from tradition pointed out by contemporary philistines—bore a sufficient family resemblance to their musical ancestors, to which his hearers were accustomed, that his new works were anticipated with obvious pleasure. In explanation, it is sometimes claimed that Beethoven and Mozart had an "intelligent" leisure-class audience who were educated in the arts. But modern audiences also include a large segment of cultivated and intelligent auditors, who are nevertheless sufficiently mystified by many current departures to raise serious questions.

The currently prevailing myth, that great composers of the past were not appreciated in their day, has its roots in the fact that the accepted manners of the day are less likely to be commented upon in current chronicles than are the departures therefrom. If this holds good for aesthetic criticism, as can be demonstrated, one can understand how certain radical aspects of Beethoven, for example, received disproportionate attention, and are now exhumed and quoted while the more conventional aspects of his compositions were accepted and enjoyed without much comment. To modernize the illustration, future historical students, reading the torrid criticisms of Franklin Roosevelt in journals and periodicals, will have great difficulty in understanding how he could have survived four elections. News records are simply not necessarily completely representative of heterogeneous public attitudes.

Changes in musical taste cannot be, and actually have not been, rushed—as impatient conductors like Theodore Thomas have been exasperatingly aware. Even revolutionary changes are less rapid than is usually implied in the concept, for all these changes have their definite antecedents. The fact that musical tastes change slowly is consistent with the very requirements of social life. Without a certain degree of uniformity and continuity in norms, no publishing enterprise, no educational system, no critical standards, no concert organization—in fact, no common social existence would be possible. This fact confers on aesthetic taste its social nature. Although there is no psychological law which would prevent the development of a perfectly unique taste on the part of a hermit-like artist, it is a sociological impossibility that such a taste could survive in a social world. In a collective world, only collective tastes can qualify for survival, because the overhead in time, effort, and financial investment necessary for the implementation of a "taste system" is so great that only collective effort will sustain it.

Musical taste systems are further stabilized by having their material embodiment in huge financial investments in auditoriums, accoutrements for professional training, pedagogical institutions, printing of scores, manufacture of instruments; and have their nonmaterial formulation in a vast corpus of literature, theory and ideology which galvanize it into a major institution resistant to changes that threaten it with extinction. Under such circumstances, a composition may, indeed, possess an individuality, but its "uniqueness" is reduced to a mere variation of a general norm which constitutes the basis of critical judgment.

For norms to exist, it is not necessary for them to be eternal. Although anyone with even a modicum of historical sense must recognize the long-term inconstancy of norms, nevertheless they are relatively stable over a period of time, and evoke considerable sentimental, ethical, and special-interest attachments which get codified into legal, religious, or cultural and critical mandates. This holds for the economic and political systems as well as for aesthetic standards. In sociological language, these general social norms are called "folkways." After they have persisted for some time—as have the norms of family life, the folkways of government and religion, and the folkways of classic musical taste—they tend to sprout a halo of uncritical acceptance, creating the illusion of general and absolute validity which condemns all deviant forms of behavior as "immoral" or "in poor taste." This predisposition to universalize the standards of one's own culture is called, in technical jargon, "ethnocentricism."

Musical norms conform to these characteristics of social folkways. The norms are codified and transmitted from generation to generation with increments of change, but are also subject to considerable sectarian fervor. They are defended, not like scientific truths, but rather by an aesthetic "conscience" which may even proselytize for what is considered "true" beauty, and declare J. S. Bach "universal" when he is quite obviously attached to time, space, and circumstance, as is every other mortal, great and small.

If the social necessity of norms in general has been demonstrated, one may still inquire how any particular norms, e.g., current musical standards, arise. By far the major portion of a given musical taste is culturally inherited from the past, as are also the folkways in religion, government, language, and other realms of social affairs. Even scientific inventions and works of art which are presumed to be "new" consist of a relatively small supplement to what has already accumulated in the past. Ninety per cent of the electric light and ninety per cent of Beethoven's First Symphony existed before Edison and Beethoven were even born. In fact, so small may be this increment that the transition, for example, between the "London" Bach and Mozart is almost imperceptible today, and the *Jena* symphony attributed to Beethoven "could have been written by various contemporaries." Beethoven is quoted as having told his friend Ferdinand Riess that "although I have taken lessons from Haydn, I have learned nothing from him." Wholly aside from the question of personal and professional honesty in this comment, sociologically it is, of course, untenable that Beethoven should have "learned nothing" from Haydn and from all his other numerous musical forebears. No artist is the free, creative spirit he sometimes conceives himself to be. There obtains a "principle of continuity" in cultural as well as biological heredity which suggests many damaging reservations to the "great man theory" which alleges that "history is but the lengthened shadow of the genius." The genius is much more the creation of history than he is the creator of it. He is as much the product of previous ages as of his own.

Furthermore, even the new "creative" elements in music can be intimately related to the past that links the new with its logical ancestry. Such devices as the multiplication of voices, juxtaposition of old keys which were formerly considered inimical, omission of modulational steps formerly required, extension of the vertical chord structure one more interval, the abandonment of resolutions of dissonant chords—all these formalities make "creation" intellectually recognizable and comprehensible. This is not intended to detract from the general mystery of nature in general, or musical composition in particular. But such a formal catalysis is in effect the grammar of music which, like a language, is spoken with great fervor and spontaneity, but in reality is the final fruition of many years of individual practice and training, of frequent correction, and much intellectual planning.

When these social principles are applied to the specific institution of the symphony orchestra and its music, there is still much more in the orchestra than meets the ear. Many of the factors which condition our tastes are quite external to music itself, but nevertheless exert significant pressures on repertoire trends.

One of the important factors limiting the performances of musical works are the inflexible boundaries of the repertoire; the fixed number of programs and the inevitable limits in playing time. Unless the length of the season is increased, the adoption of a new composition or composer will inevitably mean the reduction of the frequency, or the total abandonment, of an old one. Since music cannot live without being performed, there results a perennial struggle for aesthetic existence which is provisionally resolved every time a program is constructed. Every composition will ultimately lose its rank in the hierarchy of aesthetic survival, and every work of art may confidently look forward to the probability of its displacement by some newcomer.

The rate of this turnover is, of course, affected by the rate of production of new compositions, their character, the virility of the old compositions, and the energy of the audience in acquiring new tastes. The rising curves of Tschaikowsky, Wagner, and Brahms approximately equaled the decline of Beethoven, and new compositions today are continuously edging one another for entrance on the lower levels. As compared to a century ago, concerts have become more frequent and rehearsal time has been greatly extended, with the consequently steeper slope of the learning curve of both orchestra and audience. Such circumstances are favorable to the acceptance of new works, with the result that the repertoire today is much more diversified than a century ago.

In a strategic position to direct the course of taste changes is, of course, the conductor, whose prestige and authority seem to be reflected in repertoire policy. In fact, it is a classic complaint that the repertoire does not represent the "taste" of the audience, but rather that of the conductor who constructs the programs and whose aesthetic ideology determines his choices. With a kind of parental solicitude he is said to apportion the musical diet, not according to the likes of the audience, but according to what is "good for it." Anyone familiar with the missionary career of Theodore Thomas and the pertinacity of Gericke, will realize that many a program does anticipate the level to which the conductor aspires, rather than the actual spontaneous preferences of the audience. For reasons that have been set forth elsewhere, such program build-

ing was more characteristic of the early twentieth century than of
the time of Mozart, Haydn and Beethoven.

However, there are lengths to which even a dictator cannot go,
since there are genuine public restraints upon flouting social opinion.
Therefore, for every severely classic Gericke there is an indulgent
Max Fiedler; and for a stern Mahler, there is a popular Stransky;
and even Theodore Thomas interspersed among his symphonies the
Strauss waltzes and other delectable bits of relief. Even the most
obstinate conductor dared not, even if he would, flaunt his own
eccentricities and ignore the basic communal repertoire that resides
in the habits and expectations of the public.

The deterministic role of the conductor has been grossly exaggerated—as have the roles of all other leaders, political and social.
Regardless of who wields the "authority," there is a basic repertoire,
often referred to facetiously as the "standard fifty pieces," which is
not fiction but reality.[7] When opera-conductor Seidl, who was innocent of the standard symphonic repertoire, was injected into the
responsible position of head of the New York Philharmonic, he lost
no time in acquiring the repertoire demanded by the musical mores
of the day. The easy interchange of conductors between distant
orchestras—even internationally—is both evidence and a product of
this standardization of musical "parts." This cannot be said of men
of the cloth, national officials, lawyers, and pedagogues.

Where the conductor does manifest his individuality is on the
periphery of the repertoire, not in its core. The conductor is permitted liberty, but not license. The traditional core being taken
for granted, the conductor often indulges in tangential explorations,
at which certain elements in his heterogeneous audience may take
offense; but which other elements may applaud. Like all other
public servants, musical leaders do not meddle much with the basic
way of life of their time, although they often attract disproportionate attention for the variety with which it is spiced.

It should also be remembered that a large proportion of an
audience actually desires a program a little above its heads. To such
listeners the symphony concert is more than mere musical delight;
it is ritual and ceremony of which all the social trappings and even
the intellectual affectations are a part. To many patrons, concerts

are a fashion in which prestige of participation takes priority over spontaneous aesthetic relaxation. Concerts are often "bought" like hats—more for style than beauty. But it *is*, nevertheless, the taste of that audience. There are various types of listeners in the heterogeneous audience, ranging from the lighthearted to the intellectual and studious extreme to whom every new composition is a puzzle which they delight in solving. It is a semantic question whether this whole range of audition should be included in the concept of the aesthetic. But its diversity does go far in explaining the variety of attitudes to the items in the repertoire.

Contemporary events usually leave visible traces on the repertoire, which tend to be as ephemeral as the events inciting them. Finland, in the thirties, was unique in international annals in keeping faith by repaying the installments on her American war debts. For the American concert audience, Sibelius epitomized all that was Finland, and their gratitude and curiosity sought expression in the playing of his music, his percentage registering the intensity of American sentiment for his country. World War I, which propelled the French to unprecedented heights, and tumbled Strauss from secure pre-eminence to temporary insignificance, is a long story fully covered in this history. It is important to note, however, that most of these effects were evanescent, indicating that musical tastes are conditioned by more abiding factors than passing hysteria, however intense it may seem at the moment.

The scientific and material world has also made its contribution to the formation of aesthetic taste, remote as science and art are popularly alleged to be. Certainly, much of the scientific activity is irrelevant to matters conventionally considered artistic; however, in the orchestral repertoire the science of physics and acoustics has revolutionized the repertoire simply by revolutionizing the instruments on which the repertoires are played. The old natural horns, with their removable crooks, had become increasingly awkward as the scores became more complex, demanding numerous key changes and chromatic passage work. The valves, of course, simplified the execution of these passages and made Wagner and Strauss, to say nothing of the later moderns, possible. The woodwinds, the violin (Tourte bow), the piano, and all other instruments were at various times the beneficiaries of corresponding technological improvements, with analogous evolution in the standards of musical structure and aesthetic tastes. It can therefore be unreservedly asserted that physical science is an integral element in the formation of aesthetic taste.

To these strictly musical applications of technology and science must be added the equally important technical advances in printing, architecture, communication and transportation, without which musical developments would have remained sterile. For, what benefit the chromatic creations of Wagner and Strauss without the facility to print the huge scores, to promulgate them rapidly and economically throughout the nation and beyond its borders, and the acoustical architectural setting to exploit them? It is said that the art of printing made democracy possible. A similarly daring generalization may be made about music; the art of printing probably exerted no less influence in the creation and dissemination of aesthetic tastes than in the formation and propagation of political beliefs.

The discussion of repertoires ultimately raises the problem of "good" taste and "good" music. There is no room here for the Olympian dictum that there are only "two kinds of music, good and bad." Such alternatives do not specify the concrete quality of the music to which these appellations are to be applied.

The question of "what is good music" is often shrugged off as being both impossible and unnecessary: impossible because the inner feelings of aesthetic conscience cannot be made rationally articulate; and unnecessary, because one need only to emulate those "qualified" persons who possess "good" taste. However, the whole foregoing text is a refutation of that dual evasion. If the repertoire is the result of individual choices, there should be no objection to an attempt to determine the possible criteria on which these choices are based.

The classification of our innumerable and diverse experiences into the desirable and undesirable, into the *good*, which we seek to perpetuate, and the *bad*, which we seek to avoid, is one of the most elementary human judgments. But it is complicated by the manifold use and meaning of the concept. The concept of "good," when applied to taste or action of man, can have only four basic meanings.

(1) The instrumental or utilitarian meaning: an action or thing which is good *for something*. Spinach may be good as nutritious diet (but "I don't like it"). The study of mathematics may be good for your efficiency, but you may not enjoy the discipline. A Strauss waltz may have therapeutic value in hastening convalescence, and coincidentally be quite thrilling and "good" to listen to.

(2) Personal pleasure, as an aesthetic end in itself: an article of food may be consumed, a piece of music may be listened to, with utter delight, without any ulterior thought of health or prestige for having listened to it. It will earn from the consumer the pronouncement of "good" when he probably should proclaim more accurately, "I find it good," "I like it," "it gives *me* pleasure." He may experience such profound satisfaction that it will be difficult for him to realize that many another person may experience other and contrary reactions. However, this propensity to universalize and to dogmatize concerning beliefs and tastes that are intensely felt is a common phenomenon and results in attempts to impose on others our religious, political, and aesthetic beliefs whether or not they are appropriate. It emanates from a psychological myopia, which renders nothing more convincing than our own inner experiences and beliefs.

(3) Conformity to an established social norm: moral behavior, styles of dress, and certain art forms are labeled "good" when they conform to certain pre-established standards or norms. These norms usually reside in certain authoritarian sources, such as historical and critical documents, in tradition, or in the behavior or tastes of a social class. Thus, monogamy is undoubtedly "good," though many enjoy violating it at times. A new hat may be in "good" style prescribed for the season—"that's what they are wearing"—though "it is not becoming to me." The concert patron who lacks confidence in his own judgment may say: "I suppose it is good music, but I don't like it." These well-established technical and aesthetic standards, representing as they do the composite judgments of large groups over long periods of time, carry the weighty sanction of

tradition, and are therefore considered more valid than any individual judgment. The individual does not readily pit his momentary opinion against the judgment of time. These norms are received in the social heritage, give great intellectual security, and deserve the laudatory title of "good." They promote social solidarity, permit predictability, while social customs undergo their slow changes on the experimental growing edges.

(4) Related to the definition of the social norm, but differing in its sanction, is the criterion of Truth or Goodness which is presumably independent of any human being's belief or judgment. This metaphysical notion, characteristic of the romantic doctrines of the nineteenth century, posits a Truth which resides in cosmic nature, inherent in the Universe, which finally gains acceptance through the agency of the clairvoyant leaders who possess the genius to translate it into mundane objects of art. This doctrine makes of the musician a kind of priest who interprets by inspirational and intuitive means, Truth and Beauty. This makes of Beauty an objective entity rather than a subjective human judgment. When fervently believed in, it confers on an artist and his interpreter a sense of self-confidence attained by no other means. It is a widespread dogma which, though not always articulately explained, lies at the root of many aesthetic pronouncements among pedagogues as well as laymen.

These familiar dilemmas testify to the necessity of coming to grips with the semantic implications of our terms. If "good" music is a social norm, and "taste," which approves it, is a more or less enduring and definable pattern of preferences under given conditions, then "good taste" will fluctuate and be subject to all the laws of social folkways. This definition conforms to all the observations which have been made throughout this work. But taste is never pure. It is a pluralistic phenomenon compounded of various ingredients which consist not only of spontaneous pleasure, but also of the overtones of fashion and prestige and technical erudition that emanate from the leaders. Conductors, musicians, and other members of the elite make the decisions for the public, very much as do the leaders in politics and public opinion. The norm may therefore be strengthened by the authority of a group which practices it, by a social ideology which sanctions it, and by the fervor with which it is promulgated. On the other hand, it may be weakened by competing groups, who are, for various reasons, opposed to the conventional norms, and seek to replace the "embalmed classics" with a modern style.

Ultimately, the established taste is a grand cooperative enterprise between the external physical object—which is neutral—and the audiences who endow it with "beauty," and who have been conditioned by their past experiences, their ethics and religion, the physical environment and the innumerable factors which impinge upon their lives and determine their choices. It would be more precise, therefore, to discard the "truism" that "good music survives," and to substitute the more realistic view that music which, through various social, material, and psychological circumstances survives, and which contains features that society values, is adjudged and labeled aesthetically "good." Sometimes this judgment is held in abeyance for years, while these forces are doing their work.

The goodness or beauty of an object is therefore a superimposed quality with which an observer, according to his system of values, endows an object. If he confers beauty on an object, he also withdraws it after it has been conferred, or withholds indefinitely such a distinction.

This system of aesthetic theory, often denominated "subjectivism," may be variously criticised, but it appears to many to be most vulnerable because of its supposed nihilism in standards. If one can never assert, so runs the charge, that "this is beautiful," but is permitted to admit only that "it is beautiful to me," one must conclude that every man is his own critic, and every criticism is cosmically as valid as any other. This would, in the end, lead to rampant individualism, a negation of all standards, with the disquieting result that all aesthetics would flounder in a morass of solipsisms. If the common denominator between all good music is only that it is "thought" good, that "there is nothing good or bad but thinking makes it so," it would necessarily wipe out all genuine distinctions between "good" and "bad" and right and wrong, thereby making all judgments meaningless. It would deny the validity of a procedure which mankind has always followed.

As a matter of fact, the "confusion" of voices which the above argument deplores does, to a certain extent, exist. Historically, it is simply true that aesthetic preferences do differ, not only between epochs and between national cultures, but also between classes and groups in the same society. There is even a great diversity between the art objects that are enjoyed by a tolerably versatile and experienced individual patron.

In spite of this, there is no end to the search for objective criteria of good music which would be compelling on all rational beings. In a strictly technical sense, there may be moderate consensus on this question. Probably most musicians would agree on certain standards of workmanship, clean handling of instrumentation, and many other processes. But fine workmanship is not inevitably translated into an aesthetic thrill. The sons of Sebastian Bach, the detractors of Stokowski's transcriptions, the critics of "atonalism," the auditors who hold themselves aloof from the flamboyant Wagner—all are the final refutation of a presumed identity between an objective description of an art object and the thrill of the listener. Technically, such music is "good"; aesthetically it is "bad" to many listeners.

Consonant with these changing conceptions, the function of the musical critic has undergone a metamorphosis. The days of Hanslick and Krehbiel are past, when critics were considered pontifical authorities on the elusive questions of beauty and ugliness in musical ethics. Today, most of them eschew the function of keeper of musical conscience. They would rather express their aesthetic reactions not as final absolutes—an infirmity from which they have been cured—but as stimulants to public imagination, aids in appreciating the contents of the musical work. They have become technical specialists in the instruction of their readers. Like lawyers, they serve to bridge the gap between the expanding complexity of their field and the preoccupied layman who seeks guidance and self-assurance in an aesthetic labyrinth. This work as liaison agents will never be complete, for there is no final consummation in the social process. Society is in a constantly evolving state in which the standards of the true, the beautiful, and the just are constantly being refashioned in the context of the times.

Today most theorists are reconciled to an indeterminate prolongation of the unstable equilibrium in social, aesthetic, and other relations. Many aestheticians have sought for the relative certainty of laboratory science. But the mutability of standards is shared with all other social fields where social judgment is an issue. If aestheticians feel the need, they may seek consolation by stealing a glance at the field of law, where judgments of justice and their rationalizations constitute the essential content. Judge Benjamin Cardozo, for some years on the United States Supreme Court. affirmed his own sense of insecurity in delivering his critical opinions.

We live in a world of change. If a body of law were in existence adequate for the civilization of the day, it could not meet the demands of the civilization of tomorrow. Society is inconstant. So long as it is inconstant, and to the extent of such inconstancy, there can be no constancy in law.[8]

No legal scholar conceives of this admission of human fallibility as undermining the validity of his legal decisions, or ruining the usefulness of his profession. This is not a helpless and futile subjectivism. On the contrary, it is a constructive view which renders the fluctuations of history credible and makes peace with reality.

NOTES

INTRODUCTION

1 Harold C. Schonberg: "A Half Century of Orchestral Recordings," *Musical Courier*, December 1, 1945.

2 E. G. Sonneck: *Early Concert Life in America.* (Leipzig: Breitkopf and Haertel, 1907.)

3 H. Earle Johnson: *Musical Interludes in Boston.* (New York: Columbia University Press, 1943.)

CHAPTER ONE

1 Robert Schumann: "A Retrospective View of Musical Life in Leipzig, Winter, 1837–38"; in *Music and Musicians* (translated by F. Ritter). (London: W. Reeves, 1880) Vol. I, p. 380.

2 Eduard Hanslick: *Geschichte des Concertwesens in Wien.* (Vienna: 1869.)

John H. Mee: *The Oldest Music Room in Europe.* (London: John Lane, 1911.)

Myles Birket Foster: *The History of the Philharmonic Society of London, 1813–1912.* (London: John Lane, 1912.)

Reginald Nettel: *The Orchestra in England.* (London: Jonathan Cape, 1946.)

Alfred Dörffel: *Geschichte der Gewandhausconzerte zu Leipzig, 1781–1881.* (Leipzig, 1884.)

A. Elwart: *Histoire de la Société des Concerts du Conservatoire Impérial de Musique.* (2d. ed.; Paris, 1864.)

H. M. Schletterer: *Johann Friedrich Reichhardt, Sein Leben und Seine Musikalische Thätigkeit.* (Leipzig, 1879.)

George Dyson: *The Progress of Music.* (London: Oxford University Press, 1932.)

3 Percy Scholes: *The Great Doctor Burney.* (London: Oxford University Press, 1948), pp. 118–129.

Ibid., The Mirror of Music. (London: Novello & Co., 1949), Vol. I, pp. 144–147.

4 Some of the sources of information on playing time were the following:

Catalogue of Edwin Fleischer Private Collection of Orchestral Music: Philadelphia Free Library, Philadelphia.

Encyclopedia of Recorded Music. (New York: Crown Publishers, 1948.)

Claire Reis: *Composers in America.* (New York: Macmillan Co., 1947.)

T. C. York: *How Long Do They Play?* (London: Oxford University Press, 1929.)

CHAPTER TWO

1 John H. Mee: *op. cit.,* pp. 30–32.

2 Charles Francis Adams (ed.): *Letters from John Adams, Addressed to his Wife.* (Boston: C. C. Little and J. Brown, 1841), Vol. II, pp. 67–68.

3 Albert TenEyk Gardner: *Yankee Stonecutters, the First American School of Sculpture, 1800–1850.* (New York: Columbia University Press, 1945.)

James Thomas Flexner: *America's Old Masters, First Artists of the New World.* (New York: Viking Press, 1939.)

4 Sonneck: *op. cit.,* p. 65.

5 United States Bureau of Census: *A Century of Population Growth in the United States, 1790–1900.* (Washington, D. C., 1909), p. 12.

6 Alma M. Mahler (ed.): *Gustav Mahler Briefe, 1879–1911.* (Berlin, 1924.)

7 Eduard Hanslick: *Aus dem Tagebuch eines Musikers.* (Berlin: 1892), p. 58.

8 Ottmar Schreiber: *Orchester und Orchesterpraxis zwischen 1780 und 1850.* (Berlin, 1938), pp. 248–249.

9 *Boston Musical Herald,* August, 1881, p. 189.

10 Ernest Newman (ed.): *Memoirs of Hector Berlioz.* (New York: Alfred A. Knopf, 1932), p. 197.

11 For the stories of the British orchestras see:

Reginald Nettel: *op. cit.*

Adam Carse: *The Orchestra from Beethoven to Berlioz.* (Cambridge: W. Heffer, 1948.)

Robert Elkin: *Royal Philharmonic.* (London: Rider & Co., 1946.)

Robert Elkin: *Queen's Hall.* (London: Rider & Co., 1944.)

12 Alfred Oliver: *The Encyclopedists as Critics of Music.* (New York: Columbia University Press, 1947.)

13 Ernest Newman: *op. cit.*, p. 76.

14 Charles Burney: *A General History of Music.* (New York: Harcourt, Brace & Co., 1935), Vol. II, p. 955.

15 Thomas Busby: *A Complete Dictionary of Music.* (3d ed.; London: G. & W. B. Whittaker, 1819.)

16 Charles Burney: *The Present State of Music in Germany.* (London: T. Becket & Co., 1773), pp. vi–vii.

17 George Upton (ed.): *Theodore Thomas.* (Chicago: A. C. McClurg & Co., 1905), Vol. I, pp. 265 ff.

18 "Report of St. Louis Correspondent." *Musical Courier*, April 3, 1895, p. 31.

19 Upton: *op. cit.*, Vol. I, frontispiece.

20 Robert Schumann: *op. cit.*, Vol. I, p. 394.

21 *Musical Courier*, April 29, 1891. Address by Theodore Thomas, on his departure from New York for Chicago. Reports on Bergmann do not always agree. See Upton, *op. cit.* Vol. I, p. 36.

22 Charles E. Russell: *The American Orchestra and Theodore Thomas.* (Garden City: Doubleday, Page & Co., 1927.)

23 H. E. Krehbiel: *The Philharmonic Society of New York.* (New York: Novello, Ewer & Co., 1892), p. 7.

CHAPTER THREE

1 For histories of the Philharmonic-Symphony Society see:

    James G. Huneker: *The Philharmonic Society of New York— A Retrospect.* (New York: Privately printed, 1917.)

    Henry Krehbiel: *The Philharmonic Society of New York.* (New York and London: Novello, Ewer, 1892.)

    John Erskine: *The Philharmonic-Symphony Society of New York: Its First Hundred Years.* (New York: Macmillan Co., 1943.)

2 Miles Birket Foster: *op. cit.*, p. 4.

3 Eduard Hanslick: *Das Conzertwesen in Wien*, pp. 316–317.

4 John Erskine: *op. cit.*, p. 2. Quoted by permission.

5 R. Osgood Mason: *Sketches and Impressions, Musical, Theatrical and Social.* (New York and London: G. P. Putnam's Sons, 1887), pp. 169–170.

6 In Europe it was generally the opera which was supported by the State, although some orchestras received small subventions at times.

7 Henry E. Krehbiel: *op. cit.*, p. 41.

8 *Ibid.*, p. 85.

9 Ethel Rose Peyser: *The House that Music Built—Carnegie Hall.* (New York: Robert M. McBride & Co., 1936.)

10 *Musical Courier*, August, 1910.

11 For a gossipy but revealing account of the old Symphony Society, see Winthrop Sargeant: *Geniuses, Goddesses and People.* (New York: E. P. Dutton & Co., 1949), pp. 63 ff.

12 Andrea Della Corte: *Toscanini* (translated into French by A. Jacquemard). (Lausanne, 1947.)

13 "Symphony Finance," *Fortune*, March, 1935, pp. 78 ff.

14 In 1916 he resigned his position in Italy because the audience remonstrated against Wagner. He was succeeded by Molinari. In 1931 he was attacked by Fascisti in Bologna and physically injured. On April 1, 1933, his signature headed a protest to Hitler in behalf of the persecuted musicians. In June he declined to conduct in Bayreuth because of the "lamentable events which have wounded my feelings both as man and artist."

15 *Musical Courier*, December 25, 1934.

16 As is, of course, known, Toscanini returned to the United States in 1937 in response to an invitation of NBC, which organized an orchestra expressly for broadcasting purposes. There was some apprehension that his broadcasts would interfere with the Philharmonic series. In deference to that fear, the NBC concerts were scheduled at first for Saturday nights, until distant cities with Saturday night subscription concerts protested.

17 After de-Nazification proceedings, Furtwängler was officially cleared of collaboration. For a report of the earlier history see: Berta Geissmar: *Two Worlds of Music.* (New York: Creative Age Press, 1946.)

18 *Musical Courier*, May 29, 1937.

19 Madeleine Goss: *Bolero—The Life of Maurice Ravel.* (New York: Tudor Publishing Co., 1945.)
   See also Howard Taubmann: *The Maestro.* (New York: Simon and Schuster, 1951), pp. 177–178.

20 Walter Damrosch: *My Musical Life.* (New York: Charles Scribner's Sons, 1923), p. 22.

21 *Musical Record*, Boston, April 9, 1881.
   See also: *Musical Courier*, May 30, 1894, p. 32.

Edwin T. Rice: "Personal Recollections of Leopold Damrosch." *Musical Quarterly*, Vol. 28 (1942), pp. 269–275.

22 *Musical Courier*, March 24, 1927.

23 M. A. DeWolfe Howe: *The Boston Symphony Orchestra, 1881–1931*. (Boston: Houghton Mifflin Co., 1931), p. 16.

24 Many of these data are culled from the pages of *Dwight's Journal of Music*.

25 *Musical Record*, October 29, 1881.

26 The "fate" theme was frequently taken in slower tempo if the statement of the music critic of *Watson's Art Journal*, March 12, 1870, is to be believed.

27 *Musical Courier*, January 20, 1892 and October 29, 1902. *Ibid.*, March 8, 1893.

28 *Musical Courier*, September 8, 1897.

29 *Musical Courier*, December 29, 1898 and April 30, 1902.

30 *Musical Courier*, January 10, 1900, p. 5.

31 H. E. Krehbiel: *Review of New York Seasons, 1889–1890*. (New York and London: Novello, Ewer & Co., 1890), pp. 61–66.

32 *Musical Record*, November, 1890.

33 Felix Weingartner: *On Conducting* (translated by Ernest Newman). (Leipzig, 1925.)

34 *Musical Courier*, January 8, 1908.

35 Ferdinand Pfohl: *Artur Nikisch*. (Hamburg, 1925.)

36 *Boston Herald*, February 17, 1927.

37 *Musical America*, May 12, 1917.

38 Walter Damrosch: *op. cit.*, pp. 337 ff.

M. A. DeWolfe Howe: *op. cit.*

Olga Samaroff: *An American Musician's Diary*. (New York: W. W. Norton & Co., 1939), pp. 139 ff.

Irving Lowens: "L'Affaire Muck, A Study in War Hysteria, 1917–18." *Musicology*, Vol. I, No. 3.

Nicholas Slonimsky: *Music Since 1900*. (New York: W. W. Norton, 1938.) Assorted dates in 1918.

39 Hugo Leichtentritt: *Serge Koussevitzky: the Boston Symphony Orchestra and the New American Music*. (Cambridge: Harvard University Press, 1946.)

Arthur Lourié: *Serge Koussevitzky and His Epoch* (translated by S. W. Pring). (New York: Alfred A. Knopf, 1931.)

Moses Smith: *Koussevitzky*. (New York: Allen, Towne, and Heath, 1947.)

H. Earle Johnson: *Symphony Hall.* (Boston: Little, Brown & Co., 1950.)

40 *Boston Herald*, April 24, 1949.

41 Quoted in Geo. W. Cooke: *John Sullivan Dwight, A Biography.* (Boston: Small, Maynard Co., 1898), p. 227.

42 *North Philadelphia Musical Journal*, December, 1887.

43 *Musical Record*, July, 1887, p. 4.

44 Following are the principal works on the life and work of Theodore Thomas:

    George P. Upton: *Musical Memories.* (Chicago: A. C. McClurg & Co., 1908.)

    George P. Upton (ed.): *Theodore Thomas.* 2 vols. (Chicago: McClurg, 1905.)

    Rose Fay Thomas: *Memoirs of Theodore Thomas.* (New York: Moffat, Yard & Co., 1911.)

    Charles E. Russell: *The American Orchestra and Theodore Thomas.* (Garden City: Doubleday, Page & Co., 1927.)

    Philo A. Otis: *The Chicago Symphony Orchestra; its Organization, Growth and Development.* (Chicago: Clayton F. Summy, 1924.)

45 *Musical Courier*, December 21, 1904, p. 21.

46 Upton: *op. cit.*, Vol. 1, Appendix.

47 Henry E. Krehbiel: *Review of New York Seasons, 1886–87.* (New York: Novello, Ewer & Co., 1887.)

48 *Boston Musical Herald*, June, 1880, p. 141.

49 *Dwight's Journal of Music*, February 15, 1879.

50 Antoine Ysaye and Bertram Ratcliffe: *Ysaye, His Life and Work.* (London: Heinemann, 1947.)

51 R. F. Eyer: "America's Notable Orchestras." *Musical America*, January 24, 1937.

    For other histories of the Philadelpiha orchestra see:

    Robert A. Gerson: *Music in Philadelphia.* (Philadelphia: University of Pennsylvania, 1940.)

    Frances A. Wister: *Twenty-Five Years of the Philadelphia Orchestra, 1900–1925.* (Philadelphia, 1925.)

    R. L. F. McCombs: *The Philadelphia Orchestra.* (Philadelphia: Philadelphia Orchestra Association, 1947.)

    The Philadelphia Orchestra, Fiftieth Anniversary Season, 1900–1950. (Philadelphia, 1950.)

52 Philadelphia correspondent in *Willis Musical World and Times*, February 18, 1854.

53 The Musical Fund Society, *Charter and By-Laws*. (Philadelphia, 1930.)

L. C. Madeira and Philip Goepp: *The Musical Fund Society*. (Philadelphia: J. B. Lippincott Co., 1896.)

54 Edward Bok: *The Americanization of Edward Bok*. (New York: Charles Scribner's Sons, 1924), Chapter 32.

55 Philadelphia Orchestra Association, *Fiftieth Anniversary Season*, p. 14.

56 *Musical Courier*, March 30, 1916.

57 Frances Wister: *op. cit.*

58 Philadelphia Orchestra Association, *Fiftieth Anniversary Season*, p. 32.

59 McCombs: *op. cit.*

Musical Courier, March 25, 1933.

60 *Musical America*, October 25, 1929.

61 *Musical Courier*, November 8, 1930.

62 *Musical America*, January 8, 1927.

63 *Fortune* (Magazine), March, 1935, pp. 81 ff.

64 Ralph Hill (ed.): *Music 1950*. (Harmondsworth, Middlesex: Penguin Books, 1950), p. 18.

65 See: Ernst C. Krohn: "The Development of the Symphony Orchestra in St. Louis: An historical sketch," Proceedings, Music Teachers National Association, 1924.

66 The propriety of dating the founding of the symphony orchestra to the date of the founding of the St. Louis Choral Society (1880) is questionable. The orchestral repertoire in the present study dates to 1907, which some of the early programs after 1907 refer to as the "new series."

67 Leonora Wood Armsby: "The San Francisco Symphony Orchestra: First Decade." *California Historical Society Quarterly*, Vol. XXV, No. 3, September, 1946, pp. 229–254.

68 Adella Prentiss Hughes: *Music is My Life*. (Cleveland: World Publishing Co., 1947.)

69 Caroline Estes Smith: *The Philharmonic Orchestra of Los Angeles; the First Decade, 1919–1929*. (Los Angeles: Privately printed, 1930.)

70 Isabelle Morse Jones: *Hollywood Bowl*. (New York: G. Schirmer, 1936), pp. 39 and 67.

71 *Ibid.*, p. 5.

72 Martha F. Bellinger: "Music in Indianapolis," *Indiana Magazine of History*, December, 1945, pp. 345–364; March, 1946, pp. 47–65.

73 *A Short History of the National Symphony Orchestra.* (Washington, D. C.: Privately printed, 1949.)
Hans Kindler's Programs with the National Symphony Orchestra. (Washington, D. C.: Privately printed, 1950.)

CHAPTER FOUR

1 Otto Kinkeldey: "Beginning of Beethoven in America," *Musical Quarterly*, April, 1927, pp. 217 ff.

2 Eric Blom: *A Musical Postbag.* (London: J. M. Dent, 1941), p. 22.

3 Quoted in *Musical Courier*, December 9, 1891.

4 Quoted in Rose Fay Thomas, *op. cit.*, p. 79.
See also Henry T. Finck: *Richard Wagner and His Works.* (New York: Charles Scribner's Sons, 1907), Vol. I, pp. 267–268.

5 Henry T. Finck: *Chopin and Other Essays.* (New York: Charles Scribner's Sons, 1910), p. 256.

6 Charles Edward Russell: *op. cit.*, pp. 98 ff.
Rose Fay Thomas: *op. cit.*, pp. 111–117.
Henry T. Finck: *Richard Wagner and His Works.* (New York: Charles Scribner's Sons, 1907), Vol. II, p. 509.
Ernest Newman: *Life of Richard Wagner.* (New York: Alfred A. Knopf, 1941), Vol. IV, pp. 475, 542.

7 Paul Henry Lang: "Background Music for *Mein Kampf.*" *Saturday Review of Literature*, January 20, 1945.

8 Leon Stein: *The Racial Thinking of Richard Wagner.* (New York: Philosophical Library, 1950.)
Friedelind Wagner and Page Cooper: *Heritage of Fire.* (New York: Harper and Brothers, 1945), pp. xii ff.

9 John H. Mueller and Kate Hevner: *Trends in Musical Taste.* (Bloomington: Indiana University Publications, 1942), p. 85.

10 Eduard Devrient: *My Recollections of Felix Mendelssohn* (translated by Natalia Macfarren). (London: R. Bentley, 1869), p. 56.

11 Gerhard Herz: *J. S. Bach im Zeitalter des Rationalismus und der Frühromantik.* (Leipzig, 1936.)

12 Friedrich Blume: *Two Centuries of Bach, An Account of Changing Taste* (translated by Stanley Godman). (London: Oxford University Press, 1950.)
N. Forkel: *Uber J. S. Bach's Leben, Kunst und Kunstwerke* (translated by C. S. Terry). (London: 1920.)

E. Rebling: *Die Soziologischen Grundlagen der Stilverwandlung der Musik in Deutschland um die mitte des 18 Jahrhunderts.* (Saalfeld, 1935.)

13 Ernest Newman (ed.): *Memoirs of Hector Berlioz.* (New York: Alfred A. Knopf, 1932), p. 324.

14 *Musical Courier,* January 31, 1894, p. 7.

15 Bruno Walter: *Theme and Variations.* (New York: Alfred A. Knopf, 1946), p. 227. (London: Hamish Hamilton Ltd.)

16 Ludwig Geiger: *Briefwechsel zwischen Goethe und Zelter.* (Leipzig, 1902), Vol. II, Letters of April 5, April 21, June 9, 1827.

17 Upton: *op. cit.,* Vol. I, p. 212.

18 *Ibid.,* Vol. II, p. 107.

19 *Musical America,* March 17, 1917.

20 *Ibid.,* November 11, 1916.

21 The Schoenberg school protests the label of "atonality," but it is still the most common designation. See René Leibowitz: *Schoenberg and his School.* (New York: Philosophical Library, 1950), p. 74.

CHAPTER FIVE

1 *Musical America,* May 5, 1917.

2 *Musical America,* October 27, 1917.

3 *Willis Musical World and Times,* March 4, 1854.
See also: John Tasker Howard: *Our American Music.* (New York: Thomas Y. Crowell Co., 1946.)

4 *Willis Musical World and Times,* February 18, 1854; February 19, 1853.

5 United States Bureau of the Census: *Census of 1850,* p. c.

6 Aaron Copland: *Our New Music.* (New York: Whittlesey House, 1941), pp. 132–134.

7 Daniel Gregory Mason: *Tune in America.* (New York: Alfred A. Knopf, 1931), pp. 43–45.
Douglas Moore: "The Cause of Native Music." *Saturday Review of Literature,* January 25, 1947, pp. 24 ff.

8 The American Music Council classifies composers as native-born; foreign-born, living in the United States; and naturalized composers.

9 Upton: *op. cit.,* Vol. II, pp. 283, 286.

CHAPTER SIX

1 Emily Anderson (tr. and ed.): *Mozart's Letters.* (London: Macmil-

lan & Co., 1938), Letters of January 14, 1878; November 1, 1777; September 26, 1781.

2 Charles Burney: *A General History of Music.* (New York: Harcourt, Brace & Co., 1935), Vol. I, p. 21.

3 Richard Aldrich: *Concert Life in New York, 1902–23.* (New York: Putnam, 1941), p. 314.

4 Upton: *op. cit.*, Vol. I, p. 235.

   H. T. Finck: *Richard Wagner and His Works.* (New York: Charles Scribner's Sons, 1907), Vol. II, p. 511.

   R. Osgood Mason: *op. cit.*, pp. 199–200.

   Ernest Newman: *Richard Wagner.* (New York: Alfred A. Knopf, 1937), Vol. II, p. 115.

5 Upton: *op. cit.*, Vol. I, p. 251.

6 Henry T. Finck: "Music and Morals," in *Chopin and Other Essays.* (New York: Charles Scribner's Sons, 1910), pp. 143–182.

7 Charles E. Russell: *op. cit.*, p. vii.

8 George W. Cooke: *John Sullivan Dwight.* (Boston: Small, Maynard Co., 1898), pp. 147, 151–152.

   "Introductory Statements," *Dwight's Journal of Music,* April 10, 1852, Vol. I, no. 1.

9 William James: *Psychology.* (New York: Henry Holt & Co., 1890), Vol. I, pp. 126 ff.

10 Eduard Hanslick: *Concerte, Componisten, und Virtuosen.* (2. Aufl., Berlin: 1886), p. 312.

11 Upton: *op. cit.*, Vol. I, p. 289.

   Reginald Nettel: *The Orchestra in England, A Social History.* (London: J. Cape, 1946), p. 103.

12 Upton: *op. cit.*, Vol. I, p. 104.

13 Remark attributed to Rudolph Ganz, conductor of the St. Louis Symphony Orchestra, November, 1925.

14 In the prospectus of the New York Philharmonic for 1870–71, we read significantly: "Inasmuch as compositions in that class can seldom be fully appreciated when heard but once, the society has, for many years, made the rehearsals preceding each concert open to the public. Scale for admission: First Rehearsal and Second Rehearsal, 50 cents; Third Rehearsal, $1. Regular Concert, $2."

15 E. Creuzberg: *Die Gewandhausconzerte zu Leipzig, 1781–1931.* (Leipzig, 1931), p. 96.

   Percy Scholes: *Mirror of Music.* (London: Novello & Co., 1948), frontispiece.

Adam Carse: *The Orchestra from Beethoven to Berlioz*. (Cambridge: W. Heffer, 1948), p. 161.

16 Madeira and Goepp: *op. cit.*, p. 144.

17 Otis: *op. cit.*, p. 11.

18 Richard Hoffman: *Some Musical Recollections of Fifty Years*. (New York: Charles Scribner's Sons, 1910), pp. 63–64.

19 *Willis Musical World and Times*, December 3, 1853.

20 Eduard Hanslick: *Geschichte des Concertwesens in Wien*. (Vienna, 1869), p. 95.

21 *Musical Courier*, November 23, 1898; July 30, 1902.

22 August Schmidt: *Musikalische Reisemomente auf einer Wanderung durch Norddeutschland*. (Hamburg, 1846.)

23 *Willis Musical World and Times*, December 3, 1853.

24 Hector Berlioz: *Treatise on Orchestration*. (London, 1856.)

25 M. A. DeWolfe Howe: *op. cit.*, p. 32.

26 Reginald Nettel: *The Orchestra in England*. (London: Jonathan Cape, 1946), p. 174.

27 August Schmidt: *op. cit.*

28 *Musical Record*, October 29, 1881.

29 See photograph of Theodore Thomas orchestra in Upton, *op. cit.*, Vol. II, p. 82; and seating plan in Rose Fay Thomas, *op. cit.*, p. 372. H. E. Krehbiel: *How to Listen to Music*. (New York: Charles Scribner's Sons, 10th ed. 1900), p. 76.

30 J. J. Rousseau: *Dictionaire de Musique*, "Orchestre." (Paris, 1768.)

31 For a photograph see: *The Philadelphia Orchestra, Fiftieth Anniversary*. (Philadelphia: The Philadelphia Orchestra Association, 1950), p. 32.

32 *Musical Courier*, January 2, 1932.

33 *Musical Courier*, July 31, 1895; September 3, 1925.

34 Sir Henry Wood: *About Conducting*. (London: Sylvan Press, 1945), p. 115.

35 Sir Thomas Beecham: "The Position of Women" in *Vogue's First Reader*. (Garden City Publishing Co.: Halcyon House, 1944), p. 420.

36 Emily Anderson: *op. cit.*

37 Reginald Nettel: *op. cit.*, p. 171. Robert Elkin: *The Royal Philharmonic*, pp. 43 ff.

38 Hector Berlioz: *op. cit.*

39 Ernest Newman: *Life of Wagner*. (New York: Alfred A. Knopf, 1937), Vol. I, pp. 142–143.

40 Amy Fay: *Music Study in Germany*. (New York: Macmillan Co., 1909), pp. 108 ff.

41 Ludwig Spohr: *Autobiography*. (London: Longmans Green, 1865), p. 54.

42 Eduard Devrient: *op. cit.*, p. 59.

43 Percy Scholes: *op. cit.*, frontispiece.
Adam Carse: *op. cit.*, pp. 208, 232.

44 Spohr: *op. cit.*, pp. 54–55; 81.

45 Devrient: *op. cit.*, pp. 60–61.

46 Richard Hoffman: *op. cit.*, pp. 70–71.

47 Schumann: *op. cit.*, Vol. I, p. 37.

48 Eduard Hanslick: *Concerte, Componisten und Virtuosen, 1870–1885*. (2 Aufl., Berlin: 1886), p. 49.

49 Georg Henschel: *Personal Recollections of Johannes Brahms*. (Boston: R. G. Badger, 1907), p. 84.

50 Caroline Estes Smith: *op. cit.*, pp. 181–182.

51 *Musical America*, September 3, 1927, p. 16; August 30, 1928; August 31, 1929; June 11, 1932.
Joseph Szigeti: *With Strings Attached*. (New York: Alfred A. Knopf, 1947), p. 81.
Israel Nestyeff: *Sergei Prokofieff*. (New York: Alfred A. Knopf, 1946), p. 102.

52 Hugo Goldschmidt: *Die Lehre von der Vokalen Ornamentik des 17. und 18. Jahrhunderts bis in die Zeit Glucks*. (Charlottenburg, 1907), p. 156.

53 William F. Apthorp: *By the Way*. (Boston: Copeland and Day, 1898), Vol. I, p. 50.

54 Wilhelm Furtwängler: *Gespräche über Musik*. (Zurich: 1948), pp. 100 ff.

55 Charles Burney: *The Present State of Music in France and Italy*. (2d ed.; London: T. Becket & Co., 1773), p. 160.

56 Gerald Abraham: *This Modern Stuff*. (London: Duckworth, 1946), p. 56.

57 *Musical Courier*, October 7, 1896.

58 *Musical Courier*, October 17, 1900.

59 Paul S. Carpenter: *Music, an Art and a Business*. (Norman: University of Oklahoma Press, 1950.)

60 *Memorandum #3*, Symphony Orchestra League: Charleston, West Virginia, November 30, 1950.

61 Arthur Judson: "American Orchestras," in *Musical America,* February, 1951, pp. 8 ff.

62 The Arts Enquiry: *Music, A Report on Musical Life in England.* Political and Economic Planning, London, 1949.

63 Margaret Grant and H. S. Hettinger: *America's Symphony Orchestras.* (New York: W. W. Norton & Co., 1940.)

64 *Musical Courier,* March 15, 1893.

65 *Musical Courier,* December 20, 1893.

66 Mrs. Adolph Brodsky, the wife of the concertmaster, places this interpretation on the incident. She asserts that Damrosch deliberately maneuvered the musicians into a strike for the purpose of voiding their contracts, which would then be renewed on easier terms for himself. See Mrs. Adolph Brodsky: *Recollections of a Russian Home.* (2d ed., London: Sherratt & Hughes, 1914), pp. 187–202.

67 *Musical Courier,* May 30, 1906.

68 *Musical Courier,* December 3, 1902.

69 *Musical Courier,* August 4, 1927.

70 *Musical Courier,* December 15, 1897.

71 *Musical Courier,* October 7, 1896.

72 Otis: *op. cit.,* p. 30.

73 *Musical Courier,* May 5, 1921.

74 *Musical Courier,* November 4, 1904.

75 Emily Anderson: *op. cit.,* Vol. III, p. 1072.

76 Carl Krebs: *Meister des Takstocks.* (Berlin: 1919), p. 53.

77 Eduard Hanslick: *Geschichte des Concertwesens in Wien,* p. 59.

78 *Dwight's Journal of Music,* July 10, 1875.

79 *Musical Courier,* January 1, 1896.

80 Henry T. Finck: *Chopin and Other Essays,* p. 243.

81 G. B. Shaw: *Music in London, 1890 to 1894.* (London: Constable & Co., 1932), Vol. I, p. 5.

82 Related to the author by a former member of the Lamoureux orchestra.

83 *Musical Courier,* June 20, 1900, p. 27.

84 H. M. Schletterer: *Johann Friedrich Reichhardt: Sein Leben und Seine Thätigkeit.* (Leipzig, 1864), p. 363.

85 Percy Scholes: *The Mirror of Music, 1844–1944.* (London: Novello & Co., 1947), Vol. I, p. 219.

86 *Musical Courier,* January 17, 1900.

87 Eduard Hanslick: *Geschichte des Conzertwesens in Wien*, pp. 152–153.

88 Madeira and Goepp: *op. cit.*, pp. 66–67.

89 *Musical Courier*, January 3, 1894, p. 22.

90 Creuzburg: *op. cit.*, p. 107.

91 *Boston Musical Herald*, March, 1887, p. 71.

92 *Musical Courier*, February 17, 1904.

93 Apthorp: *op. cit.*, Vol. II, p. 62.

94 *Boston Musical Herald*, January, 1891, p. 5.

95 *Musical Courier*, March 4, 1896.

96 Upton: *op. cit.*, Vol. II, p. 19.

97 Hanslick: *op. cit.*, pp. 55–56.

CHAPTER SEVEN

1 John H. Mueller: "Is Art the Product of its Age?" *Social Forces*, March, 1935, pp. 367–375.

Idem: "Theories of Aesthetic Appreciation" in *Studies in Appreciation of Art*. University of Oregon Publications, Vol. IV, no. 6, February, 1934.

Idem: "Methods of Aesthetic Measurement." *American Journal of Sociology*, January, 1946, pp. 276–282.

Paul R. Farnsworth: *Musical Taste, Its Measurement and Cultural Nature*. (Stanford: Stanford University Press, 1950.)

2 Kate Hevner: "The Aesthetic Experience; A Psychological Description." *Psychological Review*, May, 1937, pp. 245–263.

Max Schoen: *Psychology of Music*. (New York: Ronald Press, 1940.)

George Boas: *A Primer for Critics*. (Baltimore: Johns Hopkins Press, 1937.)

3 Donald Tovey: *The Main Stream of Music and Other Essays*. (New York: Oxford University Press, 1949), p. 373.

4 Curt Sachs: *The Commonwealth of Art*. (New York: W. W. Norton & Co., 1946), p. 326.

5 Karl Marx: "A Contribution to the Critique of Political Economy." Quoted in: Karl Marx and Friedrich Engels: *Literature and Art*. (New York: International Publishers, 1947), pp. 17–20.

6 Charles Lalo: *Esthétique*. (Paris, 1927), p. 3.

For a brief critical summary of Lalo's aesthetic see:

Katherine Gilbert: *Studies in Recent Aesthetic*. (Chapel Hill: University of North Carolina Press, 1927.)

John H. Mueller: "The Folkway of Art: An Analysis of the Social Theories of Art." *American Journal of Sociology*, September, 1938, pp. 222–238.

7 Francis Perkins: "Favorites of 25 Years on Orchestral Programs in New York." *Musical America*, February, 1950.

8 Benjamin Cardozo: *The Paradoxes of Legal Science*. (New York: Columbia University Press, 1928), pp. 1–2.

Index